Discovering
Natural Israel

Northern Negev from Avdat

Discovering Natural Israel

MICHAL STRUTIN

jD | JONATHAN DAVID PUBLISHERS
Middle Village, New York 11379

Discovering Natural Israel

Copyright ©2001 by Michal Strutin

No part of this book may be reproduced without the prior written permission
of the publisher. Address all inquiries to:

Jonathan David Publishers, Inc.
68-22 Eliot Avenue
Middle Village, New York 11379

www.jdbooks.com

2 4 6 8 10 9 7 5 3 1

Library of Congress Cataloging-in-Publication Data

Strutin, Michal.
    Discovering natural Israel / by Michal Strutin
       p. cm.
    Includes bibliographical references and index.
    ISBN 0-8246-0413-X
    1. Natural History—Israel.   I. Title.
QH193.I8 S76 2000
508.5694—dc21   00-064498
                                                        CIP

  • Book design by John Reinhardt Book Design
  • Map of Israel by Rusty Nelson
  • Key maps by Kent Burdick, Geography Department,
    East Tennessee State University
  • All photographs by Michal Strutin unless otherwise noted

Printed in China

for
Michael and Talia

"He has made her wilderness like Eden,
Her desert like the Garden of the Lord."

(ISAIAH 51:3)

Acknowledgments

WITHOUT THE COMMITMENT and support of Rabbi Alfred J. Kolatch, editor-in-chief of Jonathan David Publishers, and David Kolatch, editorial director, *Discovering Natural Israel* would not be. Editor Judy Sandman helped polish the rough spots and asked the right questions. And Fiorella deLima put all the elements together. I thank them and everyone at Jonathan David Publishers. I'd also like to thank book designer John Reinhardt.

A number of dedicated people at Society for Protection of Nature in Israel (SPNI) helped enormously. Robin Gordon, director of SPNI's American branch, ASPNI, provided not only information, but also succor for a rustic writer stranded in New York. Dan Diamant, Cynthia Graber, and Sharon Hoffman—SPNI liaisons all—pointed me in the right direction and cleared many paths. Noga Watter, Tanya Moshe, and Stephanie Glickman organized complicated arrangements.

Dr. Yossi Leshem took time to explain many aspects of Israel's environment as well as the history of SPNI. Thanks, too, to Dr. Reuven Yosef at International Birding and Research Center in Eilat for allowing me to tag along on his bird research.

The men and women who head and staff SPNI's field schools are both knowledgeable and committed. I am particularly grateful to Jacob Gavish, Itzik Waknin, Judith Ayalon, Baruch Shwulewitz, Roni Saslove, as well as David Glasner and Che'ch at Kefar Ruppin. Ido Heruty provided not only good guiding, but good humor.

I appreciate the assistance I received all along from Mike Livneh, and the advice of Dr. Benny Shalmon. Tomer Kahana, Dan Ofri, Yoel Oren, and Hava Lahav helped me keep the facts straight. And Shai Gonorov and Dan Tzahor made me look better than I deserved atop Khatz the camel.

Susan Berson, a friend and librarian, provided critical information. El Al Israel Airlines provided some travel assistance.

Contents

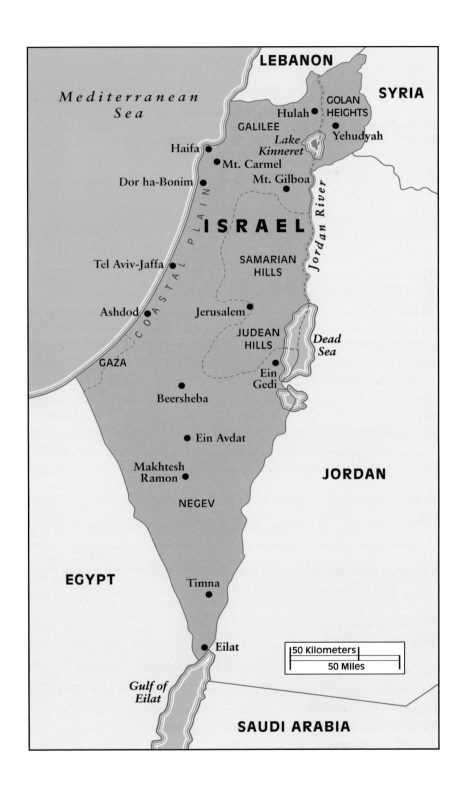

Discovering
Natural Israel

I SRAEL'S IS A GEOGRAPHY INSCRIBED upon the heart. Few places
in the world are so viscerally understood, whether known first-
hand or not. So much human history resonates so deeply there.
So many have a religious or emotional tie there. Because it is the
land of the Bible, Israel is as much an imagined land as a land with
wadis, mountains, ibex leaping in the desert, leopards lying in wait.

In his novel *Touch the Water, Touch the Wind*, Israeli author Amos
Oz reveals an old man, an immigrant from war-wracked Europe
who, though he lives in Israel, continues writing "poems of yearning
for Zion." For some, Israel imagined is more real than Israel in fact.

As the epicenter of the world's three great monotheistic religions— 1
Judaism, Christianity, and Islam—Israel is where every nuance of
our considerable spiritual vocabulary can be found. It is hard to
view this geography without a map in one hand and a Bible in the
other.

On Mount Nebo, just northeast of the Dead Sea, Moses looked
from the mountains of Moab, in what is now Jordan, to the land
God promised Israel. In the last, poignant verses of the Hebrew scrip-
ture, Moses, who was barred from entering the Promised Land, was
allowed to see from afar the Mediterranean Sea, the low-lying Jordan River Valley, the Negev Desert, and the forests that clothed the
mountains of Galilee.

On the shores of Lake Kinneret (Sea of Galilee), Jesus became a
fisher of souls. He was baptized in the nearby Jordan River, which
flows through Lake Kinneret and is itself a mythic river. In the Judean
Hills in the city named Jerusalem—meaning "City of Peace"—
Muhammad rose to heaven from a broad rock.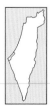

A place imbued. Yet, a place with a physical as well as an emotional geography. The land has a majesty of its own, in addition to its thousands of years of human history. This small piece of real estate, the size of New Jersey, is at the juncture of three continents: Europe, Asia, and Africa. Although much of human history has passed through here, the land has been—and still is—a crossroads for natural history as well.

Within Israel's borders live approximately five hundred bird species. All of Europe, an area more than two hundred times larger, has only seventy-seven species more. One of the world's major flyways for bird migration passes through Israel, right over the Judean Hills. So many birds—more than half a billion—travel this route spring and fall that planes must be especially alert when flying in this vicinity.

Millions of migrating raptors—eagles, hawks, and vultures—soar on thermals of warm air that rise from the base of the mountains. Birds from stilts to swallows migrate over this land bridge from Europe to Africa each winter. White storks travel the route by the hundreds of thousands.

Israel harbors ecosystems representing all three continents. When the spies Moses sent from the desert to survey Canaan returned with figs, pomegranates, and lush bunches of grapes, they said, "We came to the land you sent us to; it does indeed flow with milk and honey" (Numbers 13:27). Canaan was rich in natural wealth, far richer and more diverse than most of its neighbors because of its favorable position at the junction of so many natural divisions.

The northern and central regions of Israel are greened with Mediterranean vegetation, similar to that found in Greece, Italy, and other European countries bordering the Mediterranean Sea. To the south lies the Negev Desert, part of the Saharo-Arabian realm, the classic desert of the Sahara, the Sinai, and the Arabian Peninsula. Yet, dry highlands in the northern Negev echo areas found in Iran, Turkistan, and as far east as Mongolia's Gobi Desert.

Low, wet pockets in the Jordan Valley flourish with tropical vegetation, such as found in southern Sudan. In the center of the Jordan Valley, the Jordan River traces the planet's largest gash—the Great Rift Valley—to the Dead Sea, at thirteen hundred feet below sea level the lowest place on Earth.

From low-lying valleys to four-thousand-foot mountains, Israel is the northernmost limit for many southern species and the southernmost limit for many northern species. Biodiversity is incredibly high, with more species per square kilometer than found in California.

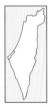

2

Within Israel's border live approximately twenty-seven hundred plant species, compared to seventeen hundred in England, fifteen hundred in Egypt, and thirteen hundred thirty in Norway—all much larger countries. Of these species, one hundred fifty grow only in Israel.

Plants range from gnarled old oaks holding onto the sides of forested slopes, to giant papyri swaying over warm waters, to brittle artemisias living in desert conditions too sear for most life. In spring, slopes in the north are quilted with the pinks, purples, blues, and whites of anemones, poppies, cyclamen, and others.

The cool waters of the Dan River are canopied by tall plane trees and luxuriant vegetation, a rarity in this land. Even the desert puts on a flower show in early spring before the winter rains end and the fierce summer sun beats down.

At Jordan Park, just before it enters Lake Kinneret (Sea of Galilee), the Jordan River ripples past banks crowded with willows and myrtles. The 186-mile river empties into the Dead Sea.

Israel is full of natural wonder. Yet, despite the fact that vegetation clothes the hillsides and fringes the rivers, despite the fact that birds by the millions travel through the land and more than seventy mammal and eighty reptile species live upon it, untwining natural history from human history is difficult if not impossible.

Human history developed in the Fertile Crescent: It is no accident

The Arbel Cliffs rise above Tiberias on the western shore of Lake Kinneret. Atop the cliffs, trails provide views of Galilee and of caves used in Roman times.

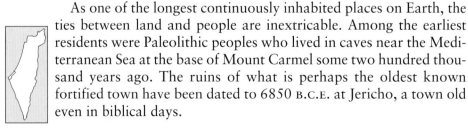

4

that humans began cultivating plants and domesticating animals here more than nine thousand years ago.

The Jordan is Israel's most important river, in terms of both ecosystems and economics. But the image of this lovely if modest waterway is shaped more by psalms and hymns than by the real river. Olive trees whose twisted, gray-green forms cling to Israel's dry slopes remind us of the dove returning to Noah with an olive branch that signaled dry land or Jesus teaching on the Mount of Olives. It is difficult to think of Mount Sodom, hard by the Dead Sea, without remembering how Lot's wife was transformed into a pillar of salt when she turned to watch the destruction of Sodom. Even lowly thorn bushes put us in mind of Moses and the burning bush.

As one of the longest continuously inhabited places on Earth, the ties between land and people are inextricable. Among the earliest residents were Paleolithic peoples who lived in caves near the Mediterranean Sea at the base of Mount Carmel some two hundred thousand years ago. The ruins of what is perhaps the oldest known fortified town have been dated to 6850 B.C.E. at Jericho, a town old even in biblical days.

Since then trees have been felled and irrigation channels cut by successive landlords: Assyria, Egypt, Israel, Babylonia, Greece, Rome, Turkey, to name but a few. The people and the land have transformed each other.

The Bible and other documents of human history serve as records of the natural history of this place. Samson the Nazirite goes down to Timnah and, "behold, a young lion roared against him" (Judges 14:5). Lions once roamed Israel, as did elephants, rhinoceroses, and bears. Job describes the attributes of the desert-dwelling ostrich (39:13–18). Nahal Tanninim—Crocodile River—empties into the Mediterranean Sea between Tel Aviv and Haifa near the Roman ruins of Caesarea. In the recent past, when this riverbed was edged by marshes, it was inhabited by the reptiles whose name it still bears.

The Song of Songs tells us what grew in Israel's valleys in the time of King Solomon: "I am a rose of Sharon, a lily of the valleys" (2:1). The rose of Sharon, a low red tulip, still grows on the Plain of Sharon. And the lily, probably a white narcissus, still graces certain lowlands.

Although most were destroyed in wars or cut for fuel over the centuries, broad forests of oaks and terebinths grew in Israel as recently as the 1800s. Old-growth groves remained until World War I, when Turkish forces, which had controlled the region for four centuries, cut them down for the war effort. Venerable terebinths, first cousins to pistachio trees, are fewer in number now, but they remain an integral part of the natural landscape.

5

Since the founding of the modern state of Israel, millions of trees have been planted under the auspices of the Jewish National Fund, to replace those lost over the centuries. Pines and eucalyptuses were imported and planted as a fast means to halt rampant erosion on long-denuded hillsides. Now, many evergreen groves are old enough to shade Mount Gilboa.

The leading force for preserving the natural wealth of Israel is the Society for the Protection of Nature in Israel (SPNI). Founded in 1953, this organization is known to visitors through their tours of the country's natural and historic areas. It was the efforts of the SPNI that led to the creation of the Israel Nature and National Parks Protection Authority. Under Israel's Ministry of the Environment, this agency is now steward of more than forty national parks and more than three hundred nature reserves in Israel.

The Bible tells of miracles. To slake the thirst of the children of Israel during their wanderings near the Wilderness of Sin, God caused

SPNI

The lithe dorcas gazelle, which can escape leopards and other predators at speeds of 60 miles per hour, roams in small bands throughout Israel's desert valleys.

6

water to pour forth from a rock (Exodus 17:6). Yet the waters that spring from rock in the Judean Desert—at the headwaters of the Arugot River and along cliffs near where the Dead Sea Scrolls were found—seem no less miraculous.

Indeed, Israel is full of miracles of nature, evolutionary adaptations and geological aggregations that can fill an onlooker with awe. Dorcas gazelle can survive without ever drinking. Flower seeds lie dormant, sometimes for years, until rains cause them to germinate then flower in just days. Brine shrimp spring to life seemingly from nowhere when rains create small, ephemeral pools. And the fossilized shells of ammonites, extinct mollusks that once roamed the seas, pave the floor of the desert.

The miracles of Israel's diverse natural history are equal to its better-known human history. Earth, wind, and water have their own compelling stories to tell. I had been reading histories of this epicenter of continents and dreaming of wandering the Negev again. Although I had spent a few months in Israel years before, roaming the country with natural history in mind would bring me face to face with hundreds of species I had read about but never met. That whetted my appetite.

From editor of outdoor and environmental publications I had evolved to writer, and one of the pleasures of writing about natural history is the research: roaming each new territory, discovering species new to me, understanding how a place is put together. Another pleasure is the people I meet, from tourists to knowledgeable park rangers, who enthusiastically explain the life stories of plants and animals under their care.

There is another reason to roam the natural world, one that is less concrete. On a three-week ramble through northern Wisconsin a few years ago, I had started out with some trepidation, a fear of unknown forests and getting lost in a strange place. Two weeks into the trip, after plenty of driving, hiking, and canoeing, I had allowed myself to relax and was bumping down an empty country road one sunny Sunday morning, singing along with a song on the tape deck. A bald eagle skimmed the trees, flying low just ahead of me. When the huge bird curved right, floating above an even smaller road, I had to follow. A couple of powerful flaps of his wings and he had reached the top of a sycamore. Before me, at the road's end, lay the broad, sinuous curves and copper-colored waters of the Namekagon, a river of classic proportions and incredible grace. I roam for moments such as this.

But returning to Israel was more than a desire to experience and write about a species-rich crossroads of nature. Some cord ties me to the umbilicus that is Israel. During these musings about the nature of Israel, my friend Talia called from Tel Aviv. "It's time. It's been too long already. Come," she said. So I did.

CHAPTER ONE

Southern Negev:
By Camel into the Heart of the Eilat Mountains

Timna Valley

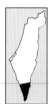

Southern Negev Eilat Mountains

UVDAH VALLEY

Shaharut •

Mount Berekh •
• Timna

Eteq Canyon •

Red Canyon •
Eilat •

I N ISRAEL IT IS BEST TO AVOID long bus rides on Sunday. On this first day of the work week, every eighteen- to twenty-year-old is returning to a military base after a Shabbat spent with family and friends. The Negev, where I was going, is dotted with military installations.

I was jammed onto a public bus filled with teenage soldiers in tan uniforms traveling south from Beersheba: tall girls with freckled noses, dark-blond hair twisted in casual loops atop their heads; boys with olive complexions jostling against big-boned red-heads; almond-eyed girls whose luxuriant dark curls made clear why Orthodox Jewish wives modestly cover their heads; and youths of both sexes who already looked tough enough to stand for the Knesset.

Squeezed against the window, I shared a seat with a young woman and her friend, who were comparing nail polish, their Uzis slung over their shoulders like handbags. The friend sat half on, half off the two-person seat. The expressions on the faces of the young people crowding the aisle flashed from innocent youth to national defender as fast as cloud shadows racing across the land, and their shouted conversations ricocheted around the bus.

Some of the teens were plugged into music headsets. More were connected to the ubiquitous third ear of Israel—the cellular phone—undoubtedly talking to friends on other buses returning to other bases.

We had all pushed aboard in Beersheba, which lies at the northern border of the Negev, that huge dry triangle of land sculpted by abyssal craters, stark red mountains, sinuous white canyons, rock towers, and pinnacles. In biblical Hebrew the word for "south" and "dry" is the same: *negev*. The great desert of Israel accounts for more than 50 percent of Israel's area and less than 1 percent of its water.

It was spring, and wildflowers glowed across the broad flat high-lands. *Rotem*'s delicate white flowers perfumed the basins of the wadis. In this season, rain can flood dry sandy riverbeds with such force that cars are swept away like toys. A few of the unwary or unlucky lose their lives every year in flash floods.

Only a month or so later, the khamsin begins to roam the Negev. When this hot, dry wind that makes people crazy ceases, overwhelming heat remains. In the breathlessness of summer, waves of hot air blister up from the desert floor. Most wildlife waits for night to tame the day's heat, emerging only when the long shadows of evening appear.

Since the time when Abraham lived there nearly four thousand years ago, Beersheba had always been the last town, perched on the edge of the vast desert. Yet a sprinkling of Hebrews and others had always—if sparsely—occupied the Negev between Beersheba and the Red Sea. To ancient Israelites who had given up the nomadic life and saw Israel from the relative civility of Jerusalem or other of the walled cities, Beersheba seemed the last outpost.

Today Beersheba is the gateway to the Negev and a fast-growing development city full of new immigrants. On the bus they were represented by young people with the light hair and broad cheekbones of Russian Jews and those with the fine-boned faces and carob-brown skin of Ethiopian Jews.

As the bus sped south past the outskirts of Beersheba, farms disappeared and a parched tan land emerged, set off by the ramshackle dwellings of Bedouin and their herds of black goats. This is the dividing line between the sown and the wild, where a sweet-water well can still mean the difference between life and death.

Although a fast car can span the one-hundred-fifteen-mile length of the Negev in a few hours, vacationers might miss the desert's three distinct sections as they hurry south to the Red Sea resorts of Eilat. A dry riverbed—called a *nahal* or wadi—marks the boundaries of each section.

The canyon of Nahal Zin divides the plateau of the northern Negev from the broken country of the central Negev. The broad swale of  Nahal Paran separates the central Negev and the giant crater of Makhtesh Ramon from the southern Negev, which centers on the wild Eilat Mountains.

At its eastern edge, the Negev is defined by the Syrian-African Rift, Earth's largest visible scar. A broad trough rimmed by mountains, the Great Rift Valley runs from Syria into Africa and forms

Israel's border with Jordan. This colossal rent between continental plates explains much of Israel's geography.

The section of the rift that runs through the Negev is known as the Aravah, a broad trenchlike desert valley that catches flash floodwaters of Nahal Paran and other riverbeds. When it reaches the Aravah, the precious rainwater seems to disappear, draining into natural underground aquifers away from the hot eye of the sun.

On its western side, the Negev is not so well defined. Painstakingly drawn political boundaries now separate the Sinai Desert from the Negev, Egypt from Israel. But ecologists consider the two deserts together. Beginning with the Negev's Eilat Mountains, a line of red sandstone peaks marches south along the Sinai coastline, only one of the obvious connections between the two deserts.

What I saw from the bus in the northern Negev was a broad plateau plated with a crust of sand-and-gravel soils, etched by riverbeds. These northern Negev highlands slope down from the Judean Hills and are well watered compared to the southern Negev: precipitation drops from an average eight inches per year in the northern desert to a bare inch per year near Eilat.

As we neared Nahal Zin, the southern boundary of the plateau, I saw the sign for Kibbutz Sedeh Boqer, home of modern Israel's first prime minister, David Ben-Gurion. A few miles beyond, another sign announced the entrance to Avdat National Park, which protects the ruined splendor of Avdat, the city that was the brilliant centerpiece of the Negev during Nabatean and Byzantine times. Some two thousand years ago, Avdat rose from a simple desert caravansary to a town studded with the fine homes of wealthy merchants and churches whose graceful arches overlooked the surrounding desert.

11

The bus crossed Mishor ha-Ruhot (Plain of the Winds) at the head of the central Negev. We passed the town of Mitspeh Ramon, then seemed to plunge off a precipice. A tightly wound descent of hairpin turns carried us into the dominant feature of the central Negev: Makhtesh Ramon, often called the Grand Canyon of Israel. The bus traversed the floor of this immense oval cavity (*makhtesh* means "crater" or "mortar") then, after a few miles, climbed the road on the other side. From the window, the choppy country south of Makhtesh Ramon looks full of plains and hills, and finally, the broad bed of Nahal Paran came into view, signaling the start of the southern Negev.

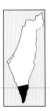

Sweeping in from the Sinai, Nahal Paran stretches nearly one hundred miles, the longest, largest riverbed in the Negev. Alongside the *nahal* lies the Wilderness of Paran, the largest, most desolate stretch of desert in the Negev. It was to this parched region that, at his wife Sarah's behest, Abraham, the patriarch, banished his concubine Hagar. There Hagar wept for her young son Ishmael, fearing the fierce aridity would devour him. A place no ancient traveler approached without concern, the Wilderness of Paran now rates little more than a casual glance from a passing bus.

By the time the bus crossed the Nahal Paran Bridge, we had been traveling more than two hours and I anxiously began looking for signs of Uvdah Airport, where I was to meet the Camel Riders. Hagar, the Queen of Sheba, King Uzziah and his generals, and the countless, now nameless traders, miners, soldiers, and slaves who toiled across these deserts were surely on journeys more hazardous than mine.

Nonetheless, evening approached, this was the last bus south, and I was worried about where to get off. Most bus stops seemed to be merely a bench and a sun covering in open vastness, miles from the nearest kibbutz or army post. The bus that had been standing-room only, now held only a half-dozen passengers.

Fortunately, Uvdah was obvious: a small airport surrounded by desert. It consisted of a departure lounge flanked by a small cafe and some offices and a large arrival room where I waited for the car coming to pick me up.

I watched planeloads of pale Europeans empty onto buses bound for the sun-soaked resort hotels of Eilat that line the Red Sea and busloads of tanned Europeans file into planes bound for Copenhagen and Frankfurt. I waited and read that Uvdah Valley is the largest water-catchment basin in the southern desert, a fact hardly obvious to a casual observer. It seems a valley in name alone, considered fertile only by the flinty standards of the mountains around it.

I waited until the sun set, the lights on the once-busy arrival and departure board had stopped blinking, and airport employees were leaving. I kept checking my watch. The pickup time came and went; the airport in the middle of nowhere became quieter and quieter. A certain concern began bubbling up.

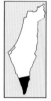

Exploring the ways in which geography, plants, and animals fit together requires a fair amount of travel. In order to devote my attention to, say, an Appalachian witch hazel or a salamander hiding along the stream at the witch hazel's feet, I plan my itinerary beforehand with compulsive detail. The hope is that the more complete the plan, the less scrabbling I'll do en route, and the more I can experience witch hazel and salamander.

But at a few points on every trip, I hit the panic button. Had I gotten off at the wrong airport? How many airports could there be in the middle of the Negev? Itinerary and maps scattered frantically around me, I was rechecking my position when a pleasant-faced young woman with a backpack and bouncy dark hair approached and asked if I was waiting for the camel trip.

We waited together. Becky, who had taken the bus north from Eilat, was not long out of college. She began telling me about her recent experiences with the Peace Corps in Turkmenistan. As she talked, the empty, echoing airport seemed much less ominous. Finally, a car roared up and a fellow hopped out. After an abrupt exchange of information, he piled our gear into the car, and we were off to the Camel Riders.

This is a quality of Israeli organization I had noticed a number of years before. Everything is a big mixed-up *balagan* until the last possible second. Then, in a rush, everything gets done and all is fine—*ha-kal beseder*—or pretty close to it. Perhaps the eight hundred thousand Russians that have migrated to Israel since the late 1980s are onto something. These are people who know irony. At the time, two journals for Russian émigrés were entitled *Balagan* and *Kal Beseder*.

We bounced off into the night, headed for the heart of the Eilat Mountains.

13

The Camel Riders

The small community of Shaharut straddles a hillside at the eastern edge of the Eilat Mountains and has attracted a community of people happy to be living away from conventional jobs and city bustle. Some are longtime Shaharut residents. Some are just passing through, spending time off the clock. A number work for the Camel Riders, as guides or in other staff positions.

Set apart from Shaharut, the Camel Riders' khan perches atop a cliff facing Jordan and overlooking the Aravah. We were escorted into the khan, a canvas-sided, palm-thatched "tent" whose walls were hung with rugs and whose dirt floor, thickly covered with multicolored carpets, could easily sleep fifty. There were two of us. We had caught that perfect period between the end of winter and the beginning of the tourist season.

A few lanterns and a potbellied stove gave off just enough light to create a circle of protective warmth while the far corners of the

Shai leads Farouk the camel across a stony stretch of hammada (desert plain) on our way to Mount Berekh and a four-day journey into the heart of the Eilat Mountains.

khan remained in shadow. Arriving at a strange place at night is disorienting. Make that place an exotic khan and you've set a mood straight from the *Arabian Nights*.

Shai, who would be our guide on the four-day camel trip, sat on pillows near the stove and ground coffee beans in a great wooden *makhtesh*, or mortar. The rhythmic thumping, he explained, was the sound of Bedouin hospitality in the desert. Anyone within earshot knew that they were welcome to sit and sip coffee with their host.

Three times, as tradition demands, Shai offered Becky and me tiny cups of coffee. Three times, as tradition demands, we accepted the cups and drank the thick, sweet liquid. This Bedouin tradition is a highly formalized icebreaker and, as we sipped, Shai told us a little about the Camel Riders.

The enterprise started with one man, Seffi, who began conventionally enough, studying as a young adult at Hebrew University. Later, the desert claimed his attention, and he began a few years of learning in an entirely different way. He lived with Bedouin, taking up traditional ways of surviving in the desert.

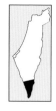

Rather than give up his desert life, Seffi turned it into a living. He started giving camel tours and, as the business grew, hired and trained guides. Now he offers tours lasting an afternoon to two weeks that focus on the Negev or roam from the Sinai through the Negev into Jordan's Edom Mountains, taking in remnants of ancient cultures as well as desert lore.

I learned about Seffi and the Camel Riders through the Society for the Protection of Nature in Israel (SPNI), Israel's oldest and largest conservation organization. Once aware of the possibility, I was sure that the truest way to see a Middle Eastern desert was from the back of a camel.

After we finished our coffee, a female staffer entered the khan carrying a bronze tray crowded with dishes. She offered us hummus, baba ghanouj, olives, sliced tomatoes and cucumbers, and pita bread.

After we ate, the Camel Riders staff returned to homes in Shaharut. Becky and I washed up in a simple but adequate palm-thatched bath-house then laid out our sleeping bags close to the warmth and security of the stove, the cavernous space of the khan all around. As my eyes became heavy, I saw a large, sand-colored rodent run along the wooden beam supporting one side of the khan. Too handsome to be called a rat, the plump animal slipped through a slit to the outside, and I let sleep claim me.

Morning was announced by the insistent caw-caw-caw of crows. Becky and I packed our bags and walked a little way down the hill to the camel corral. There Shai and Dan, an apprentice camel guide, loaded up, and we began walking from the outpost town of Shaharut.

Shai strode ahead with the agile, erect bearing of a self-contained man of the desert. But where a desert dweller of old might carry a long curved sword, Shai carried a flute made from a length of PVC pipe. Dan, who had the look and easy amble of a student on spring break, led the second camel, and Becky and I brought up the rear, four people and two camels heading south among the Eilat Mountains.

15

These jumbled mountains, a clutter of deep red sandstone peaks separated by serpentine canyons, are the crown of the southern Negev. The jewel in the crown is Timna, a valley of dark magmatic plugs, scattered green malachite, and ancient altars where Egyptian miners prayed for safekeeping so far from the Nile, in a wilderness where they smelted copper more than five thousand years ago.

Within the twists and turns of this complicated terrain ibex and a few rare leopards make their home. Hyenas and wolves live here, too, and gazelle where broad valleys like Uvdah open up. The Eilat Mountains form a backdrop for migrating raptors that soar on thermal updrafts rising along the cliffs. Reptiles, hiding among rocks to avoid the sun's burning heat, are seldom seen but found everywhere in the southern desert.

The plants that survive in the southern Negev are the toughest and driest in all Israel. Species of acacia and caper plants that live nowhere else in the country live here. Broom and saltbush, found in wadis here and throughout Israel's deserts, provide animals and humans with a few of life's barest necessities.

During the next four days we would travel more than thirty miles: trekking through wadis that feed the Uvdah Valley, scaling the shoulders of Mount Berekh, twisting among the narrow confines of Eteq Canyon, traversing the cliffs that circle Timna Valley, then descending into the valley itself.

The path rounded a hill where a few dogs barked ownership near Shaharut's last house, and soon we had passed beyond the sight of civilization. A slim man with the fluidity that comes of practicing yoga, Shai swung himself onto the back of one camel. He showed us how he could lock his legs around the pommel to secure his seat and leave his arms free for the reins.

He asked if Becky and I would like to try. He and Dan compelled the camels to kneel, and we each climbed atop saddles bound back and front by tall wooden pommels. Positioned atop the camel's hump, the padded saddle was centered between enormous, bulging camel bags that hung from either side.

Shai and Dan called for the camels to rise, and my camel staggered up on his back legs, nearly pitching me over his head. Next, he lurched up on his front legs, spilling me toward his tail. Not a graceful beginning. I envisioned blisters on my hands from clutching the pommel.

16

Unlike a horse, whose head and neck rise like a safe stanchion, a camel's head is way down there. Seated seven feet above the desert, I had unobstructed views but no feeling of security. For a while I sat bolt astride the camel as if he were a horse but found myself sliding from side to side, ineffectually gripping the pommel for balance.

After determining that I was in no immediate danger, I tried wrapping one leg around the front of the pommel and hooking it under the other leg, as Shai had demonstrated. This had the effect of causing my behind to shift slightly off the ridge of the camel's humped back. *Voilà!* Stability.

With my newfound skill, I let go of the pommel and watched the scenery unfold before me. Increasingly relaxed and confident, I twisted around to look at the desert on either side. Then I tried the hooked-leg position on the left side. It worked, too. I pulled out my notebook now that my arms were free and felt altogether smug. "What's his name?" I asked, rubbing a hand across his tight, light brown coat, thinking I should be introduced to my transportation. Dan, who walked ahead loosely holding the camel's lead rope, replied, "Farouk."

Becky decided she preferred walking to riding, but I rode for an hour or so, across rocky rises and around bare hills, until my legs cramped. With Dan holding him steady, I slid off Farouk and fell into line behind.

Relics at the Edge of the Uvdah Valley

Taking turns riding and walking, we wound our way along routes traveled by people and animals for thousands of years, beside dry streambeds at the base of mountains devoid of any tree or shrub. Mostly sandstone, the mountains are colored by minerals, here tan, there ocher, not yet the famous deep reds of Nubian sandstone found at Timna. Sometimes, ascending or descending, we crossed benches of broken black flint. Who knows how many spear points, ax heads, and other Stone Age tools are buried here?

At the time, the southern Negev was experiencing the second year of a drought. Elsewhere a drought might mean a few inches less water, but in the southern Negev there's not much to subtract from an inch. For two years, not a drop of rain had touched most of the land. Yet, plants struggled on, and where plants survive, so does the tenuous but tough desert web of life, from spiny mice and scorpions to ibex and leopards.

In order to give up as little water as possible to the blazing day, the bean caper's stomata—tiny pores that allow gas exchange—open only at night. The thick, waxy cuticle that covers each leaf helps retain moisture, when moisture is available. We saw a few plants, hidden in the shade of a boulder, that had the temerity to produce small white flowers.

That first day, we saw vegetation only in the wadis. One of the plants, bean caper, told us how bad the drought had been. In the northern Negev, the succulent leaves of this low desert shrub swell with water like tiny cucumbers, so it is called the desert cucumber. (In Hebrew its name is *zugan*, or couple plant, because its succulent leaves grow in pairs.) Here, the leaves were shriveled and the ground around littered with those that had fallen off.

In one wadi we saw a bean caper bush all twisted and black, dead except for a lone live branch. Because each of its multiple branches is tied to its own root system, if some branches die, others can struggle

on until rains finally come. In this way, bean capers can live for a hundred or more years. In the Negev, each plant and animal has some angle, some strategy for survival.

Once, in the Sinai, I met a Bedouin couple at an oasis. The wife was clothed all in black: black gown, black veil, black head covering woven with bright red and yellow threads. Why, I wondered, would anyone wear heat-absorptive black in such a hot place? The answer is that a person who has only one set of clothing is more concerned with the brutal cold of a desert winter than the heat of summer.

If it had been summer, not early spring, Shai, Dan, Becky, and I would have traveled more during the shoulders of the day, near dawn and dusk, and would have rested in what shade we could find during midday. Each day, however, we did stop when the sun was high and laid out a large reed mat for a simple lunch.

We arranged a platter of oranges, apples, and figs, dipping them in a paste of sesame and date spiced with cinnamon and ginger. A smaller platter of nuts completed the meal. And water, always water, to replace what the desert had sucked from us. After a short rest, we packed up and continued on, quiet and reflective in the waning daylight hours.

Anyone who has spent time in deserts knows they are worthy of great respect, require considerable effort, and reward effort with great beauty. To not only see but perceive what the desert offers, a person must strip away the distractions of civilization and bring only essentials to the experience. In a desert, water is the first essential.

18

I had taken plenty of trips into the desert canyons of Utah, been soothed by glowing red canyon walls at twilight, and, later, been wrapped in the quiet blanket of night, the Milky Way unmarred by city lights, the silence unmarred by the sound of motors. But the trips were always slightly spoiled by having to hoist on a bulky backpack each morning. Its straps drag at your shoulders, its bag of dead weight bangs against the posterior bones of your pelvis.

What had become obvious was that experiencing the desert without having to be my own beast of burden is exquisite luxury. Camel trekking allowed me to concentrate on the sights and sounds of the desert while camels carried gear and water.

Abruptly, Shai stopped and squatted in the middle of a wadi about as wide as a four-lane road. Even if we had noticed what he was about to point out, we would have missed its significance. Across the wadi, a low dam of softball-sized rocks had been planted to break the flow of floodwater. The faster floodwater flows, the less it penetrates the ground. Once desert dwellers slowed down the water, they could more easily capture it in irrigation canals. Since the dawn of agriculture, they have planted crops on floodplains, irrigating their fields with channeled floodwater.

In fertile valleys of the Middle East, early people first gathered wild grains, then began cultivating crops such as wheat, lentils, and barley. People farmed in Uvdah Valley as early as 5000 B.C.E. and there archaeologists have found some of the world's oldest threshing floors.

Along with the stone breakwater we found potsherds but had no idea whether they were made twenty or two hundred years ago. Shai showed us another remnant of an earlier time: a small piece of wood pierced by a hole whose edges were polished by use. A long stick fit into the hole, creating a spindle for twisting black

Farouk rests at daybreak before being loaded with gear. To keep a low profile in sun and sandstorms, camels developed specially shaped breastbones and thickly calloused kneepads.

goat hair and tan camel hair into thread. Perhaps a Bedouin relic.

The farmers were not, by definition, Bedouin. Bedouin do not farm. They have never considered themselves "slaves to the earth." Instead, Bedouin traditionally have lived a nomadic life, moving their tents and their flocks of goats and sheep from one grazing area to another.

Bedouin once roamed Negev and Sinai with their herds, each tribe within generally recognized boundaries. With the modern state of Israel came strictly monitored international borders. Like many before them, some Bedouin departed for the Sinai. The Sinai Peninsula, though governed by Egypt, has long been an area where people generally can live their lives beyond the eyes of government and state.

Some Bedouin who have settled in the Negev's northern highlands have adopted modern trappings. Their dwellings are no longer tediously made goat-hair tents, but composites of tin, plastic, and canvas. Driving by at night, it is not unusual to see the blue glow of a TV lighting an entryway.

There is a place on the continuum between the wild and the sown for each of us. Some prefer the comforts and culture of cities. Some are happiest away from crowds and the clutter of buildings, where the loudest sound is that of the wind. For me, it would be impossible to give up art museums and cafes for the stripped-down life of a desert dweller. But like my camel-trek companions, I occasionally need the solitude and space of wild places to reclaim my sense of self and my relation to the world, of nature and of people.

For most of the day, the only sounds we had heard were those of birds, Farouk bellowing, the wind, Shai's flute, and our own voices. Nothing more. Visual and aural distractions are absent in this austere majesty. The land allows the human imagination to fill its stripped-down beauty with legend, with pattern, with a sense of a greater presence. Again and again I was reminded why the great prophets had fled to the desert.

A Miracle the First Night

As we walked toward evening of the first day, Shai told us about camels, who are superbly equipped to handle aridity, sandstorms, and every other sort of desert travail. All parts of a camel's anatomy are designed to help it survive in the desert. When khamsins scour the desert, a camel will turn its back to the wind and kneel. But in case the wind doubles around, the camel's ears are fuzzy with hairs that help prevent stray sand from entering. Long, double-fringed, interlocking lashes protect its eyes from sand and sun. In addition, a light-filtering membrane extends over the camel's eyeball when the sun's glare is too bright.

The slitlike nostrils on its long, sloping nose shut tight in a sandstorm. At other times, moisture expelled from its nostrils during respiration leaks down narrow grooves into the camel's mouth. Water is precious, and a camel recycles and conserves as much as it can.

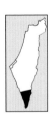

In the Negev, a person would die in just a few days without water. A camel can survive about two weeks, in part because of the most well-known part of its anatomy, its hump. The hump of a well-watered, well-fed camel is turgid with fat. As a camel travels across the

Camels were not originally desert animals. The first camels, the size of rabbits, lived in the forests of North America about fifty-four million years ago. Roaming across continental bridges, they established themselves throughout the world. Early camels came in all shapes and sizes. Most died out; some became the ancestors of South American llamas, and two—the one-humped dromedary and the two-humped Bactrian—became the largest of desert denizens.

The Bible says that Rebecca was chosen as Isaac's wife because she offered to water Abraham's camels at her father's well (Genesis 24:19). Although camels are mentioned even earlier in the Bible, when Abraham went to Egypt during a drought (Genesis 12:16), they are relative newcomers to the Middle East. Researchers believe they were first domesticated in southern Arabia more than four thousand years ago. Probably they were introduced to the Middle East by Midianites invading from northwest Arabia. Today the only wild dromedaries live in Australia—feral descendants of camels introduced to that continent in the mid-1800s.

desert, it burns fat for energy with water as a byproduct. Our camels' humps, full and rigid at the beginning of the journey, shrank and became flaccid as the days progressed. A nearly perfect desert system.

21

Walking behind a camel for a long time, you notice the most intimate details of its anatomy. For one, camel penises point backwards. The construction looks inconvenient for mating, yet reproduction is one of the most strongly hard-wired aspects of animal behavior. If it hindered reproduction, this particular configuration must have some supplemental use.

Each camel has a distinct personality and a mind of its own. Although they are infamously cantankerous, our two were generally well behaved, having gone to etiquette school. Camels are truly prized by their trainers and owners. I, too, fell for these oddly shaped ships of the desert: trustworthy, surefooted, uncomplaining . . .

Well, Farouk actually did quite a bit of complaining every time we loaded him up in the morning or led him down a steep descent. He groaned loudly and long, a terrible wailing protest reminiscent of Chewbacka, the *Star Wars* Wookie.

Switching from walking to camelback again, I was comfortably

surrounded by camel bags filled with sleeping bags, water jugs, pots, and canisters of food. In addition to me, Farouk can carry about five hundred pounds of equipment. Despite this load, Farouk sweats relatively less than I.

A camel's body temperature fluctuates: higher in the daytime and lower at night. Because its body temperature stays closer to the ambient temperature, a camel does not have to lose as much heat through evaporation. So it sweats less. Camels can tolerate body temperature variations of more than 11 degrees Fahrenheit. We consider ourselves sick if our temperature is only two degrees off 98.6 Fahrenheit.

Everything about a camel is water-efficient. A camel can lose 40 percent of its body weight through dehydration, then gulp a hundred liters of water at a time to revitalize itself. If we did that, our blood cells would burst, but camels even have desert-adapted blood cells.

Camels absorb water more slowly into blood cells that are smaller but more numerous. And they are the only mammals with oval blood cells. Small and oval allows the blood cells to travel through narrow, thick-walled capillaries—an adaptation to higher salt content in the body when the camel is dehydrated. Even camel kidneys are water efficient.

And a male camel's penis? It is said a camel's penis hooks slightly backward so that when he pees, his urine will run down his back legs, cooling him. Urine also wets the camel's tail during rutting displays. A male camel slaps his urine-moistened tail against his back, intimidating rivals with the aggressive noise.

I thought highly of our lead camel, the dignified, self-directed Khatz. Farouk had a mind of his own, but it was a childish mind, like a whining kid on a long car trip. Perhaps he could be excused for his complaining because he was, after all, only seven years old, still young for a camel.

Just before making camp for the night, we descended down a steep slope, exposing Farouk's worst fault. Khatz negotiated the difficult terrain sedately, his long legs gracefully straight while balancing the heavier of the two loads. Farouk trotted with a splayfooted gait, bouncing me and gear wildly from side to side in an uncontrolled version of the hokey-pokey.

Our first camp was on the banks of a dry, sandy wadi that eventually reaches the Uvdah Valley. Above us a cliff hid a portion of the darkening sky as we stoked a fire and chopped vegetables for dinner.

To temper our hunger while we cooked, Shai put out a bit of halva and some strong sweet tea made from a type of lemon grass he had gathered on the way.

We quickly discovered that Shai could cook three-star meals from a few basics and what the desert provided. After a vegetarian slumgullion that included potatoes, tomatoes, onions, and eggs, we scrubbed our bowls with sand and rinsed them. Then we washed our hands with a lather produced by crushing stems of the *yafruq* plant, whose name comes from the Hebrew word meaning "chapter," because each stem is neatly segmented. We hobbled the camels, wrapped ourselves in sleeping bags near the dying embers of our fire, and talked.

Although Shai talked little about himself, he explained much about the Negev as we walked each day, and he told wonderful stories.

Dan had just finished his three years in the army, including duty on the West Bank and along Israel's border with Lebanon. Young Israelis who can afford it run off to India or South America after the army, places as different and exotic as they can find. In this effort to regroup mentally and emotionally, Dan had chosen the desert.

Becky talked about her time in Turkmenistan. The city where she had worked sounded like equal parts grim post-Soviet industrial outpost and Samarkand exotic, with old women weaving rugs from wool dyed in tones of deep ruby and sapphire blue. I told of camping in American deserts. Talked out, we fell silent. I tried to stay awake as long as possible, knowing such nights are rare.

23

In the black velvet night an eyelash of moon rose above the horizon. The new moon: Rosh Hodesh, the head of the month. For the ancient Hebrews, the sighting of this sliver of new moon was a sign that the celestial clock had ticked into a new month. It was a sign of continuity in a universe whose solar systems and galaxies, gravitational pulls and quantum theories they knew little about. But they understood the universe was created with order and predictability, and they celebrated that.

The return of the moon has occurred hundreds of times during my lifetime, but the omnipresent glow of city lights and evenings spent inside has always given the moon's return more intellectual than visceral recognition. Deep within the Eilat Mountains, this perfect arc of pale light dominated the night.

Despite the fact that I had seen new moons before, the blackness of the desert night, the smallness of our group, and the wildness of the place sparked a thrill of primal recognition. Here we had a *nes*, a miracle.

Rabbis explain that a miracle can flower from something we experience regularly, even take for granted. Given a certain time and place and a certain emotional vision, the simplest act can seem a miracle. These natural transformations are powerful because we are changed by them. We see with new eyes.

Stories in Stone on the Way to Mount Berekh

The first thing I noticed the next morning was the number of darkling beetles scurrying along the desert floor. Round and darkly shiny, their bodies are perched atop legs so long they look like stilts.

As I crouched over one, it scurried out of my shadow. Its long legs are a desert adaptation, of course. The desert floor can burn fifteen degrees hotter than the air, so even a few millimeters of height will hold a darkling beetle above the worst of the heat.

Another beetle trick is to scavenge for food at night and in the cool of the morning. Negev air is so dry that it holds no heat. So when the sun sets in the desert, temperatures plummet. Mornings remain relatively cool until the ground once again absorbs the relentless heat of the sun. During the hottest part of the day, the beetles hide under rocks. Even if they do get caught in the sun's glare, an air space under their fused wings serves as insulation from heat and cold.

24   Before we packed up, Shai suggested we try some yoga-type movements to loosen us up, physically and mentally. I have always been leery of group meditative states, so I joined in reluctantly but found they were essentially stretching exercises—not a bad thing after a night on the ground.

As the sun warmed the morning air, we made our way across the desert floor to the defiles that lead to Mount Berekh. Quietly competent, Shai made camel guiding look easy. And even though his clothes looked like desert garb from some indeterminate time, they were clean every day. Certainly cleaner than mine. I had opted to stuff in wildflower and bird books rather than extra clothes, but I had bought a new hat before my journey.

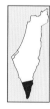

Head coverings are critical in the desert. I had an Australian bush-type hat with a broad, flexible brim; beige to reflect the sun. Becky wore a baseball cap with a long bill. Shai and Dan wore kaffiyehs. Long cloths secured around the head by a twisted cord, kaffiyehs drape down the back, protecting the neck. The loose ends can be wrapped around the face when sandstorms flare up.

By late morning we had reached the bottom of Mount Berekh and began climbing steeply. Cliffs fell sheerly from one side of the trail. The other side hugged the shoulders of the mountain as it wound up the high dome of light gray rock. Below the trail, in a narrow canyon funneling down to the desert floor, shrubs spread as sparsely as a young man's mustache. Twelve hundred or so plant species grow in the Negev, nearly half of all plant species in Israel. Only a quarter of the desert species, however, are tough enough to live in the southern desert.

As we trudged upward under a sun so bright it bleached away perspective, we were jolted from our heat-heavy effort by other travelers: three Egyptian vultures floating effortlessly just above our heads. Magnificently plumaged in bold black and white, these raptors are among the half-billion birds—from warblers to eagles—that funnel through Israel during spring and fall migrations.

Egyptian vultures roost on cliffsides at night, waiting for the morning sun to warm the air. Like other raptors we saw during our trek, they conserve energy by soaring, rather than flapping their broad five-foot wings. As the sun heats the air, the air expands, rising along the cliffs in spirals called thermals. The raptors use their broad wings to let thermals lift them, gliding from thermal to thermal north from Africa.

Near the top of a switchback we stopped to take a water break. In deserts it is important to drink water in timed intervals, like medicine. Shai also stopped us at this particular spot to show us some rudist fossils, which protruded from the rest of the rock. These mollusks, about the size and shape of an ice-cream cone, were the corals of their time, he explained, living in tropical seas during the Cretaceous period when dinosaurs ruled Earth.

25

In northern Israel, near the Mediterranean Sea, a whole reef of perfectly preserved rudists rises near the coastline. Standing on the dry slopes of Mount Berekh, it was hard to imagine turquoise seas filled with colonies of rudists and other strange sea life. But, in fact, where we stood once was sea bottom.

Much of Israel is exposed sea bottom—young land, geologically speaking. Marine sediment hundreds of feet thick spreads across nearly three-quarters of Israel. Layers of chalk and limestone, compressed from skeletons and shells that fell to ocean floors over millions of years, now mix with other sedimentary rock in the Carmel Mountains, Galilee, and the Judean Hills. Whereas northern Israel is mostly sedimentary rock, the southern Negev has it all: a magnificent mix of sedimentary, metamorphic, and igneous rock.

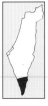

At Timna Park, our ultimate destination, the basement of Earth is revealed. There, igneous rock—primal rock, direct from Earth's molten mantle—was pushed up by the titanic grinding of Earth's tectonic plates. Timna's igneous rock dates to the Precambrian period, more than six hundred million years ago, a time before life on Earth began.

We were working our way to the top of Mount Berekh for our first look at Timna, when we stopped to rest. The flat-topped rocks at this switchback seemed a perfect place to sit down. Apparently earlier people thought so, too. Engraved in the rock were images of a man on a donkey, a camel, and some sort of female symbol. With human presence in the Eilat Mountains dating nearly ten thousand years, who knows how many centuries these petroglyphs have lain exposed to the sun.

Finally, we reached the top of Mount Berekh. And, as usual on Israel's high places, a military lookout crowns a neighboring mountain. Eight hundred feet below, Timna Valley spread out from a center of dark, igneous crags. These crags were formed when magma, thrust up from Earth's liquid mantle, cooled as granite before it reached the surface. The movement of tectonic plates pushed the granite toward the surface. Eventually, the surface rock eroded, revealing the dark crags.

The view of Timna from above is straight from an H. Rider Haggard tale of romantic adventure. A solitary road on the floor of the enormous cirque winds around jagged peaks of black igneous rock. Mine-shaft holes, piles of tailings, and other remains of mining, dating back thousands of years, score the landscape. Flat-topped acacia trees hint of Africa. Far away, at the other side of the cirque, soar natural rock formations called Solomon's Pillars.

Circling atop the surrounding mountains, it would take us two more days to reach Timna Valley proper.

After lunch atop Mount Berekh and a catnap, we packed up and moved on. Afternoons were heat-drugged. Little was said. Now comfortable atop a camel, I hooked one leg around the saddle and dozed. We had descended from Mount Berekh to high plateaus and I could hear the sound of flint striking flint as the plodding camels kicked up small stones. A fly buzzed. One of the camels swallowed—a gargling sound. Somewhere out of sight a crow complained. The hot, heavy silence seemed to smother more than soothe.

I decided to walk, hoping movement would wake me. Dan held the lead rope as I slid down Khatz's shoulder—I'd given up on Farouk and his hokey-pokey gait.

26

Dan reminded me of my son, who is a bit younger but has the same straightforward, light-up-the-world grin. A quick pang of missing family shot through me.

The move to my feet did not have the hoped-for effect. Slogging along, eyes on the ground, too logy to lift my head, I looked to one side and spotted a skull, the sun-bleached remains of an ibex.

Fascinated and instantly alert, I picked up the ibex skull and examined every orifice, noting the angle of the horn insertions, the smooth, perfect hole where the spinal cord entered, and a small, strange hole near one eye cavity. Could this asymmetric puncture be from the tooth of a leopard? the gnawing of a porcupine hungry for calcium? Or could it be from the arrow point of some ancient hunter?

Earlier, near a wide wadi, we had passed wells that held sweet water and wells whose water had become salty with desert minerals. There we had found other bones. A pile of rocks that looked unnatural drew us closer. Peering between the chinks we saw a human skull, perhaps a child's because it was small.

Desert travelers of old had little energy to spare, so the dead were carried until the next stopping point, usually near a wadi or well. Because the earth is too hard to dig, mounds of rocks served as burial sites. We had found one, and I had drawn away out of respect and from some more primitive emotion.

An ibex skull could fascinate, but the skull of one of my own kind was another matter. I had shivered—a dread of death—and understood why so many cultures have such elaborate rituals concerning the dead. Contact with even those unknown remains seemed to ask for some sort of ceremony to honor the dead and to make the boundaries between living and dead very clear.

As the sun edged closer to the horizon, I held the ibex skull but thought about the child.

27

Dinner Serves as a History of Food

We made our second night's camp in the lee of a low curving cliff not far from a wadi. By the time we were finished unloading the camels and setting up camp, the sun had left only a rose-colored memory on the horizon.

Deserts have a way of bringing the basics into focus: we were tired, thirsty, and hungry. First we drank, then we cooked. The main dish was a stew of red lentils, chunks of white potatoes, sweet potatoes, carrots, sweet pepper, and zucchini. Earlier in the day, Shai had

told us about desert saltbush, and we had gathered handfuls of its silvery leaves. These we cooked with onions—a poor man's dish, according to Job. The biblical sufferer says of the impoverished men who mock him: "They flee to a parched land, to the gloom of desolate wasteland. They pluck saltbush and wormwood; the roots of broom are their food" (Job 30:3-4).

To Job, saltbush and broom root may have been food for the lowest class of society. To me, saltbush stew was tastier than any fast-food, but I was probably too hungry to judge.

Our salad of chopped tomatoes, cucumbers, and spring onions was seasoned with wild marjoram. We roasted eggplant over the fire and liberally sprinkled its soft, smoky flesh with lemon juice and garlic. And we baked Bedouin bread: *fatir*, a thin dough thrown over a metal half-moon shell set atop the fire. Ancient people of this region ate flat breads, wheat gruels, and other quickly prepared wheat staples. They were, after all, nomads, people on the move. Leavened breads were for those who could wait for dough to rise.

With so little naturally occurring sustenance around us, we were thankful to eat such a feast. The stew of red lentils and our hunger was a direct echo of Esau's great hunger when he traded his birthright to Jacob for a red-lentil pottage (Genesis 25:29-34).

Lentils were an ancient food even then. These legumes were among the first foods cultivated, about ten thousand years ago, perhaps earlier even than wheat or barley—all of which can be traced to wild varieties in the Middle East. Lentils average 24 percent protein and not only ripen earlier than the cereals but ripen successively, with flowers and fruit found at the same time on the same plant. Lentil plants can be harvested over a longer period than cereals, which ripen all at once.

Esau is associated not only with red lentils, but with the color red in general. He was said to have a ruddy complexion, and when he left his father's land he settled in mountains whose name, *edom*, means red. The Edom Mountains lie opposite the Eilat Mountains, on the Jordanian side of the Aravah Valley. We had watched the Edom Mountains come in and out of view on our trek. Sometimes they were a wall of fiery red etched sharply on the eastern horizon. Sometimes, when dust clouded the air, we saw only an impression of looming mass.

Even the herb that flavored our salad has a history. Hyssop, or *zatar*, grows on rocky slopes in most parts of Israel. Its fuzzy, gray-green leaves, which smell wonderfully aromatic when crushed, are dried and mixed with sesame seeds and olive oil as a savory spread on pita. In Egypt, just before the Exodus, the Hebrews dipped the humble plant in lamb's blood to mark the lintels of their homes during the plague of the killing of the firstborn.

The simple act of eating had become a history lesson.

At breakfast the morning of our third day, we were introduced to another side of Khatz the camel. The four of us were seated on the large straw mat that served as a portable room, using bread to scoop up *zatar*-topped *labaneh* (thick yogurt). Some other foodstuffs lay just behind me, ready for packing. Both camels knelt on the ground nearby, their legs tucked under them.

Until now, Khatz held himself as the unflappable lead camel: patient, steadfast, a mind of his own, but always pointed in the right direction. And his large size matched his psychological presence.

So it was with some amusement that I noticed the usually dignified Khatz edging toward the mat on his knees, a few feet at a time. Whenever I turned around to see what he was doing, he froze and looked away, preoccupied with some middle-distance view. We knew his eyes were on the food.

When Khatz's muzzle hung over my shoulder, I looked up, throwing him what I hoped was an annoyed and suspicious look. Khatz looked around, seemingly surprised that he found himself so near the food.

Enough acting. We muscled Khatz back to a respectable distance. Did this huge animal think that even kneeling, he could sneak up on us? Did he think we didn't notice? But I had to give him credit for trying.

29

Music in Eteq Canyon

We were headed toward Eteq Canyon and an entirely different view of the Eilat Mountains. Until now, we had seen rugged mountains, vast plains, and distant vistas, but no real canyons. After a few hours of trekking, we reached the head of Eteq Canyon, atop a rounded knob similar to Mount Berekh. There we hobbled the camels and slung on our day packs. Although camels can negotiate incredibly steep trails, they have their limits, and Eteq was one.

We hiked down a razorback ridge and into the first section of the canyon, which was about thirty feet wide but narrowed as we descended. Here the walls were low and the floor of the canyon rocky. As we descended farther into the canyon, the walls rose higher and

Sculpted by wind and water, Eteq Canyon presents a fantasia of form. In years when the Eilat Mountains receive rain, animals come to drink at the inner canyon's clear pool.

30 higher until they confined the sky to a narrow wedge of blue directly above us. Smooth tan sandstone floored the canyon, stepping down like broad stairs.

In years of average rainfall, the stream that carved the canyon flows down the middle. Now, in the second year of drought, the canyon was dry. But the shadowed recesses gave plants a chance. Near shrubs bunched along the bottom of the sloping walls, we saw an ibex grazing on the flowers and new leaves of a thorny, bushy acacia. The ibex saw us and moved to the safety of a rocky ledge, her sleek tan body blending so perfectly with the color of the canyon walls that she seemed to disappear. Like most desert animals, the ibex's pale coat also helps reflect light and heat.

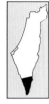

Two genera of large grazing mammals live in the Negev, and their niches rarely overlap. Gazelle, fast and light as the wind, live on plains and broad valleys and use their speed as protection from predators. Ibex, related to wild goats, prefer the rocky slopes and recesses of canyons. Their superb climbing abilities, not speed, are what give ibex the edge over Negev predators such as leopards. At the brink of extinction not long ago, due to sport-hunting and encroachment, ibex have been reintroduced to their native habitats in Israel and given strict protection. Now about two thousand ibex live in the Negev and Judean Deserts.

Just beyond where the ibex grazed, Eteq Canyon began a steep and narrow descent; the walls became smooth and water-sculpted. We came to the top of a ledge with a twenty-foot sheer drop to a recess below. Not as agile as ibex, we climbed down using metal handholds and footholds anchored to the canyon walls.

Within the cool, curved recess, I could see where in wetter years a narrow waterfall dropped cleanly into a perfectly round pool. In the middle of the sheer wall, a caper plant clung from some unseen crack. Dense with round, green leaves, caper stems streamed down like some vegetable version of Rapunzel's hair.

This is the southern Negev version of the caper. Its blue-green cousin grows most everywhere else, including from the stones of the Kotel, the Western Wall, in Jerusalem. In Israel, the caper is renowned as the king of plants because it is versatile and strong enough to penetrate rock.

All a caper seed needs is a crack in a rock face to get started. Once germinated, the caper exudes chemicals that help dissolve rock, allowing the plant to insinuate its roots deeper and deeper into a cliff face, absorbing nutritious minerals from the decomposed rock.

The caper has other desert survival strategies. Its leaves are coated with a waxy cuticle to retain moisture. And its stomata—akin to our pores—are located only on the top of the leaf, just the opposite of what one would expect in a dry climate. But the caper's stomata remain closed until triggered by rain, then they open to absorb as much of the life-giving substance as possible.

31

Like lentils, caper plants flower over a long period, a flower or two at a time. Each flower is a small showpiece with a spray of purple stamens surrounded by delicate petals, white and luminous so they will attract night-flying moths as pollinators.

Shai said the yellowish "sauce" inside the red, grape-sized fruit tastes like Dijon mustard and that Bedouin children suck the sauce and spit out the seeds. Since the caper's seeds contain cyanide, I decided not to experiment. The capers that grocery stores sell in small jars for high prices are not caper fruits. They are unopened flower buds, and they have been harvested as an agricultural crop since talmudic times.

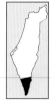

Sitting beneath the draping caper, shaded from the sun by the canyon's narrowness, we ate a simple lunch of dates and almonds as Shai told a story:

Once a proud and mighty king decided to survey his kingdom. He set out, surrounded by royal retainers, and everywhere he went his subjects bowed before him. After he had visited all the great cities and towns, even the countryside, he asked, "Is there more that is mine?" His retainers took him into the desert where they came upon a desert dweller leaning against a rock, eyes closed, basking in the sun. The man opened his eyes when the king's shadow crossed him and merely looked up.

The king was outraged. "Bow before your king or you will die," he roared. The desert man shrugged his shoulders, whereupon the king's guards seized him and were about to cut off his head. The king could not believe such temerity and said, "Wait! This man impresses me. Let us not kill him. Let him go." The desert man eased down in his former comfortable position. "Rather, I will be magnanimous. I will show you my great power and grant you anything you wish," he said to the man, as he stood over him.

The man considered, then said, "My wish? My wish is that you buzz off, you're blocking my sun."

Hidden within Eteq Canyon, we too were feeling freed from the busy world beyond the desert. But the feeling was illusory because soon the sound of many people, coming closer, jarred our ears. Eventually the group came close enough for us to distinguish the raucous sounds of teenage boys.

32

They climbed down the handholds: five, ten, twenty boys about fifteen years old, accompanied by a teacher and, as it was a school trip, an armed escort. Grouping themselves on the other side of the pool, the boys shouted and wrestled and generally woke up Eteq Canyon. At a loss, we simply stared until Shai picked up his flute and started to play.

It caught the attention of the boys and we all listened, the lilting notes resonating from the canyon walls. When he was done, Shai suggested the boys respond to his presentation with one of their own. They all looked toward a boy whose dark features suggested Middle Eastern origins.

The boy reached for his rectangular water bottle and, balancing it on his knees, beat out a rhythm reminiscent of a *tambalah*, a Yemeni drum. Then he began to sing, a high, exquisitely pure sound that rippled and wound back on itself, echoing in the canyon as the words told of Moses leading the children of Israel in the desert, not far from here.

What had begun as a disturbance ended as an enchantment.

After retracing our route to the top of the canyon, we retrieved the camels and started our march toward Timna Valley, across first one bleak rocky plain, then another. In late afternoon we reached our final descent. The trail was too narrow, rocky, and steep to ride. Even though it occasionally looked as though the camels might pitch head over heels with their loads, they negotiated the twisting trail with surprising grace.

Near the bottom, where the trail became sandy, we saw the tracks of wolves leading into the mountains. Wolves, mammals of the north, are at their southern limit in the Negev. Although relatively plentiful in the Eilat Mountains, they have adapted to a desert environment by becoming smaller, with a shorter, lighter coat. This sand-colored subspecies of the timber wolf weighs about forty pounds, half as much as the gray-toned timber wolf.

As we entered the valley, we saw tracks of gazelle leading down the sandy trail. About fifteen steppe eagles descended on thermals that ebbed as the evening air cooled. The great birds circled lower and lower toward the cliffs, where they would roost until morning.

On our last night in the wilderness, we made camp on the soft sands of a small side canyon that spilled into Timna. In the evening light, the smooth canyon walls glowed in peach and gold. By the time we finished dinner it was dark, but there was enough of a moon to dimly light our campsite. Finding a private "bathroom" before bed meant walking some distance. After picking a path around rocks and small shrubs, I found a secluded spot with a fine view of the Timna Valley suffused with moonglow.

33

I had learned the hard way to appreciate such moments. Trekking through the Himalayas, I had dutifully taken daily medicine to prevent dysentery. After the third week with no problems, I figured I was immune and stopped taking the prophylactic.

The next day, just as we were about to trek into the highest, wildest area we would visit, dysentery struck. Three nights later, I found myself shivering in a tent at sixteen thousand feet, my bowels roiling in protest. Nearly in tears, I dragged myself out into the bitterly cold black night.

Seemingly alone on the roof of the world in Nepal, I looked down on a scene of ineffable wonder. A near-full moon lit up the clear night sky. Below, a thick and endless blanket of clouds hid the world, except for a dozen or so cold and glittering peaks, whose icy white summits pierced the cloud layer. This heavenly view would not have been mine had I been a good patient.

I've come to view these inconveniences as opportunities. Timna alone in moonlight was a soft-edged dream compared to its sun-blasted face.

Wrapped in our sleeping bags, Becky, Dan, Shai, and I fell asleep under a canopy of stars.

I woke early, before dawn, to walk alone on this last morning in the wilderness of the southern Negev. Khatz and Farouk sat atop folded legs, peacefully chewing their cuds. The soles of their feet, the shape and size of pita breads and perfectly designed for crossing desert sands, were just another strange and wonderful part of their anatomy.

In Timna Valley proper, doglike tracks crossed the sand, one pair large, one pair small. A mother and youngster perhaps. I returned to camp where we ate, packed up, and moved out into the broad cirque of Timna Valley, now preserved as Timna Park. When I pointed out the tracks to Shai, he said, no, it was the tracks of only one animal: a hyena.

He explained that because hyenas move backwards as they drag animal carcasses, their front legs are longer and the paws broader than those of their back legs. For the same reason, their necks are long and their shoulders strong. Thus, hyenas' odd, hump-backed shape. Wildlife movies have cemented in our minds the image of hyenas cleaning up a lion's kill, but these efficient predators, which are distantly related to dogs and wolves, are just as likely to kill their own meal as to scavenge.

34

Israel is the home of the striped hyena, which is endangered and not as communal as the spotted hyenas more familiar to most people. These mountains are also home to the few leopards that remain in Israel. Tracking the leopard's progress are zoologists such as Dr. Benny Shalmon, who began as a nature guide with the SPNI.

Based at the Mammal Information Center at SPNI's Eilat Field School, Dr. Shalmon is hopeful that as ibex rebound in the canyons of the Negev, leopards will rebound in concert with its prey. Leopards are rarely seen, so I had no expectations. I was happy to see the tracks of a hyena.

Timna Cirque, the Fiery Furnace

Like volcanic islands in the sea, Timna's dark igneous hills rise in the midst of the surrounding desert sands. Nearly encircling the valley are the red peaks and cliffs of the Eilat Mountains. The Timna cirque, a mix of natural and cultural history, is a result of millennia of erosion.

Once the area where we walked was a broad sheet of sedimentary

At sunset, iron deposits cause Timna Valley to glow red, but the world's first miners were drawn about six thousand years ago by green copper-rock, from which they made tools.

rock. Because Timna lies near the Great Rift, however, the surrounding earth's crust is riddled with cracks. When we were descending into the valley the evening before, we could see a few of these crevices, which are, essentially, Earth's stretch marks.

Long ago, when sedimentary rock lay across the land, hot magma forced its way up through cracks far below the surface. Although this molten mass never broke the surface, it thrust against the surface rock, causing it to bulge. The magmatic rock cooled as granite, topped by a huge rounded anticline of sedimentary rock.

Like sculptors, wind and water chiseled the anticline until the harder underlying granite was finally exposed. Because eastern Israel slants toward the Great Rift, the eroded rock was washed in that direction. What was left was a large semicircular valley centered on a cluster of granitic plugs. Scenic Amram Valley, just south of Timna, was formed the same way.

Exposed with Timna's granitic core was a wealth of metamorphic rocks. Metamorphic rocks are igneous or sedimentary rocks that have been transformed by heat and pressure. Usually the transformation comes in the form of recrystallization: sedimentary limestone becomes metamorphic marble; igneous granite becomes metamorphic gneiss. The most well-known of Timna's metamorphic rocks is malachite.

As we walked along the floor of Timna Valley I kicked up some of these bright green stones. Malachite was once strewn all over Timna Valley, but as millions of visitors have taken stones with them, over time Timna's malachite has been depleted.

Malachite, which is largely copper carbonate, is a clue to the reason this area has attracted humans since the dawn of the Chalcolithic period, about six thousand years ago. (Chalcolithic is Greek for "copper-stone.") The world's oldest copper mines have been found in the Sinai and Negev Deserts.

Ancient peoples discovered that by softening green ore with heat, they could mold ornaments from it. Sometime later, people discovered that by using high heat to melt the copper-laden rocks of Timna and other areas of the Middle East, they could produce metal, which they turned into tools, weapons, and jewelry.

We are the benefactors of this astounding technological breakthrough. We carry with us the knowledge of all who have gone before; without the accretion of knowledge, we would still be foraging for food. Agriculture, metal tools, written languages—these are all legacies of peoples who were no less intelligent than we. They simply had a much smaller body of accumulated knowledge.

Even in the light of our expansive knowledge, that ancient technological advance is still profoundly impressive. How did it happen? Perhaps human curiosity combined with happy accident caused people to cook ore-bearing rocks. But what brilliance those early people exhibited by progressing from cooking rocks to creating the entire process of metal production. Their prehistoric efforts are everywhere on display at Timna.

More than seven thousand shafts, each the diameter of a manhole, Swiss-cheese the valley. One of the shafts, dug by ancient Egyptians, is more than one hundred feet deep. Many have filled in over time, but we saw a few opened by archaeologists. Like the dozens of other archaeological sites at Timna, the mine shaft openings are accompanied by park signs explaining their history and use. I peered down into one and could see slots chopped into the rock that enabled ancient miners to climb in and out of the earth.

One area has been identified as the site of a furnace and, here, archaeologists believe miners used foot bellows to raise charcoal fires to the necessary twenty-two hundred degrees Fahrenheit to melt copper. Mine workers might have used a goatskin as the bellows, pumping it with their feet, forcing air through a pipe made from the hollow stem of a phragmites reed. Giant phragmites reeds, a worldwide species that can grow fifteen feet high, form dense stands in fresh water: at Ein Gedi, at Ein Fashehah alongside the Dead Sea, in spring-fed pools throughout Israel.

A cliff face shows off an ibex, a chariot, and a pharaonic-period driver that an Egyptian carved into the rock thirty-two hundred years ago. Although Egyptians started mining at Timna much earlier, the carving tells us that Egyptian culture was using wheeled vehicles at least that far back. And they had learned to bind the rims of the wheels with strips of metal as tires.

In another part of Timna soar three massive columns of red Nubian sandstone known as Solomon's Pillars. The mines were worked in King Solomon's time, most likely by Midianites or other Semites. It is, says Deuteronomy 8:9, "a land whose rocks are iron and from whose hills you can mine copper."

At the base of Solomon's Pillars, Egyptians built a shrine to Hathor, goddess of love and a patroness of the mines. What remains of the shrine are a low wall, an anteroom, an altar, and a petroglyph of a pharaoh presenting an offering to Hathor. In this stark and rough-hewn land, miners from the flat banks of the Nile needed a familiar connection.

37

Later, Timna was mined by Nabateans, Romans, Byzantines, Ottomans, even by present-day Israelis as recently as the 1980s. Solomon's Pillars and the prominent mushroom rock, which stands alone on a stage of slickrock, are the two most famous of Timna's dramatic rock formations. One of the best is a soaring stone arch. Captured within its rocky arms is a circle of lapis-blue sky. But it was time to go. Our small group crossed the floor of Timna, passing umbrella acacia trees but little other vegetation. We started down a long decline, toward the road where we could see a couple of cars, our first encounter with the modern world since leaving Shaharut.

Astride Khatz for the last time, I turned to face the camel's tail, hooking my leg around the back pommel. Dan had suggested this maneuver as a good counter to pitching forward on a decline. On level ground again, I swung smartly toward the front. Tourists standing next to their car were pointing their camera at me, sitting jaun-

Solomon's Pillars, Timna

tily atop Khatz. Perhaps later they would show their friends the camel rider in the picture. What they did not know: if Khatz decided to break into a run or even wander off track, all semblance of masterful riding would instantly vanish and I would become just a helpless tourist on a runaway camel.

At the road our trip ended. Becky and I said goodbye to Shai and Dan, then shifted our gear to the jeep that had come to take us to Eilat. Shai and Dan turned the camels, heading back toward Shaharut.

Other Beauty Spots

Timna is not the only remarkable red rock site in the southern Negev. The Red Canyon, which lies near the road that hugs the Egyptian border, is a wonderland of sinuous rock, formed where two faults meet. The canyon itself has a dual nature: part sandstone, part conglomerate.

The upper part of the area is white conglomerate. Conglomerate is just what it sounds like: a hodgepodge of different types and sizes of rocks. Conglomerate is formed when water breaks off bits of rocks, then sweeps them downstream where they collect over time. Seas then cover the rocks and limestone forms on the sea bottom, cementing the conglomeration together. At the Red Canyon, the limestone that encases the rocks is dazzlingly white.

39

Easier on the eyes is the Red Canyon proper, also formed by water. The canyon floor twists and turns between water-sculpted red walls. Within this maze, odd angles and strange shapes create variations on a theme of red. Cavelike crevices provide shadowed red refuge for rest and a cool drink. Smooth red ledges offer ways to clamber up and see the canyon from a different perspective. Butterflies light on shaded areas damp with dew and, here and there, caper bushes grow from the walls.

Between the Red Canyon and Eilat lie Mount Shelomo, Nahal Netafim, Mount Yoash with Nahal Gishron below, and numerous other natural areas. This collection of peaks, wadis, canyons, and cirques remains the wildest in Israel—an austere, exquisite contrast to the fleshpots of Eilat.

CHAPTER TWO

The Negev's Aravah:
Wiidlife of the Great Rift Valley

Ostrich in the Aravah

TONY MALMQVIST

DURING MY FIRST VISIT TO EILAT, in 1980, the town was small enough that I could walk from end to end without thinking about it. Crossing the street was not a risky business. One of the few restaurants listed marinated fava beans, in whimsical if poor English, as "Everyday Beans and Becoming Sour." That's often how I feel about Eilat now. A modest little town is becoming soured with too much tourism: car-crowded, noisy streets and a glut of luxury hotels in every shape and style from nouveau pyramid to neoclassical.

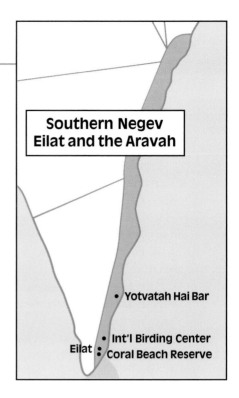

Yet, another part of me loves the gaudy, noisy contrast. Sitting at the lip of the Red Sea, framed by spartan, still desert and the red Eilat Mountains, the city of Eilat is full of life. Seaside promenades offer everything

from fast food and cheap jewelry to upscale shops and haute restaurants. Nursing an iced cappuccino, I can watch life's parade go by: Scandinavians here for some sun, Thai and African guest workers, Russian immigrant families, Israelis of all sorts.

Before Eilat lies the Red Sea with its rainbow-colored tropical fish and bands of coral. Behind lies the Aravah.

Hemmed in between the mountains of Jordan and the mountains of Israel, stretching from Red Sea to Dead Sea, much of the Aravah Valley lies well below sea level. This long, broad trench of a desert valley is part of the Great Rift that stretches from Syria into Africa. Yet, as dry and lifeless as it looks, the Aravah serves as a migration corridor for African plants and animals just as the Mideast's Spice Route served as a migration corridor for humans more than three thousand years ago.

In flood plains or where water lies just below the ground, the Aravah supports umbrella acacias, doum palms, and other vegetation that migrated north from Africa. Seed by seed, carried by birds or by wind, the plants made their way north over generations. Where it is dry, the Aravah is classic Saharan. Broom, tamarisk, and dozens of other desert shrubs and wildflowers eke out a harsh living.

Aravah animals are a mix of European and African. Hyenas, wolves, three types of fox, long-limbed, graceful caracal cats, and low-slung sand cats, Israel's tiniest, most elusive wild felines, barely bigger than kittens, are among the predators that roam the southern Aravah and adjacent canyons.

Dorcas gazelle are plentiful on the broad open spaces of the Aravah. The rare Aravah gazelle lives here also, but in much smaller numbers. Unlike the dorcas gazelle, which is perfectly adapted to desert life, the Aravah gazelle is a subspecies of Israel's mountain gazelle that had migrated south during the Ice Ages. Israel's two largest lizards, the three-foot-long desert monitor and the two-foot-long Egyptian dabb lizard inhabit the Aravah along with a host of other reptiles.

The Aravah is most famous, however, as one of the world's most heavily trafficked bird migration routes. Heading north from Africa each spring, birds make landfall near the city of Eilat.

The cranes a visitor usually sees in Eilat, however, are not the sort that fly. Construction cranes hover, like lean metallic predators, over the Red Sea coastline, as developers build one resort hotel after another. Not far from where King Solomon's fleet unloaded gold from Ophir lies the modern port where workers unload imported cars.

All of this bustle is bad for birds, and conservationists worry that the birds are, literally, losing ground. Eilat's North Beach, the first landfall for many migratory birds, is shrinking as resort development eats up precious coastline. Still, birders from across Europe come to watch the spectacular spring migration that brings more than half a billion birds annually through this, the major flight corridor between Africa, Asia, and Europe.

Gardens of the Sea

Eilat also is gateway to an opulent natural world visible only by descending into the colorful coral-fringed waters of the Red Sea. The Red Sea, which separates Africa from Asia, is part of the Great Rift.

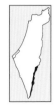

Thousands of years of coral building in this narrow, isolated gash of a sea has created a marine community unique in the world. Coral reefs that fringe the shoreline and form patches in the sea are home to more than one thousand species of fish, many of them brilliantly col-

TONY MALMQVIST

Parrotfish roam among coral reefs in the waters off Eilat, grazing on algae that cover sections of coral. The largest species of parrotfish in the Red Sea reaches about two feet long.

ored. Fully 20 percent of the species in the Red Sea are found nowhere else. And Israel's coral reefs are the northernmost reefs in the world.

43

At the southern edge of Eilat, near the Taba border crossing to Egypt, lies SPNI's Eilat Field School, which was instrumental in preserving Israel's coral reefs. Across the street is a result of these efforts: Coral Beach Reserve, which includes nearly a mile of shoreline coral reefs.

For a small sum, I rented flippers, a mask, and a snorkel and walked out over one of the footbridges that span the coral reef. Slipping into the waters of the Red Sea on a mild spring day, I felt slightly chilly. Later, when summer air temperatures soar to an average 105 degrees, Red Sea waters feel positively refreshing.

Below the surface, all I could hear was the sound of my own breathing: a calm rhythmic regularity imposed by the snorkel. I had become a fish, gliding past huge stands of coral in an opulent underwater garden.

Few places in the world's seas are as rich in life as a coral reef, and few places in the world are as colorful. Corals themselves take on hues: violet, orange, blue, green, yellow, and shades of red, depend-

ing on the species. The Red Sea's one hundred twenty species of soft corals appear spongy, feathery, or fanlike.

Hard corals take the shapes of branching antlers, finely patterned rocks, and clumps of miniature stalagmites. Large reefs are mainly aggregations of hard corals; the waters off Eilat are home to one hundred ten species of reef-building corals. Because corals come in so many shapes and sizes, a reef is not a solid wall of coral but full of knobs, islands, caves, and bowls where fish congregate and hide.

Although coral reefs look like pocked stones, they are alive. These aggregations of small rocky cells are home to thousands of animals called polyps. Usually no bigger than a fingertip, polyps are actually a plant-animal team.

The polyp, a night-feeding relative of sea anemones, captures microscopic organisms with its tiny tentacles. It is the polyps that color the coral, often becoming more vivid when they extend their tentacles to feed. The soft-bodied polyp would, itself, be a food target without protection. But within the polyp lives a type of algae that helps the polyp secrete a protective calcareous casing extracted from minerals in seawater. It is the stony casing we think of as coral.

Coral polyps, each in its tiny protective cell, build upon the casings of those who have gone before. Over thousands of years of coral building, reefs can become massive. But when humans touch coral, we scrape off the coating that protects coral polyps from bacterial invasion and death. Because access to this coral reef is so easy, the coral has declined over the years. Like many reefs worldwide, Israel's suffers from the loved-to-death syndrome.

From a crevice in the coral, a chunky grouper emerged and drifted by. Red patterned with blue dots, it is much more attractive in the water than on a dinner plate. Like a number of other marine species, groupers are hermaphroditic, possessing both male and female sex organs. And they are among the top predators of a coral reef. At the sight of this slow-moving hulk, smaller fish darted into gaps between corals, anxious to conceal themselves.

Once the grouper passed, sergeant majors, wearing black and silver military stripes, looped around stands of coral in small squadrons. One of the most numerous species on the reef, sergeant majors find safety in numbers.

Bright yellow clownfish with electric blue highlights poked tranquilly among crevices. Relatives of sergeant majors, clownfish live in symbiotic relationship with sea anemones, those stationary sea creatures whose flower-petal tentacles lure small prey, then sting them.

ISRAEL NATURE AND NATIONAL PARKS PROTECTION AUTHORITY

Stretching about a mile along the shore just south of Eilat, the Coral Beach Reserve allows visitors easy access to an underwater world in the Red Sea's Gulf of Eilat.

Anemones allow clownfish to take refuge among their tentacles because, in return, the clownfish graze off algae and other residue that impedes the anemone's ability to function.

The tropical fish at the Coral Beach Reserve must sense that snorkelers are not predators. Although human traffic along the linear reef moves as if on a two-lane road, the fish seem unperturbed by us. A man and woman passed, moving together quickly in the opposite direction. Then a young boy, twisting and turning like an eel. People, too, look more graceful below the surface, executing balletic turns with ease, flippered feet stroking effortlessly through the water.

Farther along, a Picasso triggerfish slipped between corals. Its angular, pale grey body with mouth and eyes sharply outlined in yellow, blue, and black looked a mix of high fashion model and cubist art. The triggerlike protrusion on its spine anchors it in small holes at night, so that predators cannot pull it out.

A heavy-looking, solitary, blue Napoleonfish came into view. Unmistakable with its pompadour head, this odd-shaped fish stares with an expression that falls between bemused and mournful. As counterpoint, yellow butterflyfish flashed past, like bright points of sunlight. Elegantly patterned angelfish with shimmering fins and tails added a note of genteel refinement.

45

Cobalt-blue surgeonfish flicked yellow tails, roaming the water in great numbers. Their bright tails warn that scalpel-sharp spines extrude from the base of those tails when the fish are threatened. I was delighted to come across a parrotfish grazing at the face of a coral wall. With its paint strokes of lavender, turquoise, and pink, the parrotfish looks like a Matisse painting come to life. It uses a parrotlike beak to bite off bits of coral rock, then it consumes the algae covering the rock and spits out the rest. Even underwater I could hear its loud crunching.

After seeing the fish of the reef face to face, I wanted to find out more about reef life. I had rented a car back in Tel Aviv, so I hopped into it and headed down the road to Coral World, which allows hundreds of people to enjoy the reef without even getting wet. A marine park that shows off the best of Israel's underwater life, Coral World exhibits sharks, stingrays, and a variety of fish-filled aquaria. It was one of the first to breed hawksbill turtles in captivity, returning the rare and endangered marine turtles to the sea when they are old enough to evade predators.

Coral World's centerpiece is an outstanding underwater observatory whose towerlike structure rises from the sea and is connected to the park by a footbridge. I took the stairs down to the observatory's lowest levels. Swimming past windows that looked onto the reef were familiar faces: sergeant majors, clownfish, and angels, plus wrasses and a few other species I had not yet seen. Although viewing reef fish as they glide past your arms and legs is more satisfying, the windows at Coral World did allow me to look into the heart of the coral reef.

Trapping a Hawk in the Aravah

In the late afternoon, as the sun edges toward the west, the Eilat Mountains cast their shadows over the water. At this time of day, the Red Sea takes on the ruddy hues of the reflected peaks. Come spring, at this time of day North Beach is busy with birds and birders.

To reach North Beach, I drove a mile or two on a dirt road just east of the crush of new beach hotels. Who knows how long this spot of undeveloped sand and sea will last as new hotels expand the city farther and farther east along the Red Sea shore.

The beach was dotted with about twenty people, some looking out over the sea through binoculars, others peering through huge spotting scopes set atop tripods, the barrels of the scopes the size of antiaircraft guns. In the fading light, black-winged stilts on long, spindly legs probed the shallow waters for prey. Terns and a variety of gulls wheeled over the water.

Like most enthusiasts, birders are a focused lot, and conversations generally do not stray from species and viewing technology, always in low voices so as not to disturb the birds. Bird-watching was winding down and clusters of people walked toward the line of cars parked just behind the beach. One group discussed in low tones the relative merits of zoom lenses. From the conversation of another group, I learned that I had just missed a brown booby. Although I was a little late, I was content in the quickly closing twilight.

Later, as evening overtook the day, I looked out from the broad balcony of the Eilat Youth Hostel. The buildings of Eilat glowed opalescent in the darkening sky. They make a pretty geometry, the white structures spread along the base of the Eilat Mountains, which evening had tinted the color of old bricks.

Far off I could make out the flickering lights of 'Aqaba, Jordan's Red Sea port that lies at the foot of the Edom Mountains. Down at Eilat's seaside promenade, the colored lights of amusement rides shouted in reds and blues, and I knew groups of young people strolled to the pounding beat of rock music. From the balcony, the lights from the town below flashed, but otherwise all was silent.

Suddenly, an explosion. Hostel guests rushed from their rooms onto the balcony. In Israel, such sounds must be taken seriously. But this is Eilat, and, a moment after the explosion, a glittering umbrella of gold and blue fireworks spread over the dark sea. Wands of bright light shimmered toward the water, and multicolored pinwheels brought oohs and aahs. What none of us could see were the hundreds of small birds—wrens and warblers, buntings and bee-eaters—making their way north in the night.

47

Birding in Eilat is more than a hobby. Because Eilat is the first landfall in Israel for birds migrating north from Africa, it is a perfect place to monitor bird populations. Since 1949, Israel's International Birding and Research Center in Eilat has done just that. Eilat's Birding Center has an office at Kibbutz Eilat, but its ringing station is the place to be.

Directly north of North Beach, along a dirt road, the ringing station attracts school groups, interested visitors, volunteers, and, of course, ornithologists. Here, John Morgan, in charge of banding birds, plucked a blackcap from the fine netting strung across shrubs in order to catch songbirds and other lightweight species.

Morgan weighed and measured the bird, then expertly chose a minute aluminum band from a selection of sixteen sizes and secured it around the blackcap's leg. The band is stamped with an address and a number that will be recorded along with the bird's vital statistics. Morgan opened the bird's mouth to check for spots on its tongue. Spots would indicate that the bird is quite young; the markings tell bird parents: "Put the food here."

Morgan explained that before birds make the desert and sea crossing from Africa they can double their weight in a week or two of voracious feeding. Like camels, birds break down the fat they've stored into energy and water. The energy keeps them going, and the water keeps them from dehydrating as they journey. Small birds, who fly by flapping rather than by soaring on thermals, travel at night to conserve water.

The ringing station is fitted with banding benches and wooden bleachers for school groups, but little else. Outside the station, the bird sanctuary is lush with tamarisk, white broom, bean caper, and other native shrubs loaded with nectar-bearing flowers or fruit. Adjacent are salt marsh ponds, mere shreds of the once-profuse salt marshes, but enough to attract herons, flamingos, and other wading birds. This mini-Eden was reclaimed from city landfill by Dr. Reuven Yosef and his team.

48 Dr. Yosef, who immigrated from India when he was seventeen years old and spent time studying birds in Florida after receiving his doctorate, became director of Eilat's Birding Center in the early 1990s. He secured and transformed the landfill as a bird sanctuary and, with the help of the Jewish National Fund, planted food-rich shrubs more densely than would normally be found in this dry region to make up for food sources lost to development.

Referring to the Jewish National Fund's tree-planting program, Dr. Yosef said, "My 'dump' is a good place to do that." As if to prove him right, an iridescent little green bee-eater, like a winged emerald, darted between shrubs less than an arm's length away. In an adjacent pond a glossy ibis with dark, slightly iridescent plumage waded into view.

Dr. Yosef, however, is after raptors. After piling into a jeep, Dr. Yosef, ornithologists from Norway and Hungary, and I bumped along a dirt road paralleling Route 90, the Aravah highway.

Just east of kilometer post 20, we passed a tiny reserve where the world's northernmost cluster of doum palms grows. Unlike the tall single trunk of a date palm, doum palms branch, then branch again, their skinny limbs topped by manes of fronds like crazy Dr. Seuss characters. As we passed, a half-dozen gazelle leaped away.

We reached a Yotvatah date plantation and, with as little movement as possible, set out cages, one baited with a sparrow, the other with a very nervous mouse. Then we backed the jeep off and waited in the palm-shaded grove to see who would strike.

As we waited, Dr. Yosef, who has a sharp sense of humor and a double-barreled delivery, explained something of the center's work banding, tracking, and protecting birds. From overflight counts, they expected a typical number of migrating steppe buzzards that year: between three hundred fifty thousand and half a million over a month's time. But steppe eagle numbers were down about 15 percent, and Dr. Yosef wanted to find out why.

Receiving information via banding helps, but only one in a thousand banded birds is recovered. Despite the infrequency, they've had reports of banded steppe buzzards from as far away as Finland and Russia. One ornithologist came upon Eilat's bird bands while visiting a tribe in Africa. The tribe had killed the birds for food and made a necklace of the bands. Not wanting to offend, the ornithologist copied the bands' serial numbers as fast as he could.

We momentarily froze as a steppe buzzard, the most common buteo on passage, cautiously landed and hopped toward the caged mouse, then thought better of it and flew away. Some black kites passed overhead. A squacco heron landed in a palm, and a yellow wagtail danced and wagged in another. Then a second buzzard eyed the mouse from on high. The gray-brown raptor circled, swooped to a landing near the cage, considered, moved off, came back. Then he seemed to squat, pressing himself toward the ground. The three ornithologists inhaled sharply, and Dr. Yosef whispered, "That's it."

49

In a whir of wings the buzzard was on the cage, its talons tangled atop the wire frame. We ran out, Dr. Yosef removed the buzzard from the cage, weighed the bird with a hand scale, then measured and banded him, handling him with such surety that the buzzard put up little fuss. Dr. Yosef also drew a bit of blood for an ornithologist studying bird parasites. Then he lowered an Elite coffee can over the bird's head, and the buzzard immediately became completely quiet. Without warning he thrust the "canned" bird onto my lap as we drove off to check the other traps.

The splendid wild bird lay perfectly still. Although the buzzard has a four-foot wingspan, it was surprisingly light, about three pounds. Unlike our dense bones, the bones of birds are relatively hollow, allowing air to loft them easily.

"You have children," Dr. Yosef said with certainty, noticing how I cradled the bird. I had no experience holding raptors, so I did what seemed most natural. Dr. Yosef also explained how they knew the buzzard was about to strike. When it appeared to squat, the buzzard was defecating, clearing his bowels so he had room to add more food. Raptors must remain as weight-efficient as possible, and defecating before eating is one way of doing that. It also is a clue to ornithologists that a strike is at hand.

The other traps had netted no birds so we drove out into the open, where Dr. Yosef showed me how to hold the buzzard by his talons before releasing him. Then he lifted the coffee can. I grasped the buzzard's talons, the feel of feathers and rough skin between my fingers, and, as if in slow motion, I thrust the bird upward and released my hold as he exploded into the sky, soaring beyond sight.

Animal Oasis at Yotvatah

Beneath the burning flats of the Aravah lies a cool, wet world hidden in darkness. Within the buried rock layers vast pockets have filled with water. Percolating down from infrequent rains and flash floods over thousands of years, precipitation has filled these aquifers with billions of gallons of sweet water. Here and there the water bubbles up as springs, most of them known since biblical times.

The spring at Yotvatah has been known for that long. Now, however, Yotvatah is known as the kibbutz that makes delicious yogurt and other dairy products from its cows' milk. And it produces dates dripping with date honey, completing the duality: a land of milk and honey.

Yotvatah is also the location of Israel's first wildlife park: Yotvatah Hai Bar. From the Aravah highway you usually can see ostriches loping along a fence line that encloses Yotvatah Hai Bar's four thousand acres. Although the wildlife reserve is not exactly a natural area, it is not exactly a conventional zoo.

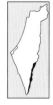

Yotvatah lies about twenty miles north of Eilat, on the east side of the Aravah highway. Visitors can rent audio handsets and drive in small, guided caravans through Yotvatah's open areas where onagers, oryx, ostriches, and other desert species roam. At the main buildings, one can walk through the circular Predators Center, where enclosed habitats hold predators no longer capable of surviving in

TONY MALMQVIST

Each spring and fall, thousands of steppe buzzards soar over Israel, traveling from Africa to Europe or Asia and back. On the way, they hunt small mammals and birds.

the wild. Nearby, the Desert Night Life Hall exchanges day for night so that visitors can see the habits of nocturnal animals.

The reserve was established in 1964 as a place to protect and breed endangered species such as the onager (wild ass) and the Arabian oryx. In the early 1900s, when guns and motorized vehicles became common in the Middle East, so many oryx were shot for sport that the species teetered on the edge of extinction. As animals such as the oryx and onager declined, so did the wolves and raptors that preyed on them. Later, towns sprung up in the Negev. Along with people and their detritus came crows, a species that helped push out lappet-faced vultures.

51

Yotvatah Hai Bar is now the only place in Israel to see the lappet-faced vulture, the largest of Israel's birds of prey. The vulture, a subspecies of the African lappet-faced vulture, disappeared from the Negev wilds in 1990. Fortunately, a breeding program had already begun.

Hunched in their large, room-sized cage, the feathers around their naked necks like dark ruffs, it is difficult to imagine lappet-faced vultures soaring above the desert, stretched to their full nine-foot wingspan. Despite their captivity, they have proven to be attentive parents, feeding their young and shading them from the sun with their wings until the babies are fully feathered.

A breeding cycle, usually producing a single nestling, takes nearly a year. Parents nourish their young by feeding it regurgitated or dismembered prey, such as rodents, and by tippling water from their crops into the baby's open bill. When the population of lappet-faced vultures reaches a certain strength, Yotvatah Hai Bar plans to reintroduce the birds to the wild.

In the Predators Center, I passed desert animals difficult to spot in the wild: hump-shouldered gray hyenas striped with black; sleek fawn-colored caracal cats whose long, black-tufted ears act like air conditioners; wild cats, whose kind were used to breed domesticated cats about five thousand years ago; Negev wolves, smaller and paler than those found on the Golan; eagle owls, who hunt at night; and a host of smaller animals.

Just before driving into the open areas of Yotvatah, I happened upon mammal expert Dr. Benny Shalmon, whose work I had heard about for years. Because Israel is so small, encounters such as this are not uncommon. A fit man who looks like he has spent a lifetime outside, Dr. Shalmon said that Yotvatah had recently reintroduced oryx to the desert near Hatsevah, in the northern part of the Aravah Valley.

Driving through the reserve, I saw these elegantly white, scimitar-horned antelopes as they milled about in small ghostly groups. Their bodies are so white and horns so straight that, from a sideview, they look like unicorns—and some say the oryx is the model for that legendary animal.

Onagers find shade under umbrella acacias. The onagers have so flourished that they have been reintroduced to Makhtesh Ramon and other areas of the Negev.

52

Male ostriches are especially visible, their striking black and white plumage enhanced by long necks and legs that turn red during breeding season—a display meant to turn the eyes of the gray-feathered females. During this period, they also attract females by dancing, but they seem to dance for females, touring vehicles, whatever is in their path.

As the car approached, the ostriches loped over, hoping for a handout. Their legs are long and strong and their talons sharp. Unlike the cliché, they are not at all shy about sticking their necks out. When they realized nothing was forthcoming, they wandered away, but left me with an impression of size and strength.

Despite their gawky appearance, ostriches can be fierce, and, with a top speed of thirty-six miles per hour, they can run. They could not run fast enough from hunters, however, who were paid well for ostrich plumes. Fashion in the nineteenth century depleted both North American beavers, whose pelts were used to make tall beaver hats for men, and ostriches, whose plumes were popular in ladies' hats.

Yotvatah Hai Bar is helping the ostrich make a comeback in Israel. They need some help because ostriches are not known for their intelligence. They leave their softball-sized eggs, which weigh about three and a half pounds and have the heft and texture of marble, lying in clutches on the ground. Job, a true natural historian, assessed the bird succinctly:

> The wing of the ostrich beats joyously;
> Are her pinions and plumage like the stork's?
> She leaves her eggs on the ground,
> Letting them warm in the dirt,
> Forgetting they many be crushed underfoot,
> Or trampled by a wild beast.
> Her young are cruelly abandoned as if they were not hers;
> Her labor is in vain for lack of concern.
> For God deprived her of wisdom,
> Gave her no share of understanding,
> Else she would soar on high,
> Scoffing at the horse and its rider.
>
> (JOB 39:13–18)

The Slowly Moving Mountains of Edom and Eilat

From Red Sea to Dead Sea, the Aravah stretches one hundred fifteen **53** miles, most of it as dry as old bones. The Aravah, which served as a highway for ancient peoples, was the traditional land of the Kenites, the seminomadic tribe whose name means "smith." The Kenites are mentioned in the Bible as the first metallurgists, descended from Cain, and they were traditional allies of the Hebrews.

Perhaps the most famous of the tribe was Yael, the Kenite woman whose tale is told in Judges 4:17–22. After the Israelites defeated the Canaanites at Mount Tabor, the Canaanite general, Sisera, fled. Yael, wife of Heber the Kenite, invited Sisera into her tent where he fell asleep. She then drove a tent pin through his temple, killing the enemy warrior.

The Bible also has much to say about the desert's natural resources. When the Israelites of the Exodus, tired of manna, cried out for meat, their cries were answered with the appearance of quail. And each year, quail do appear in the desert: once in the spring on their way to Europe, and again in the fall on their return to Africa for the winter.

When they reach landfall, exhausted from their arduous journey,

the birds "fall out," as ornithologists say. In this depleted, vulnerable state, quail are easily captured. Once, near cliffs overlooking the Aravah, I saw nearly a dozen quail straggling absently across the rocky terrain. They looked slow enough that if I had been very hungry, I think I could have caught one.

Not long after the Bible mentions quail, Exodus 28 includes a precise litany of how to make priestly vestments. In addition to jewels, dyes, and gold threads, crimson yarn is specified. Sheep and goats were the source of yarn, and the crimson was derived from the dried bodies of cochineal insects that live in the Negev. Indigenous peoples in the deserts of the American Southwest also learned to make red dye from insects of the *Dactylopius* genus. The Arabic word for these insects is *kirmiz*, the root of the word *crimson*.

Traveling slowly by camel or by foot, the people of this region were keen observers of all that surrounded them. Knowing that tamarisk trees may mean a high water table or that phragmites reeds indicate sweet water can save a life in the desert.

Travel through the Aravah today is significantly different. With tape decks and air conditioning humming, drivers keep their eyes open for a gas station or a snack shop, passing wadis whose names resonate with thousands of years of history.

I had been warned that the Aravah highway, though not crowded, is the most dangerous in Israel because it passes through the desert

54

with few distractions other than scenery. Drivers keep the accelerator to the floor and, when they doze at the wheel, they tend to veer and crash.

Once, while driving north from Eilat toward the central Negev, I turned off the Aravah highway for no reason except that time seemed to be speeding as fast as my car. I was a little drowsy, but mainly I wanted to stop moving so fast through this vast landscape. Slowing down seemed important.

I parked, stepped away from the car, and let my ears adjust to the silence. The roadside and small wadis were covered with low moricandia shrubs, whose profusion of violet flowers made a low purple haze in the bright desert light. Ahead, I could see a half-dozen storks spiraling on thermals, traveling north to Europe. Sparsely dotting the broad valley, umbrella acacias matched their name: broad, flat canopies stuck in the sand like beach umbrellas. They have the look of Africa's Serengeti Plain, and that is no accident. Like ostriches, hyrax, and other wildlife that migrated up the Great Rift from Africa, umbrella acacias are at their northern limit in the Aravah Valley.

SPNI

One of five wildcat species in Israel, the caracal was once trained to hunt birds in Iran and India. A nocturnal hunter, it needs little water beyond what it consumes as prey.

One of three acacia species in the Negev, umbrella acacias space themselves far apart because the roots of each must reach out dozens of feet to find enough moisture to survive. The acacia often provides the only shade in the Aravah and refuge for a variety of animals. **55**

The longer I stood, the more I became part of the background. Wildlife that had frozen at my approach began moving again. A mourning wheatear, formally attired in black and white, hopped down the branch of a near acacia. A gazelle moved under the broad shade of another acacia. A second, well-camouflaged gazelle became visible merely by jumping a few steps forward. Its ears were large and wafer-thin, a dark narrow stripe ran down its forelegs, and its neck was as slender as a figure in a Modigliani painting.

With beige coats and narrow profiles, motionless gazelle blend into the background. But they are plentiful in the Aravah and other Negev valleys, these incredibly slim animals that seem propelled by tightly wound springs. Though gazelle appear only in small groups, altogether the Negev and Judean Deserts are home to more than eight thousand of them.

Like other desert animals, the food gazelle eat provides the liquid

they need. Water efficiency even shows up in their scat, which is as small and dry as a BB.

As I watched, the first gazelle balanced its spindly forelegs against one of the acacia's several trunks and stretched its neck into the overhead branches, munching the acacia's feathery new leaves. Ah, this was not the dorcas gazelle, the typical gazelle of the Negev. The gazelle browsing the acacia—avoiding the tree's sharp thorns—was likely a rare Aravah gazelle.

Dorcas gazelle usually browse closer to the ground, hardly ever standing on their hind legs. Aravah gazelle commonly browse the upper branches. The unique Aravah gazelle is a subspecies of mountain gazelle, which lives in northern Israel and is common on the Golan. The mountain gazelle is a Mediterranean species. The dorcas gazelle is Saharan.

During the Ice Ages, when deserts became cooler and wetter, mountain gazelle migrated south. When the glaciers of Europe and Asia retreated north, so did most of the mountain gazelle, leaving behind a relict subspecies: the Aravah gazelle. Earlier in the 1900s, this subspecies almost became extinct, before scientists had even studied it.

Caracals were implicated as predators. Forty-pound felines whose name derives from Turkish and refers to the cat's black-tassled ears, caracals can leap nine feet to pull down prey. And they frequent stands of acacias. But scientists found that caracals preyed mostly on partridges, rodents, and hares. Human disturbance is a more likely reason for the gazelle's precarious position.

Now that areas frequented by the Aravah gazelle are protected as nature reserves, the population is recovering, but slowly. Seeing one reaching up to nibble an acacia was a lucky sighting.

Gazelle are not the only animals that eat acacias. Even a plant, the semiparasitic strapvine, or loranthus, lives off the acacia, twining through branches, killing the acacia as it sucks its sap. In Hebrew, the vine's name means "acacia strangler," but its taxonomic name is *Loranthus acacia.*

From country to country, each plant and animal is referred to by many names. To avoid confusion, eighteenth-century Swedish scientist Carolus Linnaeus devised a system for naming each species with a specific genus-species name. Although Latin may be a dead language in other respects, scientists worldwide communicate species names using the Latin taxonomic system Linnaeus devised.

Umbrella acacias are plentiful in the Aravah and are one of the only desert trees that provides useful timber. The Israelites, on their

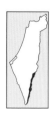

The strapvine's gaudy red flowers lure tiny, darkly iridescent Palestine sunbirds, which sip the flowers' nectar, become dusted with pollen, and fly off to pollinate another strapvine. Tristram's grackle and other birds eat the strapvine's red fruits and inadvertently carry the sticky seeds to another tree, where within two hours a new vine can germinate from the seed. Israelis have another name for the vine, "half-parasite, half dumb." On the surface, it may seem dumb to kill your host. But, by producing seed, the strapvine has accomplished the purpose most potently hard-wired into every living thing: it has reproduced.

journey to build a people and a religion, chose the acacia for building the Tabernacle and the Ark of the Covenant. Some say the burning bush that appeared before Moses was an acacia ablaze with red strapvine blossoms.

As I watched the wildlife around me, the shadows of late afternoon began sliding across the barrens of the Aravah, staining bleached surfaces with eye-soothing shade. In softer light, it is easy to see that the Aravah is still a work in progress. Across the valley, in Jordan, the red wall of the Edom Mountains floats above heat waves that obscure its base. Facing the Edom Mountains on the Israeli side are clay-colored sedimentary hills. Between is the low place where great **57** tectonic plates are being rent, one from the other.

The Edom and Eilat Mountains were once a match. Now the Eilat Mountains lie farther south, because of action along the Great Rift. The rift began forming, slowly, at the beginning of the Tertiary period some sixty million years ago. About twenty-five million years ago cataclysmic splitting shook the region. Since then, the Jordanian and Israeli sides of the Rift have separated about seventy miles, the Jordanian side moving north, the Israeli side south.

As I stood looking across to the Edom Mountains, on a seemingly still evening, the earth beneath me was moving. Oh, very slowly, only a half-centimeter per year—but inexorably.

There is a sense of the world being made here, and perhaps a sense of the Maker. The mind focuses on big questions, for a moment. But we are a species that craves answers, and sometimes the questions are too complex or beyond our comprehension. So, like cars on the Aravah, we speed off to other issues.

CHAPTER THREE

Central Negev:
Makhtesh Ramon,
Israel's Grand Canyon

Nahal Ardon, Makhtesh Ramon

MAKHTESH RAMON LIES AT THE CENTER of the Negev, like a monstrous pitfall or a crater gouged by some misshapen asteroid. In its level approaches and gaping grandeur, Makhtesh Ramon is similar to the Grand Canyon and often is called the Grand Canyon of Israel.

Nelson Glueck, a rabbi and one of the preeminent archaeologists of the Negev, wrote in his book *Rivers in the Desert*, "Looking like a gigantic footprint stamped deeply at the time of creation into the crust of the earth, [Makhtesh Ramon] straddles much of the width of the scarred and wrinkled upland of the Central Negev on the east side of the watershed."

Like the proverbial elephant in the living room, it is difficult to ignore Makhtesh Ramon. It so dominates the central Negev that one of the few main highways traversing the desert goes right through the *makhtesh*, switchbacking down its northern rim, crossing its floor, then climbing out on the way south.

Having only glimpsed the *makhtesh* earlier, I wanted to make it my destination. So I started south from Tel Aviv, driving the dreaded Ayalon, the car-clogged freeway where road rage seems only moments away from erupting. The turnoff to Beersheba is the first sign that life is slowing down to something approaching reasonable. South of Beersheba, buildings disappear, the road empties out, and the desert reclaims its place of prominence.

When I'm traveling into wild places, the moment I see the last traffic light or clot of stores recede in my rearview mirror, a sense of release overwhelms me. It seems safe to let my guard down, notice cloud patterns or wildflowers blooming alongside the road. Interest-

ing ideas bubble up. Does it matter if they are brought to fruition? Sometimes their unexpected arrival is pleasure enough.

Above, two Egyptian vultures glided past on the wind. On the seat beside me lay three small bags: one of olives, one of dates, one of almonds, plus a bottle of water. Basic Bible food.

At Sedeh Boqer, still in the northern Negev, I pulled in. The winding walk from the kibbutz parking lot leads to David Ben-Gurion's home, now preserved as a museum. This time I was there not to see the sights, merely to restock my pistachio supply. The cafe that sells the nuts always seems to be well-provisioned with a variety of attractive salads. One of the best places to stop while journeying through the Negev, the cafe is surrounded by gardens and a patio full of umbrella-covered tables.

Every kibbutz seems to be known for something: fish ponds, rock quarries, high-tech electronics. Sedeh Boqer, for instance, is known for its pistachios, just as Yotvatah is known for its yogurt, and Ein Gedi for its spring water.

Continuing south, the plain face of the hammada—rocky flats—stretched all around me. Eventually, a bus stop signals the town of Mitspeh Ramon just to the west of the highway. Mitspeh Ramon—Roman Overlook—lies along the northern rim of the *makhtesh*. A new town, Mitspeh Ramon serves as a gateway for travelers exploring the *makhtesh*.

Hotels, hostels, and shops—many of which advertise jeep tours and climbing guides—are scattered around the small development. An observatory and an SPNI field school sit at the southwestern edge of town overlooking the crater.

Where the town meets the *makhtesh* lies the Makhtesh Ramon Visitor Center, a low, round building that matches the beige color of the surrounding rock. The center was fashioned to resemble the shell of an ammonite, sea animals that lived in spiraled, chambered shells. Why a visitor center shaped like an ammonite shell? Because hundreds of millions of years ago, this desert was covered by a sea whose waters were filled with ammonites and all manner of now-extinct marine animals.

Perched as it is on the rim of the *makhtesh*, the visitor center looks more like a spacecraft poised for takeoff than a sea creature. It is part of an engaging complex that includes guest accommodations, a small wildlife park and botanical garden, a restaurant overlooking the *makhtesh*, and a rim path that offers singular views.

I made straight for the edge of the *makhtesh*. Toward the northwest rises the thick, squat profile of Mount Ramon. At thirty-four hundred feet above sea level, it is the highest point in the Negev and the third highest point in Israel—after Mount Hermon and Mount Meron, both in the north. Strange as it may seem, parts of the *makhtesh* floor are nearly as high as Jerusalem, which sits atop the Judean Hills.

Faulted and folded, twenty-five miles long, five miles wide, and about thirteen hundred feet deep, Makhtesh Ramon is one of Israel's most dramatic natural landscapes. From where I stood on the north rim, the immense oval cavity below seemed a circus of geologic shapes and events. Low black cones, like miniature volcanoes, rise from the floor of the *makhtesh*. Elsewhere, small streambeds writhe across the bottom like crazy calligraphy.

At the southern rim looms the red-ridged back of what is called

The north rim of Makhtesh Ramon rises more than a thousand feet above the floor of what is known as Israel's Grand Canyon. Trails wind through the crater past springs, wildlife, and the remnants of an ancient caravansary.

the Tooth of Ramon. Cliff walls are striped with tones of white, red, yellow, and green—a dynamic painting in the desert's midst.

The Grand Canyon became part of my emotional memory only after I had hiked it, camped on the banks of the Colorado River, capsized in a roaring rapid, and seen the Milky Way's sash of stars light the night sky. I would come to appreciate Makhtesh Ramon in the same way. It is one of those places that does not offer itself up in one easy swallow. It can be savored again and again because no one trip can show off all its facets.

Makhtesh Ramon and its environs exemplify a variety of desert habitats. Highlands around the *makhtesh* are similar to regions of Turkey and Iran. Trees that characterize those regions, such as Atlantic pistacias and almonds, grow here as well.

Hammada runs to the lip of the crater and stretches for miles across the Negev. These rocky flats support little life: low wildflowers such as sunrose and storksbill manage to survive; gerbils find refuge among the rocks and so do scorpions, which keep the gerbils' numbers in check.

Another highlands habitat forms where fine dust called loess collects. Here, colonies of fat sand rats hole up and porcupines roam. White wormwood, a silvery, finely cut artemisia that symbolized misery and bitterness in biblical times, digs its roots into the sandy soil.

The slopes of the crater provide yet a different niche, where low shrubs such as bean capers, capers, and purple-flowered fagonia cling to rock walls. Hyraxes, agama lizards, and golden spiny mice also prefer the crevices of Makhtesh Ramon's limestone cliffs.

Far below, the floor of the *makhtesh* is much warmer than the top, providing a Saharan environment. Dry streambeds that crisscross the bottom are dotted with white broom, saltbush, and tamarisk, typical floor-of-the-desert plants. Among the white wormwood, dune grass, and sand lilies that populate the sands live dabb lizards, desert hedgehogs, and sidewinder vipers.

Onagers, gazelle, foxes, hyenas, and wolves of the compact Negev subspecies are the large mammals found in and around the *makhtesh*. Small animals are legion: hares, jirds, gerbils, dormice, a variety of snakes and scorpions. And the animals that eat plants have hundreds of varieties to choose from.

62

Geologic Time Travel: the Carpentry to Nahal Ardon

The Carpentry Shop, located just off Route 40 near the floor of the crater, is a quick drive from the north rim. A sign at the edge of the parking lot announces that the path to the Carpentry is dedicated to Gadi Eran, a geologist and explorer who died soldiering for his country. Whether a walkway or stone monument, picnic area or pine forest, areas all over Israel are dedicated to the memories of the men and women who have died in one of Israel's wars.

Beyond the memorial plaque, a raised walkway made of recycled plastic encircles a hill tumbled with dark, blocky prisms of quartzite. The walkway allows close views without damage to the rocks. The quartzite prisms—large, log-shaped chunks of six-sided rock—look as though they have just been chopped off blocks of wood in a giant's sawmill. Thus, the name Carpentry.

The same forces that created the Great Rift created these quartzite blocks. A passing flow of hot lava caused the quartzite to crack into hexagonal prisms, whose sides pack together like the hexagonal cells in a beehive. Later, iron oxide coated the ranks of hexagons with a black patina.

The Carpentry is just the beginning of a journey into the geologic wonderland of Makhtesh Ramon, the largest of Israel's erosional craters. Besides Makhtesh Ramon, the Negev contains Makhtesh Gadol (Large Makhtesh), Makhtesh Qatan (Little Makhtesh), and the small, twin craters atop Mount Arif.

The conditions that created erosional craters are unique, so much so that the word *makhtesh* has entered the international vocabulary of geologists. *Makhtesh* also refers to the deep round mortar in which spices or coffee beans are ground—although the geologic *makhtesh* is more elliptical than round.

Israeli geologists explain that making a *makhtesh* is similar to eating a soft-boiled egg. First, water and other erosional forces cracked the hard outer shell of rock (limestone and dolomite). Then, the soft sandstone within was eroded away relatively quickly, leaving the outer shell as the walls of the *makhtesh*.

The making of Israel's *makhteshim* depended on a precise and unique series of events. It all started in the Jurassic period when the Negev was covered by shallow seas. Below the seas spread layer upon layer of rock: sandstone from drier times covered by harder layers of limestone and dolomite laid down by sediments of marine animals.

63

Tectonic forces within the earth pushed these layers upward, creating a mountainous dome. Horizontal rock layers domed upward by tectonic forces are called anticlines. Rising above Jurassic seas, the huge anticline was exposed to the forces of erosion: lashing waves, wind, rain. As soon as erosional forces broke through the hard limestone crust, rivers formed, eating their way down through the more friable sandstone.

Eventually, the seas receded and the Great Rift formed. With the earth now tilting downward toward the rift, the major river of each *makhtesh* found a weak point in its eastern wall and broke through. A *sha'ar*, or "gate," in the rock wall leads each *makhtesh* river toward the Great Rift. Over millions of years, the tributaries and the main river in Makhtesh Ramon scoured out the easily eroded sandstone, carrying it eastward through the gate, leaving only the hard limestone and dolomite shell.

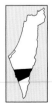

After the last Ice Age, the climate became warmer and drier and

Growing in sand at the bottom of Makhtesh Ramon, the Negev colchicum puts out graceful leaves in spring. A lily relative, it blooms in the heart of winter with bouquets of white flowers that are brightened by yellow stamens.

Negev rivers became seasonal. Yet, flash floods on the floor of the crater keep *makhtesh*-making a dynamic process. Because of the discrepancy between top and bottom, the plains above the *makhtesh* are more like an Iranian steppe environment and the *makhtesh* bottom more like a Saharan desert environment. This diversity allows about a thousand plant species to thrive here—watered by less than four inches of rain per year but helped by plenty of dew.

Unlike an eaten soft-boiled egg, the inside of the *makhtesh* is hardly empty, as a walk along the riverbed of Nahal Ardon revealed. Nahal Ardon feeds into Makhtesh Ramon's main riverbed, Nahal Neqarot, and shows off some of the most spectacular rock formations in the crater. The dry riverbed of Nahal Ardon is itself a place of beauty. Acacias lining the sandy riverbed provide shade for wildlife and add a touch of soft green to the arid landscape.

Some of the most elegant plants grow directly from the coral-colored sands of Nahal Ardon. Negev colchicum, or sand lily, whose swordlike leaves twist into fanciful shapes, blooms with crocuslike white flowers in late winter. Unseen is the thick cormous root that stores water, allowing the lily to live in this sandy, arid place.

Hoping to spot more lilies, I kept my eyes down and found, instead, tracks and droppings of gazelle, who are at home on the broad floor of the *makhtesh*. Where gazelle reside, leopards and wolves are not far off. But these predators make their living by being covert, so sightings are rare.

When white broom is blooming, you don't need your eyes at all to find this tall shrub, which grows in Nahal Ardon and other dry riverbeds all over the Negev. Your nose can lead you to it. In spring, small, fragrant white flowers cover white broom, each flower cupped

Hagar laid Ishmael under a broom bush, *rotem*, and then sat a bowshot away so she would not have to see her son die of thirst in the Negev (Genesis 21:16). Later, when the ancient kingdom of Israel was overrun by idol-worshipping priests put in place by Jezebel, King Ahab's pagan queen, the prophet Elijah annihilated them. When Jezebel heard what he had done, she threatened to kill him. Elijah fled to the Negev and there found refuge under a *rotem* (1 Kings 19:4).

Rotem has even served the voice of love. In former times, if an Arab man saw a woman he liked standing nearby, societal rules said he could not speak directly to her. Instead, he would twist a knot in the flexible branch of a broom bush to signify his interest. If the woman was similarly attracted, she would tie a knot near his. The next step was negotiating with the woman's father and, if all went well, tying a knot would lead to tying the knot.

in a deep purple calyx. The rest of the year white broom, or *rotem*, looks far more austere with its spiky profile.

Like all desert plants, *rotem* has a strategy for conserving moisture. Its gray-green leaves are narrow: the less surface area exposed, the less water lost to respiration. When a dry spell occurs, the shrub will shed its leaves, which desert dwellers have used for millennia as tinder for starting fires.

65

Rotem's roots go deep, reaching as far as twenty-five feet into the sandy beds of wadis. *Rotem*'s Hebrew name comes from the verb meaning "to harness," because with twenty-five feet of anchor, the shrub usually can withstand tumultuous flash floods. The English name comes from its use: a twiggy limb makes an acceptable broom. The branches make good charcoal, a fact recorded in a talmudic story in which two teachers cook a leg of meat in the desert. A year later they return to find the *rotem* embers still smoldering. Some believe the white broom, with its ability to burst into flame from long-burning embers, was the burning bush that Moses saw.

Little Red Canyon and the Kiss of a Scorpion

Sometimes I have to remind myself to lift my eyes from the ground. At a bend in the riverbed of Nahal Ardon I looked up from my inspection

of plants and tracks to see a tall wall of sandstone ahead, layered tier upon tier with red rock. Where the wall curves, a tall spike of stone splits through the layers as though driven by a hammer.

This startling rupture is a dike, formed when hot magma finds loose joints in rock, forces its way upward, then solidifies as it cools. More than two hundred dikes pierce the walls of Makhtesh Ramon, six of them within Nahal Ardon. Some are basalt, some are formed of other types of rock, such as gypsum.

Joining Nahal Ardon not far past the dikes is a small, parallel canyon: lovely and intimate Red Canyon, which shows off its own gypsum dikes. In soft afternoon light, the canyon glowed a deep rust-red, its sandy floor scattered with colored rocks like chunky beads: yellow dolomite, green copper-bearing rocks, white rocks embedded with fossils.

Before I bent down to pick up any of these rocks, I flipped them with my hiking boot. Zoologists at the Bio Ramon wildlife park say if you start rolling rocks, within fifteen minutes you are likely to come upon a yellow scorpion, that's how prevalent they are. The first advice I was ever given concerning scorpions was to shake out my shoes mornings after camping out. A useless gesture, I thought, until a morning in California's Sierra Nevada Range when I shook out a scorpion.

Although thirty species of scorpion live in Israel, the most prevalent—and most lethal—is the yellow scorpion. About the size of a child's hand, the yellow scorpion looks made of squishy, translucent yellow plastic. Its arching tail, however, delivers a sharp, poisonous sting that can kill children and even adults, so most Israeli hospitals keep antivenin on hand.

People often look upon scorpions and snakes as loathsome, malevolent creatures. But they have no evil intent. Like all life, their mission is merely to make a living.

During the day, scorpions usually rest in burrows that can be as much as five feet deep. If opportunity arises, they will usurp a lizard's burrow rather than dig their own. In the cool of the night, they hunt for gerbils, jirds, all of the small, scurrying mammals. Without such predators, rodent populations would explode, then crash due to disease or starvation.

One of their most remarkable characteristics is that scorpions glow in the dark when exposed to ultraviolet light. At night, UV-lit scorpions sparkle like small earthbound stars, advertising their location to suitors.

In early summer, if a male and female scorpion meet each other while hunting, courtship may take precedence over food. The male, grasping the female's pincers with his own, leads a dance that includes a meeting of the mouths—hard to call it a kiss. At some point, the male will deposit sperm on the ground, and dance the female into position so that she can absorb the sperm. Then, the male leaves or, sometimes, is eaten by the female. In either case, his reproductive mission has been accomplished.

As many as twenty or more babies develop inside the female and are born live. When they emerge, the young swarm onto their mother's back, where they cling for about a week, subsisting on stored embryonic yolk. Then the babies drop off but remain nearby for another week or so until they are ready to fend for themselves.

The scorpion gives its name to the most famous ascent in the Negev. Twisted like a scorpion's tail and once perhaps as deadly, the Scorpion Ascent, near Makhtesh Qatan, was once a camel caravan route and is now a rudimentary road. The Scorpion Ascent, Ma'aleh Aqrabim, was named in the books of Numbers and Joshua as part of the southern border of Israel.

67

Spice Route Caravansary at Saharonim Spring

One after another, tributaries join the main riverbed, which leaves Makhtesh Ramon as Nahal Neqarot, one of the largest riverbeds in the Negev. Ahead I could see the gate of the *makhtesh*, where flash floods have cut through the *makhtesh* wall in their inexorable rush downward toward the Aravah Valley. Ancient traders headed toward the Aravah took this road and, on maps, it is still called the Spice Route.

Rather than follow the riverbed down, however, I headed upstream again, into another branch of the river system, the horseshoe bend of Parsat Neqarot, which means Horseshoe Crevice. Within the great bend is a narrow, twisting gorge not to be trusted during the rainy season.

It reminded me of Dark Canyon in Utah where a friend and I had backpacked. On our second day, we noticed a few dark clouds hang-

ing over mountains far to the north. We thought nothing of it and entered a narrow, sheer-walled gorge in Dark Canyon, bisected by a trickling creek.

When we realized the creek was rising—fed by waters racing off faraway mountains—we had just enough time to clamber onto a ledge five feet above the gorge floor. There we watched as the roiling water rose one foot toward our perch, then another, and another.

If the stream took us, we would be swept into the Colorado River, but by that time we would be dead, smacked about by swirling logs and overwhelmed by water. The rising creek had become a red adobe slurry, a thick chili filled with chunks of logs. We had already started crying over our motherless children when the floodwaters, with less than a foot to spare, slowly began to retreat.

Now I am never totally off guard in a narrow canyon. As I walked through the gorge of Parsat Neqarot, I scanned the sky for dark clouds at the horizon, but could find none. Only weeks later, I read that a couple of men, foolishly motoring down a wadi elsewhere in the Negev, had been swept away in a flash flood and drowned. This sort of tragic accident happens most years.

Once I had assured myself that floodwaters were not about to race into Parsat Neqarot, I indulged my senses. When dry, few places are as evocative as this secluded gorge. Water has sculpted caves, ledges, and curves of white stone. Reflecting opalescent light, the gorge is shaped like pearls on a string, each section rounded and luminous. Caper plants form small hanging gardens on the serpentine canyon walls. Each curve brings a new perspective, seemingly more enchanting than the last.

Eventually, the canyon widens again and rises to a broad flat where giant phragmites reeds, bending their plumed heads, announce the presence of Ein Saharonim. Makhtesh Ramon's largest spring, Ein Saharonim is named for another, much rarer hanging plant. *Saharon*, or snail-seed vine—both names refer to the plant's crescent-shaped seeds—was known to desert peoples as a diuretic. Because pharmacologically important plants were used a lot, *saharon* vines are now found in only a few places within the *makhtesh*, including those near the spring.

Giant reeds, however, are in abundance. Native to most of the world, they always have been a welcome sight in the desert because they indicate fresh water. Caravans carrying spices and other valuable goods across the Negev looked forward to Ein Saharonim.

Not many steps from the spring, on a low plateau, lie the remains of a first-century caravansary, or khan. A way station for traders headed toward ports along the Mediterranean, Yemen, Damascus, or perhaps as far as India, the khan must have been a happy and relatively civilized sight. After watering their camels at the spring, traders passed by a guard room at the entrance to the walled complex. Open to the sky, the courtyard within was once busy with camels kneeling to allow traders to unpack goods. Then, the courtyard must have rung with the sound of camel bells and the voices of traders trying to subdue their bellowing animals. Within the safety of the khan they could unload valuable goods without worry that they would be prey to raiding desert bands.

Along the wall, facing the courtyard, are the ruins of a building that once contained about two dozen rooms used by guests and innkeepers. I walked toward a corner chamber and ran my hand along the smooth, curved edge of a tub that provided soothing baths to road-weary

Two thousand years ago, merchants traveling by camel stopped near Saharonim Springs, at one of the caravansaries that served as the motels of their time. Merchants once bathed in this ancient tub—a luxury in the desert.

travelers of the first century. Carved from rock two thousand years ago, the two tubs in the room look like they would function well even today. At the opposite corner of the complex a large beehive oven still dominates an ancient kitchen.

Perhaps at shared meals merchants traded information about the price olive oil brought in Egypt or the downturn in demand for frankincense, as well as tales of traveling the deserts of the Middle East.

Ein Saharonim khan was on the Spice Route, which connected Arabia, the Mediterranean, and western Asia. Stops were usually

located near springs spaced a day's journey apart—about twenty-two miles. Traveling north from Ein Saharonim over the Plain of the Winds, traders' next stop was at Avdat. The Nabatean tribes who built and staffed these caravansaries made enough money from their services to build a desert empire. Although their capital was Petra in what is now Jordan, Avdat in the northern Negev highlands was another of the Nabateans' splendid cities.

Ein Saharonim is still a gathering place, but for wild animals, not camel caravans. Onagers sometimes frequent the spring. These wild asses had been extirpated from Israel, so Yotvatah Hai Bar, the wildlife park in the Aravah, began a breeding program with Asian subspecies and eventually reintroduced onagers to Makhtesh Ramon.

The onagers I saw were not in the *makhtesh*, but were grazing on the Plain of the Winds, near the rim of Ramon. Larger than a donkey, smaller than a horse, these sturdy gray-brown animals looked not at all domesticated. Body language revealed the difference. No dull-eyed, head-hanging patience, no hooves planted in obstinate refusal, these were wild members of the horse family: bodies sleek and alert to danger, heads held high to sample scents on the wind.

> Who sets the wild ass free?
> Who loosens the bonds of the onager,
> Whose home I have made the wilderness. . . .
> He roams the hills for his pasture;
> He searches for any green thing.
>
> (JOB 39:5–8)

70

Jeep Touring Through Makhtesh Ramon

Exploring a wild place on foot is the most intimate way to learn its nature. Getting to know Makhtesh Ramon can take many pleasant visits. But the fast way to see the *makhtesh* is by jeep. With so many layers of geologic history exposed on the walls and floor of the *makhtesh*, traveling by jeep is a quick trip through time.

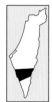

I had not planned on a jeep trip, but at the Ramon visitor center the driver said he had space if I had time. Done. Often as I traveled through the Israeli countryside, random people and events came together serendipitously—and suddenly it was soup. I always find such casual and happy accidents the most delightful part of traveling.

Soup that day was *makhtesh* gumbo, a little of this, a little of that in the great crater. Also taking the tour was a suave Parisian couple, but I cannot trust my own judgment because I see Parisians through a highly colored filter. When I wear a scarf I look like a Girl Scout—early training, no doubt. The scarf the woman had artfully twined around her throat gave her a Champs Elysées *savoir vivre*. Although my French and their English did not allow much conversation, I felt fashionable by association.

As we wound our way into the *makhtesh*, Alen, our guide, told us his dream: He was saving, he said, to buy many dunams of land in the Negev and open a dude ranch with all the tourist amenities. Right now he owns only a few Land Rovers, but crazier dreams have come true. And, with the government poised to develop the Negev, a dude ranch seems a well-timed goal.

Rotem, or broom brush, which grows throughout the Negev, anchors deep, water-seeking roots to survive drought and withstand floods. In spring, its sweet-smelling blossoms perfume the dry desert air.

Gypsum, basalt, quartzite, clay, sandstone, limestone, flint, conglomerate, shale, chalk—Makhtesh Ramon displays them all. One of our first stops was near the white gypsum hills once mined by the British. Now Israelis mine the gypsum to make cement. The presence of gypsum tells geologists that this part of the *makhtesh* was once a swamp or a lagoon full of still water. Gypsum, like limestone, is based on calcium from the remains of ancient shells and skeletons. Whereas limestone is calcium carbonate, gypsum is calcium sulfate and it forms only in still waters.

When the water evaporated, layers of gypsum were left. This happened probably about two hundred twenty million years ago, in the Triassic period, when the dinosaurs' reign was building. Scientists know that dinosaurs roamed Israel at one time because they left footprints and more. Nearby the gypsum hills is Reptile Valley, so

called because during the Mandate period after World War I the British-owned Iraq Petroleum Company found the fossilized bones of dinosaurs and other reptiles.

The *makhtesh* also is full of clays: high-quality, colored clays sought out by potters; white clay used for china; and aluminum-bearing clays that produce industrial ceramics. At a few sites, the clay has been quarried below the water table.

We rounded a bend and came upon one of these quarries. An improbable pool of Pleistocene water filled the deepest gouge, and the water, colored a milky blue-green by minerals, shimmered in the bright sunlight. Eight ducks floated on the surface of the pool, a strange sight in the desert. Unruffled, they bobbed sedately until a pair of F16s screamed by, tearing the air and causing us all to start.

We made our way along the ancient Spice Route to the Date Ascent. We, however, started at the top and descended. It is hard to imagine camels negotiating the rocky "camel steps" of this route, much less jeeps. Lurching like a cartoon car with wheels that tiptoe like feet, the Land Rover picked its way down the rocky ledges one tire at a time.

Moving at a snail's pace gave the Parisians and me plenty of time to spot wildflowers. Sunrose and fagonia make pink and purple mounds among the rocks that border the camel steps. But the queen of rockbound Negev wildflowers is erodium. From its low mat of gray-green leaves burst hot-pink flowers that lit up the gray limestone. Coveted by gardeners designing dainty rock gardens, erodium chooses to live in the least dainty scree and gravel.

It survives thanks to thick, water-retentive bulbs that are said to taste like potatoes and are a favorite food of Israel's porcupines. Related to cranesbill geranium, erodium is called storksbill because its seed pods are long and pointed like the bill of a stork. When dry, the seed pods curl like a corkscrew. When wet, erodium pods straighten, driving their pointed ends into the soil, thus planting themselves at the most opportune time.

Down in the bottom of the *makhtesh*, we followed a wadi to its juncture with a larger streambed and there met up with a gaggle of jeeps. Although only a few jeep guides tour the *makhtesh*, they subcontract with jeep owners "in the neighborhood," so their tours can swell to six-car caravans or shrink to just one, depending on circumstances.

Alen stopped briefly to chat with his compatriots, then we drove on, parked, and got out to walk along the *makhtesh* floor. The sandy streambed was cluttered with rocks of every color, which we flipped over with our feet before picking them up to examine. We wanted no scorpion surprises.

We saw white broom, saltbush, and other familiar faces, and then I found a plant nestled in the sand and wreathed with wildly curly leaves, like a present tied with too many bows or a girl with a perm. I pointed. "*Shikor Sinai*," Alen responded. *Shikor* means "drunk." Here, it is more ominous.

Alen explained that insects crawl among *shikor Sinai*'s leaves looking for nectar but are overcome by the plant's chemicals, which have hallucinogenic properties. Once the insects are *shikor*, the plant's digestive juices take over. Insects come looking for food and, instead, become food for this carnivorous plant. *Shikor Sinai*'s potent chemicals cut both ways, however, because the plant has proved effective in the production of liver medicine.

In order to survive in the Negev, every plant has a story. In order to survive in the Negev, the people who once roamed this desert, from Israelite to Nabatean to Bedouin, learned the lore of the flora. For those with fewer choices than we, the Negev was a green-grocer and a pharmacopoeia.

More Makhtesh Highlights

Even a fast-paced jeep tour cannot take in all of Makhtesh Ramon's **73** sights. Other places to visit among the *makhtesh*'s broad scope of natural and cultural diversity include Mahmal Valley, where a huge white sand dune rises at the base of the *makhtesh* wall. Near the foot of Mount Ardon the *makhtesh* contains tree fossils from a time when the area received more rain. Sea urchin fossils remain from a time when shallow seas covered the land. Prismatic curtains of black basalt, similar to the Golan's spectacular Hexagonal Pool, hang in the *makhtesh*'s Prism Canyon. Peaks, each with individual attractions, ring the elliptical crater.

In spring, the rare and endemic Negev tulip carpets areas around the Lots Cisterns with delicate pink. The Lots Cisterns, a site dating to the Israelite kingdom, reveal the remains of desert farming. During the time of Israel's kings, especially Solomon and Uzziah, small agricultural communities dotted the Negev, and fortresses protected the southern boundaries of Judea. A thousand years later, *makhtesh* strongholds belonged to Nabateans.

The Israelite-period cisterns and homes, plus other remarkable artifacts at Lots, are matched by large and venerable Atlantic pistacia trees that grow near the cisterns. Although hundreds of Atlantic pistacias, also known as terebinths, dot Negev highlands, these trees should not be in the Negev at all; they belong farther north. Scientists believe the pistacias—as well as the almond trees that grow nearby—are a relict community that migrated south from Turkey and Iran during cooler, wetter times.

During the last Ice Age, when mile-high sheets of ice covered the northern realms of Asia, North America, and Europe, plant communities edged farther and farther south, staying a few steps ahead of the slow-moving glaciers. After the glaciers melted, releasing diluvial meltwaters, plants migrated back to their former homes.

Where the climate was tolerable, however, some trees stayed on. So hemlock trees, more at home in Canada, hang on in certain cool valleys of America's deep South. And Atlantic pistacias endure in Negev highlands. Although the story of Noah tells us more about human nature than it does natural history (and geologists have discerned more recent floods), it is intriguing to think that the legend of the Flood was handed down from the end of the last Ice Age.

From Route 40 at Makhtesh Ramon's southern rim, a dirt road leads west to the Ammonite Wall. This rock face, crowded with fossils, tells of a time about one hundred sixty million years ago when seas covered what is now desert. In those Jurassic seas, thousands of different species of ammonites thrived.

Swift predators, ammonites lived in spiral shells, propelling themselves away from enemies by shooting jets of water from their shells. Because an ammonite shell looks like a tightly curled ram's horn, the mollusk is named for Ammon, ancient Egypt's ram's-head god.

Like shofars of stone, hundreds of fossilized ammonites protrude at crazy angles from the Ammonite Wall. Each about a foot in diameter, they are all the same species and, like the rest of their kind, extinct—casualties of the same cataclysm that annihilated the dinosaurs.

Fat Rats and Snakes at Ramon Wildlife Park

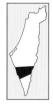

In late afternoon, after a day spent roaming the *makhtesh*, I was too full of energy to rest before dinner. I tried the visitor center, but the staff was locking up for the day, so I wandered past the parking lot until I reached a quiet compound called Bio Ramon. This unobtrusive wildlife park exhibits the small animals of the Negev and is a delight.

74

The circle of animal enclosures is surrounded by gardens that merge with the desert so that it is hard to know where botanical gardens end and Negev begins. Perhaps they were designed that way because these gardens show off Negev ecosystems: rock fall, sand dune, hammada (the desert plain), the fine loam called loess, moist spring, and dry streambed.

Paths wind through each small slice of ecosystem— here tumbled limestone ledges, there reeds rising from a water hole. At the edge of the gardens a large, fragrant white broom marks the entrance to the wildlife enclosures.

Desert hedgehogs stay cool in their burrows until sunset, when they emerge to hunt insects, scorpions, and the eggs of ground-laying birds.

The ticket office was empty, although the place did not look closed. I nudged the gate and it swung back, so I called out "hello" and entered. Porcupines, hedgehogs, scorpions, reptiles, and rodents of every sort lived in enclosures that confined them but did not look very different from their normal desert habitats.

Zoos began as nineteenth-century curiosity palaces with solitary-confinement conditions for its inhabitants. During recent decades, as species have declined—through habitat loss, poaching, and a litany of other ills—zoos worldwide have become preservation and breeding centers. Jungle ecosystems are recreated in deserts, savannas in temperate forests, all with great output of technology and energy. This is good; we should be conscientious stewards.

But there's something engaging about a low-tech zoo that shows off the very animals that live just beyond its gates. In Central America, the Belize zoo is located in the midst of a rain forest some miles outside the capital city. All the zoo's inhabitants are rain forest natives, and the place looks as if zoo keepers merely threw a few fences

around plants and animals already living there. No bells and whistles. Very natural with lots of informative signs. Simply for viewing purposes, this is my idea of a good zoo.

Bio Ramon, too, is low-key with lots of informative signs. I was concentrating on the sign at the Egyptian dabb lizard's enclosure. About two feet long with a dangerous-looking tail like that of a miniature stegosaurus, the dabb lizard prefers hot, arid spots, like the Aravah and the bottom of the *makhtesh*. Its dark, heat-absorptive skin lightens if the ground becomes too hot. Despite its fierce demeanor, the dabb lizard is an herbivore, choosing to save energy by munching leaves rather than chasing insects.

I was watching this vegetarian watching me when, from the quiet, a voice boomed and I jumped. Wearing old jeans and boots and rolled-up shirt sleeves, the man set down a bucket of water and introduced himself: Zvi.

I told him about my mission to discover natural Israel. Delighted to have an interested audience, he dropped what he had been doing and started showing off Bio Ramon's residents.

He produced a handful of flowers, reached into the dabb lizard's home and set them before her, saying, "Flowers for the lady." Lady Dabb began delicately nibbling.

Adjacent was a desert monitor, Israel's largest reptile. The sleepy-looking monitor, a three-foot-long relative of the Komodo dragon, is losing ground to development. Its sandy habitat is being taken over by apartment complexes and industry on the Mediterranean coast.

About a dozen Negev snakes are represented at Bio Ramon, including the pygmy sand viper. Buried in sand, with only its eyes showing, the pygmy sand viper is almost invisible to me and, presumably, to prey. Besides concealment, this foot-long snake has other desert survival strategies. Like the sidewinder rattler of western American deserts, the pygmy sand viper winds across hot sands so that only two points of its body touch the ground at any given moment.

Zvi stirred up the sand until the viper emerged to show off its subtle, sand-hued patterns. With a glass partition providing safety, I could appreciate the artistic coloration of this poisonous snake. Zvi explained that another of its tricks is to lift its thin tail and wiggle it like a worm on the end of a line. A passing gecko, seeing something good to eat, pounces then is pounced upon.

A snake in pursuit of prey does not need its eyes and ears as much as it needs its tongue. In fact, snakes have no ears at all, and most have poor eyesight. Instead, a snake detects movement through

ground vibrations and uses its famously forked tongue as a directional device. Animals (including us) naturally emit chemical particles into the air, and special receptors on a snake's tongue capture these particles. Depending where on the tongue the chemicals land, a snake senses whether to track prey toward the left or the right. In addition, vipers have heat-sensitive pits on their heads that help track the presence of prey.

We looked at other snakes: horned vipers and Burton's carpet vipers, desert racers, desert cobras, and Clifford's snakes. Zvi reached in and pulled out a cat snake with a shiny black head and tan body and offered it to me to hold. Thinking it rude to reject such an offer, I allowed him to ease the snake into my hands, its body coiling up my arm. I am always surprised at how dry snakeskin is. Seeing that I held the snake with a certain reserve, Zvi said, don't worry, this snake mostly eats sparrows. Ah. My last name is Russian. It comes from the Greek word for a type of small bird, a sparrow perhaps. I gingerly handed back the cat snake.

We moved on to examine fringe-toed and agama lizards, chameleons, three types of hedgehog, and skinks, which look something like a snake with four legs. I was grateful for Zvi's time and a bit shocked to discover that this zoologist was also the manager of Bio Ramon. Because modern Israel is still a relatively new country and because its founders were adamantly informal, informality still weaves through Israeli society, especially beyond the big cities.

77

We reached the habitat of Bio Ramon's lone male Indian crested porcupine, who was about the size and coloring of a soccer ball. He looked like a rodent relative, but larger, thicker, and with a blunt nose. A pompadour of quills covered his forehead, and a thick spray of quills covered his back: long and sharp with black and white horizontal stripes.

Porcupines are nocturnal animals that live over most of Israel. Renowned lovers, they can mate all year round and many times a night. Zvi told a sad tale of porcupine amour.

He showed me a breech in the fence around the male's pen where a wild female porcupine had tried to enter. Feeling sympathetic to her plight, the staff trapped the female and placed her in the male's pen. She ran straight for him. But he did not reciprocate her attentions, not at all. By next morning, he had roughed her up, so the staff quickly set her free again. Love in vain.

Zvi glanced at his watch and I knew I had claimed enough of his time. "But look for a little longer on your own," he offered.

Because they are secretive, because they slither then strike, because they can be deadly, snakes have always held a potent role in mythology. The snake that tempted Eve to taste of the Tree of Knowledge of Good and Evil is the first animal mentioned in the Bible. As punishment, God decreed: "I will put enmity between you and the woman, and between your offspring and hers; they shall strike at your head, and you shall strike at their heel" (Genesis 3:15).

A snake wrought of copper was found in the Egyptian shrine at the Timna mines. In the desert, Moses was commanded to make a copper serpent and mount it on a standard, with a curious result: "And when anyone was bitten by a serpent, he would look at the copper serpent and recover" (Numbers 21:9).

During later times, a snake mounted on a standard was the object of idolatrous worship in Israel until King Hezekiah banned it in the eighth century B.C.E. Snake gods exist in India, and the Roman god Mercury held a standard that showed two snakes entwined. Even now, the symbolism of the snake remains powerful: the caduceus, the icon of medicine, echoes Mercury's standard.

78

I did, and in one sandy enclosure saw holes similar to ones I had seen in dry streambeds throughout the Negev. What I had been looking at were the homes of fat sand rats.

Fat sand rats are another of those species that qualify for *Amazing Tales of Desert Survival*. They live in small groups, and, like the prairie dogs of the North American Great Plains, these tan rodents stand on hind legs outside their burrows, surveying the neighborhood with the look of rotund, self-satisfied merchants.

Fat sand rats never live far from saltbush. Whereas humans eat saltbush as an experience or in lieu of better food, fat sand rats eat saltbush to live. The pancreas of a sand rat produces insulin only when the animal's blood is salty enough. Without ingesting saltbush, the fat sand rat would never produce enough insulin, would become diabetic, and likely would die from this deficiency. Biomedical researchers are studying the fat sand rat's biochemistry for clues that might point to better ways of treating human diabetes.

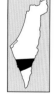

Fat sand rats also carry the leishmania parasite with no detrimental effects. Huge numbers of people in Africa, South America, and the Indian subcontinent suffer enormously from leishmaniasis. Through the bites of sandflies, leishmania protozoa infect and debilitate more than twelve million people worldwide, producing fever, spleen enlargement, and anemia. By studying the fat sand rat, researchers are hoping to tell us more about how to treat this parasitic disease.

Before I left Bio Ramon, I took a quick look at the rest of the rodent population: gerbils, dormice, golden spiny mice, and jirds. Because so many of the world's carnivores depend on rodents as a source of food, these small furry mammals are among the most important and, in terms of numbers, most successful animals on Earth.

Many of the animals at Bio Ramon do not show themselves during the day. To see them, one must become a night stalker, as I discovered one night in the Uvdah Valley. Within the space of an hour I saw a fox race across the road, a gazelle freeze in mid-step, knowing I had seen her, and a couple of jirds dart furtively across the sand. During the blazing core of day the sun chases life from the land, but at night animals emerge to search for food and each other.

A short walk back to the Makhtesh Ramon Visitor Center complex brought me to the restaurant that overlooks the *makhtesh* for a quick but filling plate of chicken and rice. The vast view was the best part of the meal. I was in a hurry to get out so I could savor the sunset.

Families strolled along the rim path. A couple asked if I would take their picture. Farther on, children pulled at their parents for dessert. Below, flame-colored shadows searched the great crater, and Egyptian vultures circled down, seeking a roost for the night. To the west, the sun hovered somewhere over Egypt, a perfect glowing globe of red with the dark shape of a date palm cast against it.

79

CHAPTER FOUR

Northern Negev:
On the Spice Route
in the Dry Highlands

Ein Avdat

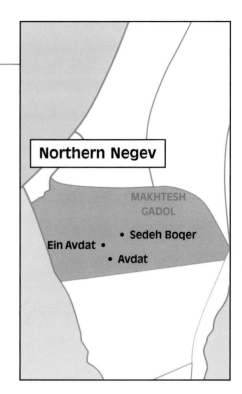

Northern Negev

MAKHTESH
GADOL

Ein Avdat • • Sedeh Boqer

• Avdat

BEERSHEBA IS A SLEEPY PROVIN-
CIAL CITY at the northern edge
of the Negev, but it is poised
to become much more. As urban plan-
ners like to point out, Israel north of
the Negev is more crowded than Hol-
land, the most crowded country in
Europe. With a growing population,
Israel seems to have no choice but to
push urban development into the
Negev. When that happens—and it
will—Beersheba, known as the "capital of the Negev," will become capital
of the desert in a much more substan-
tive sense.

Organizations such as the Society
for the Protection of Nature in Israel
are concerned that the Negev's fragile

beauty might pay a price for this expansion. The desert is a harsh
master, and every plant and animal that lives in the desert lives close
to the edge. Being pushed further by burgeoning development might
prove too much for some species. The nature preserves in the northern Negev will undoubtedly be affected by the coming growth in
Beersheba, even if only by a rise in visitor numbers.

I spent the night in Beersheba. The next day I would be going on
an SPNI tour of Negev natural areas. In the northern Negev I expected to see fewer signs of large mammals than elsewhere in the
desert because human populations are more dense.

Yet, the highlands of the northern Negev and deep-cut canyons
such as Nahal Zin provide habitat for gazelle and ibex. Ever-
opportunistic hyenas scavenge the highlands but are far rarer than
elsewhere in the Negev. Small rodents and porcupines, busy at night,
sleep in their burrows during the day.

Because more rain falls on the northern highlands than anywhere
else in the Negev, plant diversity is at its highest here, perhaps the
highest in all Israel, a country whose plant diversity is already among

the highest in the world. Even the area around Beersheba seems a veritable garden, blooming with spikes of ivory leopoldia, tall, pink-veined white asphodel, and other wildflowers. Feathery tamarisks flutter near every water catchment.

I had put up at a hostel within walking distance of the *midrahov*, the pedestrian mall that lies near the heart of Beersheba. Like many of the hostels and field schools I have stayed in, the one in Beersheba was decorated in Scandinavian Spartan with streamlined cabinets and simple furnishings. Stone-faced floors helped allay the heat much better than dark, heavy woods. Besides, in the desert, and throughout Israel in general, stone is widely available; wood is not.

Looking out over the hostel's garden, filled with purple-flowered tropical trees that visually cooled the end of a white-hot desert day, I called my husband at home, a college town in the Appalachian Mountains of Tennessee. With its shadowed, wet green forests, the southern Appalachians are a world away from this Middle Eastern desert in more respects than distance.

"I'm staying in Beersheba," I said. The phrase had a certain resonance. The Bible says this of Abraham. After he came down from the mountain, having nearly sacrificed his son Isaac, Abraham "stayed in Beersheba" (Genesis 22:19). Between Abraham and me stretched more than thirty-seven hundred years.

Beersheba means "well-of-seven" or "well-of-oath" because there Abraham made an oath with Abimelekh, king of Gerar, and paid for the well with seven ewes. Then Beersheba was little more than a collection of tents and shepherd settlements along Bronze Age trade routes leading from Egypt and the Mediterranean to Mesopotamia.

Beersheba took on greater geographical importance after the Hebrews returned from slavery in Egypt. Until the Romans destroyed the Second Temple in 70 C.E., Beersheba was thought of as the southern border of Israel. It was said, in both Judges 20:1 and 1 Samuel 3:20, that Israel stretched from "Dan to Beersheba."

After phoning, I went out to find some dinner. Daydreaming that perhaps the ground under the very sidewalk where I walked was where Abraham had trod, I headed toward the *midrahov*. Appliance stores and shoe stores had shut down for the day, but Russian-language newspapers were on display in front of small shops selling nuts, headache remedies, a little of everything.

A large falafel stand was doing a lively business, and I queued up for falafel and a beer, carrying it to one of the outdoor tables clustered below a mounted TV. A soccer mom who had become a soccer player,

I groaned then cheered along with the rest of the falafel-eaters as the Israeli team vied with a European team.

Abraham still flickered at the corner of my consciousness. The juxtaposition seemed absurd. Would a sage forebear, encountering this scene, sit down with a beer to watch soccer with us? But these comparisons of then and now are hard to avoid in Israel: King David and Dead Sea spas, Deborah the Judge and gas stations near the foot of Mount Tabor.

The next morning at breakfast I happened to talk with a professor on sabbatical from the United States. He was living at the hostel for a few months, part of a multifaceted urban-planning team examining Negev development. As we passed each other yogurts and cheeses in a variety of flavors, spreading a bit of this and a bit of that on our rolls, he told me about the efforts at planning for the growth of Beersheba and the surrounding desert.

Whereas today desert development is studiously technological, in the early 1900s it was a zealous mission. The dream of modern Israel's founders was to make the desert bloom. And, to a great extent, they have. Thousands of date palms lift tall plumed heads in plantations that line the Aravah. Orange groves sweeten the air of the Judean Desert with their perfume. Almond blossoms turn orchards into a sea of delicate white not far from Beersheba.

But the desert blooms wonderfully on its own, as does the rest of Israel. In spring, scores of people turn out to see the show: the first red anemones of the season, the pink flowers and heart-shaped leaves of cyclamen. School groups and conservation groups make floral pilgrimages. Israelis are mad for their wildflowers, and with good reason. Hundreds of wildflower species meet at this continental crossroads, from those that flourish in Europe to others happy in the heat of the Sahara Desert. Each month of the year is graced by some blooming wildflower.

83

Israel has taken a hint from nature and developed a flourishing industry of flower production. In winter, Europeans not only eat Israeli fruit, but also brighten their homes with Israeli flowers.

The wildflower that beguiles most people is the iris. Named for the Greek rainbow goddess, irises come in a rainbow of colors. For its size—for any size—Israel harbors some of the greatest iris diversity in the world.

Twenty species live in Israel, each in its own particular habitat. These habitats span the length and breadth of the country and cycle through the year, so that in any month there usually is some iris in

flower. Narrow-leaved Vartan iris blooms a pale blue on Mount Hermon in autumn. In late winter, the rare Grant-Duff's iris glows in swamps with delicate, creamy yellow blooms.

Hermon irises thrust up huge purple-and-white freckled flowers on the Golan in early spring. About the same time, deep purple irises bloom in sandy patches of coastal dunes, their color as velvety as night over the nearby Mediterranean. Found in only a few spots in northern Galilee, the large Lortet iris seems delicate only because of its oh-so-pale pink tint. Come summer, low, swampy places like the Hulah are brightened by nodding yellow heads of yellow flag iris.

Some species are rare, and some live only in Israel. It is no wonder that the SPNI has chosen the iris as its symbol.

A Walk Back in Time at Makhtesh Gadol

The SPNI bus passed the sign marking the Yeruham Reserve near Dimona in the northern Negev. SPNI, which sponsors trips as well as conservation and educational initiatives, was formed in 1953 to save the last remnant of northern Galilee's once-vast Hulah Swamp. The Hulah became the first of Israel's nature reserves, a system initiated by SPNI and now under government authority.

Yeruham Reserve was designated to protect an iris. Typically a deep purple, Yeruham irises already had bloomed by the time we passed the reserve. But we noticed that the small development town named Yeruham had planted flowers and splashed attractive colors on fences and street lamps in an effort to win tourism associated with the nature reserve. As Negev development grows, Yeruham's efforts will pay off.

Carrying our group of about fifteen, including our guide, Itzik, the bus passed Makhtesh Gadol's high white outer walls, banded with dark bracelets of flint. Makhtesh Gadol is the second largest of Israel's unique craters, and we would be hiking through it. After entering the *makhtesh*, the bus deposited our group at a trailhead near Nahal Hatirah, the riverbed that bisects the *makhtesh* and empties into Nahal Zin, one the Negev's main riverbeds.

Caravans once passed this way, bound for Nahal Zin and other main routes through the desert. Most important to ancient people who stopped here was the pool at a bend in the Hatirah riverbed. Guarding the path down to the Yeruham Pool are the ruins of a small fort. In Israel, a land that is half desert, water has always been—and will always be—more valuable than any other natural resource.

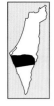

Scientists believe the tamarisk developed on salt flats created after primordial seas retreated. Tamarisk still lives on salt flats throughout the deserts of Israel, as well as in Old World deserts from China to Namibia.

In order to survive such caustic conditions, tamarisk excretes salt in solution through glands on its leaves. An added advantage to this metabolism trick: the liquid evaporates, leaving salt crystals that drop to the ground. This salted desert crust keeps other plants from encroaching. In addition, tamarisk provides one-stop shopping for desert insects, offering both pollen and nectar—a tremendous expenditure of energy for any plant, much less one living in marginal conditions.

As Hebrew University botanist Avi Shmida said, "Since the tamarisk is the only 'shop' for insects in the area, it functions as a general store for its patrons, offering an entire range of merchandise, so to speak."

The timeworn fort had been built by desert traders to protect the water for themselves and their clients.

From the fort, we stepped from ledge to ledge, down camel stairs chopped into the rock more than fifteen hundred years ago. At the bottom is a tiny blue-green jewel of a pool, cool in the shadow of an overhanging cliff. When the rains come, waterfalls splash nearby. Tamarisks hug the banks of the riverbed. With its cloud of dusty pink flowers and its tangle of thin trunks, tamarisk is attractive in an unobtrusive way. But this is one plant that does not need to call attention to itself. It is among the hardiest of desert survivors, with more species than any other type of tree in Israel.

In fact, tamarisk is so successful that when it was planted in gardens near America's western deserts, it "went native," escaping to desert riverbanks. The beaches at the bottom of the Grand Canyon and along the Rio Grande are now thick with tamarisk, which crowds out native willows and poplars. In North America, tamarisk is an invasive alien.

But it is hard to fault such a successful desert dweller. Abraham, when he purchased the well at Beersheba, promptly planted a tamarisk to mark the spot (Genesis 21:33). When King Saul and his sons were slain by Philistines, their bodies were buried beneath a tamarisk—a lasting marker (1 Samuel 31:13).

From the Yeruham Pool, a trail leads along the clifftops of

85

Makhtesh Gadol. Near the pool, the trail is only a few feet above the Hatirah riverbed. But as it cuts a deep canyon, the riverbed recedes hundreds of feet below our path.

Our group included Americans from San Francisco and Boston, and a couple from Canada who visit Israel often. As we rock-hopped, a young couple from Switzerland spent time telling me about efforts to revive the ancient Romansch language and culture centered in one part of their country.

The half-dozen or so German tourists included an older woman who worked as an administrator of plant patents. She and her companion, in their sensible brown shoes and nubby sweaters, both soldiered forward, keeping up with the group's quick pace.

Another German, a young man, added a new dimension to the image of minister. Anything but staid, he leaped here and climbed there, interested in everything, translating English to German for his wife. She, a lithe gazelle of a woman, was as athletic as her husband despite being four months' pregnant. At times, Itzik looked as though he would like to lasso the minister in order to keep him tied to the group.

Itzik, a longtime SPNI guide, speaks Hebrew, Arabic, English, and some German. Of medium height and age, he has the kind of wiry fitness that looks like he could walk the length of Israel on a bet and not be any worse for wear.

His grandfather was a peddler in the Atlas Mountains of Morocco. Following the path of many other peddlers' sons, Itzik's father became a store owner. The whole family was set to immigrate to Israel in 1956 when Morocco finally won its war for independence from French colonial rule. In the confusion, the Jewish Agency was forced to halt work on Jewish emigration, so Itzik's family had to put its plans on hold. A few years later, the family made it to France and, in 1963, on to Israel.

Itzik's olive complexion and dark hair hint at his Middle Eastern origins. Although Jews from Middle Eastern countries have had problems moving into the mainstream of Israeli society, Itzik is mainstream anywhere he pleases to be, having friends in Europe and America.

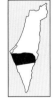

As we walked along the *makhtesh* cliffs, he pointed out a stork in flight. With their seven-foot wingspans, boldly patterned in black and white, storks in flight make you catch your breath. We did not see porcupines, because they are nocturnal, but we saw their scat and disturbed soil. Where porcupines dig up the hard ground, they create microclimates that become tiny oases of vegetation.

In sandy pockets at the edges of the rock grow fat green rosettes of sea squill, a bulbous perennial related to lilies. As summer wears on, their broad fleshy leaves wither and die. Then, just before the autumn showers that mark the beginning of the rainy season, sea squill sends up spires of white flowers. So vital is the water that the first autumn rains have their own name: *yoreh*. They fall around the harvest holiday of Sukkot. At the other end of the rainy season are the spring rains, *malqosh*, which fall around the Passover holiday. These spring rains are the last before the sun grips Israel in its hot grasp. Because rain is so critical in an arid land, the Jewish prayer book includes a special prayer for rain, to be said between Sukkot and Passover.

Rainy and sunny—these are the two basic seasons in Israel. The sunny season signals the beginning of school vacations. When children see the tall white spikes of sea squill, they know their summer freedom is over and school is about to start.

Because their bulbous roots are large and deep and few animals eat them, squill has been used since ancient times as a boundary marker. It is said that Joshua used squill to mark the boundaries of the twelve tribes. Squill makes an effective marker because it is difficult to dig up all of its deep roots. What inadvertently remains tells the guilty tale of those who would extend their boundaries at their neighbor's expense. The Talmud says squill "trips up the feet of thieves" (Beitza 25b).

87

Dotted alongside the trail are low, white-flowered Negev colchicum—sand lilies. Like squill, colchicum and sternbergia have large tuberous roots that store energy and slowly feed the plant during the worst of summer's baking heat. The bright yellow cups of sternbergia sprout directly from the earth in autumn, anticipating the rain.

As the trail narrowed and the canyon floor fell ever farther from the clifftop, we had to watch where we put our feet. Eventually the trail led to an exposed cliff that narrows to a point like a ship's prow. Delicate-looking sand lilies bloom even on this forbidding point, where canyon walls drop hundreds of feet to the riverbed below. Just beyond the cliff face, small desert swallows put on a dizzying performance of aerial acrobatics, whirling and diving toward the cliff, turning and soaring, then dropping with explosive speed toward the canyon bottom.

Edging closer, we looked down on the backs of black-and-white Egyptian vultures and a much larger, darker griffon vulture carving lazy circles in the air. Among the cliffs overlooking nearby Nahal

Zin, colonies of griffon vultures nest. Unlike Egyptian vultures, the griffons live here year-round.

On chalk-colored cliffs opposite we could see broad stains where water washes to the canyon floor when it rains. We sat on warm rock near the cliff's edge and sipped water. Having walked together and talked together, reaching this prow poised above the deep canyon and a sea of stone was a satisfying culmination of our hike. As we relaxed, Itzik told us stories of Ma'aleh Palmach—the Palmach Ascent, a tenuous-looking trail that scales the cliff across from us.

Now paved roads crisscross the Negev. In the 1940s, none existed. During the War of Independence, Palmach commandos climbed the seemingly sheer cliff face opposite, opening a route south. Moving quickly, the group trekked down to Eilat to claim the land for Israel.

Then, the only development that existed was the small mud-brick dwelling of Umm Rashrash, a Bedouin woman who nursed Muslim pilgrims making their way overland on the arduous *haj* route to Mecca. Umm Rashrash, which means "mother-nurse," was the site of a British post during the Mandate period between world wars.

In 1949, not far from the dwelling of Umm Rashrash, Palmach soldiers planted the famous Ink Flag in the seaside wilderness of what is now Eilat. Not having an official flag, they took a scrap of cloth and inked on the intersecting triangles of the Magen David. But a splash of ink in the middle marred the design, so they filled in the entire Magen David with ink. In commemoration, the Magen David on the Israeli Air Force insignia remains filled in to this day.

The men and women of those times seem larger than life. Perhaps it is because goals were simpler then, so more focused. Early Zionists' goals of re-creating a state are accomplished, but what are the goals of those who follow? In some ways, the paths are more complicated. Not only must Israelis find paths to real peace with those around them, they must find ways to forge accord among factions within. The zealous single-mindedness of sheer survival is gone. And people not only want peace, they want cameras and cars.

Sedeh Boqer: Home on the Range

Sedeh Boqer was the home of the quintessential Zionist, a man who lived a life considerably larger than most. David Ben-Gurion, Israel's first prime minister, emigrated from Poland in 1906 and was at the center of the independence movement, declaring Israel's independence

Found all over Israel, the striped hyena is solitary, unlike its sub-Saharan cousin, the spotted hyena. It emerges at night to scavenge carrion, fruit—whatever is available.

on May 14, 1948. A few years after becoming prime minister, Ben-Gurion visited Sedeh Boqer and was impressed by the young people who dared to build lives and a successful kibbutz in what was then a dry, roadless nowhere. When he retired, he chose Sedeh Boqer, which translates as "Cowboy Fields," appropriate to the wide-open land and the kind of energy it took to make this place.

Ben-Gurion's modest cottage, where he and his wife, Paula, entertained the world's leaders, is part museum, part pilgrimage site. And Ben-Gurion's dream of expanding into the Negev is well on its way. One of the engines for fulfilling that vision is Beersheba's burgeoning Ben-Gurion University.

Just down the road from the kibbutz lies Sedeh Boqer Academy, a complex that includes Ben-Gurion University's Blaustein Institute for Desert Research and its small but effective zoo, devoted mostly to desert reptiles. The academy also houses one of SPNI's field schools with attached visitor accommodations. Here we would stay the night.

As evening drew on and we drove from Makhtesh Gadol to our lodging, we passed fields full of storks picking at the ground, preening

their wings, preparing to roost for the night. One grove of trees was covered with what looked like white handkerchiefs caught in the branches, fluttering with each passing breeze. As our bus passed, the storks rose, wheeled in the air as one, and alighted again on the trees. We saw maybe five hundred of the large, long-necked birds within a few miles. They were a small contingent of the half million storks that fly over annually during migration.

After dinner, a young biology student opened the small zoo for us and told us about the feeding station for foxes, hyenas, and wolves that lies a few miles from here, a growing necessity as humans tame wild lands. Forty snake species live in Israel, many of them curled in enclosures around us, including a few of the eight poisonous species. In an aside, the student mentioned that one of the best places to see birds is the garbage dump near Ben-Gurion International Airport, just east of Tel Aviv.

The clustered rooms of SPNI's field school overlook the canyon of Nahal Zin. The next morning I rose early, while dew still clung to the ground. Dew, *tal*, has always been precious in this land of little water: "I will be to Israel like dew; he shall blossom like the lily," says Hosea 14:6.

The prophets and kings of Israel were not merely waxing poetic in their references to dew and other aspects of the natural world. In ancient days, the natural world was the source of everything. To a larger extent than most of us imagine, it still is.

I walked to the edge of the highlands and looked down into the great maw of Nahal Zin, where the dry riverbed twisted and turned far below. Nahal Zin writhes past Makhtesh Gadol, veering northeast toward the Dead Sea. Even in the soft light of morning, the eroded slopes of Nahal Zin's canyon looked raw and forbidding. Yet, canyons can change character dramatically, as we would see.

The Pools of Ein Avdat

A few hours later, the bus took us to a trailhead at Nahal Havarim, a tributary of Nahal Zin. We would hike down Nahal Havarim to its juncture with Nahal Zin, then hike Zin upstream, through Ein Avdat National Park. The two canyons present a visually dramatic geology demonstration: the first canyon is mainly marl, a pale clay and lime mix; the second mainly limestone.

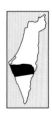

At the head of Nahal Havarim, whose name reflects the rock found there, pink tamarisk blooms screen a cistern carved into the rock

Occasional rains that sweep the northern Negev sculpt the sedimentary rock that floors Ein Avdat National Park. Where the water carves pools, ibex and other animals gather to drink. Because this is one of Negev's well-watered canyons, fourth-century Byzantine monks chose it as a place of retreat.

centuries ago by Nabateans. The cavelike cistern, supported by a central pillar, might have served thirsty travelers or perhaps desert farmers who terraced and planted fields on the plains above the canyons. Almost invisible on sand-colored rock near the tamarisk, a squat lizard warily watched us pass.

As we walked deeper into the canyon, its walls rose high above us. In one sheltered spot, a small pool of water was thick with tadpoles in a race to become frogs, mate, and lay eggs before their universe dried up.

As we walked along the sandy canyon floor, the woman from San Francisco mentioned that she was in the midst of changing careers. A small woman with sculpted features, in her late twenties, she explained that she was making a major switch, from high-pressure advertising to homeopathy. The subject turned to plants as medicine.

We passed thorny broom, the odor of the bush's deep yellow blossoms sweetening the air. At our feet pheasant's-eye scattered its lacy leaves, its brown-eyed yellow flowers winking across the sand. In the canyon all was calm and quiet.

"Nature itself is medicine," commented the plant patent woman.

Walking downhill toward the canyons' confluence made conversation easy and we discovered that the man from Boston was between jobs, the secretary from Berlin had quit her position and was looking for a new line of work, and the fifty-something woman from Peoria was picking up and moving to Portland.

All deep in transition, yet here, deep in a canyon in the Negev. Their reactions to change were illuminating. Perhaps these people had the right idea: When faced with career crisis or similar life muddles, instead of frantically trying to steer back into the stream, direction may come by drifting a bit and examining things.

My reverie was interrupted by a fat chukar, who darted in front of me then disappeared behind a bush. Chukar partridges appear all over Israel. Plump, the size of a large chicken, they start when discovered, flapping so awkwardly it looks as though they have not learned how to fly. They seem near the bottom of their class in intelligence—called "bird-brained" for a reason.

But looks are deceiving. Populations of these tan birds, with black striped wings and thin black face masks, are on the rise. Hunting laws and the decline of predators allow them to multiply readily. And, unlike many other wild species, chukars don't seem to mind human bustle. In fact, agricultural fields suit them well.

Where Nahal Havarim feeds into Nahal Zin, the larger canyon is strikingly scenic. On the clifftops far above, we could just make out

Among Israel's loveliest desert pools, Ein Avdat tempts hikers to take a cooling dip. Important in ancient times, the pool was protected by a guardhouse on the clifftop.

the buildings of Sedeh Boqer. In the tan sands, a crimson desert tulip blazed. Just one. It was enough.

93

Ein Avdat National Park is a short walk from the canyons' confluence. For those with cars, it is also accessible by road through Nahal Zin and from a short, easy road at the upper end of the canyon. Announcing the entrance to the park are palms, a parking lot, a ticket office, and a large, centuries-old Atlantic pistacia or terebinth, the kind of tree mentioned so often in the Bible.

Near the park entrance lies Ein Mor, a spring named for the spice myrrh, a valuable commodity to the ancients. Myrrh was extracted by cutting the small *Commiphora myrrha* tree. When wounded, this tree of eastern Africa and the Middle East protects itself from infection by oozing a sticky, chemical-rich resin. The fragrant resin was used in medicines, but even more so as incense and perfume. Not far lie the ruins of Avdat, a prominent city along the Spice Route, which saw the travels of many camel caravans carrying myrrh northward.

Before the formation of the Great Rift, Nahal Zin and other Negev rivers ran northwest into the Mediterranean across fairly level plains. After the Rift formed and tilted all of Israel eastward, the waters of Nahal Zin, seeking the land's lowest level, changed course and cut eastward, carving its present canyon. Now, its ivory walls soar thirteen hundred to nineteen hundred feet.

Caves gouge the walls here and there. In some of the caves farther upstream, Byzantine monks once sought refuge from the secular world, including, some say, Saint Theodore, the fourth-century C.E. Greek martyr.

Rain had splashed the Negev highlands recently, and rivulets of water ran across rocky sections of the canyon floor. The rivulets became a stream running through the middle of the canyon, its quiet, blue music a fluid contrast to the stark white canyon walls.

Itzik mentioned that Ein Avdat and Ein Gedi were the best places to see ibex. As if on cue, two females came into view. A few more steps and a herd of fifteen appeared on the opposite side of the canyon. Farther on, a dozen more.

The ibex grazed along the brush-covered sides of the canyon, a mix of females, kids, young adults, and one older male. About the size of goats, to whom they are related, the tan, short-coated ibex chewed their cuds unconcerned, as if they knew they were protected within the park.

Israel's wildlife, especially endangered plants and animals, are protected by law both within and without nature reserves. Israel's nature reserves, which are akin to U.S. national parks, do not allow any disturbance to the natural or historic features. Although ibex are protected wherever they occur, they congregate in nature reserves, which protect not only them but also their natural habitat.

94

As we walked, with the stream on our left, we saw mourning wheatears, bulbuls, and other birds flitting among the bushes that dot the meandering stream. Here grows rope plant, or *yitran*, a shrub with small yellow flowers and tough fibrous bark that was used for centuries as rope. Delilah, it is said, used ropes of *yitran* to bind Samson. But, since Delilah and Samson lived in the Judean Hills and *yitran* grows only in sandy soils, it had to be brought from the coast or the desert.

Near one white broom bush we could not help but notice an extravagant low plant called broomrape. Broomrape is a strange sight: a foot-high pyramid of fat, yellow flower cups grows directly from the sandy soil—no leaves, no stems, just outrageously large blooms. Desert plants, in order to conserve energy, usually produce small blooms. Yet, broomrape has the audacity to flaunt its great flowers. Life is energy efficient. So why does broomrape produce such blossoms?

Why not? Broomrape is not expending much energy; others are doing all the work. This parasitic plant plunders other plants, particularly

Both male and female ibex have horns, but the females' are shorter. And the tuft of hair that hangs from the chins of males—their goatees—looks like the model for the chiseled chin tufts of the pharaohs. Male ibex, when they are battling for dominance, engage in head-butting contests that ring with the clash of their extravagantly curved horns.

Unless challenged, a male will mate with all the females in his band during autumn rut. Except during rut, the sexes generally live apart, the females and young together, the males either in small groups or singly. In March or April babies are born. Then the ewes form a sort of child-care center, Itzik explained. Two or three will watch the kids as the others go off to graze.

Ibex is the favorite prey of leopards, but the cycle of both species' lives—as well as those of many other wild animals—was disrupted with the introduction of the gun. Over the past century, humans killed so many ibex and leopards that their populations plummeted, bringing each species to the brink of extinction. Now, with protections in Israel, the ibex is making a steady comeback. Zoologists hope that as ibex populations recover, so will the leopard, which once lived over most of the country. Cheetahs, too, once lived in Israel, but the last of the region's cheetahs was killed in the early 1900s.

white broom, by attaching its roots to the roots of the host plant and sucking away nutrients.

Upstream, the canyon narrows, and a low rock dam forms a pool that nearly fills the canyon from wall to wall. The still water is a reflecting pool, mirroring the white walls of Nahal Zin, creating art from rock and water.

At the base of one sheer wall, we followed a narrow footpath back to where the canyon is plugged by a natural rock wall. From the ledge above, water spills into the pool when it rains and, over thousands of years, the waterfall has carved a shallow cave at the base of the wall.

Before we hiked up to the next level of the canyon, some of us sat cross-legged on the rocky floor and talked. The minister, making the most of opportunity, climbed high among the rocks with his camera.

Itzik, whose interests include the history of names, as well as the history of nature, asked if my name had Greek origins. He was

correct, but I wondered how he guessed Greek from a Russian name. The pool of Ein Avdat reminded him.

In Jerusalem, he said, near a certain monastery, lies a pool mentioned by Josephus in *The Jewish War*, which chronicles the first-century Jewish revolt against Rome. I had read that the name Strutin refers to the Greek for a small bird. Itzik said the pool was called Struthion Pool, referring to the small birds that drank there. I promised myself that next time I was in Jerusalem I would look.

We gathered our belongings and climbed shallow stairs cut into the cliffside near Ein Avdat's pool. The stairs lead around and above the waterfall where the trail continues at its upper level. Eventually we reached a grove of streamside Euphrates poplars. From there, we could see that the trail made a precipitous, giddy ascent to the top, probably with views of the pool and canyon below. But at the top the bus waited, so we lingered in the poplar grove to delay leaving lovely Ein Avdat.

The Euphrates poplars, or willow poplars, shading the stream are relicts from a cooler, wetter time. Most of Israel's willow poplars hug the banks of the Jordan River in Galilee.

The sun-flecked shade, the stream, and the Euphrates poplars here in Nahal Zin conjure a memory of the Babylonian exile. In 587 B.C.E., the Babylonians conquered Jerusalem, after having marched most of Israel's leaders to the Tigris-Euphrates Valley. There the exiles sat under the willow poplars of Babylon, remembering the willow poplars of home:

96

> By the rivers of Babylon,
> there we sat,
> sat and wept,
> as we remembered Zion.
> There on the poplars
> we hung up our lyres,
> for our captors asked us there for songs,
> our tormentors, for amusement,
> "Sing us one of the songs of Zion."
> How can we sing a song of the Lord
> on strange soil?
>
> (Psalms 137:1–4)

Framing the northern Negev is an arch at Avdat, which grew from a camel caravansary to a wealthy fourth-century city complete with homes and churches.

Learning Ancient Ways at Avdat   97

Stately remains of ancient arches and pillars cover a low, broad hill on the Negev highlands just north of Sedeh Boqer. These are the ruins of Avdat, which tell more of history than of nature. But, because the people who built Avdat understood the desert so well and used its resources wisely, their society is instructive for ours.

During the fourth century C.E., at the height of Avdat's glory, the northern Negev was filled with towns, and the land was terraced and farmed more intensively than any other time, including the present. Avdat, one of the great caravansaries along the famed Spice Route, was remarkable for its architecture as well as for abundance in such an austere location.

Itzik showed us the vestiges of a wine merchant's home with its graceful arches and wine storage area. On the ceiling of what is left of a Byzantine church we saw a cross and a bull's head: a mix of symbols from early Christianity and ancient pagan bull worship. Forts, homes, and churches terrace the white chalk hill, which is riddled with Nabatean cisterns.

The Nabateans, who began building Avdat in the fourth century B.C.E., were originally Arab nomads who became an economic force along the famed Spice Route. This highway system of the ancient world brought spices, precious metals, and rare woods from the Arabian Peninsula and Africa to the Mediterranean and Mesopotamia, where trades were made for grains, oils, weapons, and other goods. Nabatean fortunes rose by providing caravans with supplies, escorts, and rest stations. Some stations developed into cities such as Avdat. Petra, in present-day Jordan, became the Nabatean capital.

The Spice Route followed the Aravah, then a main branch proceeded westward, past Avdat, to ports on the Mediterranean coast. As the Avdat caravansary grew to a town, then a city, Nabateans became farmers and merchants. Managing with little technology, in an area that receives about five inches of precipitation annually, they were the first people to make the desert bloom.

Nabateans, who later became Byzantine Christians as Roman rule spread south, dug cisterns and terraced their fields to capture as much water as possible. They even slowed waters racing off hills, channeling them down zigzag courses by placing small piles of rocks like pinball baffles on the slopes.

Nelson Glueck, who studied the Nabateans and the Negev, wrote eloquently of them in *Rivers in the Desert*:

> They were indeed a wonderful people, whose abilities were directed to the arts of peace rather than to the science of war, to the fructification of deserts rather than to the sowing of their neighbors' fields with salt, to the conservation of the soil and the skillful gathering and utilization of water rather than to the squandering of natural resources. . . . They sought out drops of moisture with the same eagerness that hunters display when stalking game.

Avdat Farm, a joint project of Ben-Gurion and Hebrew Universities, lies within view of Avdat, only a hill away. Established by botanist Michael Evenari in the 1950s, Avdat Farm employs Nabatean methods of water capture. The farm also studies indigenous Negev plants.

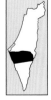

Remarkably, although the Negev and Sahara Deserts are related, researchers have found twelve hundred plant species in the Negev and only seven hundred in the Sahara, an area six hundred times larger. Just as surprising, more plant species grow in the Negev than in the moister, Mediterranean regions of Israel.

The reason for such botanic diversity is the Negev's incredible topographic and geologic diversity: rocky slopes, flat hammada, low-lying wadis, high cliffs, seeps and springs, and soils composed of every type of rock, from flint and granite to sandstone and chalk. Because of the Negev's severe conditions, plants learn to fine-tune themselves to microhabitats in order to survive. The other reason for such plant diversity—the same reason all of Israel's diversity far outreaches its compact boundaries—is its position at the juncture of three continents.

The broad bed of Nahal Zin was one of the great highways that linked continental travel. Meandering past Avdat, Nahal Zin is the thread that binds the northern Negev. This sinuous gray-green snake of a riverbed winds through tan canyons, past Sedeh Boqer, past Makhtesh Gadol toward the northeast, passing Har Zin Reserve and Mount Hor. Nahal Zin was one of the routes for the Hebrews of the Exodus, and Hor ha'Har is where Aaron is thought to be buried.

Just east of the Scorpion Ascent (Ma'aleh Aqrabim), Nahal Zin passes two springs, Ein Aqrabim and Ein Zin. One is an intermittent spring; the other spring is salty. But palms are adapted to drinking salty water, and Ein Zin's palms compose a picture of the classic desert oasis: deep, emerald fronds standing out from the faded, wind-carved cliffs of the *nahal*.

Nahal Zin continues on its way, heading northeast past Makhtesh Qatan, past Aravah Junction and the beginning of the Aravah highway. Finally, just short of Mount Sodom and the beginning of the Judean Desert, it spends itself in the salt flats of the Dead Sea.

Nahal Zin stretches sixty-six miles across the desert, one of the longest riverbeds in the Negev. It links events in history as well as linking the Negev and Judean Deserts. Venturing north of Nahal Zin I headed toward the Judean Desert, physically narrow but broad in both natural and human history.

CHAPTER FIVE

Judean Desert:
Exploring the Lowest Place on Earth

Ein Gedi pools

Judean Desert

Wadi Qelt •
Ein Feshehah •

Ein Gedi •
Nahal Arugot •

Masada •

Arad •

Mount Sodom •

C AUGHT BETWEEN THE TOWER-
ING WALLS of the Judean Hills
and the salty waters of the
Dead Sea, which fill the center of the
Great Rift, lies the narrow strip of
the Judean Desert. A place of canyons,
salt mountains, and sheer cliffs, this
monochrome of white, like the Ti-
betan Plateau and North America's
Great Basin, is a rain-shadow desert.

Moist air flowing northward toward Tibet from the Indian Ocean is
blocked by the Himalayas, producing
the high, dry plateau of Tibet. Moist
air sweeping eastward from the Pacific
Ocean is blocked by California's Sierra Nevada Mountains, causing
the Great Basin Desert to the east.

Although they are not of the magnitude of the Himalayas or Sier-
ras, the tall Judean Hills are just as effective at trapping moist air
coming from the Mediterranean Sea. At the eastern foot of the Judean
Hills lies the Judean Desert, a barren rain-shadow desert—except
for the springs.

At springs such as Ein Gedi and rivers such as Nahal Arugot, water
bubbles up, splashes, spills, and creates oases of ferns, shrubs, and tall
palms. These lush oases are world famous and provide homes for
Palestine sunbirds, Tristram's grackles, and myriad other birds. Leopards hunt ibex and hyraxes in the deep, narrow canyons. At night,
when tourists sleep, jackals, hyenas, and wild cats roam springs that
edge the Dead Sea. Though its summer temperatures average a blazing 100 degrees Fahrenheit, thanks to its springs the Judean Desert is
dotted with pocket paradises.

And, always, there is the Dead Sea—or Salt Sea as its name means
in Hebrew. A changeable body of water, it sparkles crisp and cobalt

blue after rain has washed the air. Sometimes, when the slanting rays of evening or morning strike the water, the sea is plated gold or silver. In the heat of the day, water evaporates in a misty layer above the sea, and winds whip up dust, hiding the base of the four-thousand-foot-high mountains of Moab on the eastern shore. Then the Dead Sea and its banks become a ghostly dreamscape.

The Dead Sea is so salty nothing can live in it. Nothing can sink in it either. Mark Twain, writing in 1869 in *Innocents Abroad*, describes

---

At thirteen hundred feet below sea level, the Dead Sea is the lowest place on Earth and the saltiest body of water in the world. Our blood is 0.9 percent salt, an echo of the fact that life was born in the sea. Oceans average a bit more than 3 percent salt. The Mediterranean Sea measures about 3.3 percent salt, the Great Basin's Great Salt Lake nearly 20 percent. The Dead Sea is 33 percent salt—a slew of salts.

---

with wit as caustic as the water all the ways in which a person cannot sink: on his back, on his stomach, legs out, legs in. When he and his companions were done splashing, they "came out coated with salt till we shone like icicles. . . . It was the variegated villainy and novelty of it that charmed us. Salt crystals glitter in the sun about the shores of the lake. In places they coat the ground like a brilliant crust of ice."

And, like ice, the Dead Sea salt burns bare feet. I had come to the shore of the Dead Sea because I felt I must. I had been hearing about its salty effect since I was a child.

Small family groups dotted the dire, rocky shores, their blankets spread with lunch, children's plastic toys, and grandma. The blankets seemed islands of safety amid a barren of salt-covered stones. With the steep-sided mountains of Judea and Moab sloping up on either side, I felt like a Lilliputian trapped near the bottom of some monstrous bathtub full of briny water.

Why had these people chosen to come here, rather than to Eilat, Lake Kinneret (Sea of Galilee), or the Mediterranean? For the novelty?

That's why I was here, my salt-sensitive feet now firmly strapped back in my Teva sandals, sidling into bath-warm water devoid of any life but me and a few other novelty-seekers. I waded in just past my waist when some unseen force flipped me onto my back. I tried to right myself and wade deeper, but the force flipped me onto my back again.

There's a reason tourist brochures of the Dead Sea show bathers sitting in the water, reading. The Dead Sea tolerates no other position. Every time I tried to turn and stroke, the buoyant saltwater pitched me onto my back, helpless as a cork.

At the same time that the saltwater forced me onto my back, it found every small tear and fissure on my body: hangnail, skinned knee, chapped lips. Actually, every pore of my body tingled from the brew of salts.

For me and most other tourists, dipping in the Dead Sea *is* a novelty. For some, a test of the sea's buoyancy proved a life-or-death event. The astute chronicler of the first-century Jewish war against Rome, Josephus told what happened when Vespasian, who led the Roman assault, came to examine the Dead Sea:

> He ordered non-swimmers to be thrown into deep water with their hands tied behind them, and found they all came to the surface as if blown upwards by a strong wind. . . . Moreover in many places [the sea] throws up black lumps of asphalt, which float and resemble headless bulls in shape and size.

Asphalt, potash, salt, magnesium, bromine—all products of the **103** Dead Sea—are valuable today. Some have been used for centuries. In embalming their dead, Egyptians used Dead Sea asphalt as well as perfumes such as balm and henna from this region.

But the Dead Sea is not what it was. Overuse has caused the sea to shrink. Even recently built spas are now farther from the shore. Water diverted upstream at Lake Kinneret and from springs in both Israel and Jordan lessens the flow into the Dead Sea. And the southern portion of the sea has been sectioned into great evaporation pans by the Dead Sea Works, which extracts potash, bromine, and other chemicals for export.

Although the northern portion of the sea drops to depths of nearly one thousand fifty feet, the southern portion is less than seven feet deep. A canal connects the two.

During the last Ice Age, more than fifteen thousand years ago, the Dead Sea was much larger. It was part of a vast sea stretching from Lake Kinneret in the north to Hatsevah, an ancient and modern settlement in the Aravah Valley of the northern Negev. Lashon (Tongue)

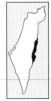

Sea, as it is called, was about seven hundred feet higher than today's Dead Sea.

Dramatic change occurred even more recently, perhaps within the memory of man. Dense salt and gypsum layers, crushed by thick beds of rock accumulating above, swelled in a violent uplift and Mount Sodom was born. Perhaps this event and the memory of the destruction of Sodom and Gomorrah are linked.

Located on the plain near where Mount Sodom rises today, the ancient cities of Sodom and Gomorrah were known for wickedness and sexual perversity. Abraham's nephew Lot was warned to flee Sodom before God destroyed the two cities. With his two daughters and wife, Lot headed up toward the Judean Hills and was warned not to turn to see the "sulfurous fire" (Genesis 19:24) that rained down upon the evil places. Lot's wife made the mistake of looking back on the wreckage of Sodom and Gomorrah and was turned into a pillar of salt. Mount Sodom is crenelated with salt crags, any one of which could be Mrs. Lot.

At eight miles long and one mile wide, Mount Sodom is a narrow loaf that forms the gateway between the Negev and Judean Deserts. Yet, this flat-topped sentinel, this mountain of salt, is still five hundred twenty-five feet *below* sea level.

Drillings into Mount Sodom have found that the salt pack plunges more than eleven thousand feet into the earth, layer upon layer of salt laid down when ancient seas ebbed and flowed. If the base of this massive plug of salt were raised to sea level, it would soar far higher than Mount Hermon, Israel's highest peak. Mount Sodom is still growing, but only a few millimeters a year. Erosion continues as well, so the mountain stays about the same height. Yet it is ever dynamic.

Although precipitation averages only three inches a year, over the years rain has carved not only crags but caves in the mountain, some dangerously unstable. Negligible rain and a mountain of salt: not a prescription for a lush environment. Indeed, Mount Sodom is probably the most life-forbidding place in Israel. Despite its parched features, or perhaps because of them, Mount Sodom is brilliantly austere.

The Road to Arad

All along its length, the Judean Desert is scored by canyons. Rain that gathers in roaring flash floods carves these canyons as it rushes down from the Judean Hills toward the Dead Sea. Some canyons, such as that carved by Nahal Arugot and the area around Ein Gedi, are spring-fed, so cooled by water most of the year. Except for occasional rains, canyons without springs are dry.

Nahal Peratsim, a narrow, white-walled gorge just off Route 90 near the foot of Mount Sodom, is dry, but its walls are galleries of whorled etchings. The artist is water, rushing through occasionally, its currents gouging and grooving the marl walls. Within the canyon's walls is the Flour Cave (Ha-Qemah Cave), one of the Sodom area's stable caves and so called because those who enter exit dusted with a fine, floury coating of white marl.

From there, an ascent leads to the Ammi'az Plain, which looks toward the southern end of the Dead Sea. A short walk back to an overlook at the edge of Nahal Peratsim shows how water cut its way through the plain's soft marl, cleaving this gorge. The marl was once the floor of the Lashon Sea, when that ancient inland sea filled the entire basin between the mountains of Moab and the Judean Hills.

On a trip from the Negev back to Tel Aviv, I decided to take the long way. Rather than turn west toward Dimona at the Aravah Junction, I turned east toward the Judean Desert. I wanted to follow Nahal Zin to its end at the Dead Sea salt flats. I wanted to see how the Negev and Judean Deserts connected.

My husband, Michael, is used to my curiosity about topography. On long drives, I am usually at the wheel and forever asking, "Where does this river begin? Where does it end? Will you check?" His groans have become ritual as he unfolds the map. By visualizing the topography of a place, I can better understand its history.

105

Following Route 90, I crossed the bridge spanning Nahal Zin at the northern edge of the Negev and looked out over fantastically eroded tan and white badlands. Curving northeast, the road traverses the narrow neck of desert that passes from Negev to Dead Sea. Then the Dead Sea Works came into view: convoluted metal towers; skeletal conveyor belts; vast, segmented evaporation pans. Even on a sunny day, there is something about this industry in such a brutal-looking landscape that reminds me of a 1930s German expressionist film.

Across, the Ammi'az Plain looks out over the Great Rift. Then the highway traces a route along the base of Mount Sodom, past the turnoff for Arubotayim Cave (Cave of the Chimneys), which visitors can enter to see how water carved two chimney-tall caves. A few miles north, at Zohar Junction, Route 31 winds alongside Nahal Zohar but climbs steadily toward Arad.

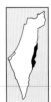

I pulled the car into one of the observation sites along the Zohar

The parched hills of the Judean Desert roll north to the Samarian Hills. This desert is squeezed between the Dead Sea to the east and the Judean Mountains to the west.

ascent. From there, I had a sweeping view of the Judean Desert, the Dead Sea, and, directly below, Nahal Zohar. The name *zohar*, meaning "radiance," derives from the glow of light reflected off the white marl walls of the river canyon. It shares its name with the Zohar, a classic of kabbalah, which encompasses the range of Jewish mysticism. Near the mouth of Nahal Zohar lies a second- or third-century Roman fort built atop a marl butte, the ruins forlorn looking in the blindingly bright and sere canyon.

Climbing higher along the twisting, mountainous road, I was amused to see a sign that announced "sea level." Wildflowers in pinks, blues, purples, and yellows softened the strict landscape as the road approached Arad. On a hillside just before the city, sheep and goats grazed on one side of the road, camels on the other: a reminder of the way life was for centuries. Just west of Arad, on the road to Beersheba, the fields were splashed with drifts of gold field chrysanthemums. Among one of these golden fields I saw a dozen camels grazing. If they all belong to one man, he is a wealthy man indeed.

Arad itself is perched dramatically at the edge of the Negev highlands, overlooking the Judean Desert. It is a new city, small and clean, a little out of the way but maybe pleasantly so. It is also the namesake of ancient Arad, one of the oldest cities known in Israel, whose tell lies a few miles to the west.

Although a tell may be covered with grasses, flowers, shrubs, or just dirt, unlike a hill it is the product of people. Centuries of human history are layered in tells, the detritus of city upon city, some, like Arad, reaching back to the dawn of civilization. Over these layer cakes of history, soil settles and plants take root. It is the opposite of the usual process: we build atop nature. At a tell, nature overlays us.

The Arad Visitor Center provides a fascinating look at the natural and cultural history of the area. As I wandered through the museum, I was taken by a display of barley, wheat, peas, lentils, and chickpeas, all foods cultivated from native plants. At the head of the Judean Desert, near Jericho, archaeologists have found evidence of the earliest domesticated grains, cultivated from wild wheat and barley that grew nearby. In the display case, curators had set ancient grains and peas side by side with our modern equivalents, which are about one-third larger, the result of millennia of selective propagation.

With evidence of humanity everywhere, the nature of Israel and the nature of people are so intricately woven as to be inseparable. As nature affected us, so we affected nature.

Back when ancient Arad was *the* city of the region, merchants sent olive oil and lumber, asphalt and salt to Egypt's earliest rulers. They made sickle handles from wood or bone and sealed flint blades into the handles with bitumen from the Dead Sea. They buried their dead in caves, a common ancient practice. Perhaps the most famous such burial place is the Cave of Machpelah, which Abraham bought as the resting place for his wife Sarah's remains.

> Hidden in a cave at Nahal Mishmar, a few miles north of Masada, archaeologists found a treasure of Chalcolithic artifacts from the fourth millennium B.C.E.: mats made of reeds, woven palm-frond baskets, crowns adorned with figures of ibex, copper scepters, flax cloth, maceheads of limestone and hematite, hippopotamus-tusk objects, and an ivory box made from an elephant's tusk. The ivory may have come from Africa, or from Syria, where elephants lived until hunting decimated their numbers in the first millennium B.C.E.

107

Masada, Naturally

The Roman siege of Masada, which ended in the suicide of the Jewish Zealots in 73 C.E., so overshadows the mount that it is hard to see Masada as the singular landform it is. A lone, flat-topped mountain standing more than fourteen hundred feet high, eroded gulches all around, Masada offers a superb view of the surrounding Judean Desert. A walk to the top brings plants and birds into focus.

At the base of the Dead Sea side, it is hard to ignore the noisy bustle of gift shop, food stands, ticket booths, cable cars—a whole megillah. But at the foot of the Snake Path, the clamor subsides.

I had started the snaking hike to the top early in the morning; the later you start, the more heat and sun will be your enemies. Near the bottom, I passed white broom and moringa, which grow in pockets where moisture collects. Farther along the winding trail, low mounds of purple-flowered fagonia and the swollen, paired leaves of bean capers grow. About halfway up, heat and the effort of slogging to the top, switchback after switchback, take the joy out of seeing such familiar plants.

Just below the top I peered into a cavernous cistern, once sealed with chalk to retain water. Soda-straw formations, like the kind found in caves, hang from the cistern's ceiling, revealing the rock as limestone.

108   Atop the mount, raucous Tristram's grackles vied for my attention with the silent ruins of Masada. The chatty bird is named for Henry Baker Tristram, the British clergyman and naturalist who made the first survey of the region's animals in 1863.

Although Tristram first described them, it would be hard to miss these gregarious inhabitants of Masada. The glossy black males flash brilliant orange wingtips as they speed around the slopes, squawking and cackling. Ornithologist Lars Jonsson accurately described their calls, noting that their meandering whistles recall "tuning in short-wave radio."

Scientists building on the knowledge of their predecessors have found that Tristram's grackles are among the numerous North African species that have migrated up the Great Rift. They are common in the Judean Desert and are expanding their range northward into the Jordan Valley and beyond, nesting on apartment buildings as well as on the rocky cliffs they usually call home.

The grackles perform a service for another species common to the rocky cliffs of the canyons. Perched on the back of an ibex, a grackle picks out many meals' worth of insects, relieving the ibex of pests at the same time. Another behavior noticed by Israeli ornithologists seems less worthy. Male Tristram's grackles have been observed attacking females on their nests in order to drive them off and kill their nestlings. Then the males mate with the females to produce their own offspring.

A grim way to reproduce. But if competition for mates becomes fierce, the males of many species, including African lions, will go to these lengths to make sure their genes are the ones passed on. Richard III fits this pattern, too, as does the behavior of other notorious bygone rulers. In his quest to become king of England in the late fifteenth century, Richard III is believed to have killed his two young nephews, who were heirs apparent to the throne.

Herod, who with Rome's blessings reigned as king of Judea from 37 to 4 B.C.E., used similarly heinous tactics. Fear and jealousy of the Hasmoneans, influential descendants of the Maccabees, caused him to kill his Hasmonean wife Mariamne, his mother-in-law, his brother-in-law, and his own two sons, among many others.

Palestine had something of a tradition of cleric-naturalists: Canon Tristram and Pater Ernst Schmitz, a German Catholic theologian. Assigned to Jerusalem in 1908, Pater Schmitz's writings include descriptive reports on cheetahs just east of the Jordan River, leopards roaming near Jerusalem, bears on Mount Hermon, and crocodiles in the Crocodile River north of Tel Aviv. Pater Schmitz saw or heard about some of the last of those species seen in Israel.

Israel Aharoni, modern Israel's first zoologist, arrived in 1902 with training from the University of Prague in zoology and a personal mission to study the animals of the Middle East and the Bible. When Palestine was under Ottoman rule, Aharoni made zoological surveys for the sultan, then served as a zoologist when the British ruled the area, and eventually worked in Israeli academia. In addition to cataloging wildlife, Aharoni added ecological depth to the study of the region.

It is the ruins of one of Herod's splendid palaces that top Masada, now a national park. At this combination fortress and pleasure palace that spreads over much of Masada's twenty acres, the king could enjoy himself, knowing he was safe from his subjects, who hated him. Rows of storerooms and a dozen or so cisterns holding a total

of ten million gallons of water made sure that Herod would not want at Masada. Far from it.

The elegant complex, its rooms fitted with fine tiles and frescoes, represented the apex of Roman architecture. The bathhouses included cold rooms, warm rooms, and a large hot room. Ceramic pipes carrying hot air from a nearby furnace ran below the floor and within the walls of the hot room, creating a luxurious salon for steaming away the cares of empire. The terraces and balconies stepping down the upper slopes of Masada look elegantly classic yet modern even today. And the views from those north-facing terraces are still stunning. From these terraces, during spring, Herod could see waterfalls tumbling off the scarps of the Judean Hills.

Seventy-five years after Herod's death, this homage to opulence revealed its merits as a fortress. During that time, relations between Jewish subjects and their Roman overlords deteriorated, and rebellion broke out across the land. After the Romans burned down the Second Temple in 70 C.E., one group of Jewish Zealots retreated to the Judean Desert, which has harbored many dissidents throughout history. They took possession of the stronghold Masada.

The Romans laid siege. Day after day, for eight months, they used Jewish slaves to build a massive earthen ramp from a low ridge on the western side of Masada to the top of the plateau, where they could direct their battering rams against the fortress's walls.

110

Each day the Zealots watched the ramp come closer; each night they saw the Roman campfires glimmering on the floor of the Judean Desert. The day before they knew the Romans would breach the walls, nine hundred sixty Zealots decided to die at their own hands rather than live as Roman slaves. In *The Jewish War*, Josephus wrote of the mass suicide that occurred on Masada in 73 C.E.:

> Expecting further resistance, the Romans armed themselves at dawn, bridged the gap between platform and ramparts with gangways and then made their assault. Seeing no enemy, but dreadful solitude on every side, fire within, and silence, they were at a loss to guess what had happened.

My view of Masada held no such horror. Below, I could see the Dead Sea, a silver and turquoise jewel under the glinting rays of the sun. Palms swayed in the wind, their fronds tousled like heads of hair. And the desert all around—a moonscape of eroded gullies running to the Dead Sea.

At the northern edge of Ein Gedi Reserve, the cliffs are pocked by caves similar to those in which the Dead Sea Scrolls were secreted. Beyond lie the Dead Sea and Jordan.

111

Ein Gedi: Garden in the Desert

Floodwaters pouring off the Judean Hills have cut deeply into the escarpments and plateaus lying between desert and hilltops, carving canyons that are among the loveliest in Israel. One is so full of natural riches and profound human history that the United Nations has designated it an International Biosphere Reserve. It is the oasis of Ein Gedi.

The United Nations Educational, Scientific, and Cultural Organization (UNESCO) program that designates the world's most important natural sites as International Biosphere Reserves puts Ein Gedi in the company of Everglades and Great Smoky Mountains National Parks in the United States, Australia's Ayers Rock, and Tanzania's Serengeti National Park. The origin of the name Ein Gedi, or Spring of the Kid Goat, is lost in time as Ein Gedi was already well known in King David's reign. And no wonder. Surrounded by the scorched, spare Judean Desert, the lush greenery of Ein Gedi Nature Reserve soothes all the senses.

George Adam Smith, a Bible scholar from Scotland, traveled through Palestine for his 1894 book *The Historical Geography of the Holy Land*. Smith was lyrical about the Judean Desert and Ein Gedi:

> There is the view from the Mount of Olives, down twenty miles of hilltops to the deep blue waters, with the wall of Moab glowing on the further side like burnished copper, and staining the blue sea red with its light. . . . And, above all, there is the view from En-gedi under the full moon, when the sea is bridged with gold, and the eastern mountains are black with a border of opal.

Ein Gedi Nature Reserve is part of the Israel Nature and National Parks Protection Authority's system of more than three hundred reserves throughout Israel. And Ein Gedi is much more than a spring. Because the reserve's approximately sixty-seven hundred acres encompass desert, springs, and high ridges, it is a meeting point for all four of Israel's major botanical divisions, representing hundreds of species: tropical trees such as Sodom apple and moringa from the Sudanian zone; desert plants such as bean caper and acacia from the Saharo-Arabian zone; Irano-Turanian steppe plants such as willow and globe thistle; and Mediterranean temperate plants such as maidenhair fern and chaste-tree.

112 Besides the springs, the reserve includes the canyons of Nahal David and Nahal Arugot, caves, waterfalls, pools, a Chalcolithic temple, an ancient synagogue, a ruined fortress, Roman bathhouse, youth hostel, and SPNI's Ein Gedi Field School and museum.

Because of its fame and because its lower trails are easy to walk, Ein Gedi often is crowded with sightseers. I stepped into the stream of people walking up toward Nahal David, passing acacias, thorny canopies of jujube trees, giant phragmites reeds, and hundreds of other plants, some at their northern limits, some at their southern limits. One standout is the Sodom apple. A migrant from Africa, nothing about the tropical Sodom apple tree is demure except its height.

Its leaves are bold gray-green ovals. Its flowers are clusters of pink and white. And its pale green fruits are the size of small apples. But the "apples" are nothing more than hollow casings for hundreds of seeds attached to silky filaments. These filaments, which the Talmud says were used as wicks, are like small parasols that float on the breeze until they land, giving the seed a chance to germinate.

The Bible calls Sodom apples "grapes of gall," a metaphor for bitterness (Deuteronomy 32:32) because the green promise of its casing covers dry, bitter seeds rather than sweet fruit. Likening the Sodom apple to the destroyed city of Sodom, Josephus says it has "all the appearance of eatable fruit, but when plucked with the hand dissolved into smoke and ashes."

Like its relative the milkweed, all parts of the Sodom apple contain milky, poisonous sap. And, like milkweed, Sodom apple is the food of choice for the monarch butterfly. The butterfly has adapted to the poison, but its predators have not. As with many other brightly colored species, the monarch, with its orange and black wings, warns that it is a meal to avoid.

A little way into the hills, the first waterfall at Ein Gedi drops twenty-five feet, splashing and creating wet banks for water-loving plants. It is fed by rainfall and by springs. Farther north along the Dead Sea, Ein Fashehah spouts springs, too, but its springs well up from tectonic fissures deep in the earth. The four springs that bubble up in Ein Gedi—Ein David, Ein Shulamit, Ein Gedi, and Ein Arugot—have a different source.

One of Ein Gedi's most unusual species is the relatively large weaver ant, which lives in the reserve's tamarisks and Euphrates poplars. An African species, the weaver ant is rare in Israel, living only in a few tropical oases. Weaver ants live a life rich with relationships. Like farmers, they tend and milk herds; in their case, herds of aphids. Small insects that suck the sap from trees, aphids excrete some of this sweet sap as "honeydew," which ants eat.

Both insects are adapted to this mutual relationship. Weaver ants use their antennae to stroke the backs of aphids, spurring honeydew secretion. "Herd" aphids, unlike free species, eject their honeydew slowly. The sweet drop is held in place by a ring of specially developed hairs, giving the ants a chance to sip.

The ants protect their valuable herds from predators and from the sun with woven nests, using the silk extruded by the ants' own larvae. Each ant holds a larva in its mandibles and shuttles it back and forth across the margins of leaves, weaving a silken canopy for all.

When rain falls on the Judean Hills, the rain falling on the west side of the hills flows toward the Mediterranean, the rain falling on the east side flows toward the Dead Sea. This is the topographic watershed. Far below the surface of the hills lies a geologic watershed, and this watershed favors the Dead Sea.

Rain seeps into the soils that cloak the Judean Hills, then percolates down through permeable limestone. Eventually the water hits an impermeable layer: marl. The marl layers are tilted toward the Great Rift, so even though water may have percolated through limestone on the west side of the Hills, it will follow the tilt of the marl eastward. When water finds a crack between the marl and limestone layers, it bursts out as a "layer" spring.

Geologists discovered the difference between these topographic and geologic watersheds the hard way. As part of a national water project, dams were constructed across streams on the west side of the Judean Hills to provide water for a growing Israeli population. But the water seemed to drain away, so hydrologists tagged it with isotopes.

Isotopes of water have extra neutrons in their nuclei, making these molecules heavier than molecules of normal water. Scientists can detect the presence of isotopes by measuring the weight of a sample using an instrument called a mass spectrometer. They found samples of the tagged water on the shores of the Dead Sea and, with that clue, figured out the rest.

The layer springs allow incredible diversity of life to exist in the oases of the Judean Desert. They create tropical bio-islands for species that normally thrive more than a thousand miles south, in Africa. Although the Aravah is more southerly, it is too dry to support the range of tropical species found at Ein Gedi.

114

Following the trail farther up Nahal David, I noticed a fig tree that seemed to grow from the rocks. A thick bank of reeds blocking the path had been cut, creating a reed tunnel, and I stooped as I passed through on my way to Shulamit Falls. The tale of Shulamit Falls is a tale of lost . . . well, perhaps it was love.

Consumed by jealousy because of David's popularity among the people, King Saul had sworn to kill him. So David fled to the wilderness at Ein Gedi. It is said that at the top of these very falls he saw a maiden—Shulamit, perhaps a vision of the Shulamit who appears in Song of Songs (7:1).

Shulamit's lustrous hair enchanted David, so he followed after her to the cliff's edge. Just as he reached her, she slipped. David caught Shulamit by her tresses, but they slid from his grasp and she fell to her death in the pool below. Now Shulamit's hair, bathed by David's tears, covers the damp, shady walls.

Shulamit's Hair, *Sa'arot Shulamit*, are the scalloped ferns that tremble at the slightest breeze or when mist from the falls passes over them. *Sa'arot Shulamit*, or maidenhair fern, grows where shade and splashing water meet. Although most of Israel's ferns live in the cooler, wetter north, wherever they are, they are protected by law.

Dainty, deep green ferns seem out of place here, surrounded as they are by the fiery scarps of the Judean Desert. But, in the heat of the day, the temperature at Shulamit Falls is noticeably cooler. The falls drop prettily—sixty-five feet into a small pool created by the constantly crashing water.

Climbing still higher, I passed moringa trees. Their roots seeking out unseen groundwater, the trees mark the line where dolomite or limestone cliffs meet a layer of marl, the line where Ein Shulamit and other layer springs burst forth. Gracefully pendulous, moringa trees arch long gray-green stems from secure spots on cliffsides. Leafy they are not. Perhaps their twiggy nature is why their name in Hebrew means "broomlike." In spring, these tropical trees, which live in only a few places along the Rift and no farther north than the Judean Desert, are dotted with small flowers, white with pink throats.

Farther up, I found myself in Dodim Cave, a grotto of open arches centered on a small pool and hung with maidenhair ferns. Were it not for traipsing tourists, myself included, Dodim Cave—Lovers Cave, from the lovers in the Song of Songs—would be a graceful, intimate spot. The grotto's limestone ceiling is adorned with small stalactites, with rock fins shaped like elephant ears, and with braided ripples of rock.

115

Dipping my hand into the clear, shallow pool, the water cool in the heat of the day, I scooped up small black river snails. Shaped like whorled coronets, these tiny freshwater snails live only in unpolluted water. Wherever I encountered these snails in Israel's streams and springs, I knew the water was relatively pure. Indeed, the springs of Ein Gedi spill some of the purest water in all of Israel. Large quantities of this water are bottled at Kibbutz Ein Gedi for consumption all over Israel. Like cell phones, bottled water is ubiquitous, for Israelis and tourists alike.

Until now, I had been climbing a trail that winds up through Nahal David, a canyon fringed with myriad plants and running with spring waters. Most visitors reach Dodim Cave and then return the way they came. The trail leads still higher, though, to the Dry Canyon and Mount Yishai. Backtracking from Dodim Cave to Shulamit Spring brought me to a trail leading to a plateau overlooking the Dead Sea and the delta where the waters of Nahal David and Nahal Arugot flow into the sea.

Atop the plateau stand acacia trees and the remains of a Chalcolithic temple some five thousand years old. The temple was found devoid of any objects. Archaeologists believe the ritual objects used here were cached farther south and discovered as the treasure in Mishmar Cave. No one knows why the objects were removed or who the temple served. Perhaps it was a pilgrimage site for wandering nomads since no other dwellings from that period have been found at Ein Gedi. Without the people who gave it purpose, the temple seemed poignantly solitary.

Nearby, Tristram's grackles beat the air. A sand partridge called from somewhere out of sight. Among Ein Gedi's most commonly seen birds are wheatears with formal black-and-white plumage; blackstarts, small gray birds distinguished by black tails and a sad song; fan-tailed ravens similar to ravens anywhere in the world; and bulbuls, gregarious birds once rare in Israel, now seen all over. Large birds frequent Ein Gedi as well and, during migration, the skies may be full of storks and raptors.

If it were not for their coloring, which allows them to blend with the sand-colored slopes, plump little partridges would seem especially vulnerable. Perhaps that is why David, when King Saul came chasing him, lamented, "For the king of Israel has come out to seek a single flea—as if he were hunting a partridge in the hills" (1 Samuel 26:20).

116

David and his men had hidden from Saul in one of the caves near Ein Gedi. King Saul entered that very cave, not suspecting David's presence. Rather than kill the king, David stealthily cut a corner of Saul's cloak to prove his fealty and compassion (1 Samuel 24:1-13). Midrashic commentary says a small spider saved David's life: King Saul entered the cave because a spider had woven its web across the mouth of the cave, making the entrance look little used.

David spent time at Ein Gedi, resting on the rocks as he composed psalms, looking over the stepped escarpments and bony hills whose canyons are extravagant with rushing water and green life, an Eden for ibex and other animals.

Much of Israel has changed, often drastically, since David's time. The hills of Judea are nearly devoid of the forests that once covered them. The last forests of the coastal plain were cut in the early 1900s. More recently, the coastal dunes are giving way to high-rises and industry. Although Ein Gedi, too, has changed, nearly all the wildlife of David's time is here today.

Rock Badgers at the Spring of the Kid

Psalm 104:18 sings, "The high mountains are for wild goats; the crags are a refuge for rock badgers." And rock badgers, or, more properly, hyraxes, do appear on the crags at Ein Gedi.

Shaded by a huge umbrella of a jujube tree, Ein Gedi, the spring itself, lies a short walk from the Chalcolithic temple. When afternoon shadows creep across the rocks that skirt the spring, hyraxes begin to emerge. They know that when shadows are long, humans will soon leave and the spring will again be theirs. I sat on the low rock wall that now rims the spring and watched as hyraxes stole out from crevices, edging ever closer to the water.

Not quite two feet long, the hyrax looks like a round brown rug wearing a hopeful and endearing expression on its pointed face. Also called coneys, hyraxes belong to an old order of animals. Two of the families within the order Hyracoidea are extinct. The single family remaining contains only three genera with a total of eight or nine species. By comparison, the order Rodentia contains thirty-five families with three hundred fifty-two genera and seemingly countless species, from mice and squirrels to porcupines and woodchucks. As much as a hyrax looks like it should be related to a woodchuck, similarities in foot structure and dentition make its closest living relative . . . the elephant.

117

Hyraxes live together in gregarious groups of six to fifty, chattering among themselves and sunning on rocks. Staring into the sun does not bother them because, having evolved under the hot sun of Africa, hyraxes have adapted. A special translucent covering protects the tops of their pupils from direct sunlight.

Another adaptation allows them to run among the rocks as if they had suction cups on their feet. In fact, they do. The naked, rubbery pads of a hyrax's feet are continually moistened by special glands. In addition, the foot muscles are arranged so that the middle of the sole contracts, forming a hollow suction cup.

In *Mammals of South Africa*, the nineteenth-century naturalist W. L. Sclater says this adaptation "gives the animal great clinging power, so much so that even when shot dead it remains attached to almost perpendicular surfaces as if fixed there."

Their suction-cup soles allow hyraxes to race up cliffs with ease. And race they must because hyraxes, which live in rocky natural areas throughout Israel, are everybody's dinner. Leopards, raptors, snakes, foxes, even humans will eat them.

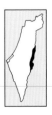

TONY MALMQVIST

Hyraxes themselves primarily are vegetarian, although they also eat locusts. Historically, locusts have been food for desert-dwelling people as well. John the Baptist, when he roamed in the wilderness of Judea, ate what was available: "His meat was locusts and wild honey" (Matthew 3:4).

As I watched, even baby hyraxes dashed around on the rocks, regrouping at the chucking sounds of an older "baby sitter." A fat-headed agama lizard scurried past. The shapes of two or three ibex separated from the tan camouflage of the rocks, and a sand-and-peach-tinted

Hyraxes, the size of woodchucks, race over the rocks at Ein Gedi Nature Reserve. Eons ago, they migrated up the Great Rift from Africa. Their closest relative is the elephant.

Arabian babbler, its long tail helping it balance on a branch, called "pik-pik-pik" from the canopy above.

On the trail returning to the Ein Gedi Field School, a partridge flashed across the path. Perhaps it was the same bird I had heard earlier. Beyond, a large, circular memorial commemorates eight youths who died in an explosion here in 1942. Not far are the remains of a sixth-century synagogue with mosaic tiles figured with Hebrew and Aramaic script, zodiac signs, and water birds.

In modern times, the sweet, heavy odor of pomelo (grapefruit) blossoms, grown in Kibbutz Ein Gedi orchards, perfumes the air. During the third to sixth centuries, when the ruined synagogue was in use, the perfumes were different and, if anything, more valuable. Ein Gedi was famous for its perfumes and spices, which were the economic essence of the community.

The first settlements at Ein Gedi date to biblical times, and cultivated palm groves at Ein Gedi probably date to that time as well. Thanks to year-round warm temperatures and perennial springs, Ein Gedi was one of the few places in the region where farmers could grow rare and valuable plants such as balm. As the Judean Desert was one of the paths of the Spice Route, Ein Gedi, with its rare plant groves, became a major trade point.

Jacob urged his sons to go and appease Pharaoh's vizier, not knowing the vizier was his lost son, Joseph: "Take some of the choice products of the land in your baggage, and carry them down as a gift for the man—some balm and some honey, gum, ladanum, pistachio nuts, and almonds" (Genesis 43:11). The balm probably came from Ein Gedi or Gilead, north of the Yarmuk River.

Nearly a thousand years later, King Solomon wrote: "My beloved to me is a bag of myrrh lodged between my breasts. My beloved to me is a spray of henna blooms from the vineyards of En-gedi" (Song of Songs 1:13–14).

From the time of Israel's kings through Roman and Byzantine times, Ein Gedi was not only full of natural gardens but farmers' gardens. Archaeologists have found evidence of aqueducts, holding ponds, and agricultural terracing. Jewish farmers grew valuable balm, ladanum, and gum at Ein Gedi over a span of fourteen hundred years.

Ein Gedi's importance declined after a conflagration destroyed the community's synagogue in the mid-sixth century. The fire occurred around the reign of Emperor Justinian I, who incited the destruction of synagogues.

Present-day horticulturists are not even sure whether the biblical Hebrew that describes the spices refers to the plant or the product that ancient people manufactured from the plant. But what were these spices used for?

119

In biblical times, burials required rituals involving one or more precious spices. Egypt, for instance, imported spices from the Judean Desert for burials. Balm and other spices grown at Ein Gedi were nearly as valuable in world trade as frankincense, the prized resin from southern Arabia.

The incense burned on the Temple altar was certainly a mix of these spices or their derivatives. Incense was so important to Temple ritual that the Mishnah speaks of its critical qualities. A particular family, the house of Avtinas, was charged with producing the incense according to closely guarded secrets. So valuable were these horticultural secrets that an inscription on the floor of the Ein Gedi synagogue leveled threats at those who would reveal them.

Similar to myrrh, the small *Commiphora gileadensis* tree—the source of balm—oozes resin when its bark is cut. Collecting the resin, or balm of Gilead, was a tedious and lengthy process, so balm became a costly yet sought-after commodity. It was used as a medicine for headaches and an antidote to snake bites, as well as in ritual incense and in perfume. The economic importance of balm was such that during the Jewish revolt against Rome, Jews and Roman soldiers fought over the balm, plant by plant.

During Roman times, spices had yet another use. Rome had adopted much of Greek culture, including admiration of the body. Although baths were available, they were not as readily available as they are today, so perfumes blended from these spices were used to mask unpleasant odors.

Henna, mentioned in the Song of Songs, is still grown near Jericho. Its rust-red extract is used medicinally, as well as to color hair. In addition, Jews from Yemen brought to Israel the tradition, widespread over the Arabian Peninsula and North Africa, of painting intricate henna patterns on a bride's hands and feet. Not long ago, an update of this practice appeared in New York where young women had henna patterns painted on shoulders or hands to make a fashion statement.

Once Israel was known for its balm and henna. Now it is known for oranges and other fruits and vegetables. And the most valuable export of Arabia is no longer frankincense, but oil. Markets change.

Feet in Water, Head in Fire:
Palm Groves Near the Field School

One thing all visitors to SPNI field schools have in common is that they have come to see nature—not to lounge in the lap of luxury—but that's where commonality ends. The dining room, fitted with school-cafeteria tables and molded plastic chairs, is the place to survey the always intriguing mix of people.

Israelis come in couples with backpacks and hiking boots. Family groups include moms and dads, aunts and uncles, and clutches of kids. School groups fill tables with Jewish or Arab middle-school students. And spotted throughout are visitors to Israel, who come from all over and for all sorts of reasons.

Our hike in Nahal Arugot the next day would include a midwife from Australia who was testing the waters for immigrating to Israel. Another traveler—a New Jersey college student—was in Israel visiting relatives in Bene Beraq. Bene Beraq is a traditional religious community near Tel Aviv: women with covered heads and modest clothing. The student was dressed casual-American in a stylishly long sundress with slits up the side, loose hair, and long purple nails. She had been signed up for the trip by her uncle.

One young woman, now living in Israel, had immigrated from France. On a trip to Israel, the French woman had met a fellow in

At Ein Gedi, groups of ibex often come down at dusk to graze on the lawns of SPNI's field school. Males, such as above, bear horns that can grow to four feet.

Eilat. They liked each other, visited one another, had fallen in love, and become engaged. Only weeks before the wedding, while completing Army duty, he was killed, another casualty of a conflict that kills some and wounds all. Still, the young woman had come. She had moved in with his parents, believing it best to face their tragedy together.

121

The German minister and his wife, whom I had met on the trip to Makhtesh Gadol, arrived. We had a small, ebullient reunion, she and I smiling and gesticulating our way beyond language barriers. Ido, our guide, does not work full time with SPNI but guides all sorts of groups: nature lovers, history buffs, Christian pilgrims, and others. His encyclopedic knowledge, a trait of SPNI guides, is matched by his sense of humor.

After dinner, a few of us walked out on the patios of the Ein Gedi Field School, cool in the dark though the day had been hot. Stone paving glowed white in the lamplight. Edging the patios are gardens full of shrubs whose flowers were bent by a slight wind. We lingered, lulled by the softness of the night. We could hear the palms rustle in the palm plantations as the wind shook their fronds, making Middle Eastern rhythm.

The date palm, *tamar* in Hebrew, was considered regal enough for the company of high priests and kings in ancient Israel: "The righteous bloom like a date palm; they thrive like a cedar in Leba-

non. Planted in the house of the Lord, they flourish in the courts of our God" (Psalms 92:13–14). The courts of King Solomon's Temple were lined with palm gardens, and the Prophet Ezekiel describes palm designs carved on the inner and outer Temple walls (Ezekiel 41:18–20).

Date palms were first cultivated some eight thousand years ago. And they were as economically important at Ein Gedi a few thousand years ago as they are today.

A date palm can produce more than five hundred pounds of dates annually for a hundred years. A hundred is its ultimate height in feet, the number of fronds it bears, and its uses. Mats and baskets are woven from its fronds and rope from its fibers. Fronds thatch the roofs of desert homes and palm trunks support them. Oil is extracted from the tree. Desert dwellers made an alcoholic drink from the fermented fruit of the date palm. And, when the Bible speaks of the land of milk and honey, the honey it refers to is the viscous, sugary liquid that drips from dates.

The lulav, used during the autumn holiday of Sukkot, is a young palm frond taken from the heart of a palm, just as the word lulav derives from *lev*, the Hebrew word for heart. When Jesus entered Jerusalem, some scholars say during Sukkot, he was greeted by followers waving palm fronds, and so Palm Sunday.

Date varieties range from dry to juicy. Bedouin used meal made from ground dry dates as long-lasting survival rations. Yet, the juiciest, highest quality dates are as succulent and sensuous a food as exists.

The first date palm oasis I ever encountered was at Wadi Feiran deep in the Sinai Desert. It was summer and hot. So, as Middle Eastern people have done for centuries, my traveling companion Yedida and I slept on the flat roof of a home. In the morning, a string of camels trotted past, under the canopy of a meandering line of palms. Arabs have a saying, "A date palm keeps its feet in water and its head in fire." The palms, snaking across the sands, gave away the presence of an underground stream.

A day later, in the garden at Saint Catherine's Monastery, near the foot of what is thought to be Mount Sinai, the keeper of the garden offered us a simple meal. Surrounded by palms and carefully tended flowers, we drank thick bitter coffee from small cups and ate dates as big as plums, soft and wrinkled and dripping with honey. It remains in memory as one of the finest meals.

Reaching the Upper Pools of Nahal Arugot

The midwife and college student decided they preferred soaking in the mud baths of a Dead Sea spa to hiking Nahal Arugot. So we dropped them off, and the remaining five of us—the minister and his wife, Ido, the French immigrant, and I—continued to the canyon of the Arugot or "garden beds."

While many people have heard of and visited Ein Gedi, far fewer are familiar with Nahal Arugot, the river canyon just south of Ein Gedi and part of the same ecosystem. A pity, but with fewer people treading the path, the natural beauty of Nahal Arugot had greater opportunity to shine.

The stream rushes down from the Hebron Mountains in the southern Judean Hills. One of the largest streams in the Judean Desert, Nahal Arugot drains a broad area and runs year-round, feeding acacias and other trees that line its lower reaches. Musical blackstarts flitted through the acacias, ignoring our presence.

At first, we walked up a gentle grade, a broad platform of rock so smooth it seemed paved. The trail, which follows the north bank of the stream, looks down on a small gorge the stream has cut at the bottom of the broad, high canyon. Less than ten feet wide and fifteen feet deep, the sheer, water-carved walls of the gorge are smooth and rounded like a Henry Moore sculpture. Running through the bottom of the gorge, the Arugot stream is milky blue from minerals.

123

As we hiked upward, the grade became steeper. Sometimes the stream was just at our feet, sometimes the trail rose high above the water, clinging to the side of the cliffs. From vantage points, we watched the stream drop from ledge to ledge, the lilt of tumbling water a strange sound in the desert.

The trail passes side canyon after side canyon, all of which pour water into Nahal Arugot when it rains. Ido pointed out the mouth of one especially large side canyon whose walls are chockablock with the rough rocks of conglomerate. A sign, he said, that long ago an enormous deluge surged through here, driving an assortment of rocks before it.

In places, the canyon walls are stained with light, bright lines, revealing where waterfalls spill when it rains. Across the stream a dirt bank is riddled with holes made by little green bee-eaters. These tiny emerald birds live in colonies and nest in holes that they excavate in sandbanks or eroded streambanks. Where the streambed widens, balanites and moringa trees grow.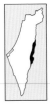

Near one such oasis, we stopped to watch four ibex, two of them little more than kids. Standing on their hind legs, they reached into the trees to munch small leaves. An older female moved downstream a few paces and, suddenly, it became clear why tan ibex have black tails. One mother ibex flicked her tail. Her young one saw the signal and immediately followed the flickering black flag.

Trails lead all over Nahal Arugot. Some lead up and over into Nahal David, the main canyon at Ein Gedi. It would not be exercising too much imagination to think that the leopards of Ein Gedi use these trails as we do, but at different times.

Seeing a leopard, the top predator in the Ein Gedi ecosystem besides us, is unusual. For one reason, they generally hunt at night. For another, even here they are rare. And if a predator could easily be seen it would not be very good at its job. Leopards, which are solitary and eat only live prey, depend on stealth and surprise to hunt down ibex, hyraxes, and porcupines, which are its main prey. As a top predator, leopards also are fewer in number than the animals it preys upon, providing fewer chances of being seen.

Shot by shepherds protecting their herds and by others for sport, and pushed out by development, the leopard of the Middle East was close to becoming merely a memory. It has been extirpated from Jordan and nearly so from Saudi Arabia. A distinct subspecies, smaller than the species, its last home is in Israel. Leopards are known to live in the Judean Desert and Negev mountains, and researchers suspect they may remain in Jordan Valley river thickets as well. But they number only a few dozen altogether. Fortunately, leopards are now protected by the Israel Nature and National Parks Protection Authority.

124

Once leopards lived all over Israel's hill country, from the Golan and the Galilee to Mount Carmel and Judea. When Tristram made his 1863 fauna study, cheetah and brown bear still lived in Israel. Of the large predators, only the lion, the symbol of the tribe of Judah, had been extirpated.

Lions used to roam the Jordan Valley and the hills of Judea. Samson vanquished an attacking lion in the Judean Hills. Returning to the spot later, he found a swarm of bees and golden honey among the lion's bones (Judges 14:5-8). When he was barely more than a boy, David convinced King Saul to let him meet Goliath's challenge by recounting that he had killed both lion and bear while protecting his sheep near Bethlehem (1 Samuel 17:34–37).

Although the lion and a few other species have been extirpated, the Judean Desert retains 96 percent of its original species, the highest "conservation coefficient" in Israel. By comparison, the Aravah retains 61 percent, and the Galilee and other Mediterranean forest regions merely 51 percent of the species that existed originally.

Following the Arugot streambed through a narrow-walled section leads to the Hidden Waterfall and its luminous pool. Farther upstream, the trail is crowded by balanites, moringa, tamarisk, caper, fagonia, and *rikhpetan*, a tall shrub with wands of yellow flowers found all over Israel's deserts.

Rikhpetan bears white fruit that, though slightly astringent, are full of vitamin A, not an easy nutrient to find in a desert. Bedouin used to use a *rikhpetan* wash to clean their hair.

Not far from the Hidden Waterfall and the trail branching off to Nahal David, the Arugot trail seems to end. Here we stopped for a moment to regroup. Ido asked if we would like to continue to the upper pools. Sure, we answered, but how? The terrace where we had stopped seemed surrounded by rock walls.

Some rungs, anchored in a low cliff, showed the way. The German minister's wife, though pregnant, vaulted up to the first rung—a good seven feet off the ground—and then climbed from rung to rung to the top. She probably could have free-climbed to the top of the next cliff, too. I had to admit a certain envy for her youth and agility. With shoving and grunting, Ido somehow boosted enough of me up to the first rung so that I could manage from there, but it was not a pretty sight.

125

On the high trail we passed moringa roots clinging to the rocks in intricate patterns and a huge, shapely acacia leaning over the gorge. Frogs croaked noisily from the stream, and a bulbul sliced through the air, landing on the tilted acacia.

About the size of a blackbird with a gray back and head and yellow belly, the yellow-vented bulbul is seen everywhere in Israel. Earlier in the century, the bulbul lived mainly in desert oases such as this and along the southern coast. But the bulbul fancies fruit, and fruit production has exploded in Israel this century. So, the bulbul has followed the food. Farmers consider the bird a pest, but in the canyon it sounded an upbeat note as we pushed on.

Finally, the upper pools. Exquisite, cool blue in a white-hot day, the pools spilled shallowly from one small basin to another between high tan cliffs. At a break in the cliff near our feet, the steady stream of a layer spring seeped out from under the rock, adding its waters to the flow.

We sat on the slickrock banks of the stream, surrounded by smooth, soaring canyon walls. We shed our shoes and eased hot and tired

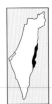

feet into the perfect water, wiggling our toes into the shallow bed of sand.

Near the end of the day, we stopped at the spa to pick up the midwife and the New Jersey student, then made our way back to Jerusalem. The others were staying on in the city, but the student and I had buses to catch: I to Tel Aviv, she to Bene Beraq.

Crowning the Judean Hills, Jerusalem lies only a thirteen-mile ride from the Judean Desert, yet it receives more than twenty inches of precipitation a year compared to the desert's two or three. That evening, heading toward Jerusalem in Ido's van, we were met by light showers even before we fully ascended to the city.

The student and I waited together at the bus station as dusk became night. Rain drizzled down steadily, distorting the pools of light cast by street lamps. We pulled our jackets around us; the cold Jerusalem night against our sun-baked skins made us shiver.

Soldiers milled around. Pudgy grandmothers talked in groups of two or three, their arms hung with shopping bags. A tall, bearded Hassid passed, his broad-brimmed fur hat—his *shtreimel*—wrapped in plastic against the rain, his long black coat covering everything.

I chatted affably with the student, she with bulky jacket over long, slit-sided dress, her loose hair now in long wet ropes. My bus came and I said goodbye. As I leaned against a rain-streaked window, three Asian workers sitting around me conversed animatedly in a high-pitched oriental language. The driver had his radio tuned to Israeli bus music: melodies of love and loss, sometimes religious, sometimes secular, sung against the pulse of eastern instruments and western backbeat—an urban lullaby as lights sped by, dim and muddy in the rainy night.

Ein Fashehah Jackals

Exploring the Judean Desert can take many trips, the place is so scored by side canyons full of natural and human history. From Matsukei Deragot to Ein Fashehah, near the road leading up to Jerusalem, the northern third of the Dead Sea's shores are fringed by bone-dry canyons and wet marshes fed by springs.

From Route 90, a road twists into the hills toward the trailheads of Matsukei Deragot, which, loosely translated, means "ranked cliffs." The name describes the canyon's dramatically stepped cliffs, sheer rock walls, and goat trails with precipitous views. A popular place to climb, rappel, and do other dances with rock walls, Matsukei

The wildcat is the ancestor of the house cat and about the same size. It was already domesticated in Egypt more than five thousand years ago. Egyptians so worshipped the cat, which destroyed mice and other agricultural pests in the Nile Valley, that it became the center of a sacred cult for more than two thousand years. Special cemeteries preserved thousands of their mummified bodies. The wildcat is not so pampered. Nocturnal and solitary, the small gray feline with the black-ringed tail hunts at night and is found throughout Israel.

Deragot also harbors squared-off caves where people lived for millennia. In one cave a letter was discovered signed by Shimon bar Kokhba, the leader of the famed but ultimately unsuccessful revolt against the Romans that ended in 135 C.E.

North of Matsukei Deragot, the road narrows until only a strip of asphalt separates cliff and sea. At one point, the cliff face bears the red-painted letters PEF, standing for Palestine Exploration Fund, founded by a group of Britons from the Royal Engineer Force. In the 1880s, these British engineers convinced the Ottoman sultan, who ruled the region, to let them conduct the first comprehensive modern survey of Palestine—for archaeological purposes, they said. The PEF maps helped the British win Palestine from the Ottomans during World War I, but the red letters also tell a tale about the Dead Sea itself.

127

When the British were mapping the Judean Desert, the only way to reach the bottom of the cliffs was by boat. The Dead Sea was so much broader that it lapped at the base of the cliff. Over the years the Dead Sea has shrunk from overuse of its tributaries. What used to be sea bottom are now low fields carpeted by red poppies in spring.

Near the caves of Qumran, where the Dead Sea Scrolls were found, a jungle of phragmites reeds rises along the northern banks of the Dead Sea, announcing the springs of Ein Fashehah. Bubbling up from cracks in the Great Rift, the springs at Ein Fashehah Reserve range from sweet to salty and harbor abundant life. Cichlids and other fish swim in Ein Fashehah's waters, attracting wildcats, among the smallest of Israel's wild felines.

Members of the dog family frequent Ein Fashehah, too. Foxes live here, and hyenas. The striped hyena, always an opportunist, emerges from Ein Fashehah and other areas of the Judean Desert to seize the

bodies of animals killed on the highway. Too often, this tactic makes the hyena a road victim as well.

More hyenas are killed by cars than by any other means, a problem the Israel Nature and National Parks Protection Authority is trying to remedy in order to save this endangered species from extinction. Striped hyenas, which used to live throughout Israel and in all surrounding countries, now have stable populations only in the Judean and Negev Deserts.

Jackals also live at Ein Fashehah. Its taxonomic name, *Canis aureus*, means "golden dog," but the jackal is more tawny than golden. During a study at Ein Fashehah, a field researcher discovered two groups of jackals at the reserve with a sharp, scent-marked boundary line between their territories. Like humans who once practiced tribal raiding, each group would sneak across the boundary to steal from the other.

Unlike the hyena, the jackal population flourishes. Like the coyote of North America, the jackal is the ubiquitous wild canid of Israel. It lives everywhere but the central and southern Negev and eats anything, from rabbits to radishes, with an especial fondness for melons.

Because they damaged vineyards and agricultural fields, scores of jackals were destroyed by mass poisoning in the mid-1960s. (During the same decade, coyotes were poisoned indiscriminately in North America.) In Israel, rural people quickly saw the results of this decimation. Small rodents, rabbits, and porcupines were suddenly everywhere, causing at least as much trouble as the jackals.

Fortunately, jackals are scrappy survivors, and their numbers have recovered. But learning that balance exists in nature, and that we are part of the balance, not above it, is a lesson hard won all over the world. All species—including ours—are in great or small stages of flux, each adjusting to the other across a skein of relationships. Some of the more difficult adjustments in these parts of the world are between groups of people.

Now part of the Palestinian Autonomous District is what some believe to be the oldest city on Earth: Jericho. Lying just north of the Dead Sea, near where Ma'aleh Adummim (Route 1) rises to Jerusalem, Jericho has been known since biblical times as "the city of palms." Jericho is known, too, for the rose that bears its name. The rose of Jericho, a tough desert dweller, survives by biding its time.

This annual plant protects its seeds by wrapping them in its outer stems, which dry and curl around the seeds. Near Uvdah Valley in the Negev, I saw dozens of dry, crumpled roses scattered in a small valley that probably serves as a rain trap. Colored a dead gray-brown, they looked like gnarled talons wrapped around dried balls. When enough rain falls, the outer fibers swell because of hydrostatic pressure, drawing back to release the seeds, which germinate in just hours. If no rain falls, the seeds will wait, for decades if necessary.

Palm trees still sway over Jericho, but few roses live there now. Christian pilgrims saw the rose of Jericho as a symbol of resurrection and, beginning with the Crusades, took so many back to Europe that populations of the plant plummeted, a victim of devotion.

Monastery Hidden in Wadi Qelt

Ma'aleh Adummim, the Red Ascent, is so named for its red rock. This break in the Judean Hills served as a distinguishing boundary between the tribe of Judah to the south and the tribe of Benjamin to the north. Ma'aleh Adummim seems tame enough going uphill, but hurtling down in a car, surrounded by buses and trucks and grim-faced drivers in a hurry, the precipitous drop between the Judean Hills and the Judean Desert becomes palpable. Ibex once roamed into the desert north of the highway, but now Ma'aleh Adummim and its speeding traffic mark that animal's northern boundary.

About a third of the way up, Nahal Perat Reserve, which encompasses Wadi Qelt, lies on the north side of the ascent. Like Nahal Arugot, the stream that flows through this canyon system is large and consistent. With a fairly constant supply of water, the margins of Wadi Qelt seem like a leafy arboretum full of flourishing trees. But because the area is something of a political hot spot, SPNI nature lovers must travel with an escort, a euphemism for a man with a rifle.

129

Our tour began at the top of Wadi Qelt. From there, the low, tan and white hills of the Judean Desert roll away to the horizon, sparse stubbles of gray-green shrubs marking the creases where water runs down. The trail we would hike enters the canyon of Wadi Qelt and eventually reaches the Monastery of Saint George, which has served as a retreat for monks from the fifth century to the present.

We shifted through a herd of black goats moving in the opposite direction. Ahead were our guide David, Dalia, two Norwegian brothers, a Canadian, and a few others. Behind me were grandparents from Buffalo, New York, visiting their son and daughter-in-law, and an Australian woman. After we rounded the first switchback, it became obvious that the Australian woman and I had a common interest.

"Oh, look, it's an *Orobanche*," she whooped. Instantly I was at

Come spring, the rocky upper reaches of Wadi Qelt, at the northern edge of the Judean Desert, are ablaze with red poppies and a host of other wildflowers.

her side, peering down at blue broomrape, a parasitic plant with blue trumpet flowers—and no leaves. It doesn't need them. It extracts what it needs from the roots of other plants.

130

Nearby, where rock had crumbled to sand, half-moon holes revealed the doorways to scorpion burrows. A tall stalk of white salvia tilted toward the trail, the top petal of each flower arched over the lower lip like a canopy, protecting precious pollen from rain.

The rains had been good to the Judean Hills that spring. Though flash floods had destroyed a section of Route 90 along the Dead Sea, the rains also had watered the slopes of Wadi Qelt, and bouquets of red, white, yellow, and blue flowers seemed to sprout from bare rock. Each bend brought gasps at the different and stunning arrangements of these natural gardens.

We hopped from garden to garden and plant to plant, ecstatic at each new discovery. Dark-eyed, hot pink erodium clung in clumps to bare sand. Blazes of poppies nestled among pale purple Maltese cross and yellow chrysanthemum daisies. A tumble of white limestone creates chance terraces red with buttercups.

Though rare most places, vast carpets of crimson wildflowers are common in Israel. The three most common red wildflowers all bear shallow cups of delicate petals, but the first to bloom, in late winter, is the red crown anemone. Come spring, red buttercups flower, with red poppies right behind. The poppy is easy to distinguish because black "thumbprints" mark the inner face of its red petals.

"Here," I called to the Australian woman, pointing to a purple pea flower with gray-green pinnate leaves. "What do you think? An astragalus?"

"And a pimpernel." Its tiny sapphire-blue flowers winked from the rocky slopes.

We could not look hard enough or fast enough to keep up: squill; golden henbane, a deadly plant of the nightshade family; purple-flowered garlic; a dozen ivory cousins of Queen Anne's lace; blue geraniums; and others, many others.

I have become, I fear, what I once thought of as "sapsucker people." Bird-watchers with binoculars on the lookout for yellow-bellied sap-suckers were the ultimate in uncool when I was young enough to be concerned about such things. Then, I had more energy than I knew what to do with, and a hike meant going up a trail as fast as possible, eating a lot at the top, then falling asleep on warm rocks before a sprint back down to the bottom.

Over the years, however, I slowed down and began paying attention to plants, animals, rocks, even the grid of holes left on a log by yellow-bellied sapsuckers. There are worse fates.

Eventually, we left the rock gardens of upper Wadi Qelt and descended deeper into the canyon. Where the canyon narrows, capers cling by their tough roots to beige walls of chalk: old leaves blue, new leaves and edible buds a purple-green. Capers were a delicacy even in talmudic times and caper-curing was a reputable profession.

The dozen or so miles between Jerusalem and Jericho through Wadi Qelt were part of an ancient trade route, continuing west to the Mediterranean and east through Amman in Jordan, across the plains of Iraq, to the Persian Gulf. During Hasmonean times, when Herod ruled Israel for Rome, Wadi Qelt was fitted with an aqueduct. Rather than allow all of Wadi Qelt's water to flow into the Dead Sea, water was diverted to irrigate Jericho's crops.

At one point, the trail passes through a hole in a crumbling, ill-built brick wall. The wall is a later addition, an inexplicable patch of bricks filling in the soaring curve of the graceful Muslim-era arch that carries its own eighth-century aqueduct over the canyon. Later we passed another arch rising near the trail, this one a natural rock arch shaped by the elements.

Farther downhill, the trail parallels a modern-day aqueduct bubbling with water used for irrigation, its edges crowded with mint

131

and small black snails. Unseen frogs kept up steady chirruping dialogues as we passed the water-filled trough, heading ever downward. Where the wadi widens, Bedouin families live in a small but pretty grouping of homes near a flour mill, all built by the el-Husseinis, an influential Palestinian family.

The buildings stand in the shade of balanites trees, palms, and large jujubes with canopies of arching, thorny stems. The jujube, a tree that migrated up the Great Rift from Africa, is also known as the Christ-thorn tree because it is believed the crown of thorns worn by Jesus was cut from a jujube.

Resident in wadis near the Great Rift, along the coastal plain, and even into the north of Israel, the jujube withstands flash floods with long, deep roots. Its roots finger their way far beyond the spread of its branches, gathering nutrients and, in doing so, depriving other trees. As a result, jujubes often seem to stand alone.

If the weather becomes too severe, the jujube protects itself by dropping its leaves, a defense mechanism used by other tropical trees. It has no defenses against the semiparasitic strapvine, however, which winds through some of the trees, flaunting its red tubular flowers.

With both straight thorns and hooked thorns, the jujube would seem strongly defended against browsers, but goats outmaneuver the thorns to get to the tree's small oval leaves and its grape-sized fruit. Orange-red when ripe, the fruit is sour like a green apple and has long been used to make preserves, despite the fact that the seed is covered by only a thin wrap of pulp.

As we neared Ein Qelt and the waterfall, the bright turquoise back of a kingfisher flashed from a tree and disappeared downstream. A sign in Arabic, painted on the rock walls that enclose the stream, thanks Allah for ownership of the spring. Not far, another sign says, in Hebrew, "No Diving." Just below the sign, a group of exuberant Army teens on their day off dove into the rockbound waters and splashed where small waterfalls pour into pools.

Our group threaded past the soldiers, those dripping with water and others whose brown, dry bodies glittered ever so slightly with salt. We found seats on rocks a bit removed from the pools where we unwrapped our lunches. We, with our cameras, long pants, and hats, were some contrast to the swimsuited soldiers, whose clothes and Uzis were scattered around them.

Then I noticed the soldiers who sat apart and above, fully dressed, weapons at hand, watching.

Not far from the "No Diving" sign, I could see where an arum plant

132

had taken refuge. In shade formed by damp rocks, the arum's large, elephant-ear leaves cloaked a tall purple spathe. The spikelike spathe is composed of leaves rolled tight as cigars around the plant's flower stem. Fig trees grow near the water as does a large carob, a tree that usually lives farther north. Perhaps both are here by human doing.

Another surprise: a yellow-flowered tobacco tree, native to South America, has wedged itself near the water. With their dramatic yellow trumpet flowers, tobacco trees probably were imported as ornamental garden plants whose seeds eventually escaped to the wild. In Israel and in countries worldwide, this garden-to-wild route allows countless nonnative plants to escape, often becoming pests.

As we headed deeper into the sun-baked canyon, saltbush and bean caper shrubs let us know that we were descending toward the Judean Desert, past a Bedouin camp where Tristram's grackles called.

The canyon dropped below us, and caves on the opposite wall foretold the Monastery of Saint George. It was caves that first attracted Byzantine monks to this wadi and a solitary, contemplative life. On narrow ledges connecting the caves, plump chukars scurried.

Far below, the waters of Ein Qelt raced between the walls of the deep gorge. A bank of tuliplike androcymbium, flowering later than usual, splayed their white blooms across the slope. David pointed out a Bonelli's eagle circling on thermals high above, its six-foot wings allowing it to vault against the sky.

133

The eagle glided on its spiral of warm air as we continued to descend. Finally, in the heart of the canyon, we approached the Monastery of Saint George, which seems to grow directly from the rock walls. The compact, finely wrought buildings stand among lush green gardens of palms and cypresses, jujubes and wildflowers—dramatic contrast with the surrounding stark desert canyon. Unfortunately, we had spent too much time enjoying nature and had reached the monastery a few minutes past closing time, so saw only the courtyards.

Originally built in the fifth century by Byzantine monks, the monastery was destroyed in 614 by invading Persians. Except for some original mosaics, the present complex of domes, arches, and cliff-hung buildings is only a century old.

Many have come to the desert to seek wisdom and grace in austere solitude, including the first monks of Saint George. Ironically, they attracted disciples, then pilgrims, which caused a monastery to be built, which prompted some monks to build wooden chambers high on the cliffs, pulling up baskets of food and water in order to remain isolated. Social beings have difficulty remaining solitary.

Monastery of Saint George, Wadi Qelt

In the 1970s, sighting a Bonelli's eagle would have been rare. As elsewhere in the world, the widespread use of DDT and other pesticides caused raptor eggs to become fragile and break, killing the chicks inside. Before DDT use was cut, populations of Bonelli's eagles plummeted. Once the most common eagle in Israel, Bonelli's eagles are gradually rebounding.

Named for the Italian naturalist who wrote a catalog of birds in the early 1800s, Bonelli's eagles prefer the gorges of the Judean Desert. There they nest on rock ledges and hunt rock doves and partridges. Occasionally, the territory of a Bonelli's eagle overlaps that of a golden eagle. In *The Birds of Israel*, ornithologist Hadoram Shirihai points out that while Bonelli's eagles eat birds and prefer narrow canyons, golden eagles like open desert where they prey on chukars and hares. Shirihai has even seen golden eagles catch tortoises, then drop them in order to break their shells and get at their flesh. Like ibex and gazelle, these two raptors have filled noncompeting niches.

Because of the political situation, we did not continue into Jericho. Our hike ended at the quiet, lovely monastery on a day of blue skies and flowers. But quiet, lovely places all over the globe have **135** seen horrors. Two weeks later, two young women went for an unescorted walk in Wadi Qelt. They never came out. They were found with their throats slit.

I could not and cannot mesh Wadi Qelt's natural grace and our careless, sunny day with murder. But this was not the first time I was bewildered by evil in a place of seeming peace.

Once a friend and I started on an early-morning hike over a high mountain pass above Telluride, Colorado. Halfway up a rocky path surrounded by soaring, sculpted peaks and a wildflower-bedecked basin, we came upon a young man covered with blood, beaten so badly we feared he was dying. Help arrived and the young man was taken to the hospital. He lived, but with brain damage from the blows delivered by drunk men on a violent bender.

What great works of art and science we produce; what industry and appreciation we have. Yet—as I have witnessed with such visceral intensity—we are a contradictory species, our brilliance easily matched by ready brutality.

CHAPTER SIX

Judean Hills:
Once and Future Forests

Neot Kedumim Biblical Landscape Reserve

NEOT KEDUMIM

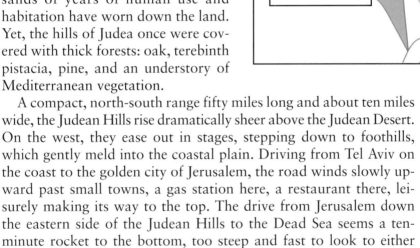

Judean Hills

THE FIRST TIME I FLEW OVER THE JUDEAN HILLS, I looked down over what I thought was the aftermath of a late winter storm. The rounded hills were white and glittered like snow in sunlight. I flew over the same hills in the heat of summer, and they still glittered. Clearly, not snow.

What I saw were hills stripped of their earthen mantle, their white, limestone bones glinting in the sun. Thousands of years of human use and habitation have worn down the land. Yet, the hills of Judea once were covered with thick forests: oak, terebinth pistacia, pine, and an understory of Mediterranean vegetation.

A compact, north-south range fifty miles long and about ten miles wide, the Judean Hills rise dramatically sheer above the Judean Desert. On the west, they ease out in stages, stepping down to foothills, which gently meld into the coastal plain. Driving from Tel Aviv on the coast to the golden city of Jerusalem, the road winds slowly upward past small towns, a gas station here, a restaurant there, leisurely making its way to the top. The drive from Jerusalem down the eastern side of the Judean Hills to the Dead Sea seems a ten-minute rocket to the bottom, too steep and fast to look to either side.

At the southern end of the Judean Hills, the Negev begins. To the north, the Judean Hills face the Samarian Hills, a more complicated, broken range that parallels the Great Rift for a while, then tacks diagonally toward Mount Carmel and the coast.

The average height of the Judean Hills is about twenty-four hundred feet, but the range is shaped something like a clothesline. It hangs from higher hills at Bethel in the north and at Hebron in the south. The Jerusalem Hills, which are part of the Judean Hills, lie in the low middle of the range.

Although the Old City in Jerusalem was built and rebuilt over the course of three thousand years, it is still graced by flowering trees and shrubs, both native and newcomer.

It is no accident that Jerusalem was sited where it is. As trading routes took shape in the ancient world, it provided a good choice for east-west traffic, offering a relatively low-lying pass over the range. And Gihon Spring provided water. With dependable water and a prime location, Jerusalem was bound to become important.

Signs of settlement date back at least five thousand years, and a walled city existed on the spot a thousand years before the reign of King David. Built on hills and surrounded on three sides by the valleys of Hinnom, Kidron, and Tyropoeon, the city was fairly defensible. Despite its position, Jerusalem was conquered again and again over time.

About 1000 B.C.E., King David took what was then a Jebusite city and made it his capital. His son, King Solomon, commenced Jerusalem's architectural glory with the building of the First Temple on Mount Moriah. In 586 B.C.E., the Babylonians destroyed the Temple and exiled the Jews to Babylon. Seventy years later, the Jews returned to rebuild Jerusalem and the Temple. In 70 C.E., the Romans destroyed the city and the Second Temple, and Jerusalem languished until the fourth century.

After Constantine of Byzantium became the first monarch to adopt

Christianity, in approximately 312, church-building began in Jerusalem. In the mid-600s, Islam arose and Jerusalem came under Arab rule. In 1099, Crusaders took the city, intending to expunge it of Jews and Muslims. In 1187, Saladin took the city back for Islam. From the 1400s to the end of World War I, Jerusalem became dilapidated under Ottoman administration, which was followed by British rule during the Mandate period between the two world wars.

Jerusalem was a small piece of real estate, only two and a half miles in circumference, enclosed by walls. Nothing existed outside the Old City until the 1860s. From then to now, especially since the city was reunited in 1967, Jerusalem's growth has been exponential. Urban sprawl, rather than the Judean Hills, now dominates the landscape. In the early 1990s, when an extensive, modern mall opened in a new section of the city, it was touted as the largest in the Middle East.

Yet, at its heart, the warm limestone walls of the Old City, quarried from the surrounding hills, glow golden in the setting sun, making Jerusalem seem timeless and serene. Here and there outside the walls, trees hint at the hills' original state.

In the earliest days, travelers crossing the Judean Hills trekked through wooded areas—the Bible is full of references to trees. When Abraham came to Canaan and the Judean Hills, he stopped at Shekhem (now Nablus), then marked by terebinth trees. Later, three strangers announced the impending birth of Isaac to Abraham and Sarah where they dwelt near Hebron, among the terebinths of Mamre.

139

When Joshua led the Israelites back into the land more than half a millennium later, several of the tribes complained about the size of their allotment: "The hill country shall be yours as well," Joshua said. "True, it is forest land, but you will clear it and possess it to its farthest limits" (Joshua 17:18).

And cleared it is. Although David protected his sheep from lions and bears in the hills around Bethlehem and shepherds had to watch for leopards even as late as the 1800s, the hills are no longer thick with the forests of Joshua's time, and the large predators are no more. The Judean Hills have been a center of civilization for so long that centuries of clearing for olive and grape orchards and centuries of black goats browsing greenery to its roots have taken their toll.

Some slopes are still shaded by Aleppo pine. Oak and pistacia still live in the hills. And small valleys are still dotted with wildflowers, from spring's pink cyclamen to autumn's pink crocus with hundreds of varieties and colors in between. The Judean Hills are still home to

Conservationists point out that monocultures of pines make the soil too acid, and thick layers of needles prevent the growth of other plants. As the highly inflammable needle layers build up, they become a fire hazard.

In addition, a monoculture of any one plant does not provide enough variety for diverse wildlife. It also is highly susceptible to devastation by disease: one hefty infestation of pine borer could ruin the entire forest. That is why natural forests are full of diversity, and that is why the Jewish National Fund, which planted nonnative pine forests, is now moving toward more mixed, native forests.

small mammals and even gazelle. The Book of Judges (15:4) says that Samson caught three hundred foxes (*shualim*) in the Judean Hills. Some say that the biblical word *shualim* then meant jackals. No matter, both foxes and jackals live here still.

But natural areas are shrinking in the face of development, and some of the area's largest forests are not really natural. Swaths of nonnative pine, planted in the 1950s and 1960s, during the early years of statehood, resulted in monocultures, forests full of only one species. Monocultures can be dangerous, as the region found out in the 1980s, when devastating fire swept through pine forests near Jerusalem.

140

Attempts are being made to save what natural areas remain, including preserving a "green necklace" around Jerusalem. Yet, much of the Judean Hills has long been snowy with limestone terracing, not green with forest. Planted and prodded by peoples for centuries, the soils have thinned and dried without their covering of trees. The Judean Hills still experience drenching dew, rainy winters, and even light coverings of snow, but without forests to trap moisture the hills have become more desertlike. Ever opportunistic, plants from drier regions, such as poterium, are inching in.

Sorek Cave's Subterranean Treasure

Rain that falls on the Judean Hills percolates into the ground through cracks in the limestone. Some water hits an impermeable rock layer canting east, and so spills out as springs in the Judean Desert.

Some springs rise in the Judean Hills and flow westward, forming streams and rivers. The Sorek is not a large river—no rivers in Israel are—but it is the major river draining the Jerusalem Hills, flowing westward until it meets the Mediterranean north of Ashdod.

Sorek also is the name of the central feature in the Avshalom Reserve, a reserve unique in Israel. From its northern terminus at Route 1 (the Tel Aviv-Jerusalem highway), Route 38 meanders southwest toward Bet Shemesh. Just north of this Judean Hills town and directly west of Jerusalem lies a stone quarry. In 1968 a blast to loosen rock in the quarry revealed an underground world of dark beauty: Sorek Cave.

Averaging about two hundred feet in both length and width and totaling about an acre in area, Sorek is Israel's largest cave. Compared to Mammoth Cave in Kentucky, Sorek is tiny, but makes up

Sorek Cave, whose stalactites began forming about five million years ago, displays a wealth of cave formations, from huge stalagmites and flowing curtains to soda straws and fragile-looking, crazily twisted helictites.

for what it lacks in size with an incredible diversity of cave formations. While generations of people worked the land above ground, water was working below, eating away the limestone, reforming it as stalactites, stalagmites, tiny crystalline helictites, and shapes like elephant ears that ripple from the ceiling of Sorek.

The Avshalom Reserve is named for Avshalom Shoham, a young man devoted to nature, who died from war injuries sustained in 1970. Sorek means "grapevine," having more to do with what was found along the river than underground.

The way to Avshalom Reserve and Sorek Cave winds past the Sorek River and hills dotted with pine and pencil-thin cypress. The white-and-pink blossoms of the almond have already faded. The

ISRAEL NATURE AND NATIONAL PARKS PROTECTION AUTHORITY

Caves form when rain combines with carbon dioxide in the air, becoming carbonic acid. As this acidified water percolates through the soil, decaying vegetation adds humic acid to the water. Over time, enough of this weak acid filters down, dissolving limestone along fracture lines. Below the surface, cracks widen, becoming a cave.

Dissolved limestone continues to drip into the nascent cave, depositing layer upon thin layer of limestone that hangs like icicles from the ceiling: the beginnings of a stalactite. As lime-saturated water drips from the end of a stalactite onto the cave floor below, buildup forms the beginnings of a stalagmite. If the lime water slips down the curving side of a cave ceiling, the precipitate forms stone draperies and elephant-ear shapes.

almond's Hebrew name, *shaqed*, comes from the root *shaqad*, meaning "watchful": the almond keeps a vigil for spring and is the first tree to burst into bloom. The blossoming almond signals Tu bi-Shevat, the Jewish New Year of the Trees celebrated on the fifteenth of the month of Shevat.

Weeks later, bright masses of yellow flowers cover thorny broom. Redbud trees keep their deep purple-pink buds furled, waiting for the right moment. Extravagantly red anemones flutter across terraced fields.

On a trip to Avshalom Reserve, I followed a pathway from the parking lot down stone steps through a grove of pines. The dark green of the needled trees was brightened by rosettes of cyclamen wedged between rocks. At their freshest and fullest, the cyclamen flowers nodded in all shades of pink. A stone terrace leads into the bright and welcoming Avshalom Visitor Center, all stone and glass and overlooking the valley that contains the quarry whose blasting revealed Sorek Cave.

The world within the cave had its birth millions of years ago. Where the Judean Hills stand, shallow seas once ebbed and flowed, and marine detritus accumulated, layer upon layer. Eventually, the pressure of its own weight caused these layers to become limestone twenty-five hundred feet deep. About the time tectonic plates were beginning to rumble, creating the Great Rift, the Judean Hills were uplifted and exposed to erosion—both without and within.

Caves formed by the dissolution of limestone are called karstic, after the Karst Plateau in the Balkans, which is riddled with such caves. Karstic caves lie elsewhere in the Judean Hills and all over the limestone layers of Israel. Although Sorek Cave is of modest size compared to the world's largest karst systems, what makes it exceptional is that it contains all known types of formations: stalagmites, soda straws, cave corals, stalagnates, helictites, water-lily deposits ringing small pools, and others.

Most of the world's famous caves were discovered decades, even centuries, ago and have suffered from deliberate and unwitting abuse, everything from breaking off formations for souvenirs to merely touching the rock. Fortunately, Sorek Cave was discovered after environmental awareness taught us how to care for invaluable natural features. More than many other caves worldwide, Sorek's high quality has been protected as pristinely as possible from the start.

Stalactites grow only 0.2 millimeters per year, so it takes thousands of years to form one of the sixteen-foot columns found at Sorek. Because oils from a person's hand can keep deposits from forming, cave interpreters warn against touching the spectacular array. The Israel Nature and National Parks Protection Authority also keeps the lighting as low as possible because light promotes algae growth in the cave.

Following a reserve guide in, I pulled on a light jacket. The cave is always cool, and has a faint, earthy odor. Our small group of six followed the guide along a paved path that twisted dimly past a phantasmagoria of shapes and colors.

143

Describing cave formations is like describing clouds: here stands the Lion of Judah, there a bunch of broccoli. Angular sculptures reminiscent of Giacometti emerge from the gloom. Frozen curtains of stone hang in rose and rust hues, colored by iron deposits. Rare and tiny helictite crystals tangle together like the gnarled fingers of a witch.

In some parts of the cave, stalactites and stalagmites have met, producing thick columns called stalagnates. Elsewhere, formations cluster like Red Sea corals and handfuls of marbles. Others look like castles made by children dripping wet sand through their fingers.

In one corner of the cave, our guide pointed out Romeo and Juliet, a stalactite and a stalagmite only a half-centimeter apart. She explained that they will never "kiss": the formations have stopped growing because that part of the cave is drying out. Lighting and the body heat of visitors contribute to the drying process, which can result when earthquakes cause rocks to shift away from seeping water.

Recent earthquakes have shaken the cave, but compared to past earthquakes, such as the one that devastated Safed in 1837, these have been minor. Earthquakes actually promote cave formation by causing rock faults and fractures that allow dissolved limestone to drip through.

Perhaps the latest earthquakes began the process of cave-making somewhere else beneath the Judean Hills. Who knows how many hidden worlds the hills hold? Now that Mount Everest has been conquered countless times and organized foot races span the Sahara, now that Antarctica and the jungles of South America are open to tourism, how much of Earth's splendor still lies unseen? It is pleasing to think that beauty is being made away from our eyes.

Ancient Landscapes: the Vale of Elah to Amatsyah Caves

South of Sorek Cave, Route 38 intersects with Route 375, which heads east toward Bethlehem. Only a mile or so east of the intersection lies the Vale of Elah, a picture of the pastoral past. A small stream cleaves the green, narrow valley, whose south slope is a wall of white chalk.

Elah is the Hebrew word for pistacia, and these trees grow in the valley that bears their name, as do African white acacia, which are rare in Israel. A relict species, the white acacia is more typical of Sudanese vegetation from tropical Africa. Its presence in the Elah valley reveals a time, about three hundred million years ago, when the climate here was tropical, before the deserts of the Middle East had yet developed.

144

Beyond the streambed, cows graze amid red buttercups and yellow-flowered mustards. It is hard to imagine that in this idyllic spot the armies of Philistines and Israelites were massed, camped on opposite hills overlooking the small Vale of Elah. Day after day, Goliath, the giant Philistine warrior, strode out to shout his challenge to the Israelites: "Choose one of your men and let him come down against me. If he bests me in combat and kills me, we will become your slaves; but if I best him and kill him, you shall be our slaves and serve us" (1 Samuel 17:8-9).

Perhaps his challenge echoed off the tall chalk wall, adding weight to Goliath's words, because for forty days none would meet him. David, a shepherd and the youngest of Jesse's eight sons, had traveled from his home at Bethlehem to bring bread and cheese to his oldest brothers and their commanders. He heard the giant's challenge, saw no one go out to meet the Philistine's champion, and offered to do so himself.

King Saul admonished him, saying he was just a boy. But David, who had felled wild beasts while protecting his sheep, chose some smooth rocks from the Elah streambed, took up his shepherd's slingshot, and felled Goliath, too. The Philistines saw their hero dead on the ground and ran toward Gat, about five miles west of Bet Guvrin.

Farther south, Route 38 terminates at the town of Bet Guvrin in the lower Judean Hills. The heights overlooking the Dead Sea are capped by limestone and dolomite, but these low western foothills reveal thick chalk layers. Bet Guvrin National Park protects the ruins of the ancient city for which it is named and myriad caves carved not by weathering but by human hands.

A bit farther south, the Amatsyah Caves (Hazan Cav-

Red crown anemones and other wildflowers dance over the narrow Vale of Elah, where David slew Goliath.

145

erns) reveal similar ancient ties between people and nature. Thousands of chalk caves honeycomb the lower Judean Hills, most of them dug during the Hellenistic and Roman periods. They provided storage areas and, later, hiding places. Easily excavated, chalk also provided construction materials and the basic ingredient in plaster. Chalk was exported throughout the Roman Empire and, more significantly, was used to seal cisterns and mikvahs (ritual baths) throughout Israel.

In *Rivers in the Desert*, Nelson Glueck says:

> It is hard to realize what a revolutionary change was effected in the history of civilization when cisterns were invented—that is, when men learned to dig holes in any kind of ground and plaster them so that they could serve as storage places for water. Without cisterns, few of the Judean fortresses and villages in the Negev could have been constructed.

Olives sparked another industry. When the Israelites were about to reenter Canaan, they were told they were entering "... a good land, a land with streams and springs and fountains issuing from

plain and hill; a land of wheat and barley, of vines, figs, and pomegranates, a land of olive trees and honey" (Deuteronomy 8:7–8).

One of the seven species mentioned in the verse, olive trees were invaluable. People ate their fruit, used pruned branches as fuel, and carved their wood into household objects such as bowls. The sanctuary doors of the Temple built by King Solomon (1 Kings 6:31) were fashioned from olive wood.

The most important product of the olive, however, was its oil. Olive oil was used for cooking, as an unguent, in medicines, and for ceremonial anointing. The Hebrew word *mashiah*, "messiah," comes from the verb meaning "to anoint." Olive oil was also a source of light. Clay lamps filled with olive oil and a wick made of plant fiber allowed people to light their homes and priests to light the Temple. Olive oil was so important that orchards of olives covered much of the Judean Hills, and the olives of Israel became renowned throughout the Roman Empire.

Because it was such a critical commodity, first-century Romans taxed olive oil heavily. Defying the tax collectors and the Roman Empire, Jews hid a whole olive-oil processing plant underground in the Amatsyah Caves, a seven-hundred-foot complex of rooms and tunnels.

At the beginning of the cave complex stands an olive press, its heavy, hewn grindstone the size and shape of a wagon wheel. Olives for oil were harvested when the fruit had fully ripened to black because black olives hold 50 percent more oil than green.

The harvested olives were crushed on the stone press, then loaded in beret-shaped baskets woven of palm fibers. These flexible, loose-weave baskets were piled one on another and stone weights laid atop to press out the oils, which dripped into troughs cut from rock. The first golden oils were sent to the Temple in Jerusalem. Subsequent pressings were kept for general use.

Stooping between the low ceiling and the chalk walls, I passed a small cistern, then arrived at one of the rooms in which olive oil was stored in hundreds of clay jars. Because the jars were round bottomed, the floor of the underground storage room was hewn into a grid of round-bottomed sections, like an egg carton. Amatsyah's hidden storerooms could hold more than ten thousand liters of oil worth $100,000 today.

Farther on lie deeper cisterns and longer tunnels. Because the chalk is so white, even a little light reflects well, and the chalk's soft texture keeps the caves from seeming claustrophobic. A good thing because in 132 C.E. this mazelike complex hid not oil but the men and women of Bar Kokhba's revolt against Rome.

The First Jewish Revolt against oppressive Roman rule resulted in the destruction of the Second Temple in 70 C.E. and ended with the fall of Masada in 73. The Bar Kokhba Revolt, which lasted from 132 to 135, was another disastrous attempt by the Jews to free themselves from the heavy hand of Rome.

Hadrian, Roman emperor during this time, banned Jewish ritual and began building a pagan city atop the ruins of Jerusalem in an attempt to subdue this most difficult part of his empire, thus setting the stage for the Bar Kokhba Revolt. Stockpiling weapons and preparing hideouts such as the Amatsyah Caves, the Jews bided their time until 132 when, under the leadership of Shimon bar Kokhba, they rose up. Though fighting centered in Judea, it spread throughout Galilee as well.

The oil-processing plant at the Amatsyah Caves was transformed into a labyrinthine bunker. Major entryways to the cave were sealed off, and a secret shaft to the main cistern was dug deep within the subterranean complex. New chambers were hastily excavated, and the tunnels connecting them were cut narrow with many twists and turns to thwart assaults by Roman soldiers. The tight corridors still require slow going, and the cistern shaft is an intimidating twenty-plus feet deep with footholds chopped into the shaft's chalk sides: a desperate way to retrieve water.

147

Niches chopped in the walls to hold oil lamps were crudely cut; war is no time for niceties. In one of the chambers, black streaks from an oil lamp still stain the chalk-white wall, a poignant reminder of what occurred here nearly two thousand years ago.

In the end, Rome sent legions from all over the empire to crush the revolt. They persecuted Rabbi Akiba and other great religious leaders of the time, and killed hundreds of thousands, depopulating some cities of Jews. This catastrophe spurred emigration, swelling the Diaspora that had begun as a result of the Babylonian exile in 586 B.C.E.

Neot Kedumim: a Modern Biblical Landscape

About three hundred years before the Bar Kokhba Revolt, another momentous revolt had begun farther north in the Judean foothills. The revolt started in Modi'in, which lies just off Route 1, the highway connecting Jerusalem and Tel Aviv. Alexander the Great had

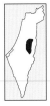

NEOT KEDUMIM

Ducks ply palm-shaded Solomon's Pool at Neot Kedumim Biblical Landscape Reserve, which tells Israel's natural and human history along its winding paths.

148

introduced Hellenism to Israel in 332 B.C.E., but by 167 B.C.E. one of his successors had imposed an intolerable regime. Antiochus IV Epiphanes, the Seleucid ruler, taxed his Jewish subjects exorbitantly, outlawed their religion, and forced them to commit sacrileges.

Antiochus' soldiers went to Modi'in, the village of Mattathias, to compel the highly respected Hasmonean priest to make pagan sacrifices. Mattathias refused and killed a Seleucid soldier. He and his sons then fled to hiding places in the hills, igniting the Maccabean Revolt, which gave focus to the unrest already among the people.

At first the Jews waged a guerrilla war against the Seleucid army. Eventually the Maccabees became more organized, finally routing the Seleucids, a victory commemorated by the holiday of Hanukkah. Ironically, not too many generations later, Hasmonean leadership degenerated, becoming as oppressive as the Seleucids from whom they had won their freedom.

The Modi'in district, where the Maccabean Revolt began, still lies among the low foothills (*shefelah*) that roll out from the Judean Hills onto the flat coastal plain. And very near Modi'in, just off

Route 443, the landscapes of those early days have been restored. In 1965, Nogah Hareuveni, a botanist and the son of botanists, fulfilled his and his parents' dream to reclaim the classic landscapes of biblical Israel.

Barren, ravaged soils, worn out by centuries of use, were amended and terraced to re-create the original terrain. Olive and wine presses, cisterns and ritual baths were reconstructed from millennia-old fixtures and set among plantings of pine, olive, almond, and hundreds of other trees, shrubs, wildflowers, and grasses that represent the ecosystems of Israel.

Now Neot Kedumim Biblical Landscape Reserve meanders over six hundred twenty-five acres, allowing Israelis and others to step back in time, or perhaps into a future landscape, healed and sustained. Although they are re-creations of bygone vistas rather than completely natural areas, the gardens of Neot Kedumim are both evocative and informative, and one of my favorite places in Israel. They bring the languid grace of the landscapes in the Song of Songs to life.

The trails that wind through Neot Kedumim are keyed to booklets that explain dozens of species and their place in history. Guides lead schoolchildren, foreign tourists, family groups, and a variety of other visitors, explaining as they go. The "white path" passes almonds, capers, figs, hyssop, and the Pool of Solomon, a quiet pond ringed by graceful date palms. The "blue path" traces history past grain-threshing floors, olives, and the spices that once drove the Middle East's economy. The "yellow path" winds among grapevine arbors, fig trees, terebinths, and beehives. The "green path" stops at an olive press, a water wheel, the seven species mentioned by the spies of the Exodus, and the four species of the Sukkot holiday.

149

Botanist Aviva Rabinowitz has said, "The land does not forget." She was speaking of all the insults sustained by the land over centuries, as people raised crops and grazed herds, dug and built, took and did not give back. Neot Kedumim is a place where people are trying to help the land remember what it once was.

Amid the peaceful landscape, I found a fine rock to sit on and, opening a book I had brought, began to read. But, surrounded by a mirror of the Judean Hills' former glory, I fell into a reverie. I dreamt about working as a gardener in this *Gan Eden* (Garden of Eden), helping to restore the land of Israel plant by plant.

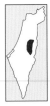

Tornadoes, Human and Otherwise

Not far from Neot Kedumim, at the Latrun interchange of the Tel Aviv-Jerusalem Highway, the Latrun Israel Raptor Information Center is growing. Part of a planned string of bird-migration and ecotourism centers, Latrun will share information with bird stations in Israel and with stations along migration corridors in other countries of the Middle East and Europe. The vision for Latrun and the string of centers comes from the indefatigable Dr. Yossi Leshem.

Yossi Leshem is a force of nature. So I was told. I was staying in the Golan when I learned he was available, his cyclonic energy at rest momentarily. I wasted no time. I spun down from the Golan; past the eastern shores of Lake Kinneret; past the fish ponds that line the road near Bet She'an, where hungry long-legged birds look for a bite; down through the Jordan Valley.

As I reached the head of the Judean Desert and the turn leading up to the Judean Hills and Jerusalem, I noticed tornado funnels moving slowly above the western shores of the Dead Sea. Raised in tornado country of the American Midwest, I looked for some safe place but saw none. I considered stopping to hunt for a cave or a rock niche in which to wait out the fury of the roiling winds. But time was running out as the funnels approached.

150 Then I looked again. Tornadoes do not writhe through the Judean Desert. What I was seeing were funnels of storks in dark colonies of tens and hundreds. They circled over a "land in the deep shadow of wings" (Isaiah 18:1).

With their long bills and legs, white bodies and seven-foot wingspans caped dramatically with black, storks have always been an auspicious sight. In Europe, where they breed each summer, sometimes on people's roofs, they are symbols of good luck.

More practically, they are valued for their eating habits. Storks graze in marshlands and croplands where they feast on a variety of small animals, from reptiles to rodents, clearing fields of agricultural pests. Coasting on thermals from Africa to summer breeding grounds in Europe, a half-million storks fly over Israel each spring. "The stork in the sky knows her seasons," said Jeremiah (8:7).

Storks also have been a special area of study for Dr. Leshem. A professor of ornithology at Tel Aviv University, Dr. Leshem has served as executive director of SPNI and was instrumental in starting the International Birding and Research Center at Eilat. He also helped establish Migrating Birds Know No Boundaries, a program that allows high school students to relay information on migrating birds to each other via the Internet. Besides tracking and learning about birds, the program promotes cooperation among Israeli, Palestinian, Jordanian, Dutch, South African, and other teens.

Dr. Leshem's most daring bird studies, however, were a result of his training as a pilot in the Israeli Air Force. As one of the world's major flyways, Israel becomes a bottleneck during spring and fall migrations, with about half a billion birds flying over the country.

Israeli pilots use the same air space as these migrating millions. In past decades thousands of bird-plane accidents occurred. "Bird strikes" are fatal to the birds and occasionally fatal to humans. And the cost to planes—fighter planes, helicopters, transports—is in the millions of dollars.

Beginning in the early 1980s, Dr. Leshem took to the skies in a motorized glider and spent hundreds of hours flying among the birds, phoning down information to trackers below on which species flew at what altitude within which migration paths. In recent years, he and his colleagues have strapped lightweight transmitters to storks and raptors to help track their movements. Radar pinpoints the narrow paths big birds take along coast and mountain cliffs. Radar also shows the broad smear of paths where small birds cross over much of Israel at night.

The collated information gives pilots hard data on how to avoid bird flight patterns. As a result, bird strikes have decreased 88 percent since the program started, saving lives and about $30 million a year.

151

I met up with Dr. Leshem—Yossi—in Jerusalem, in the lobby of a large hotel, which was filling up with people decked out in finery for bar mitzvah celebrations that would begin that night. A tall man with unruly red hair topped by a flapping *kipah*, Yossi talks, drives, and thinks fast. Leaving my car at the hotel, I hopped in the passenger seat of Yossi's van. First we had to stop at Jerusalem's large modern mall to pick up some family photos. Yossi deftly maneuvered his van across a few lanes of traffic and onto the sidewalk while talking to me and arranging a meeting with an associate on his car phone, writing down date and time on the clipboard he uses to make notes as he drives.

Up onto the sidewalk to park, photo pickup, then off to his home at Mount Gilo as Yossi showed me pictures of his son—one of five children—at basketball playoffs with a friend, their faces those of teenage boys cheering a winning team. At the same time, he was

Lesser kestrels nest in Jerusalem and in coastal towns. Because they are hole-nesters, lesser kestrels have found that the opening formed at the corners of red tile roofs makes a fine nesting space in the absence of more natural accommodations. Although their population in Israel is not at the brink yet, they are endangered worldwide and are losing their homes in Israel as tile-roof houses come down to make way for larger buildings. Dr. Leshem and company are starting school projects to build nest-box homes for the displaced kestrels.

explaining the need for green space in Israel, especially in the Judean Hills.

At their pleasant home atop Mount Gilo, site of an SPNI field office and a community where environmental and wildlife researchers live, Yossi introduced me to his wife, Rivke, then disappeared to find some background on green space. Small, lithe, and dark-haired, Rivke seemed perfectly composed despite my feeling of being in the wake of a whirlwind. I said to her, "You probably meet all the environmentalists who pass through Israel right here in your living room."

Her grin told me she agreed with my assessment and her brisk competency told me this household was a binary system, a smaller, darker star and a larger, lighter star, each centering the other. She had prepared a light meal, a thick vegetable soup and a salad, which we gulped down as Yossi speed-talked and I speed-wrote. A neighbor, a botanist, came by for a moment. The neighbor is an expert on irises, and I had many questions, but before I had a chance to ask a thing, he was out the door and Yossi was explaining how he and some colleagues had devised a means of protecting lesser kestrels.

After a three-hour jet stream of talk, ranging from protections for endangered species and the migrating birds program for schoolchildren to the crucial need for green space in the Judean Hills, we walked a few blocks to the top of Mount Gilo. At three thousand feet, Mount Gilo is the highest peak in the Jerusalem section of the Judean Hills. We could see Jerusalem spread out to the north, Bethlehem to the south. We could see valleys and peaks that looked like aeries. But the Sabbath approached, and I had more than two hours driving to return to lodgings on the Golan. So I wished the Leshem family a *Shabbat shalom* and left.

Primed by Yossi's speed, I bulleted down Ma'aleh Adummim, flew around Jericho on the bypass, and kept a heavy foot on the gas pedal north through the Jordan Valley. Absent at that hour were Palestinian women picking produce and the Palestinian boys who sold produce along the road. The roads, too, were empty. A haunted feeling hovered over the place.

The base of the Judean Hills became ever smaller in my rearview mirror. Unlike the sparsely settled Negev where the sweep of the natural landscape is obvious, the Judean Hills require a more careful eye to see past millennia of human edifice. The natural Judean Hills are more like its premier city, Jerusalem, full of hidden places, contradictions, competing interests—a checkerboard land.

CHAPTER SEVEN

Southern Galilee:

Sapphire Sea amid the Mountains

Arbel Cliffs

S OUTHERN GALILEE IS WHERE the Mediterranean forests of Israel's cooler, wetter north meet the desert. Crossed by trade routes in ancient times, with a climate benign enough for intensive agriculture, the midsection of Israel has always been busy with people. After so many millennia of use, southern Galilee has been thoroughly altered by human activity, and little is left of the natural landscape.

The great beasts of the past are gone; what remain are hedgehog and porcupine, mongoose and fox, gazelle, hyrax, and a host of rodents. Yet raptors still roost in the hills, and smaller birds are abundant. Ironically, as the number of fish ponds and farm fields have grown—providing new food sources—so has the number of birds.

From the Judean Desert, I drove north on Route 90, the Samarian Hills rising high on my left. The Jordan River, full of kinks and curves and thickly bordered by brush, meandered along the Great Rift on my right. Linking Lake Kinneret (the Sea of Galilee) with the Dead Sea, the Jordan River also forms Israel's border with Jordan. Beyond the river, I could see the mountains of Moab rising to the east.

Depending on the political climate, this is my route of choice between southern and northern Israel. Part of the reason is because I am bewildered by the political whim-whams of the Israeli-Palestinian patchwork in the Judean and Samarian Hills and have no desire to get caught in the middle. Perhaps some day Palestinians and Israelis will work out their differences and become a joint economic powerhouse. My mind played with imagined scraps of peace and shreds of dual prosperity.

Besides, most of the highways connecting Israel's north and south are clogged with traffic bottlenecks. By comparison, Route 90, which

Arbel Cliffs •

Mount Tabor •

Mount Gilboa •

Kefar Ruppin Birding Center •

Southern Galilee

stretches the length of Israel, from Eilat to Metullah, is a breeze until it reaches Lake Kinneret and knots of civilization. On Route 90 I can spend time watching for storks rather than traffic lights, looking at shrub-dotted hillsides rather than housing developments.

The route up the Jordan Valley from the Dead Sea is by no means nature at its most pristine. Between the Samarian Hills and the Jordan River lies a weave of Israeli farms, small Arab villages, date and banana orchards, and tomato crops—not natural, but easy on the eyes.

Happily, dense thickets still rim sections of the Jordan. And, within these thickets in the no-man's land where the borders of Israel and Jordan meet, leopards live. That is the assessment of Dr. Benny Shalmon and other mammal researchers. But leopard numbers are so low that the great cats do not leave their usual territorial scent markings because there are too few other leopards to notify. As Dr. Shalmon has said, "You don't phone if there's no one on the other line."

Within the Jordan Valley, the river's twists and turns are so tight it seems the Jordan is nervously hugging itself. Although peaceful now, it has seen more battles than most rivers. It also has seen many more animals. Between Jericho and Bet She'an, the thickets of the Jordan were once home to not only leopards, but also the king of beasts. Jeremiah warns that the land of Edom will come up "as when a lion comes up out of the jungle of the Jordan" (49:19). The verge of the Jordan is still thick with tamarisk, Euphrates poplar, and vines. But where lion and bear once roamed, only jackals and small wildcats survive.

Where the Samarian Hills crowd in toward the Great Rift, civilization drops away, and it is just me, my car, and the tall scalloped barrier of dry white scarps that are visually akin to California's Death Valley. Ophra Haza's voice shimmers from the tape deck, adding an opulent tapestry of sound to soften the severe scenery. Like the Judean Hills to the south, the east side of the Samarian Hills lie in a rain shadow, becoming a rain-shadow desert.

Past the turnoff for Ma'aleh Ephraim, the next sizable road arcs into the heart of the Samarian Hills. Although I was not pointed in that direction, the road leads toward the city of Nablus or Shekhem, depending on which side of the Palestinian-Israeli political fence you live. The city is flanked by the prominent peaks of the Samarian Hills: Mount Ebal and Mount Gerizim, known in the Bible as the mountains of blessing and curse. Upon entering the land, the Israelites were to pronounce blessings from Mount Gerizim on those who followed the law and curses from Mount Ebal on those who did not.

North of Nablus, a long finger of the Samarian Hills points diagonally toward Mount Carmel. Once they begin veering westward, the hills are scored again and again by valleys, so that they seem to hopscotch toward the coast. On the side of the hills facing the Mediterranean Sea lies an apron of coastal plain. On the other side lies the Valley of Jezreel, Israel's largest valley. Fertile and level, the Jezreel has produced crops for thousands of years. Today orchards, grain fields, and fish ponds are harvested there.

Soon I sensed the westward drift of the Samarian Hills, because the mountainous walls fell away and the Jordan Valley opened up. The land began to roll comfortably, covered by green and tan grasses, and I knew I was now in the northern half of Israel. I started looking for signs of Bet She'an. Along the Rift route, this development town is the first urban area north of Jericho and the site of a magnificent, millennia-old Roman city.

Over decades, archaeologists have been uncovering and restoring the ruined city, which was destroyed by an earthquake in the eighth century. Because the Earth's interior is active under Israel, signs of earthquakes are legion. At Bet She'an, pillars that have been cleaned but allowed to lie in position just as they fell provide palpable proof of the Earth's ferocious power.

157

From Bet She'an, Route 71 follows the small Harod Valley as it drifts northwest along the line of hills. Beyond lies the Valley of Jezreel. Between the two valleys, Mount Gilboa rears its vast bulk. Dark green pine forests cover its slopes and broad shoulders, but Mount Gilboa's open, windswept crown is full of wildflowers.

North of Gilboa, a clutter of low hills and ridges crowd the southwest quadrant of Lake Kinneret. Mount Tabor, the most famous among them, stands alone, overlooking the Valley of Jezreel and guarding an ancient trade route. The trade route that angled through the valley toward the east and India connected with the Via Maris, the famous trade route that paralleled ancient Israel's coastline. The Via Maris, or Sea Road, connected with southerly routes that crossed the Negev and the Arabian Peninsula, creating the most important trade network of its day.

Lake Kinneret is the blue jewel of the region. Set like an aquamarine in a ring of mountains and high plateaus that glow green in spring and golden in summer, Lake Kinneret is thirty-three miles in circumference and Israel's only large body of fresh water. It is known in Hebrew as Yam Kinneret because, tradition says, it is shaped like a harp.

Route 90 hugs the western shore of Lake Kinneret, traveling past historic sites, resorts, and the city of Tiberias. Just north of the lake, the road intersects Route 85, which divides southern Galilee from northern Galilee.

The sages had a more vegetal view of this dividing line. In the Mishnah, they clarified the division between upper and lower Galilee this way: Where the heat-loving Egyptian fig (sycomore) grows is lower Galilee; where it does not is upper Galilee. Route 85 seems a good enough demarcation line for me, but I was not headed that way that day. I was off to see the birds.

Bird World at Kefar Ruppin

Having heard of a relatively new bird-watching center in the Jordan Valley, I turned east onto Route 71 at Bet She'an. Near the turnoff are fish ponds where storks and wading birds hunker at certain times of year, looking for an easy catch. The ponds are a taste of things to come.

The road ends at the Peace Bridge, which links Israel and Jordan. But less than a mile before the border, a small southbound road leads to Kefar Ruppin. A kibbutz that lies alongside the Jordan River, Kefar Ruppin and its fish ponds are an important stopover for migrating birds and the site of spectacular heron and cormorant rookeries.

Eucalyptus trees line the entrance to Kefar Ruppin. As I approached, the long, drooping branches were flayed apart by the huge flapping wings of first one steppe buzzard, then another: a dramatic welcome in a flurry of dark feathers. Seeing raptors up close is always a thrill, but with sightings of up to two hundred thousand steppe buzzards a day during a spring migration that can last from mid-February through April, kibbutz residents are more blasé than I.

The kibbutz is peaceful with shaded lanes, fish ponds, and croplands, but it is certainly no nature reserve. It is the birds that choose to stop here that make Kefar Ruppin an international bird-watching center and, with more than three hundred species sighted, a magnet for bird-watchers worldwide.

After entering Kefar Ruppin's gates, a lane passes a fenced date palm plantation on one side and lawns lined with pathways and one-story kibbutz homes on the other. The parking lot at the end of the lane leads to the low arc of visitor lodgings, where I stashed my stuff in a light, clean room and left for a walk.

Almost immediately I came face to beak with a white-breasted kingfisher. In his *Birds of Israel*, Israeli ornithologist Hadoram Shirihai explains that white-breasted kingfishers had always clung close to the Great Rift Valley where their presence has been recorded since Canon Tristram's sightings in 1865. With the coming of agricultural settlements, irrigation canals, and fish ponds in the 1940s, the kingfishers have spread throughout northern Israel.

Their bright turquoise backs give them away as they fly, but at rest the compact, ten-inch birds with the white bib and rust-colored crown seem more head than body. A favorite perch is on a limb directly above water so they

Near dusk, a lone tree amid the sod and grain fields at Kefar Ruppin provides a roosting place for storks. During the day, storks, spoonbills, and dozens of other species fish or nest at this bird-watching center in the Jordan Valley.

can watch for small water prey. When Israel began modernizing, electric wires strung above watery roadside ditches became new kingfisher habitat. Once they spot a fish or frog, they attack with long, outsized beaks.

In addition to dates, Kefar Ruppin grows sod, alfalfa, wheat, and fish, including ornamental fish that it exports to Europe. With ponds to fish and fields to glean, birds migrating along the Great Rift flock to Kefar Ruppin, especially in spring after flying hungry and thirsty over southern deserts. Kefar Ruppin's birding route simply follows kibbutz roads, weaving around fields and fish ponds.

The first time out, I went with Che'ch, a kibbutz guide. A short

stubby man originally from Czechoslovakia, Che'ch's life has been long and remarkable, and I was torn between watching birds and listening to his story. A German couple walked with us, and we took turns letting Che'ch lean on our arms, as his legs are not as sturdy as they once were.

At the first fish ponds, he pointed out a few pygmy cormorants perched on small dead limbs floating at the edge of the water. Dark, shiny, and pointed like arrows, pygmy cormorants are half the size of great cormorants, which stood on tamarisks lining the pool. Now endangered, the pygmy cormorant was common in northern Israel before the swamps and marshes where it roosts and breeds were drained in the 1940s and 1950s. Making a slow comeback, the greatest number of pygmy cormorants are found at Kefar Ruppin.

While we drove to the next set of ponds, Che'ch told us he had come to Palestine in 1939 on a ship trying to evade official entry ports. This was during the Mandate period after World War I, when Britain governed Palestine. Despite the growing Nazi threat, Britain had blocked Jewish immigration, so Che'ch's ship was stopped and sent to the Indian Ocean. Later that year, Che'ch made his way back and into Palestine where he fought as part of the Palmach, one of the first Israeli defense forces.

The German man looked up and pointed to a lesser spotted eagle soaring overhead. I was struck by the irony of German tourists offering their arms to this old fighter. But the thought passed quickly as the next few minutes were full of birds. An osprey hunted high over a pond. Over another pond, a marsh harrier cruised low, looking for food, its distinctive flight like a huge gray cape smoothly and silently skimming the reeds. Beyond, over the fields, a crowd of storks, spooked by something, rose as one in a great billow.

The narrow dirt roads drop in stages toward the Jordan River and the Great Rift. As we eased the car downward, Che'ch explained that he had settled at Kefar Ruppin in 1939, a year after the kibbutz was founded. Between 1967 and 1970, he and other members of the kibbutz survived recurring shelling from Palestine Liberation Organization (PLO) strongholds in Jordan. Since the Jordanians routed the PLO beginning in Black September of 1970 and ending in 1971, the border has been quiet. In 1994, peace with Jordan became official.

At the river, we waved to Jordanian soldiers in their metal watchtower, and the soldiers waved back. An odd scene: four bird-watchers, two soldiers, and a skinny river caged in by tall link fences topped by razor wire. Che'ch joked that "our side" had just won a hill. The Jordan, which can run more than twenty feet high in spring floods, changes its channel at will, claiming a piece of land here, giving up a chunk there.

Seemingly imprisoned between the fences, the Jordan and its waters will certainly be the resource fought over in the future. The region is water poor, and everyone wants as much of the Jordan and its tributaries as they can get.

Parking the car alongside the dirt track, we sneaked through thistles and brush, and peered down over a marshy area thick with tamarisk trees and hundreds of birds. Every tamarisk seemed to contain two or three nests in this crowded rookery, and we saw night herons, cormorants, great white and cattle egrets, and a lone gray heron.

Through binoculars we saw the palest of blue eggs in the nests of the cattle egrets. A few of the night herons were already tending fuzzy gray babies. In a month, after all the chicks had hatched, the noise would be deafening with the squawks of hungry fledglings. Where dog and cat babies look furrily adorable, just-hatched herons look like tiny dinosaurs, betraying their common ancestry with the long-gone reptiles.

Completing the circuit of ponds banked with red poppies and other wildflowers, we passed one where they were drawing down the water and siphoning off Saint Peter's fish for market. Where the muddy banks were exposed, storks and egrets hovered hungrily by the dozens, looking for tender fish fry or tasty frogs. Among the white storks were ten or so black storks, rarer than the white and ever so elegant. The German man explained that while white storks will nest in Europe's urban areas, black storks are more secretive, seeking out the least disturbed remnants of European forests to make their nests.

161

Leaving the drained fish ponds, Che'ch told us that when Leon Uris came to gather stories for a book he was working on, *Exodus*, he and his companions told Uris stories of their exploits in the Palmach. He related how one Christmas they plied English officers with drinks and, when the officers were in their cups, he and his comrades stole their arms *and* smuggled some more Jews into Palestine.

Back near the center of the kibbutz we passed other fish ponds fitted with small paddles whirring round and round in the water to aerate them. Fish production is big in Israel; Kefar Ruppin alone produces three hundred tons of fish each year, some of which is exported. Strings flutter across the tops of the ponds to keep pelicans

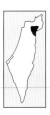

from swooping down and eating the profits. Gulls stand around the edges, picking out dead fish, helping keep the ponds clean.

Che'ch continued his narrative, explaining that many years later, visiting England, he wanted to bird-watch on a particular island he had heard about. He was told he would have to ask the owner of the property, an English gentleman who lived in a nearby manor house. Che'ch went straight to the door of the manor and asked to see the owner of the property.

He was invited in and came face to face with one of the officers he had deceived on Christmas long ago. The man, who had become a member of Parliament, was known as an anti-Semite. Che'ch later learned the anger stemmed from the fact that the Englishman's best friend had been killed by the Irgun, another of the early Israeli forces. They began trading stories and reliving the past, and the Englishman made sure Che'ch received access to the island. Linked by history, the two began trading yearly greetings.

We returned to the common buildings of the kibbutz and parted ways. Since there was still time before dinner, I continued on my own onto dirt tracks that led away from the Jordan, past more ponds, past the alfalfa fields and the bird-ringing station where European ornithology students were helping to track species. A ruddy shelduck bobbed on a pond along with a few coots. Crested larks dashed out of the way as I drove on.

162

A hoopoe flew from the fields in a flurry of black-and-white-striped wings. When they are probing the ground for insects, tan, foot-long hoopoes—their wings and crown folded demurely against their bodies—are almost unnoticeable. When they launch themselves, their fabulous, feathery displays and extravagant crowns fill the air with commotion.

More birds: the black-and-white flash of a pied kingfisher and the shiny blue head of a small Palestine sunbird. A spur-winged plover ran ahead of me on stilt legs, shrieking protests at my presence. Neatly attired in a suit of black, tan, and white, the plover is common near all water in northern Israel.

It was near evening, and I spotted a picturesque eucalyptus tree full of roosting storks and a scattering of pygmy cormorants. The tree stood alone in a field yellow with flowering mustard. The peach-colored sky framed the stork's black-and-white wings as the birds flapped and fussed, settling for the night. The tree filled my camera frame with a near-perfect, unexpected moment.

Beyond I could see a line of trees—just the tops of trees, really—

hinting at the path of the Jordan River a level below. I edged closer, for a more perfect picture. Suddenly, a mongoose crept across the road, an indignant plover called out, and the storks rose from the tree like an exploding nebula, beyond the eye of the camera. But in my mind's eye, I keep the image still.

At dinnertime, I made my way back to the kibbutz dining room, about the size and shape of a high-school gymnasium and as brightly lit, where I filled my tray with soft cheeses, hard cheeses, black bread, salad, and eggplant in tomato sauce. It was said that an Arab bride, before she married, had to learn one hundred one ways to cook eggplant and that part of her dowry was jars and jars of olive oil in which to cook the eggplants.

At one of the long tables I chose a seat across from a woman who was on the staff of a British bird magazine. She was visiting her daughter, who had recently married an Israeli psychology student. As part of her visit, she had decided to come to Kefar Ruppin to see the birds and add to her life list.

The English birder and I made a plan to meet the next morning and, after dinner, I gave her a ride to her room. As we rounded a corner near the date palms, we both spotted yellow eyes at the same moment, and I stopped the car in the dark. Atop the chain-link fence at the date plantation, a tiny Scops owl perched.

She and I watched in the dark, waiting to see who would blink first, the owl or us. The hand-sized Scops owl seeks out smaller **163** prey, mainly insects. And it was at the beginning of its night shift. The Scops owl looked at us, its ear tufts peaked like the eyebrows of a quizzical wizard. Then it launched a silent glide into the palms.

Of the approximately ten owl species found in Israel, the larger ones prey mainly on rodents. During past decades, chemicals such as DDT were used to kill off insects and other agricultural pests. But the poisons weakened bird eggs, thus reducing bird populations and depriving farmers of allies in the war against crop raiders. The director of Kefar Ruppin's bird-watching center told me that they had recently mounted a number of barn-owl boxes around the kibbutz in order to keep the rodent population in check.

I took this information home with me and put it to good use. Small rodents plague crops in Israel . . . and my garden. When they ate my favorite lily bulbs, leaving gaping bulb holes as evidence, I too mounted an owl box, probably to the horror of the smaller birds that frequent my bird feeders.

Nocturnal predators, owls have large eyes packed with many more rods and cones than we, so it can see what we cannot at night. Because an owl's eyes are positioned in the front of its head, rather than to either side, it has developed the ability to swivel its head faster and farther than most species.

The feathers around its face work as a gathering dish, for light but especially for sound. Even more than its sight, an owl's ears have developed as precision instruments. Proportionately larger and more intricate than our ears, an owl's ears are positioned asymmetrically on either side of its head, allowing it to locate a sound with an accuracy far surpassing ours.

Early next morning, just after the dew had evaporated, I drove the Englishwoman through the bird areas of Kefar Ruppin, having become an instant expert on the route. Storks, again, stood in groups at the nearly drained pool. I wondered, can storks seem mundane? Graceful white spoonbills threshed shallow water with their black spatulate bills in search of tasty prey.

We passed the outsized nests of Dead Sea sparrows on tamarisks alongside the Jordan River, in the no-man's-land between fences. The tiny beige-and-brown birds are only five inches long and lay only a few eggs per brood. Yet their nests, made with dry grasses, are more than a foot across and quite deep, purposely huge to deter snakes from climbing in and stealing eggs or chicks.

Among the fields, plump chukars race-walked ahead of us. Like plovers, Dead Sea sparrows, and others, chukars have expanded their range as irrigation and agriculture have expanded. On our way back, we were lucky to see a mated pair of francolins part the alfalfa, run up the road together, then disappear again into the fields.

With its white cheeks and delicately fretted wing pattern of cinnamon, black, and white, the francolin looks like a bird from a Dutch master still life. The bird used to be much more populous in the Jordan Valley, but intensive, high-tech agriculture and the increasing presence of people have driven it out. Where the francolin once reigned, chukars have taken over. Both are related to partridges, but chukars do not seem to mind human populations while francolins do.

In Israel, the francolin is at the southern edge of its range, which extends north and east into Turkey and Asia. Once it lived as far

west along the Mediterranean as Spain, but some birds cannot adapt to human intrusion. Elsewhere in the Jordan Valley, I had heard the loud call of a francolin male before I saw him. Extremely territorial, the male stands on a mound and calls out, again and again, that he is king of a tiny mountain.

Tree of Light Below Mount Tabor

Traveling through the Valley of Jezreel, it is difficult to avoid the sentinel presence of Mount Tabor. A perfect dome, Tabor looks like the bald crown of an immense giant rising from the earth.

From Mount Tabor, Deborah the prophet-judge and General Barak launched their successful campaign against the Canaanites. Mount Tabor traditionally is considered the place where Jesus' disciples saw him transfigured. Between then and now, battles were fought, churches were built, and little remains of the natural—except the view of southern Galilee from the top of Tabor.

In his 1894 *Historical Geography of the Holy Land*, George Adam Smith said, "Tabor is covered with bush, and on its northern side with large, loose groves of forest trees." He went on to describe the natural sights of southern Galilee as he traveled from Mount Carmel toward Nazareth, which lies near the foot of Mount Tabor:

165

> The road which goes up from the Bay of Carmel to Nazareth winds as among English glades, with open woods of oak and abundance of flowers and grass. Often, as about Nazareth, the limestone breaks out not less bare than in Judea, but over the most of lower Galilee there is a profusion of bush, with scattered forest trees—holly-oak, maple, sycomore, bay-tree, myrtel, arbutus, sumac, and other—and in the valleys olive orchards and stretches of corn-land.

Olive orchards still cover parts of the valleys and reach up the slopes. Driving through southern Galilee I came across one such orchard at an extraordinary moment. The olive trees, row upon row, were neither young nor old. Beneath their twisted trunks, the ground was covered by a magic carpet of red poppies, so that the trees seemed to float atop an undulating bed of red.

That day clouds chased each other from hill to hill, breaking into patchy sunlight across southern Galilee. A tree of light is the olive. Olive oil was the source of light in the lamps of early Israel, but there is another reason for the tree's association with light. As I passed this particular orchard, rays of sunlight pierced the clouds. The light caught the tossing, silvery leaves of the olive trees and transformed each into a shimmering tree of light.

Mount Gilboa: the Muezzin's Call

In spring, wildflowers ring the lower slopes of Mount Gilboa with a necklace of yellow. These sunny, sloping, yellow-brushed meadows are spiked with tall stalks of purple thistle and pink hollyhock. Above lie dark, cool pine forests. It was on just such a day that I decided to revisit Gilboa. I had a feeling about irises.

Irises grow in severe places, places that are either too wet for most wildflowers or too dry. Despite tough conditions, these plants with the broad, swordlike leaves produce large, showy flowers. Of the twenty species that grow in Israel, eight are unique to the nation, including Haynei's iris, more commonly called Gilboa iris because it mainly grows on Mount Gilboa. Aficionados make pilgrimages to the mountain to see these magnificent blooms, and I thought my timing might be right.

Winding up the creased slopes of Gilboa, the road passes from a bright Mediterranean landscape into the shade of pine forests. Planted by the Jewish National Fund, these forests are a collection of groves, each bearing a memorial plaque dedicated to a person or group.

Toward the top, a dirt road beckoned, leading deep into the pines. A short way in, I parked and walked on in the cool quiet. Drawn to a break in the pines, I made my way to the sun-drenched spot and a chest-high stand of flowering giant fennel. Finally, when I was only a few feet away, I saw them, fat clumps of Gilboa iris. Their huge purple blooms swelled like costumed opera stars, surrounded by an escort of red anemones, blue bellflowers, and grasses.

The iris is a relative of the grasses, but a relative that has gone to great trouble to get noticed. The petals that arch downward, called "falls," are marked in the middle: a visual clue to insects that says, "land here." The delicately veined purple of the Gilboa iris is marked by a black landing pad that leads bees and other insects inward toward the nectar. The path to the nectar leads through a tunnel created by the sepal and style. In this tunnel, the bee inadvertently rubs pollen collected from a previous flower onto the stigma, thus fertilizing the iris. As it leaves, the bee is dusted with more pollen that it will carry to the next flower.

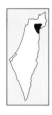

It is the beauty of the iris, not its biological endgame, that is foremost in our eyes. I darted from clump to clump, looking as hard as I could to fix this visual feast in my memory. Then the pines took over again. Alone with the pines and the wind, I thought I heard the haunting sound of a muezzin's call to worship. I ran down the road, looking for the minaret of a mosque, but saw only pines. I returned to the car, with a barely heard *Allahu akbar* —"God is great"—echoing from the forest.

Twisting upward, the road eventually leaves the pines, and the tops of Gilboa's string of peaks appear, one after another as the route levels out just below the mountaintop. The highest area of the mountain is protected as Gilboa Reserve. Wind-swept and rocky, it is lands such as this,

Endemic to Israel, Haynei's iris grows mainly on Mount Gilboa: atop the mountain and in sunny areas among the pines. In spring, when this dramatic flower blooms, it draws school groups and flower-lovers alike.

167

lands that are too hard to tame, that remain in their purest state.

On that day, the nature reserve parking lot was crowded with yellow school buses, the trailheads busy with groups of children who had come to see the irises and other wildflowers. I walked to the edge of the road and stood looking down at the Harod Valley with its blue puzzle of fish ponds. I have a picture taken with my friend Talia's family at this spot years ago. We had camped lower, in the pines, and sang old halutzim (pioneer) songs around a campfire. The next day, we had hiked to the top of Mount Gilboa, to this very spot. I'm not even sure the road was paved then.

Turning back to the mountain, I maneuvered past schoolchildren and found myself along one of the reserve's stone-lined trails. All around me, the high, rocky meadows were crowded with flowers: white salvia, purple clover, white daisies and yellow daisies, purple thistle, pink flax, bluebells, fennel with towering yellow heads, and, of courses, Gilboa irises.

Between clumps of flowers, white limestone protrudes everywhere. With just enough moisture in the air, much of the rock is covered by lichen, that formidable association of fungus and alga. Spreading colorful patches of tan, orange, and white, lichen usually is the first life to colonize rock. Along with wind and water, it begins the process of breaking down rock to create soil; it often is followed by sedum.

Rummaging among the rocks, I found what I was looking for. In places alongside the Gilboa trail, limestone lines the ground like pavement and, within one shallow stone bowl, I discovered rosettes of red sedum.

Sedum grabs hold where crumbled rock, dust, and organic material collect in the cleft of a rock and sedum adds organic matter from its own dead leaves. The humic acid produced by this decay dissolves even more rock. Eventually, sedum breaks enough stone to allow other plants to gain purchase. In not too many years, bare rock can be covered with plant life.

When the plants and animals of a forest, or any natural community, reach a collective peak, it is said to be a climax community. In cooler, wetter parts of northern Israel's Mediterranean zone, oak and one type of pistacia (*Pistacia palaestina*) hold sway as the climax trees. Beneath their boughs, small trees, shrubs, wildflowers, and a host of mammals, birds, reptiles, and insects thrive.

In warmer, drier parts of the Mediterranean zone, carob and mastic pistacia are the main climax trees. At the top of Gilboa, where soil has covered rock, carob and mastic pistacia struggle. Wind, thin soils, and, formerly, grazing have stunted the trees and sculpted them into artful shapes.

As I, too, struggled against the wind, making my way back along the spine of the mountain, I noticed that the school buses were loading up and leaving. Above, a kestrel beat its wings against the gusts, working hard to remain in a near-stationary stall. Nearby, a patch of green, unripened wild emmer, a parent of modern wheat, bent under the rushing wind. A twisted carob was backlit by an angry, stormy sky. It was time to leave.

Kinneret—a Lake Like a Harp

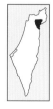

About twenty miles north of Mount Gilboa stand the Horns of Hittim, the softly pointed, paired hills where, in 1187, Saladin led the Muslims to victory over Crusaders. The horns themselves are the remains of a volcano that once occupied the spot, then blew its top. The jagged rim from that blast was softened by time, leaving the horns as evidence of a fiery past.

Just north of the Horns of Hittim and west of Lake Kinneret's widest point, the Arbel Cliffs tower like mammoth entry gates above Tiberias. Once the soaring cliffs were one long rampart of limestone, but the Arbel River split the long wall, eating through the limestone little by little, creating a wedge-shaped valley between the sheer cliffs.

My friend Ido and I had driven the road that winds up from Tiberias to the top of the cliffs, ending at a moshav and the remains of an ancient synagogue. Beyond the new and the old buildings, grasses and tall pink hollyhocks stirred in the wind, a pretty covering for the flat cap of the cliffs.

We walked a path that runs along the top of the cliffs to an overlook of Lake Kinneret, laid out still and blue below. The other direction leads to broken, rocky trails that seem to end almost as soon as they begin at the edge of the cliff.

Ido urged me forward, but I could not see how that was possible. Forward to what? Thin air? Then, looking closer, I noticed the series of metal handholds and small ledges that zigzag down the sheer face. This was the way down.

I got a firm grip on the rock, then tentatively stretched my leg down as far as it would reach, and hooked my foot on a rung. I reached out my hand and grabbed the closest rung. A foot, a hand, reaching, feeling my way down rungs and ledges until I was vertical with the cliff face.

Hyssop and other small plants cling in crevices. Flowering vines depend from the rock walls like hanging gardens. I saw them all up close, then turned to look out over the Arbel Valley and Lake Kinneret spread out below, nothing but air beneath my feet. Doing my high wire act, I was exhilarated by wind.

The thrill is less than fifty feet, however, and soon I was on terra firma, a long sloping hillside that ends its slide at the bottom of the Arbel Valley. Near where the sheer wall meets the gentler slope, a number of caves cluster. When the Jews were fighting Roman rule in the first century, rebels from Tiberias hid in the Arbel caves. The rebels figured the caves would be easily defended, but Roman forces lowered soldiers on ropes from the clifftop. When they reached the caves, the soldiers fired burning arrows inside, smoking the rebels out.

The trail switchbacks through sloping meadows colored blue with lupine in spring, ending at Wadi Hammam, an Arab village that lies near the modern community of Migdal. Closer to the shores of Lake Kinneret lay the ancient town of Migdal (Magdala), the home of Mary Magdalene and a center of shipbuilders. Some years ago, archaeologists recovered a boat in Lake Kinneret dating to the time of Jesus.

The Arbel Valley ends at one of the three great tectonic depressions that lie along Israel's Great Rift Valley. The Dead Sea and the remnants of Hulah Lake are two. The third is Israel's greatest single freshwater reservoir: Lake Kinneret, the Sea of Galilee.

Descriptions of Kinneret stretch back in time to Christian pilgrims visiting in the fourth century. One of the most famous early accounts was written in the twelfth century by a visiting European Jew. Between 1165 and 1173, Benjamin of Tudela traveled from his home in Spain, documenting places where he found his coreligionists. In his journal, he described Kinneret thus:

> The Jordan at this place flows through a valley between two mountains, and fills the lake, which is called the Lake of Chinnereth; this is a large and broad piece of water like the sea. The Jordan flows between two mountains, and over the plain which is the place that is called Ashdoth Hapisgah, and thence continues its course till it falls into the Sea of Sodom, which is the Salt Sea.

As Benjamin of Tudela described, the lake is bounded by the hills of southern Galilee on the east. On the west, the great plateau of the Golan looks down on the lake. Rushing between thickets of willows, the Jordan River spills into Lake Kinneret from the north. On the lake's southern shores, the Jordan continues, cleaving a path southward along the Great Rift to the Dead Sea.

In between, waters gather in the huge, harp-shaped bowl of blue called Kinneret. Thirteen miles long and about five wide, the lake provides one-third of Israel's water. Although it seems open and airy compared to the walled waters of the Dead Sea, Kinneret lies nearly seven hundred feet below sea level.

In addition to centuries of Jewish and Arab history, the lake and the area around it are full of early Christian history. With a few loaves and fishes, Jesus is said to have miraculously fed thousands by the shore. He was baptized by John the Baptist in the Jordan River south of Kinneret. Saint Peter's fish, which inhabits Lake Kinneret, is named for the disciple who made his livelihood fishing the lake waters.

At Tiberias, the awning-covered promenade that hugs Lake Kinneret is lined with restaurants, each boasting that it grills the best Saint Peter's fish, a fish from the Tilapia genus whose ancestors originated

From a Crusader-era fortress at Tiberias, Lake Kinneret presents one of many moods. Kinneret, which lies nearly seven hundred feet below sea level, is Israel's largest lake by far.

in Africa. Saint Peter's fish is one of the cichlids, a family of fish that seems to adapt to any circumstance, fill every available niche in freshwater ecosystems all over the world. Bottom-feeders? Some cichlids are designed to do it. There's a cichlid specialized for algae grazing. Mollusks? Small fish? Each has cichlids as predators.

171

Sitting at a lakeside table in Tiberias, I ordered Saint Peter's fish, accompanied by French fries and the ubiquitous bowl of olives. My main reason for stopping was to enjoy the view of the lake, so I picked at my food much as one would nurse a drink, just to keep the waiter at bay. I needn't have bothered. It was that time in the afternoon when people return to their homes and hotels to prepare themselves for dinner and the evening. Besides me, only a couple caught up in their romance sat under the canopy of the restaurant.

So I sat undisturbed, watching gulls and terns wheel over the water. Grebes dove for fish near shallow margins. Kingfishers, too, flitted past. The air was soft, subduing sound. It was one of those afternoons so relaxed that everything seems to happen in a muzzy haze.

The waters of Lake Kinneret lay calm and milky green. But, like most bodies of water, the Kinneret has a chameleon face. Some mornings the sun rises behind a cloud of mist, washing Lake Kinneret in golden light. One afternoon the water glows a dull pewter to match the sky. Another day, it is teal blue chopped with white-foamed rollers.

Many fish that ply the waters of Kinneret have historic names. *Tristramella sacra* and *Tristramella simonis* both carry the genus name of their discoverer, Henry Baker Tristram, the nineteenth-century clergy-naturalist. *Haplochronis josepii flavii* is named for Josephus, the first-century Jewish historian. Catfish, whose Hebrew name means "mustache fish," from its long barbels, is another Kinneret native. Fishermen also catch carp and mullet in Kinneret, but they are later, human additions.

Circling the lake, on the lookout for food, are water birds of all sorts. Mammals, too, are drawn to the water, some to fish, some to hunt small animals that hunt fish.

Once, rounding the northern shores of Kinneret near the Bet Tseda Reserve, I saw a long tube of dark brown fur slinking through reeds toward the shoreline. It was hard to say: mongoose? otter? I had seen plenty of mongooses, but never any of Israel's otters, a less numerous species. So I thought, with as much hope as truth, "must be an otter."

And as much truth as hope, since otters are most numerous where the streams of the Golan pour into the northeast arc of Lake Kinneret. Sleek water lovers, otters thrive on fish but also eat freshwater crabs and small mammals. And, oh, they can play. Otters spend hours performing aqueous acrobatics, sliding down muddy banks after each other in exuberant games of tag, or simply floating on their backs in a stream. But as wetlands were drained and increased development polluted streams, Israel's otter population has plummeted.

If the otter is at the southern end of its range along the Jordan River, the Egyptian mongoose is at its extreme northeastern limit. Tamed in Egypt more than five thousand years ago, *Herpestes ichneumon*, which means "creeping tracker," was and still is valued as an expert in rodent and snake control. It is an efficient killer, plus it has particular chemical receptors in its muscles that neutralize snake toxin. But if bitten enough times, even the mongoose loses the ability to ward off the effects of snake toxins.

Although its numbers are protected in Israel, the mongoose is not hard to see. It lives near fresh water—the Jordan, Kinneret, fish ponds—and it's not fussy about its food. Mongooses will eat just about anything small enough to catch. Mongooses also are adaptable and can be seen night or day. Since the eastern side of Lake

Kinneret is by far the more natural, less urban side, the three-foot animal I saw could have been either mongoose or otter.

It is not surprising that species from north and south meet here. The edges of Kinneret have always been fruitful. Josephus wrote:

> Alongside Lake Gennesaret [Kinneret] is a stretch of country with the same name, wonderful in its characteristics and in its beauty. Thanks to the rich soil there is not a plant that does not flourish there, and the inhabitants grow everything: the air is so temperate that it suits the most diverse species. Walnuts, most winter-loving of trees, flourish in abundance, as do palms, which thrive on heat, side by side with figs and olives, for which a milder air is indicated. . . . Those royal fruits the grape and the fig it furnishes for ten months on end.

Centuries later, in the 1860s, Mark Twain had a much different reaction to the lands around the lake. Twain was one of many Americans and Europeans who popularized travel to the Holy Land in the nineteenth century, but he was not enchanted with the place. After years of childhood Bible stories, he expected Lake Kinneret to be as broad and imposing as an ocean. Another example of Israel the Imagined.

In no uncertain terms, Twain blasted Kinneret, its shores, and surroundings as desolate and desiccated. In *Innocents Abroad* he contrasts his bleak examination of Lake Kinneret, worn out by three thousand years of constant use, with what amounts to an ode to the beauty and purity of northern California's Lake Tahoe.

173

Twain would be sorely surprised if he could visit each today. Centuries of war and occupation, most recently by the Ottoman Turks, had exhausted both land and people around Kinneret. But the landscape has been revived in recent decades. Lake Kinneret is now ringed by flower-edged beaches, nature reserves, and kibbutzim that have enhanced seaside beauty by planting oleander, palms, lantana, and ornamental banana.

Conversely, Lake Tahoe no longer lies pristine. Since Twain's time, Tahoe has seen its northern and western shores cluttered with shops, marinas, homes, and car-clogged intersections within sight of the water.

Nothing remains static. Every day, one mountain erodes a little more as another is being built. The Atlantic Ocean and the Syrian-African Rift widen, if imperceptibly. And Australia moves a hairbreadth closer to collision with Southeast Asia millions of years from now, on the way to making mountains that will dwarf the Himalayas.

Except for earthquakes and other cataclysms, we cannot see the shifts that occur naturally over the vast sweep of time. What we can more easily see are the changes we humans effect, sometimes in less than a lifetime.

A Middle East Tale

Kibbutz Ma'agan, at the southern end of Lake Kinneret, has been transforming itself to attract vacationers. The plain-faced agricultural kibbutz has added a holiday village overlooking the lake where pleasant bungalows are grouped in arcs, like raised eyebrows, above a lovely face of manicured lawns. Terraces and winding walks are edged with blue sea lavender and splashes of hot pink flowers.

Yet, the natural weaves itself into this planned beauty. My husband, Michael, had joined me late in my rambles around Israel and, one morning, as we walked toward the beach at Ma'agan, we saw a pair of hoopoes who had made Ma'agan's neat lawns their hunting grounds. With long sturdy beaks protruding in front and combs protruding in back, hoopoes have heads that look something like pick-axes, pointed in both directions.

174 Michael laughed at my efforts to sneak up on the nearer of the two birds. I took a few steps, then stopped, pretending to be a post, a tree, something nonthreatening. Then I took a few steps more, just to see how close I could get. Just close enough to flush it into flight, its drab tan body suddenly awhirl with bands of black and white, as wings and comb flashed into action. Rather childish, but provoking this glorious explosion had been my goal all along.

Toward evening we walked to another part of the shoreline, at the edge of the kibbutz. Just beyond we noticed a tiny bay faced by a clay bank. The clay bank was riddled with round holes. On the tamarisk trees that screened the bank sat a dozen or so black-and-white pied kingfishers. The holes were nests they had dug, some three-feet deep, all with "nurseries" at the back.

From time to time, one pied kingfisher would rise up, shrill its piercing cry, and dart over the water, a fury of wings. When prey appeared near the water's surface, the kingfisher would hover on beating wings, its face bent toward the target below. Then, the little bullet of a bird would hit the water and snatch the morsel in its thick bill. Or, just as often, the kingfisher would miss, circle around, and try again.

From Kibbutz Ma'agan, at the southern edge of Lake Kinneret, the tableland of the Golan Heights glows golden near sunset. The Golan edges the eastern shores of the lake.

We watched until the setting sun backlit the massive bulk and peaks of Mount Meron. A crown of flickering lights marked one peak as Safed, the highest city in Israel. Some call it the closest to heaven. I was reminded of a tale about Lake Kinneret and Middle East angst told to me by a friend who lives in Safed. She and I were sitting in Safed's kosher Chinese restaurant when she shared the following story:

175

Once a scorpion, who wanted to cross Kinneret, saw a fox nearby on the bank, ready to swim into the lake. The scorpion pleaded, "Oh, fox, please take me with you. I will ride on your back and be no trouble at all."

"Do you think I'm crazy?" asked the fox. "You are one of the deadliest of animals. Why would I risk my life?"

"What risk?" replied the scorpion. "Why would I sting you? I would only endanger myself. I have no desire to drown."

This made sense to the fox, so he agreed, and the two set out, the scorpion riding safely on the fox's back. Suddenly, when they were about halfway across, the scorpion lashed its tail and stung the fox on the back.

"Ayyy," cried the fox, "Why did you sting me? Now we will both die."

"Nu," shrugged the scorpion as they began sinking. "It's the Middle East."

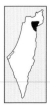

CHAPTER EIGHT

Golan Heights and Mount Hermon:

Roaming the "Wild East"

Gamla Falls

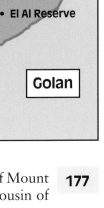

Mount Hermon •

Odem Forest •

Mount Avital •

• Meshushim Pool

• Qatsrin

Gamla Falls •

• Yehudyah

Gamla •

• El Al Reserve

Golan

THE GOLAN HEIGHTS LOOM DI-RECTLY ABOVE Lake Kinneret and the Hulah Valley, massive but not particularly mountainous. In the American Southwest, the broad plateau of land would be called a mesa, a table. In the Bible, the Golan also is referred to as "the Tableland" (Deuteronomy 3:10).

High and wide—Big Sky country—the Golan is Israel's version of the Wild West, except it is east and much smaller. At its western feet lie the Jordan River and the Great Rift. On the Golan grasses sweep across plains to the horizon. Deep canyons score the plain, one after another, their streams racing down to Lake Kinneret. The soaring, massive peaks of Mount Hermon fill the northern sky. Yes, the Golan looks like a cousin of Wyoming, somewhere near the Grand Tetons.

But the Golan is a place apart. It has always been that way, claimed as the outer boundaries first by one group, then another. The name Golan first appears in Deuteronomy (4:43) as the city in Bashan chosen as one of Israel's cities of refuge, places of sanctuary for those who have killed people accidentally. Both the word *golan* and the Hebrew for Diaspora, *Golah*, come from the verb "to exile."

If living in the Golan is exile, it is exile to a high and wild Eden, a place of vast, open meadows fluttering with wildflowers. The streams that carved the canyons tumble over rocky shelves, cascading with Israel's highest waterfalls, pooling in quiet rock-rimmed basins ringed by pink-blossomed oleander. On the plains above, cattle graze against an arching sky.

Except for the slopes of Mount Meron, the Golan is the only truly wild area left in northern Israel. Wolves roam hills and canyons, colonies of huge griffon vultures nest on cliffs, and gazelle leap away at the sight of hikers. Many other animals have homes here as well:

otter, badger, wild boar, marten, jackal, and all sorts of rodents. Fish swim the Golan's numerous streams. Stately oaks dot the plain, and undulating grasses woven with wildflowers cover much of the rest.

Although it has always been far beyond urban centers, over the centuries even the Golan has changed. Isaiah would not recognize it. In biblical times, the plateau known as Bashan was famous for its oaks; forests thick and broad with oak and pistacia covered much of the Golan. Isaiah (2:12) proclaims:

> For the Lord of Hosts has ready a day
> Against all that is proud and arrogant,
> Against all that is lofty—so that it is brought low:
> Against all the cedars of Lebanon,
> Tall and stately,
> And all the oaks of Bashan.

Later, Isaiah allegorically predicted the lofty trees' demise, saying Bashan had been stripped bare (33:9). Perhaps he could see through the centuries because Bashan literally was stripped bare. The Golan's trees had been logged since biblical times, and agriculture and grazing took their toll. But the end came in the 1880s when Ottoman Turks brought in Circassians from the Caucasus Mountains, just northeast of present-day Turkey, to settle in the Golan. The Circassians stripped what remained of the Golan's trees. Until then, nearly 20 percent of the Golan was covered with trees. Now a mere 3 percent is forested.

Ya'ar Odem Reserve, the only forest of any size in the Golan, lies in the northern third, which is bathed by about twice as much precipitation, including snow, as the southern edge. There is a reason.

A few main roads meander over the Golan. I've taken them all and noticed that the vegetation becomes sparse and the trees fewer as I headed south. It was only when I read statistics on the Golan that I realized the Golan slopes from nearly four thousand feet high in the north, near Mount Hermon, to about one thousand feet in the south. South and lower equals hotter and drier.

Nahal Sa'ar forms the northern boundary of the Golan, dividing it from Mount Hermon, the enormous massif that rises on the north side of the river. The Golan's southern boundary is the deep valley of the Yarmuk River, which separates Israel from Jordan. (Farther east, the Yarmuk River also forms the border between Syria and Jordan.) Between the Sa'ar in the north and the Yarmuk in the south, the Golan stretches about thirty-six miles long.

On the west side of the Golan, cliffs plunge down to Lake Kinneret and the Great Rift. On the east is Syria. The eastern border is purely military and has nothing to do with topography because the Golan plateau splays across part of southwestern Syria. Damascus, the capital of Syria, is only thirty miles or so northeast of the Golan.

The Golan has always been a land of shifting boundaries. Two thousand years ago, King Herod moved Jews onto the Golan to extend Israel's boundaries. The Turks imported Circassians at the end of the nineteenth century for the same reason. The present border, set after Israel won the Golan during the Six-Day War of 1967, makes Israel's portion of the plateau approximately twelve miles wide.

Some thirty-five kibbutzim and moshavim are scattered across the Golan. Qatsrin, the Golan's only sizable town, lies in the middle, overlooking the Hulah Valley and the north end of Lake Kinneret. And, with the Syrian border so close, military presence is ubiquitous.

The first time I drove onto the Golan I took Route 87, which veers northeast from the shores of Lake Kinneret, winding upward, paralleling Nahal Yehudyah, one of the major river canyons on the Golan. On my way up, I passed a hyrax sitting, unconcerned, at the side of the road. These bundles of brown fur dwell among rocky areas, and are conspicuous in inverse proportion to human bustle—a good sign.

I finally crested onto the plateau and felt completely at home. I knew why immediately.

179

I grew up on the eastern prairies of the American Midwest and spent years living at the western edge of the prairies, in Colorado. I've traveled the broad plains between Colorado and Illinois countless times.

To me, the Golan with its rolling sweep of grasses and broad, horizontal views looks like home. It is the sort of place where a person can take a deep breath and stand still for a while, allowing the sense of space to wash over and cleanse tension away. Ironic, considering how close the Syrian border is.

Mirroring the Rocky Mountains in my mind's eye, Mount Hermon and other peaks of the Anti-Lebanon Range march in a line toward the northeast, diminishing toward the horizon like a study in perspective. One big difference between the plains of the Midwest and the plains of the Middle East is the cone-shaped hills that cluster here and there on the Golan, reminding me of gumdrop hills on a child's Candy Land game. I would learn about those later.

El Al and Signs of Vulcanism

At the southern edge of the Golan—actually at its feet—lies Hammat Gader, the hot springs of Gader. While people are fastening coats against snow an hour's drive to the north, bathers submerged in the hot baths are oblivious to weather.

Hammat Gader, which lies alongside the Yarmuk River, is a spa whose history dates from the third century. Roman ruins and the remains of a fourth-century synagogue attest to its long use. Its *raison d'être* are its hot springs. Like those at Hammat Tiberias, the hot springs that fill Hammat Gader's pools are heated when underground streams pass near hot magmatic rock deep within the earth. These pools are not the only indication of great geologic forces on the Golan.

Today Hammat Gader is lush with palms, shrubs, and lawns. Paths connect the bathhouse, steamy mineral pools, a freshwater pool, imposing Roman ruins, and ancient mosaics. The resort even has an alligator farm where visitors can watch the great reptiles sun beside a pool.

From Hammat Gader, narrow Route 98 coils around cliffs hung with capers and other dryland plants as it switchbacks up to the Golan. Although it is a road that requires one's full attention, while twisting through the hairpin curves I caught quick glimpses of hyraxes scampering on roadside rocks.

180

Hyraxes live on the Golan and on the lower slopes of Mount Hermon, but no farther. Mount Hermon is the northern limit of their range. Elephants, hyraxes' closest relatives, once lived this far north as well, and remains of a prehistoric elephant are displayed in the Golan Archaeological Museum at Qatsrin. Hippopotamus fossils, too, have been found in the area.

On the Golan proper, El Al Reserve's stream-cut canyon reveals a tale of geologic extremes. Below, near the streambed, white walls tell where limestone was laid down in ancient seas that retreated eons ago.

More recently, lava solidified as dark basalt atop the white limestone. Black and white, fire and water. This light-and-dark layering is visible in canyons throughout the Golan. Even more dramatic examples are the light and dark waterfalls within the reserve, one tumbling over limestone ledges, the other over basalt.

El Al Reserve's artistic study in black and white hints at the fiery birth of the Golan. This tableland was created by rivers of molten rock. Thick and black, pushed up from pockets in the Earth's crust, blistering rivers of lava built the heights of the Golan.

Layer upon layer of lava spouted from volcanoes and oozed slowly over the land like honey. The lava layers cooled, creating an enormous rampart of dense, black volcanic rock overlooking the Great Rift Valley.

The Earth's crust is a puzzle of gigantic plates of land twenty miles thick that ride atop Earth's two-thousand-mile-thick molten mantle. Where tectonic plates collide or rip apart, cracks form in the crust and magma thrusts upward. Magma, or molten rock, can gush from volcanoes at temperatures as much as two thousand degrees Fahrenheit. As it cools, it hardens as basalt, the rock that forms the platform of the Golan.

Most of the Golan's eruptions are associated with the enormous faulting that occurred along the Great Rift during the Pliocene epoch about five million years ago. That ripping and cracking of the Earth's crust was one of the latest of the Great Rift's great upheavals. The last lava surged over the Golan only some thousands of years ago—practically yesterday considering that dinosaurs became extinct sixty-five million years ago and Earth's oldest exposed rock is more than three billion years old.

The gumdrop hills that dot the flat surface of the Golan? Dormant volcanoes. Spring-green when I first saw them and rounded by age, Mount Peres, Mount Avital, Mount Bental, and other inactive volcanoes rise near the border with Syria. Altogether about a hundred cones lie on the Israeli side of the Golan.

181

Most of Israel is built of limestone, chalk, and other sedimentary rock. Except for the Negev's Eilat Mountains, the Golan is the only part of Israel composed predominantly of volcanic rock. Once the groundwork was laid on the Golan, thick forests grew on the dark, mineral-rich volcanic soils, forests that are no more.

Wildflowers of Daliyot

Fed by springs and meltwater on Mount Hermon, all Golan streams empty into Lake Kinneret or the Jordan River. The central Golan, in particular, is heavily veined with rivers, most of them flowing into the northeast arc of Kinneret. The two biggest river systems are the Zavitan and the Yehudyah, which are protected in the Zavitan Reserve and the Yehudyah Reserve, respectively.

Of all the reserves in the Golan, at one hundred sixty-five thousand acres Yehudyah is the largest and most spectacular. Forests, streams, and canyons reach across its breadth; raptors fill the sky;

At Yehudyah Reserve, bold lupine blooms and their palmate leaves anchor a riot of meadow wildflowers. Nearby stand "dolmens," massive, prehistoric stone grave markers similar to structures at Stonehenge.

forty-two bird species nest here; and, on a modest hill, lie the remains of Gamla, some of the most poignant ruins in Israel, a nation full of poignant ruins.

My first trip to Yehudyah Reserve, along with a dozen or so other hikers, was with Society for Protection of Nature in Israel. Just after our bus turned onto the reserve road, we saw, squatting alongside the road, our first dolmen, one of more than two hundred within Yehudyah. Dolmen is an old Celtic word meaning "stone table," and the dolmen near the road was exactly that: two massive upright stones capped by an even more massive stone.

Shorter, but similar to structures at Stonehenge, these dolmens are grave markers. Dr. Claire Epstein, who won the Israel Prize for her archaeological work at Yehudyah, found forty-two-hundred-year-old skeletons from the Bronze Age, plus jewelry and pots, buried under dolmens here.

182

It was spring and the flowers blooming atop the Golan were at their peak. The somber gray stone of dolmens and more haphazard rocks were brightened by masses of yellow daisies nodding in the winds that sweep the Golan. Those of us with cameras ran across the meadows from one bunch of wildflowers to another: sheets of yellow chrysanthemums were splashed with red poppies, blue lupine, hairy pink flax, and dozens of others.

Panoramas, closeups, artful compositions—we took frame upon frame of photos of the remarkable variety and sheer numbers as if the flowers were a first child. My actual children, upon seeing the plethora of photos months later, said, "Mom, we think we got the idea on this blue flower. Why'd you need all these other shots?"

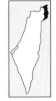

Full of earnest concern that they see the subtleties of something they had not a whit of interest in, I replied, "Well, here's a close-up so you can see the lupine's petal structure. This composition with the pink flax was just too perfect. And see how that poppy peeks through? This one—look how this enormous swath of yellow surrounds this one patch of lupine." They gave each other looks.

At some point in the photo shoot, our tour guide rounded us up and got us pointed on the trail. Yehudyah trails lead to Gamla, Gamla Waterfalls, the Raptor Overlook, and Daliyot Waterfalls, our destination that day. The trail to Daliyot begins on the mesa, tracing a line along the edge of canyon cliffs.

Like the road, the trail was framed by flowers. Almost immediately, we came upon a plant I had never seen before but had heard about in school when I had to memorize the three types of columns used by ancient Greeks. Acanthus, or bear's-breeches, whose leaves and dusky purple flowers march in fat ranks up a sturdy stalk, looks architectural and sophisticated, a perfect example of order in the universe. The Greeks thought so, too. They were impressed enough with the plant's design that they carved the capitals of Corinthian columns with acanthus leaves.

Far below us, seeming too small to have cut this large wedge of canyon, the Daliyot River ran narrowly between the thick fringe of green alongside the water. More visible was the line between igneous and sedimentary rock. As at El Al Reserve, a thick crust of dark basalt lies above a sheet of white marl.

The Daliyot River, which marks the southern boundary of the Yehudyah Reserve, flows from springs that rise around Mount Peres. Peres is the Hebrew name for the bearded vulture, which once lived among mountains ringing the Mediterranean and is endangered throughout its range due to hunting and habitat destruction. Bearded vultures were last seen in Israel during the 1980s, but wildlife experts are working to reintroduce the rare raptor. Although the bearded vulture does not live here, other raptors do. Black-and-white Egyptian vultures circled above us; in the canyon below, the huge wings of a circling griffon vulture seemed to scrape the slope.

183

We passed the ruins of a Chalcolithic structure, so old that its use is unknown. Across the canyon, almond trees gave themselves away, their pale blossoms glowing against the sloping canyon walls.

Another find among masses of flowers lining the trail: the big thistle with the brown-and-yellow flower head, called *galgal* in Hebrew, meaning "wheel," because the large, spherical flower heads break off and spread seed by rolling along the ground. Growing most everywhere north of the Negev, the tumble thistle was a biblical symbol for those whose lives were wind tossed: ". . . make them like thistledown, like stubble driven by the wind" (Psalms 83:14).

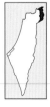

In the third century, they were mentioned in Jewish writings as a common wild food. In subsequent centuries, monks of the Judean

Where the *galgal* thistle depends on the wind to help spread its seed, another thistle has developed an intricate relationship with harvester ants. If bees are important for pollinating plants, ants are important for dispersing plant seeds.

Botanist Avinoam Danin found that milky thistles grow especially large and in dense clumps near harvester ant nests. The reason, he discovered, is that ants find milky thistle seeds and carry them to their nests. After eating the oil-rich seed coating, the ants remove the seeds from their nests and deposit them in the colony's refuse "dump." The refuse dump—full of castoff plant parts, remnants of dead ants, and other organic waste—is the perfect place to plant a thistle. In this nutrient-rich garden plot, thistle seeds sprout and flourish. Such examples of natural gardening also are found wherever hyrax deposit plant material or where herbivores such as gazelle leave droppings.

Desert subsisted on diets of wild foods such as saltbush and thistles, including tumble thistle. Young thistle leaves were used as salad greens. Thistle stalks were peeled and eaten raw or cooked. Thistle roots also found their way into meals.

Israel is full of thistles, and they are well represented on the Golan. Some thistle flowers are small and spiky; some look like old-fashioned shaving brushes. Some are blue, most are purple-pink.

As we began our descent into Nahal Daliyot, we found gazelle tracks. Because of its low people population, the Golan has a relatively high animal population. Gazelle and ibex were reintroduced and now gazelle are plentiful, perhaps too plentiful. This overpopulation has attracted canids such as wolves and jackals. When canid populations occasionally become overloaded, outbreaks of rabies can occur—a natural brake to soaring numbers.

Herbs attract herbivores. Herbivores attract carnivores. The food chain includes all its links but depends on one resource: water. Unlike streambeds in warmer areas, those in the Golan flow most of the year. Much of the water comes from Mount Hermon, whose limestone bulk absorbs water like a giant sponge. The absorbed water finds its way to underground streams, which bubble up as springs near the base of Mount Hermon.

Because rain drains from the plateaus into the canyons, the tops of the plateaus are somewhat dry. Grasses and wildflowers prevail with occasional Tabor oaks anchoring the flat expanses.

As we zigzagged into the canyon, flowers continued to crowd the trail, but the species changed to those that prefer rocky slopes. Sedum and cyclamen clung to rocks. Mallow unfolded delicate pink trumpets in soil-filled pockets between boulders. Blue bugloss sinuated itself into crevices. So did reptiles. Half of Israel's reptile species, including one poisonous snake, the Palestine viper, live on the Golan.

The farther we descended, the higher the temperature and humidity rose. The rock walls both hold and reflect heat and the stream leaks moisture into the air. It felt a little like descending into a greenhouse, although in spring's mild weather it was pleasant. Later, in summer, hiking into these hothouse canyons is made tolerable by two things: occasional dips in cool natural pools and magnificent rose-pink oleander blooms that edge the streams.

Down near Nahal Daliyot, willows and feathery tamarisk pressed against us as the trail became a jungle walk alongside the stream. Berry brambles, reeds, and ferns hug most of the streams in the Golan. The vegetable air had settled, close and moist, over the trail until we reached the stream crossing, where the bubbling water washed the steamy air. Above us slid the demure aqueous veil of Daliyot Falls.

Vulture Face-Off at Gamla   185

I had visited Gamla before and had been so moved by the place that when Michael arrived, late in my travels, I decided he must see Gamla as well. We bought cold drinks at the snack bar next to Yehudyah Reserve's visitor station. The rains had stopped, the day was hot, and we sat in the shade drinking before setting out.

It is only a short walk from the visitor station to the Raptor Overlook, a point of land overlooking the Gamla River canyon. We had come to see griffon vultures and any other raptors that might be about. In the 1860s, cataloguing animals farther west in Israel, Henry Baker Tristram observed that the skies, north to south, east to west, were rarely void of griffon vultures. He once saw a group of five hundred near Ginnosar, site of an ancient community and a modern kibbutz at Lake Kinneret.

Now the only place to see large numbers of griffon vultures is on the Golan, where they nest in gregarious communities along cliff ledges. Even on the relatively remote Golan, the population of several hundred griffon vultures is at risk: from pesticides, Army exercises, and

SPNI

Griffon vulture

hiker disturbances, even from accidental electrocution caused by flying into power lines.

Michael and I walked out to the overlook past lavender Maltese cross growing between blocks of basalt covered with brightly colored lichen. The wind was up, and clouds chased each other across a brilliant blue sky. Yet Yehudyah Reserve was nearly empty. The only sound was that of our voices, bled over the meadows by the wind. Laconic we are not.

Globe thistles clustered along the path. Each spiked ball of a flower would soon turn steel blue. I explained to Michael that, in Hebrew, globe thistles are called *kipodan*, after the hedgehog (*kipod*), who rolls up when threatened to become a similarly spiky ball. Michael and I have a time-sharing arrangement on our conversations: he listens to my raptures and rants on natural history, and I listen to the latest on his biochemical discoveries.

Nearing the observation point, which juts like a parapet over the canyon, we fell silent. At the edge of the overlook I touched Michael's elbow so he would turn to see the two griffon vultures silently gliding past. Although they were just seven or eight feet away at eye level, we heard only a whisper of their nine-foot wingspan, the ends of the wings upturned like the fingers of a Hindu dancer.

As we watched, one turned its head toward us. The vulture was so close we could plainly see its bare head and neck stretching from a collar like an ermine ruff above a brown robe of feathers. It looked at us for a moment, then away, searching the canyon floor, and I sensed the stirrings of its ancient simple predatory brain.

187

Fascinated, we stood watching in silence for a long time as griffon vultures singly and in pairs soared past, eyes focused on the ground seeking prey far below. They circled over the canyon, five minutes, ten, then landed on a ledge deep within the canyon's mouth. These magnificent birds reign in the canyons of Yehudyah and were the great birds celebrated in the Bible.

Nearing the end of his long life, Moses sang to the Hebrews a song of God's greatness as a caring parent:

> Like an eagle who rouses his nestlings
> Gliding down to his young
> So did he spread his wings and take him
> Bear him along on his pinions.
> (DEUTERONOMY 32:11)

An incredibly compassionate and tender image, but not of an eagle. The Hebrew word is *nesher*, "vulture."

English translations always switch *nesher* to "eagle," as though speaking of God as a vulture were a public relations faux pas. In English, vultures have a bad image, gathering in evil groups to scavenge dead carcasses. Although most eagles scavenge dead carcasses, too, they get better press.

It is true that many vultures have bare heads in order to keep themselves clean after ripping into a carcass, but priggish associations too quickly dismiss this regal bird. The griffon vulture is a caring parent. Its large nest, which rests on a cliff ledge secure from jackals and other prey, can take two months to build. Griffon vultures usually produce only one chick, and both parents spend nearly a year raising it.

Other raptors nest on Yehudyah's cliffs: Egyptian vultures, Bonelli's eagles, and kestrels among them. But the griffon vulture is the largest and requires large prey: gazelle, goat, mammals of that size. As available prey decreased over the years due to human development, so did the numbers of vultures.

Griffon vultures specialize in ripping open large carcasses with curved beaks as thick as metal meat hooks. About two-thirds the size, Egyptian vultures are designed for a different purpose. Using their long, slender beaks, they will clean up the bits griffon vultures have left: eyes, tongues, and flesh between the bones. Egyptian vultures also pick up eggs—pelican eggs, even griffon vulture eggs—and drop them on rocks to get at the nutrition inside. They will eat reptiles, mole rats, and other small prey. For most species on the planet, fastidious eating is a luxury.

We watched as Egyptian vultures soared past the overlook, flashing elegant black-and-white plumage and fully feathered heads. The white feathers on their heads often stand erect, as if the birds had just been roused from sleep. We roused ourselves and descended from this aerie, spooking some gazelle in high grass, proceeding toward the trail that leads to the ruins of Gamla.

Gamla is well named. Meaning "camel," it refers to that animal's most prominent feature, its hump. Lying between the Daliyot and Gamla Canyons, Gamla is a lean hump of land surrounded by sheer dropoffs except where it is connected to the plateau by a narrow saddle. A place made for a siege. That is exactly what happened here nearly two thousand years ago in the Jewish war against Roman occupation.

Gamla was the central city of the Golan in the first century,

188

surrounded by farms and orchards. A wall had been built around the city when tensions with the Romans became ominous, and behind the wall rose a citadel. An exquisite synagogue stood just within the main gates, the oldest synagogue known in Israel. Homes lined the hilly lanes, some of them built with mikvahs (ritual baths)—clearly homes of the wealthy. Olive presses provided residents with oil for cooking and light.

Tensions erupted, and, finally, the Jewish rebellion broke out in northern Israel. Beginning in 66 C.E., rebels and townspeople held off Roman legions for seven months at Gamla. The Romans finally breached the walls, and the slaughter was calamitous.

Gamla, within Yehudyah Reserve, is so named because the hill is shaped like a camel's hump. Atop the hill are the ruins of a Jewish town, destroyed in 67 C.E. when Roman legions massacred thousands of its residents.

Josephus, a Jewish general eventually captured by the Romans, chronicled the war and, in doing so, provided a compelling written record of that time and place. In *The Jewish War*, he wrote:

> In a moment, news of the Roman entry reached the centre of the town. Some snatched their children and, dragging their wives with them, fled to the citadel, wailing and shouting; others went to meet Titus and were without exception killed. Many were prevented from running up to the heights, and in their helplessness fell into the hands of the Roman guards. There were heart-rending cries as men were slaughtered on every side, and the whole town was deluged with the blood that poured down the slopes.

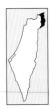

By Josephus' count, the Romans felled four thousand Jews, but an even greater number—five thousand men, women, and children—threw themselves off the cliffs, plunging to their deaths in the deep ravines below.

As we made our way down the rocky path to Gamla, we saw four gazelle in the distance and, closer, heard the fumbling grunting of a wild boar. Then we crossed the slim bridge of land to the ruined town. We were struck by the stark contrast between past and present, between blood-soaked battles two millennia ago and gentle gazelle today.

The view from the camel's hump is dramatic. Far below, the Gamla River Gorge angles in from one side and the Daliyot River Gorge from the other. Looking toward Lake Kinneret, the hump of Gamla rises sheer and edgy, like a colossal arrowhead between the gorges.

Past the ruined gate of the city, the remnants of the synagogue stand: here stone benches, there the stubs of columns. The citadel stood on the highest point.

An upper street reveals homes of the wealthy with their ritual baths and oil presses built of the dark basalt that underlies the Golan. Wildflowers twine through broken walls and around black lintels of the barely excavated ruins. The only sound is the soughing of the wind.

On one side of the bluff, where the grade is gentler, narrow streets step down the slope. We picked our way down, level by level, talking about history and the killing fields of today's world.

Gamla, now, is serene. In this peaceful place that, as Josephus said, "hangs in air," it is hard to imagine such carnage and the cries of the dying.

The remains of Gamla feel intimate and immediate, more so than busier, restored sites. Nothing but time lay between us and the people who lost their lives here.

Yehudyah's Goddess Trees

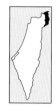

Some days stand out with unusual clarity; everything in sight, from the geometry of a thistle to the pattern of clouds, seems preternaturally illuminated. I had spent time on the Golan before meeting up with Michael, making the SPNI field school my base and exploring a variety of natural areas. The day I set out on the trail to Gamla Falls, north of the Yehudyah Reserve Visitor Center, all my senses were centered on my surroundings. Alone, you not only sense nature more

In general, the highlands of central and northern Israel are dominated by two types of pistacia and three types of oak. In the southern Golan, Tabor oak reigns, its rounded crown dense with small-lobed, pliable leaves. In the northern Golan, where rainfall is greater and summer temperatures milder, calliprinos (kermes) oak prevails. In the central Golan, the two types mix.

Calliprinos oaks are evergreen, retaining their leathery, hollylike leaves all year. Tabor oaks lose theirs, but only for a few months in winter. Then they sprout another set of shiny new leaves.

Another difference between calliprinos and Tabor oaks is that calliprinos like limestone slopes and Tabor prefer chalk and clay soils, which lie closer to sea level than limestone. About two thousand feet lower than the north, the southern Golan is closer to sea level and has a larger share of Tabor oaks.

Much of north and central Israel lies on a limestone base, however, so calliprinos is the most common oak. Its name in Hebrew, *alon matsui*, means just that: "common oak."

Tabor oak was more common in the past than it is now. Once it grew on the Plain of Sharon along the coast, but it was stripped from the plain beginning in the 1800s. The Boissier (Cyprus) oak, the third commonly seen oak, still lives in the north. Two other species of oak—turkey oak and Look oak—are extremely rare and grow only on Mount Hermon.

Besides the Atlantic pistacia, the other pistacia common in Israel's northern highlands, especially in the mountains of Galilee, is the Palestine pistacia. A third type of pistacia, mastic pistacia, is found on lower slopes of northern Israel, where sunny, dry conditions exist.

sharply, but the lack of human conversation allows you to see animals that would flee at the sound of voices.

Immediately, seven gazelle emerged from the tall grass, browsing their way over the hill. Their short tan coats stood out against the green grasses. Later, when summer crisped the grasses golden, the gazelle would be hidden by their color. Behind me, storks, white with black wing tips, probed for food among the grasses of the flat plateau.

Amid the grasses were spaced broad Tabor oaks. Atop each short, thick trunk spread an enormous green canopy—a tree Isaiah could assuredly call "stately." The Tabor oak often lives in association with another imposing tree, the Atlantic pistacia or terebinth. These two giants, the Tabor oak and the Atlantic pistacia, form the climax trees of the southern and central Golan.

When the Hebrews returned from exile in Egypt, they repeatedly were cautioned against worshipping idols. At that time, cults devoted to pagan fertility goddesses were widespread, and, often, the living representation of these goddesses were trees. Tree worship was common. In fact, the Hebrew name for pistacia, *elah*, means goddess. To see the girth of the greatest of the oaks and terebinths is to understand why ancient peoples revered them.

The other conspicuous tree along the trail to Gamla Falls is the jujube. Originating in Africa, the jujube reaches its northernmost range on the Golan and the lower slopes of Mount Hermon. As I walked across the Golan plain, the jujubes I passed were showing their "bones": an intricate structure of dense white thorns that had just begun to sprout young chartreuse leaves.

Not far from a huge, spreading jujube, dark ruins sprouted in the long, quivering grasses. I left the path for a closer look and found black blocks of basalt that formed a square of low walls. But what was left of this structure was shrouded by vegetation.

192

A sudden movement above caught my attention. In the sky, a short-toed eagle hovered, head bent, intent on small prey that I could not see.

I was delighted to be audience to all the dramas on the plain. To me, trees have character. Birds, of course, have character. The eagle that hovered above, angular and intent, is a very different being from, say, a chubby, chatty chukar.

My husband claims—only half-jokingly—that I am an animist, believing that every living thing has a spirit. No, that is not quite right. I grew up in a household where science was god and Mr. Wizard had all the answers. But science can hardly tell us how the universe was created, much less why. This is where science and religion intersect. And, as for goddess trees, I have enjoyed good, if one-sided, conversations with them.

Birds, trees, and dark ruins masked by grasses—I was lost in looking, when a young couple, whose approach I had not heard, made me jump. They were returning from their walk, each carrying a small sleeping child. He wore black slacks and a white shirt, she a long skirt and covered head. Their plain, clean clothes and demure demeanor somehow fit the place. Sensing their religious propriety, I focused a smile toward the woman, who bent her head and flashed a small, brief smile in return. They were the only people I saw on the trail that day.

Birds, however, were plentiful, especially shrikes. Great gray shrikes seemed perched on each thorny jujube. The shrike's pearl-gray head and breast contrasts strikingly with its black wings and tail. Its narrow black mask gives it the appearance of a theatrical bandit. The shrike strikes like a bandit: insects, lizards, small rodents, and birds. Then it stores its catch by impaling it on a jujube thorn, the thorns of other trees, even on barbed-wire fences.

The size of a blackbird, the "great" gray shrike is only ten inches long, but large compared to others in the genus, such as woodchat shrikes. These, too, seemed everywhere in the meadows. Perched on the tops of grasses and thistles, their copper caps gave them away.

Finally, I could hear the sound of the falls. I meant to hike down to the river first and save the falls for last, but the sound was too compelling. I ran along the canyon's edge to an overlook.

Israel's highest perennial waterfall, Gamla Falls plunges nearly one hundred seventy feet to a deep green pool it has cut for itself in the riverbed below. Like a pitcher pouring a stream of bubbling milk, the falls foams white as it drops off the plateau. The walls on either side are interlocking hexagonal pillars of dark basalt, which appear all over the Golan, wherever water has cut through the basalt. They are at their most spectacular at the Hexagonal Pool, a few canyons north of here and a site high on my must-see list.

193

The tumultuous patterns of falling water were hypnotic, and I stood at the falls overlook for a while, absorbed. Then I retraced my steps along the top of the cliff to where a path leads down to the riverbed.

The cliffside trail cuts between rocks patterned with orange, black, and gray lichen. Niches between the rocks are filled with rock-garden wildflowers: red sedum, navelwort, cyclamen's heart-shaped leaves and pink flowers, and hens-and-chickens, whose central rosette had spawned a number of smaller rosettes around its fleshy-leaved skirts.

As I hiked down the narrow, rocky trail, small brown lizards darted into the foliage. Near the riverbed, temperature and humidity rose suddenly, matched by a lavish growth of vegetation: fig trees, reeds, mint, willows, and masses of bluebells.

Parting thick greenery, I rock-hopped upstream along the bank to view the falls from below before turning back, thinking dinner in Qatsrin would cap this perfect day.

Capital of the Golan

Qatsrin is as much the capital of the Golan as Beersheba is of the Negev. Although it is a development town with a high proportion of immigrants, Qatsrin seems a little like a town from a television set, an Israeli version of *Leave It to Beaver* perhaps. Soccer fields and parks ring neat streets lined with palms. Low white homes in orderly rows surround the small central shopping district where the pizza parlor is the place to be on Saturday night.

Kids come in waves: from 7:00 to 7:30 p.m. the booths and tables were crowded with children under ten. During the next half hour, preteens made their way in, tight cliques of girls and loose-knit groups of boys. They reminded me of ibex bands I had seen in the Negev. As groups mingled and shifted in and out, the decibel level rose, and the young waitresses became worn out and damp around the hairline, shouting in food orders and trying to make change.

From about 8:30 on adults filtered in: army recruits on weekend leave, Russian immigrants, and naturalists from SPNI's Golan Field School, where I was spending the night. I was ready to leave but could not get my harried waitress's attention, so I added up the amounts from the menu, figured in tax and tip, and closed in on her. She gave me a desperate, don't-bother-me-now look, but seeing I had what looked like correct change, took it, said thank you, and that was that. In the cool night air and quiet, I made my way back to the field school, feeling unusually tired.

SPNI's Golan Field School lies on the edge of town, a small town within a town. Like other SPNI field schools, it includes offices, a large dining room, and spare but clean rooms for overnight visitors like me. Set into a slope, the stone terraces of the field school provide some of the best views of distant Lake Kinneret.

The next morning I was awakened early by the whine of the wind. I sat atop a stone wall enclosing one of the terraces and looked out toward the lake, wondering what to do with my day. It was one of those uncommon days with nothing particular scheduled.

I decided to take a busman's holiday and find one of the rare patches of Hermon iris. A ranger at Yehudyah Reserve had suggested a particular, out-of-the-way intersection, as most of them are in the

Golan. As I approached, a few soldiers hunched against the chill wind near a lonely bus stop. They heard my car's engine and looked up, hopeful a ride had arrived. I wheeled to the opposite side of the intersection, parked the car, and could see their scowls as they shrugged back down into their jackets.

Where the rough dirt from the intersection met the meadows of the Golan, clumps of Hermon iris bowed under the wind. As big as a baby's head, as one biologist puts it, the irises were a study in purple: ruffled falls freckled midnight purple and pale lavender standards veined with violet. The wind ripped at them, but the irises merely bent a little more, belying their delicate appearance.

Being out on the Golan felt so exhilarating that I pushed on, though shivers coursed through me even as the day warmed. Near a bridge that crossed the narrow beginnings of a canyon, I parked the car and followed a small trail along the rim. My reward was a modest waterfall whose spray was driven my way by the wind.

By the time I returned to the field school, I knew I was sick. I brewed hot water in the coil-heater pot standard in each room. The pot stood on a table along with cups and assorted packets of hot drinks.

Some days earlier, sensing a cold coming on, I had purchased cough drops and a packet of antihistamines in Qiryat Shemonah. Qiryat Shemonah is to the Hulah Valley what Qatsrin is to the Golan. But Qiryat Shemonah has been around long enough to have become a small city with a broad array of amenities, including a large, well-stocked pharmacy.

195

I took the blankets from the four beds that lined the walls of my field school room and piled them on top of me, burrowing in with a Batya Gur mystery, getting up only to pour cup after cup of hot liquid. The sun slanted into my room, and I could hear children playing on the terraces outside. Day eventually faded, and night came on as I used up tissues and drank my way through tea, coffee, and cocoa, feeling lonely and sorry for myself.

Meshushim: the Hexagonal Pool

Two days later, well (and bored), I met Roni, and we pointed the car down Route 888, in the direction of the Hexagonal Pool. We turned onto a dirt track and, for the first couple of miles, drove without incident, paralleling Nahal Meshushim. Soon rocks and deep, water-filled ruts made the route too much of an obstacle course. We parked and went on by foot.

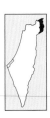

Roni, who has the gamine face and bone structure of a tall Audrey Hepburn, is among the growing number of women trained as SPNI guides. The army saw her test scores and wanted her for intelligence, but Roni managed to hold out for an SPNI assignment, one of the few alternatives an Israeli girl can choose for army duty. A good match with SPNI, Roni has an infectious enthusiasm and an overarching curiosity about nature.

As we trudged down the dirt track in the heat, she waved her arm in the direction of a rusting wreck by the side of the road. "Russian," she said. The vehicle had been used by the Syrians until it was abandoned during the Six-Day War. The Golan is littered with Syrian military remnants: lookout towers, hulls of military vehicles, battlements overlooking Israel's Hulah Valley, and the huge scar of a canal dug to redirect Israel's water sources into Syria.

We passed pink salvia, purple thistles, and blue lupine in full bloom. Roni called me over and we crouched in front of a lupine. The watcher in me stepped back and saw two kids—despite our ages, even the difference in our ages—absorbed in discovery.

I have seen countless lupines in my life, but she pointed out something I had never noticed. The blue flowers at the bottom of the stalk had purple lines running down their centers, while the flowers at the top were striped with white. The white lines, Roni explained, served as bright runways for bees, showing them where to land and guiding them toward pollen and nectar.

196

Bees collect nectar and convert it to honey, which they eat, and pick up protein-rich pollen, which they feed to their larvae. Some of the pollen they carry fertilizes successive flowers the bees visit. Once fertilized, each lupine flower receives a chemical message that causes its bright landing strip to darken so that bees will not waste their time visiting an already-pollinated flower. Very efficient.

As we walked, goldfinches flew between bushes, and a chukar raced down the road ahead of us. We noticed chopped-up dirt next to the road where a small bulldozer seemed to have been at work: wild boars rooting for food. We passed first porcupine scat, then a black-and-white striped quill.

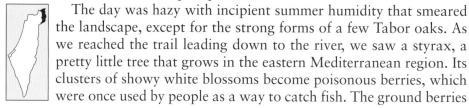

The day was hazy with incipient summer humidity that smeared the landscape, except for the strong forms of a few Tabor oaks. As we reached the trail leading down to the river, we saw a styrax, a pretty little tree that grows in the eastern Mediterranean region. Its clusters of showy white blossoms become poisonous berries, which were once used by people as a way to catch fish. The ground berries

Hexagonal basalt columns that ring the pool in the canyon of Nahal Meshushim are the result of volcanic activity, which has occurred all along the Great Rift.

were cast onto water, and the poison stunned the fish, which then floated to the surface to be scooped up.

197

We turned off the road and started down a rocky slope into the canyon of Nahal Meshushim. Lizards ran across the trail, and hyrax watched cautiously from perches atop rocks. In the shade of a large boulder stood an arum, its spathe and spadix straight as a stick. Surrounded by a sheath of fused leaves called a spathe, the spadix is a fleshy flower spike that pokes above the spathe like someone sticking out a tongue. Although arums are native to Mediterranean countries, they have a North American counterpart: jack-in-the-pulpit.

As we continued downward, we could see the narrow canyon walls of black basalt. The pillars of basalt, with each hexagonal side married to an adjoining pillar, looked like dark, creased curtains above the water. At my feet I noticed pods of storksbill. Israel is home to twenty species of erodium, commonly called storksbill because the pods are long and thin and look just like storks' bills.

The flower provided poor cover for an agama lizard who held still, trying to remain unnoticed. No matter, agama lizards are the fastest, most athletic reptiles in Israel, able to leap more than three

Arums, exotic-looking flowers that live in damp, shady places in central and northern Israel, are deceivers when it comes to reproduction. They give off unpleasant, rotting odors to attract flies looking for a meal. Carrying pollen from another arum, the fly is led into a chamber near the bottom of the plant, where it pollinates tiny female flowers on the rodlike spadix. The fly is then trapped within the arum until the male flowers mature. When the male flowers release pollen, the arum releases the fly, which carries pollen to the next flower. By these tricks, arums are assured of cross-fertilization. Orchids scattered throughout Galilee use similar stratagems.

feet though they are only a few inches long. The second we moved in its direction, the lizard danced away over the rocks.

"It's a male," Roni said, pointing to the lizard's head, a fat blue triangle. During breeding season, the heads of the males turn blue. So, in Israel, a guy with his mind fixed on sex is called, "What else," said Roni, laughing, "a 'blue-head.'"

Stepping over muddy stones, we arrived at an opening shaded by a broad Syrian ash tree. This tree of the Levant is found only in Israel's north, and is rare there. Before us lay the large, quiet Hexagonal Pool whose curving walls are crenelated with hexagonal columns of basalt. Packed together like organ pipes, they are one of the celebrated sights of the Golan, a spectacular example of "hexagonal close-packing."

As we sat at the edge of the pool, Roni explained that, here, magma cooled at optimum conditions, assuming the most dynamic possible shape: a hexagonal column. Each of the column's six sides fits with the side of an adjoining column. Beehives are another example of hexagonal close-packing.

In summer, large clusters of rose-pink oleander set off the columns of dark gray basalt. The pool's cool, spring-fed water is a refuge from summer's heat. In the calm quiet, it was hard to imagine Nahal Meshushim raging between its walls, a deadly roaring river, sweeping people to their deaths. But it has happened.

After our day exploring, we decided to go to Qiryat Shemonah and treat ourselves to a meal at the Nargila, one of a popular chain that serves Yemeni food. Their specialty is *malawah*, a flaky, folded pastry similar to unsweetened Greek filo dough. We wolfed down orders of *malawah*, using pieces of the pastry to scoop up spicy tomato sauce. Happy with the walk and the food, we made our way back to the Golan, where I dropped off Roni at the field school and continued into Qatsrin.

But not every day ends perfectly. As a result of a flat tire, my car limped into Qatsrin's small industrial park. I drove to the end of a short, broken road lined with businesses, where I was told I would find an auto repair business.

The entryway was cluttered with batteries and various parts from old cars, all coated with dirt and grease. A roly-poly puppy ran toward me, barking, delighted for a reason to bark. Perhaps he would grow up to be a junkyard dog, growling and guarding old engine blocks.

Two squat middle-aged men approached, and I slowly and carefully explained that I needed my tire fixed but that my Hebrew was not very good. The men seemed pleased, and the one with the gap-toothed grin said in Hebrew thickly accented with Russian, "Us, too."

A Lone Wolf, a Lone Forest

In the northern Golan, rivers are fewer and flow into the Jordan upstream from Lake Kinneret. What fills the northern plateau, besides military installations, are apple orchards, cattle ranches, and some vineyards. Cowboy country and fine wines—an odd couple. In addition, a number of natural areas highlight this part of the Golan.

199

I was roaming the northern Golan with Baruch, one of SPNI's staff who previously had spent time in the United States. He found that the secular Judaism of Israel does not work well where the dominant culture is not Jewish, so he studied in a yeshiva to help maintain his identity in the States. Back in Israel, however, he wakes up without wondering about his Jewishness, without working at it. Here he is a naturalist, not a yeshiva bocher.

The day was sharp and clean, the sky the simple blue of a child's drawing. As we drove, we saw pillows of spurge draping roadside boulders, their chartreuse flowers glowing. Forests of giant fennel, their five-foot stalks domed with yellow blooms, swayed in the slight breeze. A member of the carrot family, fennel is related to Queen Anne's lace and all the varieties of white-capped, lacy flowers that line Israel's roads and dot fallow fields.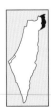

We passed Mount Shifon (Rye), and there among the tan rye grasses a canid looked out. Once spotted, it immediately disappeared. Too dark and heavy for a jackal, the animal was a wolf. Seeing one of the planet's top predators is always a thrill. Not only is it rare, there is something primeval about the encounter.

Predecessors of domestic dogs, wolves used to be one of the most widespread carnivores on the planet. But they have been killed off indiscriminately, even purposefully. With habitat and prey diminishing as well, wolf populations have been on the decline worldwide. Like vultures, wolves have an image problem.

In the past, especially in Europe, wolves were looked upon as the embodiment of evil: bloodthirsty creatures, fangs dripping with gore. This view, transplanted to the United States, resulted in federal bounties paid to wolf killers. When wolf populations teetered on the brink, the policy was dropped and the wolf put on the endangered species list.

Like most animals, wolves kill to eat. Hardly ravening monsters, wolves live extremely orderly lives. They hunt together and reside together in packs of about four to seven, more if range and prey are plentiful. Each adult requires up to ten pounds of meat daily, whether in cattle, gazelle, even mice or birds.

Only the top male and female breed. Anyone who has seen mating dogs stuck together, helpless in their inextricable coupling, has seen wolf biology at work. To make certain his genes will be advanced, the alpha male's penis swells once coupled. This biological strategy makes it impossible for the pair to part and gives sperm time to find their target. Male and female can remain bound together for as much as half an hour, but they are not entirely vulnerable. Standing tail to tail, they face out so that each can defend against possible attack.

The rest of the pack serve as aunts and uncles, bringing food to the den and helping to raise each new litter of pups. Facial expressions, howls and yips, tail position, and scent marking are part of their complex communication system. This language lets each wolf know about critical events and his or her standing in the pack. And they howl together. Once heard, the sound of wolves howling at night is never forgotten.

Wolves used to live throughout Israel and are mentioned a few times in the Bible. The prophet Habakkuk says of the Chaldeans, "Their horses are swifter than leopards, fleeter than wolves of the steppe" (Habakkuk 1:8).

In present-day Israel, wolves are scarce: a small desert subspecies lives in the Negev; remnant populations live on the Golan "steppes." Wolves remain on the Golan because it is less populated and because of a plentiful source of food: cattle. SPNI and other conservation groups are working on creative solutions to keep ranchers from killing wolves who eat into their profits.

Northwest of Mount Shifon, near Mount Avital Reserve, lies one of the Golan's many observation points. Some overlook Lake Kinneret, some the Hulah Valley. This one overlooks Syria and mountains to the east. Mount Avital and Mount Bental are adjacent volcanic cones, whose Hebrew names mean "Father of Dew" and "Son of Dew," respectively. But, like many geographical features in Israel, the hills have Arabic names as well. The Arabic name of one of these hills is the Lover, complete with sentimental story of unrequited love.

From the paired cones, we drove north to Masadah Junction, where Routes 98 and 99 meet. The Ram Pool, near the junction, is a reminder of the Golan's fiery genesis. A perfectly round pool, it is thought to be the remnants of a volcanic caldera. In King Herod's time, his son Philip claimed that chaff he threw into the Ram Pool arose in the waters of Banias in northern Galilee, thus proving a connection between the two. Although modern tests refute the connection, both the Ram Pool and the Banias River are fed by underground springs whose "plumbing" is connected to Mount Hermon—all resulting from rumblings along the Great Rift.

Also near Masadah Junction is the best of what remains of the **201** Golan's great forests, Ya'ar Odem Reserve: Odem Forest. This forest still stands because the Syrians used it as cover in their attacks on northern Galilee. Odd, that what served as protection for the Syrian Army also served as protection for the forest.

We left the car near a picnic area and walked into Odem Forest where calliprinos and Boissier oaks stand in groves separated by grassy swards. Though the oaks are broad, they are not high, so the place feels open and green, more park than forest. As we walked toward one thick stand of oaks, Baruch pointed out churned-up earth between the trees: evidence of mole rat pathways and wild boars rooting for acorns. Blackbirds and bulbuls, among Israel's most obvious and gregarious birds, were here, too.

In places, oak groves are so thick they completely shade the forest floor. In these dim areas, beneath spreading boughs, moss glows emerald on tree trunks and rocks. In sunny, open spaces, anemones and tulips grow and Syrian veronica hugs the ground, forming bright blue mats of tiny fleur-de-lis flowers. Despite their official name,

Baruch pointed out that they are patriotic flowers, the blue touched with a splash of white, the colors of the Israeli flag.

Pink-flowered Anatolian orchids live here as well as rare green orchids. We poked around in the underbrush, looking for orchids, but had no luck. Another rare wildflower, round-leaved cyclamen, blooms here in winter, sometimes pushing up through snow.

Though I've never been to a Provençal country estate, the grassy meadows between Odem's groves is how I imagine such painterly, sunlit places to be. We crossed through one grove that gave onto a meadow framed by trees. The long green *allée* directed our vision to towering, snow-covered Mount Hermon, cool and distant against the verdant grass.

This astonishing unspoiled scene reminded Baruch of its antithesis. Modern Israel's pioneers were focused on draining swamps, planting orchards, and building roads and towns. With the humor of hindsight, he voiced the opening to one popular song that lauded all that human industry: "We will clothe you in a robe of cement and concrete . . ."

Now groups of Israelis are just as enthusiastic about rehabilitating nature for its own sake. The urge to protect the land from layers of asphalt and cement is a modern notion, everywhere in the world. In prior centuries people sought to insulate themselves from ferocious creatures and the rigors of the wild. Animals were killed with little thought because nature's bounty seemed limitless.

John James Audubon, one of the first modern ornithologists, drew wonderfully precise pictures of birds from specimens he shot. Early zoologists, including nineteenth-century zoologists in Israel, collected and studied specimens killed either by them or for them. The brown Syrian bear, for instance, had lived throughout the eastern Mediterranean since biblical times. Ironic, Baruch said, that in the early 1900s modern Israel's first zoologist, Israel Aharoni, killed a brown bear, not knowing that it was one of the last—if not the last—bear in Israel.

Yet, where modern agriculture has flourished in Israel, bird species new to the region have appeared. As new species move in, others fight to survive. Galilee forests were reestablished even as its wetlands were drained.

In tropical areas of the globe, rainforests are burned in the wake of human industry. In temperate grasslands, the opposite often occurs. We suppress fire on prairies and other areas that require fire to flourish.

Inexorably, the pace of environmental change has increased. Yet, we hardly know what we do. We are still in the early stages of learning the complicated relationships among all elements of our world: plant diversity, balances of predator and prey, air pollution and climate change.

Base hunger interrupts the best of musings. Baruch and I drove to Buq'ata, one of the Golan's four Druze towns. At a small sidewalk restaurant where he is a regular, Baruch and the owner traded news of the day as we ate smoky babaghanouj with pita and dipped large balls of savory falafel—the best falafel in Israel, some say—into tahini.

Later, we climbed the hill of a small botanical reserve, home to more than six hundred plant species because of all its econiches. Rivulets with swampy borders course down the sides of the hilly reserve, boulders provide hot sun on the south side and shade on the north, and small gullies hold rich organic soil.

We were looking for orchids, but we were either too early or too late. What we found were a large, dried-out, oval reptile egg; badger tracks; tiny yellow flowers of the lily family; lupine; and, directly overhead, a short-toed eagle. The Golan has been home to short-toed eagles throughout recorded history. The short-toed eagle's presence is even "documented," appearing as a stone carving in a remnant of a fifth-century Golan synagogue.

Like kestrels, the short-toed eagle suspends itself in a stall, beating its wings in a stationary hover while focusing on its prey. With its six-foot wingspan, the short-toed eagle is far larger than the kestrel and the only large raptor to hover when hunting. The pale, short-toed eagle usually hunts for reptiles on sunny hillsides, and we have seen small lizards aplenty on this sun-warmed hill. But no orchids.

203

The White Shoulders of Mount Hermon

The heights of Mount Hermon rise with such dramatic presence that any trip up its flanks is worthwhile. But in summer, when the rest of Israel is either baking or steaming and the green of spring has crisped to tan, Hermon is just coming into its own.

The top of Mount Hermon, at ninety-two hundred feet, is in Syria. Of Hermon's many secondary peaks and shoulders, the highest in Israel is seventy-three hundred feet, high enough to boast a subalpine community. A bio-island of rare species, most of Hermon's subalpine plants and animals are found nowhere else in Israel.

When the snows finally melt in late spring, Mount Hermon's plants

Seen from the oak groves and meadows of Odem Forest Reserve, the snow-covered flanks of Mount Hermon rise more than seven thousand feet.

rush to flower in an effort to survive the short growing season. The plants that hug the mountain's slopes are adapted to Hermon's predominately limestone and dolomite soils. The fact that the underlying rock is sedimentary explains how it was formed. Millions of years ago, when seas covered the region, shells and skeletons of marine animals accumulated, layer upon layer, eventually compressed as limestone. When the seas retreated, a flat limestone plain remained, embedded with marine fossils that are still visible.

It took the Great Rift to make the mountain. Fissures in the Earth, like the Great Rift, are not ruler-straight. Where the Great Rift made a dogleg turn, tectonic plates ground together, wrinkling the land, thrusting up Mount Hermon. The same forces caused the rest of Israel's sedimentary mountains.

Part of the Anti-Lebanon Range, which parallels the coast, Mount Hermon is a twelve-by-thirty-mile behemoth composed of numerous shoulders, saddles, and peaks. Only 7 percent of the mountain—

the southwestern mass—lies within Israel. The majority falls to the east in Syria and to the northwest in Lebanon.

Clouds snag on Hermon's peaks, releasing rain and dozens of feet of snow in winter. Wreathed in clouds or glittering with a cap of snow, Mount Hermon looms majestic from many points of the Golan and Galilee.

"Sidonians call Hermon Sirion, and the Amorites call it Senir," says Deuteronomy 3:9. Hermon, the "lofty one," was also called *sirion* and *senir* because it was "armored" as a "glacier." Elsewhere, it is called *sion*, the "peak." The more prominent a place, the more names it bears.

Rain and snowmelt percolate down through Mount Hermon's porous limestone and, where water hits an impermeable chalk layer, it cascades out as a spring, such as the one that feeds Nahal Sa'ar. The stream that divides Mount Hermon's white limestone from the Golan's black basalt, Nahal Sa'ar is dry much of the year, its water drawn off for irrigation. But in late winter and spring, filled with snowmelt, it spills down the mountain, crashing as waterfalls near Route 99, fulfilling the words:

> Oh my God, my soul is downcast;
> therefore I think of You
> in this land of Jordan and Hermon,
> in Mount Mizar,
> where deep calls to deep
> in the roar of Your cataracts;
> all Your breakers and billows have swept over me.
>
> (PSALMS 42:7-8)

Mount Hermon is ringed by three distinct vegetation zones. The woods of the lower slopes are familiar Mediterranean vegetation, found also on the slopes of Mount Carmel and the Galilee. Some of the oaks are giants, six feet in diameter.

At about forty-two hundred feet deciduous oaks grow, including two rare species indigenous to Hermon. In this belt, too, wild almond, rose, and juniper flourish.

In the subalpine zone above, where wind scours the surface, plants lie low, forming ground-hugging cushions. The low mounded shape of milk vetch and other plants not only keeps foliage from being torn by the wind, but it also helps preserve heat and moisture.

Besides the usual rodents and other small mammals, Hermon is home to animals found nowhere else in Israel. The country's only squirrels live here, their presence recognized in the name of one of Hermon's peaks: Mount Sena'im (Squirrels).

The rock nuthatch, a compact bird the size of a sparrow, lives on Mount Hermon, usually above thirty-three hundred feet in altitude. It prefers rocky limestone terrain and uses its long, strong beak to pry insects from rock crevices and tree trunks. For such a compact bird, the nuthatch has extremely strong legs and feet, which it uses to walk *down* tree trunks—the only bird that can manage this odd-looking feat.

Hawthorn, ash, maple, and buckthorn are found here and only in a few other places in northern Israel. Pink Mount Hermon tulips; snow romulea, whose white-and-violet blooms hug the snow line; a purple nepeta, cousin to catnip; an arum; and two types of iris are among Hermon's rare wildflowers. One type of milkweed and a species of Saint-John's-wort are also distinctive to Hermon.

Like many of the world's plants, Saint-John's-wort has been used medicinally for centuries. Hippocrates prescribed it in Greece around 400 B.C.E. Today it is prescribed by German doctors to ease depression, and it has become a popular item in American health-food stores.

Stinging nettles, which grow over much of Israel near water, are still used medicinally here and have been used in Russia to treat gallbladder problems. It is said that Caesar's soldiers brought nettles to England, rubbing the stinging hairs against their bare legs to keep warm. (Dulled by heat and humidity, my son and I once rubbed nettles against our legs to keep alert as we slogged up a trail in the Appalachian Mountains.)

White willow, whose inner bark was chewed to relieve headaches, grows along the upper Jordan River; it is the precursor of one of the world's most common medicines, aspirin. Ephedra, desert shrubs full of green, sticklike branches, yield ephedrine, an alkaloid used to treat respiratory ailments. The tuber of the lion's leaf plant, which grows in the northern Negev, contains saponin, sometimes used as a remedy for epilepsy.

Fully 25 percent of all prescription drugs include an ingredient based on a flowering plant. The percentage soars to 40 percent when you count drugs that include ingredients taken from some source in nature, be it flowering plant or fungus. Scratch a plant, find a medicine.

To the Top of the Mountain

Tempestuous weather had swept down from Mount Hermon across the Golan and the rest of northern Israel, scattering rain, sleet, and, higher up, snow. Finally, the winds subsided and rays of sun picked out a patch of grass, a tree, a cat crossing the terrace of the Golan Field School. I could not wait. I was off to shake loose the storm's confinement.

Although once tree-covered, the Golan in early morning sunlight seemed a vast primeval prairie of undulating grasses under the gaze of Mount Hermon. Soft green cones of dormant volcanoes edged the horizon, and imagination easily conjured long-gone grazing elephants and a hunting party of primitive humans.

Mantled with snow from the late spring storm, Mount Hermon rose above the plain, thrusting its hulking white presence into the deep blue sky. I passed pastures of grazing cattle. At the feet of the cattle, white cattle egrets probed the ground for insects. Black-eared wheatears, conspicuous in stark black-and-white plumage, flew past. Near one pasture, white water buttercups half-covered an ephemeral pool, a depression that fills with water during the spring rains, provides a place for frogs to spawn, then dries up in the heat of summer. It is one of a few such pools left in the Golan.

A row of tall metal windmills lines a low rise. Their blades whirred like airplane propellers. At Masadah Junction, I thought to turn left and perhaps visit the ancient burial place of the revered Druze prophet Nabi Hazuri, whose tomb was set among huge old oaks. Along Ma'aleh Gideon, below Mount Dov, lies the site where it is said that God promised Abraham the land of Israel, a site marked with giant oaks.

My impulse was mostly for the oaks. Throughout the world, some of the most undisturbed and carefully preserved nature is found at tombs, cemeteries, and other hallowed places. People are loathe to disturb the dead or the sacred. So trees are not cut, grasses and wildflowers are not stripped away, and natural grandeur becomes a living memorial.

But I had not contacted any authorities, was not sure about the rules for visiting either of these sites, and was too determinedly headed upward to stop, so I continued on.

The roads leading to Mount Hermon are lined with orchards. Although many who live in Mount Hermon's four Druze villages now hire out as workers, most still maintain small farms, and their main crop is apples.

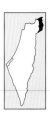

207

I passed through Majdal Shams, Tower of the Sun, so called because as the highest Druze village—in fact, the highest village in Israel—it is the first to catch dawn's light. The village is situated near the spring that flows out to feed Nahal Sa'ar.

I wound through narrow streets where women were enveloped by long black skirts and voluminous kerchiefs, out early to start the day's chores. Men I passed wore the traditional Druze white hats and unintentionally stylish baggy pants. The Druze religion developed from Islam but is its own closely held faith, centered in the mountains of Lebanon and Syria.

The Druze who live in the Galilee and on Mount Carmel have more or less become integrated into Israeli society, serving in the Army if they wish, even standing for the Knesset. Druze on Hermon are divided in their allegiance. Some want a return to Syrian statehood, some prefer the opportunities and modern conveniences of Israel. Mostly the Druze of Mount Hermon would prefer to be left alone.

Although it is hard to get beyond the reach of politics in a land never beyond the reach of an enemy missile, I had no use for politics that sun-burnished morning. Looping from switchback to switchback, the car climbed ever higher into the mountains until all signs of settlement lay below. Even evidence of terracing was faint.

Within a bright wedge of a meadow between rock walls, cushions of wildflowers beckoned. I pulled the car to the side and roamed among the natural rock gardens of Hermon's slopes, hiking higher into the cleft. Growing among tumbled limestone boulders, in artlessly exquisite designs, were pink mallows, blue veronica and bugloss, yellow gagea, and others. Myrtle, with its trim evergreen leaves had wedged itself between rocks, its feet now covered with a dollop of snow that the sun had not yet found.

I had an uneasy feeling that wandering at will, alone, on Mount Hermon was not only unwise but frowned upon. Back in the car, my feeling was fed when I looked behind and saw a car following me and another behind the first. What reason for these cars on a high, lonely two-lane during a workday morning if not to stop me and question my movements? I grew anxious but could not turn around on the narrow, winding mountain road. Soon, snow packed the sides of the road, and the asphalt grew slick with melting slush—the results of the storm.

Finally, I reached a broad area and pulled to the side, expecting plainclothes military authorities to pull up next to me and cite me,

208

fine me, who knows what. But the car behind sped by, as did the next car, and the next.

A whole line of cars passed. Each was bearing skis mounted on racks or stuffed in the back and sticking out the windows. They were all headed toward the gates of the Mount Hermon ski area, doing what a skier with any sense does on a rare powder day in Israel.

CHAPTER NINE

Northern Galilee:
Beneath a Green Canopy

Nahal Ammud

Northern Galilee

Ayun Reserve •
Nimrod Fortress •
Dan Reserve •. Banias
Qiryat Shemonah •
Hulah •
• Mount Meron
Nahal Ammud •
Jordan River Park •

TRAVELING FROM METULLAH TO EILAT, from the northernmost city in Israel to the southernmost city, is like traveling from southern Europe to the Sahara—in less than three hundred miles. Eilat seems a mirage, shimmering white on the hot desert rocks. The area near Metullah looks like a European forest, with leafy trees shading cool streams and a lush green understory. Such extremes, in so compact an area, is what makes Israel one of the most biologically diverse places on Earth.

Northern Galilee itself is a world of extremes. At Tel Dan, waters sing over stones as they rush beneath the

deep shade of laurels and plane trees. Yet, less than twenty miles south, steamy marshes thick with tall, swaying papyrus and waterlilies look like an Egyptian frieze come to life. Hulah Swamp lies little more than two hundred feet above sea level while, looming above, Mount Meron soars to nearly four thousand feet.

Difficult terrain plus thick vegetation made northern Galilee harder to tame than southern Galilee or the coastal plain. Its mountains, canyons, and spongy swamps repelled settlement over the centuries. In large part, the terrain saved itself.

Lebanon borders the Galilee region's northernmost tip, called the "finger of Galilee" because it is shaped like a long finger. On the western edge of the finger, the Naphtali Hills drop a steep twenty-three hundred feet toward Qiryat Shemonah and the Great Rift.

Near the border with Lebanon, streams gather: Hermon, Dan, Senir, and Ayun—the lifeblood of a dry land. They join as the long artery of the Jordan River, which continues down the Great Rift until it enters the Hulah Valley, a broad basin approximately eighteen miles long and four miles wide.

Much of the Hulah Valley was once covered by a vast shallow lake and teeming swamp but is now crowded with cotton, fish ponds, and other crops—except for one incredibly fecund wildlife reserve. At the southern end of the Hulah, the Jordan re-forms and continues down the Great Rift to the Sea of Galilee.

Southwest of the Hulah Valley, massive Mount Meron and all its attendant peaks dominate the view. The Meron Range, which separates northern and western Galilee, is so rugged and thickly forested that nearly all of it is a nature reserve.

Most people traveling through northern Galilee see farms and towns, but little that is natural. A closer look reveals enchanting nature reserves filled with wildlife. Fire salamanders stay moist in streamside leaf litter. Frogs croak and chirp from ponds. Otters and fish thrive in the Galilee's cool streams.

Wild boars root for acorns on the slopes of Mount Meron. Fox and jackal are the only members of the wild canids who roam here, while porcupines and other rodents are the most populous family. Eagles and owls, herons and moorhens, bee-eaters and goldfinches, and hundreds of other birds make the Hulah Reserve a natural aviary to compare with any in the world.

Seeing the splashing sources of the Jordan or Meron's rain-streaked mountains in January, the saying comes to mind: 50 percent of Israel's land has less than 1 percent of its water, and 50 percent of Israel's water comes from 1 percent of its land. There's the difference between the Negev and the North.

212

Temple in the Woods

We were overlooking one of the Jordan's sources, Nahal Hermon (Banias), from Nimrod Fortress. Surrounded by spreading oaks, this imposing medieval stronghold commands a point of land in the shadow of Mount Hermon. Hyrax raced furtively along the thick castle walls. In its cracks, lamium spread white-splashed leaves, and red and blue anemones danced in the wind at the feet of the walls.

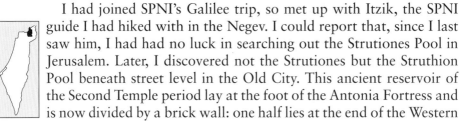

I had joined SPNI's Galilee trip, so met up with Itzik, the SPNI guide I had hiked with in the Negev. I could report that, since I last saw him, I had had no luck in searching out the Strutiones Pool in Jerusalem. Later, I discovered not the Strutiones but the Struthion Pool beneath street level in the Old City. This ancient reservoir of the Second Temple period lay at the foot of the Antonia Fortress and is now divided by a brick wall: one half lies at the end of the Western

Wall Tunnel, the other in the lower level of the Sisters of Zion Convent on the Via Dolorosa. I still have not found any connection between my name and the pool, but some things are better left veiled in mystery.

It had been raining, on and off, for a few days. We pulled rain jackets and ponchos close to keep out the sputtering drizzle and watched our footing on the slick stones at the base of the fortress. Roaming Nimrod's arches and keeps were a group of about a dozen of us: six people from the Netherlands, a tall Swiss shift-worker, a psychologist from Australia, a Boston pediatrician, and a couple from New York, he a lawyer, she a recent medical school graduate. Another doctor, also a woman, was on sabbatical from the United States.

We clustered around Itzik to hear about Nimrod. SPNI guides are trained by experts in biology, geology, archaeology, and other disciplines to know a great deal about all aspects of Israel. Although my focus was natural history, it is hard to ignore human history in this land, and who would want to? Just as Israel was the meeting place for many of the world's plants and animals, so was it the meeting place of peoples.

Nimrod Fortress was built not long after 1100 C.E., probably by Muslims. One of a chain of fortresses, Nimrod was constructed at a critical point along the ancient trade route of the Middle East. The fortress was probably not known as Nimrod until more recent times, named enigmatically for the biblical hunter and king of Babel, "the first man of might on earth" (Genesis 10:8). **213**

Early on, the fortress was occupied by members of the Ismailian sect of Islam, fanatic warriors who would heighten their courage with hashish before going out to kill. They became known as *hashshashin* and the word has come down to us as *assassins*. The fortress switched hands a few times: to Crusaders, then again to Muslims. In 1187, Saladin launched his successful assault on the Crusaders from the fortress. Nimrod overlooks a much older site, the Greek temple of Banias, and Banias Spring, one of the sources of the Jordan.

From Nimrod, we descended to Nahal Hermon Reserve, the Hermon River, and Banias. As we began walking down the reserve's trail, which was wet and slippery from the rain, we saw a school group of young teens exiting. Most were smeared with mud from head to foot: mud in their hair, coating their clothes, caked on their boots. I considered my own boots and pants and decided a little mud would not be so terrible, until I realized that the teens with the

Banias Waterfalls

most mud also had the broadest smiles. Aha! Head-to-toe mud was an option not a requirement.

The channel of the Hermon River is outlined by tall, straight plane trees, similar to those that grow throughout Europe and to those in eastern North America. Near the river, we walked beneath the canopy of plane trees, and the sides of the muddy trail immediately became thick with a clamor of plants: willows hung with long yellow catkins, styrax, shiny-leaved laurel, an understory of ferns and cyclamen, and a tangle of thorny brambles where jumpy Cetti's warblers live, feeding on berries.

Holy bramble, which produces sweet blackberries in summer, is so named because it is another of the plants said to be the burning bush that appeared to Moses. But, like the plane tree, it usually grows near the kind of streams not found in the desert. In the old days, a thirsty traveler who spotted a tall plane tree or tangled mounds of bramble would know a drink was near.

A huge old carob spreads its branches near the trail. Carob trees usually prefer dry slopes, so perhaps it was planted. Where the slopes alongside the trail are too rocky to support trees, tall wands of hyacinth squill sway, topped by airy blue flowers. Avoiding the crowd at streamside, redbud trees look down from above. The redbud is also called the Judas tree because Christian tradition says that Judas Iscariot hung himself from just such a tree.

As we walked, we learned that the Swiss shift-worker was an ascetic who refused to watch TV but liked listening to classical music on the radio. The doctor on sabbatical was working in Beersheba, treating Bedouin. The couple from New York were relative newlyweds, and she, a new doctor, had previously worked as a potter and a sculptor. She and I found we shared an experience, trekking in Nepal. We traded stories with each other as we slipped and slid along the muddy path.

The trail winds past stout oaks whose old, gnarled trunks lean over the river's rushing water. Soon spray spread a moist, gauzy veil across the view, and we could hear the roar of a waterfall. Finally, the trees parted and we could see Banias Waterfalls, crashing down as twin falls of bubbling whitewater. The waters catch their breath in the pool at bottom, then race as rapids through a streambed strewn with boulders and enclosed by greenery.

Following the river, we crossed a bridge then hiked upstream on the other side toward Banias Spring. We passed an old swimming pool built for Syrian army officers before reaching the confluence

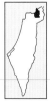

of the Hermon River and the Sa'ar River, which pours down from Mount Hermon. An ancient flour mill, used until recently, lies alongside the stream. Not far upstream, Nahal Guvta adds its waters to Nahal Hermon. Guvta often is dry, but in the rush of recent heavy rains and a melting snowpack it pushed aggressively into Nahal Hermon.

At the confluence of Guvta and Hermon, an underpass leads below a two-thousand-year-old Roman bridge, old enough so that water dripping from the limestone bridge above our heads had already formed small stalactites. Beyond lies Banias Spring and all manner of ruins. The spring, a significant holy site for thousands of years, is layered with history: Hebrew, Greek, Roman, Crusader, Maronite Christian, Arab.

Below a cliff and a collapsed cave entrance, Banias Spring flows from beneath the rocks into an open area where it shimmers in a series of lovely, stepped pools. Judging from numbers carved in the cliff, the temple to Pan dates from 87 C.E. Although excavations continue to reveal remains of the temple, the most obvious vestiges are exquisite niches that etch the cliff, some with delicately scalloped arches. The spring takes it name from the Greek god Pan, the goat-legged god of forests and flocks who played songs on his panpipes. Because Arabic has no sound for the letter *P*, the name was corrupted to Banias.

216

Christian, Jewish, Muslim, Druze, and pagan lore is associated with Banias. At this place Jesus told Peter he would give him the "keys to the kingdom" (Matthew 16:19). Herod, the Jewish Hasmonean ruler, built yet another of his extravagant palaces here. The remains of the palace's broad terraces overlook the stepped pools. Despite his ferocity, Herod knew how to live well. Of Herod, Banias, and Mount Hermon poised above, Josephus said:

> At a later date, when Caesar had enriched him by the addition of further lands, there also he erected a shrine of white marble dedicated to his patron, near the sources of the Jordan at a place called Paneum. There is a mountain here whose top is lost in the clouds; in the lower slopes is a cavern with its mouth concealed by vegetation, inside which a sheer precipice descends, nobody knows how far, to a cavity filled with still water: no plummet has ever reached the bottom, however long the cord. From the roots of the cavern outside well up the springs which some consider to be the head-waters of Jordan.

Banias, we know now, is only one of the headwaters of the Jordan. I looked forward to exploring the others.

In a light rain Itzik shepherded us back to the bus, and we made our way to Kefar Giladi for the night. Kefar Giladi, which lies on the northern flanks of the Naphtali Hills, is a kibbutz whose contemporary hotel is one of a chain of kibbutz hotels spread throughout the country. Next to the hotel dining room is a cozy bar where some of us repaired for a warming drink after a raw, gusty afternoon. I sipped Sabra, a smooth orange liqueur made with Israel's famous Jaffa oranges.

After dinner, a group of us made our way to the recreation center to try Israeli dancing. On the paths that crisscross the kibbutz, we passed older people making their way from one area to another in the transportation of choice: golf carts. We reached the large, bright recreation hall where the dancing had already started. A compact man with expressive hands and quick feet started each dance by running through the opening steps.

For years, folk dancing has been a national passion. Annual folk dance festivals draw groups from across the country to dance, seemingly nonstop, for days. Among urban young people, the folk dance passion has waned, but I know grandfathers and grandmothers who dance a marathon's worth of folk dances several nights a week.

The next day brought more gray weather. On this trip, Itzik had to negotiate with rain, snow, floods, wind, and our group's deluge of conflicting suggestions as weather fouled up our schedule. We tested his patience and good humor. He decided that hiking up to the Arbel Cliffs near Lake Kinneret might be a good way to avoid rain.

217

Our bus pulled up to the trailhead, but the rain had followed us south and began a gentle but ominous patter on the roof. Having already hiked the Arbel and preferring to stay dry, I opted to wait in the bus with the driver. We watched as the group made their way up the mountain in gentle then driving rain.

The bus driver checked his watch and turned on the radio to catch the latest news. By the time the news concluded, the hikers had raced down the mountain and jumped onto the bus, dripping and muddy.

Tel Dan Reserve: Emerald of the North

It is impossible to visit Tel Dan Reserve too many times. The home of the Dan River, headwaters of the Jordan, is one of the most idyllic sites in Israel.

Not only is the Dan River the largest, most important source of the Jordan, but it wells up from the largest karstic spring in the Middle East, fed by waters percolating down from Mount Hermon. The Dan also is the source of the Jordan River's name: the Jordan, Yarden in Hebrew, "descends" (*yarad*) from the Dan.

In places, the Dan River roars through Tel Dan Reserve with rollers and whitewater, cascading over boulders that strew its bed. In places, it flows smooth and deep. The Dan flows vigorously year-round, with more than 7.8 billion cubic feet of water pouring from its source per year.

Though small, the Tel Dan Reserve is a good place to linger. When the rest of Israel bakes in summer, the paths of the Tel Dan Reserve are cool, shaded by a canopy of plane trees, laurel, and Syrian ash, here near its southern limit. So well-knit are the tree boughs above that light cannot part them. In their damp shade, banks of maidenhair ferns tremble in the dim light. Greenbrier and other vines twine up trunks and branches, further binding the green canopy.

Brambles line the waterways and myrtles grow like giants at the Tel Dan Reserve. Laurels, too. Elsewhere in Israel laurel grows to about twelve feet. Here, the splendid gray trunks of *dafnah* reach twice that height. In spring their flowers perfume the air with sweet scent, but bay laurels are best known for their shiny, spicy leaves. Used by ancient Greeks to crown Olympic athletes and poets, bay leaves are still used to flavor food.

218

Paths twist and turn through the understory, and a damp, vegetable odor pervades. So many rivulets and small streams braid the reserve that the land seems to be leaking water. Occasionally, the path becomes a chain of stepping stones across a stream. Rare marsh ferns sprout from shallow, backwater pools. The place seems to have been imported from England, so atypical is it in dry, sunny Israel.

Like other spring-fed streams of northern Galilee and the Golan, the Dan River is home to black river snails, freshwater shrimp and crabs, and fish. An introduced type of trout, called *forel*, thrives in the Dan's cold, oxygenated water. Pink fleshed and mild tasting, *forel* is being farmed by nearby kibbutzim.

Jumbled like pickup sticks, fallen, moss-covered logs clutter a small pool. On a limb above, a kingfisher lets loose his piercing cry against the low drone of dragonflies. Where shadowed banks thick with leaf mold meet spring-fed rivulets, salamanders live.

Leaving the river, the trail climbs to the low plateau of Tel Dan, and the country opens up. Wheatears and swallows course through

Only one species of salamander inhabits Israel, and it is found only in three isolated populations: on Mount Hermon and the sources of the Jordan, on Mount Meron, and on Mount Carmel. These are the only places constantly wet and cool enough to support the fire or spotted salamander, an amphibian that lives throughout most of Europe and is at its southern limit in Israel.

To see them to is to understand their "fire." The salamanders' shiny black bodies mottled with bright gold or orange flash a warning: "Stay back." Like many frogs, salamanders are equipped with glands that coat their skin with a mild poison. About ten inches long, the fire salamander emerges at night from damp rock crevices to hunt insects and other invertebrates.

the air, the wheatears a blur of black-and-white, the swallows shimmering iridescent blue-black, then swooping to reveal buff-colored breasts.

Typical Mediterranean vegetation fans across the plateau: olives, oaks, and Atlantic pistacias—terebinths. Here lived giants. Until vandals burned it, the largest terebinth in Israel grew on Tel Dan, its trunk twenty feet in circumference. The venerable and majestic terebinth was approximately six hundred years old.

219

Although calliprinos oak grows around Tel Dan, most of the open forest is Tabor oak. Researchers believe deciduous Tabor oaks migrated from more northerly parts of the Mediterranean where colder winters require them to lose their leaves to conserve energy. In Israel, however, losing leaves is not as necessary. Researchers suspect that dropping their leaves each winter may cost the trees more in energy consumption than it saves. So, they are trying to discover if Tabor oaks in Israel hold their leaves longer.

With its streams and a plateau crowned with oaks, Dan became an important cultural center in ancient times. The first city on this spot was the Canaanite city of Laish, later conquered by the tribe of Dan. Later still, after the Jewish people split into two kingdoms, Judah and Israel, King Jeroboam decided to promote Dan—which replaced Laish—as a rival to Jerusalem in Judah. The remains of Jeroboam's temple have been uncovered on Tel Dan: "So the king took counsel and made two golden calves. He said to the people,

Plants, like animals, expend the energy needed to survive and no more. Fine-tuned to their environment, northern conifers of the planet's boreal realms bear tight needles that conserve energy during cold winters and sloping branches that allow snow to slide off.

Deciduous trees, living in climates with cold winters and hot summers, unfold broad leaves that quickly gather lots of energy in summer. The energy is stored and the leaves fall off in autumn. Besides releasing too much of the plant's energy in winter, broad leaves would be ripped to shreds in a snowstorm.

Tropical plants of Israel, such as Sodom apples, have drip-tip leaves. When it rains, their broad evergreen leaves funnel the precious liquid to their pointed leaf tips, where it drips toward thirsty roots. Desert trees maintain narrow, silvery leaves in order to conserve moisture and to reflect heat and light.

'You have been going up to Jerusalem long enough. This is your god, O Israel, who brought you up from the land of Egypt!' He set up one in Bethel and placed the other in Dan" (1 Kings 12:28–29).

While revisiting favorite parts of northern Galilee with Michael, we emerged from Tel Dan Reserve near dusk, the last visitors of the day. A stylish glass and wood-beam restaurant nestles among the trees just outside the reserve, and we decided to stay for supper. The restaurant's decks and broad windows overlook the tumbling waters of the Dan River. We ate grilled *forel* with three sauces. The air was still, the banks of the river emerald with foliage.

As we ate, we talked about the story told by the signs at Tel Dan, how King Jeroboam saw that because Jerusalem was a religious magnet, it also became an economic magnet. Why not Dan? the king thought. Why should pilgrims' shekels head straight to Jerusalem?

Returning south, we took the route that curves west around the Hulah Valley beneath an awning of tall, leafy eucalyptus trees. The trees evoke a country-lane ambience, but they were planted for a 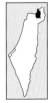 much different reason. Israelis established this line of fast-growing Australian trees to camouflage trucks and cars from Syrian guns aimed at them from the Golan directly above. In the 1967 Six-Day War, Israel won the Golan. Now, the road *is* a quiet country lane lined, in places, with small holiday homes that provide a cool summer retreat for Tel Aviv vacationers.

A francolin crossed the road ahead, its damask-brown plumage quivering in the rising wind. Flocks of swallows dove, daring the windshield of the car, flicking their wings in our faces. Then they turned and spiraled up as one, an aerial ballet.

Drumming River and Oven Falls at Ayun Reserve

On the grounds of Kibbutz Dan, near the Lebanese border, Bet Ussishkin Museum provides a rich and varied view of northern Galilee's natural history. Associated with SPNI, Bet Ussishkin Museum of Natural History and Archaeology is one of the country's numerous regional museums, with exhibits on birds, mammals, plants, and geology that explain how nature's parts fit together and why. Situated among the sources of the Jordan, the museum makes a pleasant and informative stop.

Nearby spreads Hurshat Tal, Grove of Dew, a national park dotted with Tabor oaks. Waters of the Dan River and the lure of old oaks counteract planted lawns and an artificial lake. A nature reserve within the park protects numerous orchid species and birds, both rare and common.

Just to the west, the Senir River parallels the Dan. Flowing from the slopes of Mount Hermon in Lebanon, the Senir is also called by its Arabic name, Hatsbani. Although at thirty-six-plus miles the Senir is more than four times longer than the Dan and drains a much larger area, its water is not as reliable. Part of the reason is because upstream water is drawn off for irrigation.

But in winter and spring, the Senir is often tumultuous, boiling through the narrow ravine it has cut along its course. Between Gesher ha-Tsinorot (Bridge of the Pipes) and Route 99, a trail meanders alongside Nahal Senir, weaving close to the river, then back through the dense vegetation, and again to the river.

Where the water is not hazardous, people play in the stream. Otters used to play here, too, but with development they are seen less frequently. Plane trees and willows crowd close to the river. Horsetail reeds grow near the water's edge here and in only a few other places in Israel.

The fourth of the Jordan's main sources, Nahal Ayun, also rises in Lebanon, in the Ayun Valley, and flows into Israel near Metullah, the nation's northernmost town. Skirting Metullah along the north and east, Nahal Ayun Reserve lies near the Good Fence, which divides Israel from Lebanon.

The sweet-smelling yellow flowers of thorny broom and other shrubs soften the look of Nahal Ayun Reserve's sheer cliffs. Just beyond, Tanur Falls sweep over hundred-foot cliffs in a broad sheet of water.

As it drops from the ridge separating the two countries, Nahal Ayun has carved a course that steps down in stages over four waterfalls. The sound explains the river's Arabic name, *Dardara*: Drumming River.

Because of the sheer cliffs, the scenery here seems more open than among the dense foliage of the Dan or even the Senir. Pouring over ledges, the river has fewer places to collect, leaving fewer places for large plants to flourish. Oleander and willow have grabbed spaces streamside, and buckthorn, a shrubby tree that tolerates poor soil, settles where it can, providing late-summer berries for birds.

Where the terrain opens up, around slopes and cliffs, wildflowers abound. Michauxia, whose white, recurved petals make the flower look like a dart, is rare, a treat to see. It is named after the French botanist who traveled the world in the late 1700s. André Michaux searched out hundreds of species, from Palestine and Asia to the Appalachian Mountains of North America. During his travels he suffered everything from starvation to attack by American Indians, eventually dying from disease in Madagascar.

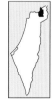

White sea squill blooms from bulbs around the time of the first autumn rains. Tall blue hyacinth squill flowers at the other end of the rainy season, in spring, along with rose-pink snapdragons, which cling to rocky crevices. A Mediterranean native, snapdragons are now grown all over the world, bred in colors to suit every vase.

Another Mediterranean plant that has wandered far from its origins is purple loosestrife, which forms bold clumps along Nahal Ayun. Brought to North American gardens because its tall purple spikes are extremely showy, loosestrife escaped to the wild, where it has bullied North American plants from streambeds all across the continent. In some areas of the United States, loosestrife has become so aggressive that it is banned, hunted down, and destroyed.

As the world has become smaller, every nation now has its share of nonnative plants. Sometimes nonnatives stay politely within reasonable bounds. Sometimes they don't. And sometimes nonnative plants are accompanied by insect pests and diseases that can wreak havoc in new environments.

> In talmudic times, Nahal Ayun was specified as a northern border for Jewish observance. Those who lived farther north were not required to observe the laws of the sabbatical year (*shemittah*), which say: "In the seventh year the land shall have a sabbath of complete rest, a sabbath of the Lord: you shall not sow your field or prune your vineyard. You shall not reap the aftergrowth of your harvest or gather the grapes of your untrimmed vines; it shall be a year of complete rest for the land."
>
> (Leviticus 25:4-5)

Israel's aliens come from around the globe: eucalyptus, weeping acacia, and casuarina from Australia; flame tree from Madagascar; flowering tobacco and tipuana from South America; wiry parkinsonia from Central America; black mulberry from the Far East; fan palm and sabra cactus from North American deserts. Even the pomegranate probably came from elsewhere in southwest Asia, but so long ago that the round red fruit has become part of cultural memory.

Following Nahal Ayun downstream, past Ayun Waterfalls, the trail zigzags across bridges to the Mill Waterfalls, the second of the reserve's cascades. A broad swath of water that sheets down about sixty-five feet, the falls once drove an Arab flour mill, whose remains are still visible. In the late 1800s, Baron Edmond de Rothschild purchased the mill for Jewish settlers, but it was abandoned in 1920 when Metullah was evacuated to protect its citizens from attack.

From there, the trail leads past Sucra Springs and Squill Hill, which overlooks a steep-walled gorge where the river is broken by cascades. Rock doves, seen throughout Israel and the rest of the Mediterranean, are at home here on the cliffs even as their close relatives, pigeons, are on the "cliffs" of Tel Aviv high-rises.

Pigeons are descended from rock doves (*Columba livia*) domesti-

cated about five thousand years ago in Egypt. Bred in *columbaria*—dovecotes that often were dug in chalk caves—pigeons were and still are a delicacy, cooked Middle East-style in flaky pastries. And they had other uses: as early as the twelfth century, Baghdad sultans used specially trained pigeons to speed messages.

A far rarer bird at Nahal Ayun is the wallcreeper, seen at Ayun, Arbel Cliffs, and a few other difficult, rocky places in northern Israel. A small gray bird, it flashes red wings as it creeps around rocks, probing crevices for insects with its long, slender bill.

Near the Metullah cemetery an overlook allows the first glimpse of Tanur Falls, a long dramatic drop of crashing water. Switchbacking down the slope, the trail leads to the bottom of the hundred-foot falls. During its drop, streaking water dashes against the rocks, sending up arcs of spray that catch the light, forming and reforming tiny rainbows.

Tanur, in Hebrew, means "oven." Perhaps Tanur Falls was given its name because the shape of the falls resembles beehive-shaped Middle Eastern ovens. Or perhaps it is because, in summer, close canyon walls can seem hot as an oven—except for the spray. But *tanur*, in Arabic, means "gown." So the name also could refer to the long white gown of water or the equally sweeping white rock wall behind it.

224 Below Tanur Falls, Nahal Ayun once flowed down the valley to merge with Hulah Swamp. Now, during summer, water is drawn off for irrigation in Lebanon, and, downstream from the nature reserve, the water is channeled for use in Israel.

Harnessing water certainly has improved societies, bringing reserved water, hydroelectric power, and flood and disease control. But it also has changed the environment to unprecedented extents. While draining Hulah Swamp helped control malaria by curbing mosquitoes, it destroyed habitat for rare amphibians and drove away migrating birds.

In Egypt, pharaonic temples and tombs were moved to accommodate the Aswan High Dam, but upstream sediment no longer renews the crucial Nile Delta. Glen Canyon Dam in the United States flooded 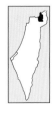 ancient Indian artifacts and breathtaking canyons, and changed the ecology of the Colorado River. The scheduled Three Gorges Dam in China will flood extraordinary gorges of the Yangtze River and thousands of archaeological sites, as well as forcing relocation of a million-plus people.

We have become proficient at remaking nature. We have constructed things useful, even noble and uplifting. But we also have constructed things of questionable wisdom, some solely to feed egos or line pockets. Sometimes it seems we do things simply because we can do them.

Living in the Material World

Qiryat Shemonah is the city of the north. Still not much bigger than a town, it once was all shabby storefronts with roll-down metal shutters and squat apartment blocks fitted with bomb shelters—defense against the missiles that rained in from southern Lebanon, and sometimes still do. It still is a development town, but one with new buildings, a tennis club, and banks of flowers lining streets.

At the edge of town lies a *qanyon* that I had heard young people excitedly talking about. I was anxious to see this canyon, surprised that high-school students would be so enthusiastic about a natural area.

The *qanyon* to which I was directed was no rugged gorge. Instead, I found myself in front of a broad white edifice—a shopping mall. In the atrium people nibbled pastries and drank coffee at a chic cafe. Circling the atrium were two stories of shops: women's clothing, a Steimatzky bookstore, a stationery shop, a pharmacy, and more.

*Qanyon*s are popping up all over the country. The Hebrew name *qanyon* comes from the word *qanah*, "to buy."

Plenty of real canyons cut through the hills of northern Galilee, many protected in nature reserves. Perched above the Hulah Valley, Mount Nezer Reserve crowns the Naphtali Hills. Owls live within the partially collapsed great hall of Nezer Cave, and hyrax scurry among the rocks. The reserve is a place of iris and orchid, berry bush and rockrose. Rockroses are graceful shrubs that cover hillsides throughout the Galilee and Carmel. Come spring, they are covered with large roselike flowers, one species blooming pink, the other white.

Located at the south end of the "finger of Galilee," where the border with Lebanon makes a ninety-degree angle, lie the canyons of Nahal Dishon and Nahal Avivim. Within Nahal Dishon Reserve, the stream has cut a long rocky gorge, baring layer upon layer of sedimentary rock—an *in situ* geology lesson. Surrounding slopes are a garden of wildflowers in spring.

225

Nearby Nahal Avivim shows off caves and tall rock towers, which stand alone, like sentinels, on the slopes. Called "girls" by some, the towers look more like oafish *djinn*s magically frozen in place. While wind and water ate away the softer rock around them, these towers of harder rock remained, withstanding erosion.

Fight to Save the Hulah

Nahal Dishon flows into the Jordan just south of what may be the most famous nature reserve in Israel: Hulah. Hulah Reserve seems placid enough, a turn off Route 90 and a short drive down a shady country lane to a parking lot under eucalyptus trees. A visitor center complete with audiovisual displays, dioramas, books, and maps is an excellent introduction to the boardwalks and marshes of what remains of Hulah Swamp.

Placid as the Hulah seems, it was the site of a major battle in the early 1950s. Not a battle of armies and guns, but of ideas. The vision of "making the desert bloom" had become so ingrained that creating useful land was a near unshakable tenet.

In 1900, Hulah Lake and its surrounding marshlands filled more than fifteen thousand acres of Hulah Valley with water, birds, fish, and myriad other life, including disease-carrying mosquitoes. Early Zionists who settled in the area contracted malaria in scores.

The idea of draining the swamp and exposing more arable land grew, and, in 1951, the draining of the swamp began. Establishing useful agricultural land—who could argue with that?

A growing number of conservation-minded scientists and citizens did. The Hulah is a critical stopover for millions of migrating waterfowl. After long, energy-depleting flights, these birds forage at Hulah for water plants or gorge on insects that hatch on the water's surface.

The Hulah serves as a filter, purifying water traveling to Kinneret. And the Hulah is critical habitat for rare species that live nowhere else. It is the northernmost point on the globe for papyrus and the southernmost point for a number of other species. A water-rich environment in a water-starved land, the Hulah is an ecosystem without peer in Israel.

Conservationists argued that incalculable natural resources would be lost were Hulah drained completely. They reasoned that the white-tailed eagle should be the indicator species for preserving part of Hulah Swamp. An indicator species is a plant or animal that indicates the health of a particular environment or an aspect of an environment. For instance, in the eastern forests of North America healthy populations of lung lichen indicate relatively clean air.

Although white-tailed eagles can be found as far north as Greenland, they are not a common species, and only a few winter in the Hulah Valley. These rare and majestic birds require considerable range, and Hulah Swamp, which combines open waters with woods, is the white-tailed eagle's preferred type of terrain. Save at least enough of the Hulah to support white-tailed eagles, biologists said.

They won their case. About 10 percent of the swamp was saved, and Israel's conservation movement was born. The growing numbers of conservationists organized themselves as the Society for the Protection of Nature in Israel: SPNI or *Ha-Hevrah la-Haganat ha-Teva*.

In 1964 Hulah Reserve's eight hundred acres became the first nature reserve in Israel. SPNI then embarked on a mission to protect other wild lands from development. Mount Carmel was saved from quarrying and established as Mount Carmel National Park. Eilat coral reefs were spared ecological disaster from a potential oil refinery. The Tanninim River, the last undisturbed coastal river, still flows—but not in the shadow of a planned power station. SPNI convinced officials to site the huge power station elsewhere.

SPNI saved so many places that, in 1963, the government passed a law that collected them all under its official purview in a nationwide system of reserves and parks. Since that time, the Israel Nature and National Parks Protection Authority has added numerous properties to its system. Israel's more than three hundred nature reserves are just what they imply, places that preserve nature. The forty-plus national parks are more of a mix. Many preserve ancient synagogues, Roman ruins, and other significant antiquities. Some are more recreational parks with lawns and pools.

Alarmed that Israel's botanical wealth was unwittingly being plundered, SPNI launched a campaign in the 1960s to stop wildflower picking. A law was enacted in 1963 and an educational program begun in the schools. Wildflower picking is no longer a major threat.

The SPNI tree has three main branches: protection, education/research, and experience. Its protection limb still works to protect the natural areas of Israel. A system of field schools throughout the country provides research facilities for scientists as well as accommodations for visitors.

SPNI's array of field trips, ranging from a day to two weeks, of-

fered in Hebrew or English, allow both Israelis and visitors to enjoy and learn about the country's natural diversity. More than a million people participate in SPNI activities each year, including 70 percent of school children via class field trips. Israeli Arabs are part of SPNI, serving as field guides and spreading environmental awareness within Arab communities.

As SPNI has grown, other environmental organizations have sprung up in Israel: Israel Union for Environmental Defense, Guardians of the Environment, and EcoNet Israel are just a few. Two major issues facing Israel's conservation community are the rapid loss of a green belt in the Judean Hills and shrinking natural areas along the coast.

Turtles cluster on papyrus mounds amid Hulah's marshes, where ducks nest and marsh cats roam.

A Taste of Hulah

I had been staying at the field school atop Mount Meron and left early one morning for Hulah. Despite the fact that mountains lie all around, in plain sight, I am always slightly surprised by how hilly the Galilee is, as if I had not noticed it before. Winding down the steep curves of breeze-blown Mount Meron, I could feel the three-thousand-foot descent as well as see it. The fresh mountain air became progressively hotter and heavier, still and moist.

In the Hulah Valley, drifts of mustard plants undulated alongside the road, their sweep of yellow broken by springy mounds of green poterium. Standing amid the mustard were redbud trees, their deep pink flowers the color of a steamy tango.

High above, the hills were capped by white and gray limestone boulders, softened by chartreuse banks of Jerusalem spurge.

Between top and bottom, thorny broom blazed, suffusing the entire valley with its sweet scent. To the north, I could see the Naphtali Hills, glowing yellow with broom washed by morning sunlight.

On raw, gray days, the Hulah Valley can seem as austere and cerebral as the music of a Schönberg psalm. That day there was no such chill. I was listening to the bright, pulsing rhythms of Brazilian jazz as I drove through the newmade morning. I can close my eyes, see that golden scene and hear the rhythms still.

About twenty thousand years ago, the scene would not have been so sunny. That was one of the periods when Golan volcanoes were spewing lava. During that time, a thick rim of basalt oozed down to block the southern end of the Hulah Valley, forming the Korazim Plateau. This rim held back ancient Lake Hulah, but not the channel of the Jordan River flowing through the lake.

Inexorably, the Jordan chipped away at the Korazim Plateau, cutting a narrow canyon through it down to the Sea of Galilee. Over time, the river deepened its canyon, creating what is called the "mountainous Jordan." The deeper the Jordan cut, the faster water drained from Lake Hulah until only a shallow basin surrounded by swamps remained.

But shallow lakes and marshlands mean life. Terrestrial life was born in such places. At Hulah, among the thickets of papyrus, fish swim, turtles hide, ducks build nests, wading birds hunt.

The name Hulah aptly derives from the Hebrew word meaning "paper reed," for the tall papyrus reeds that crowd the marsh. More than forty-five hundred years ago, Egyptians discovered how to make paper from this plant.

229

Spring or fall migration presents the broadest number of bird species at Hulah. In winter, birds from the north congregate. Whatever the season, early morning is a good time to wander the paths and boardwalks of the Hulah Reserve. Not only are more birds visible in early morning, but people are absent, leaving reserve and birds undisturbed.

More than half of Israel's five hundred bird species either live or pass through Hulah. At the observation point near the visitor center, I could see Mount Hermon in the distance and, close up, a host of birds. A white-breasted kingfisher flashed its brilliant turquoise back as it darted past. A bulbul perched atop a ten-foot-tall phragmites reed, a blackbird on another reed.

A small flock of red-faced goldfinches swirled in to find perches among the reeds and were soon hidden among the rustling stalks. A

formation of bee-eaters swooped by in supple flight, catching insects on the fly, the morning sun dancing across their green, yellow, and cinnamon plumage. Finished with their night's hunting, a clutch of night herons hunched on the limbs of patchy shrubs, pearl gray bodies crowned by velvety black. Frogs sang a dissonant song from hidden places, having survived hunting herons yet another night.

In addition to birds, mammals, fish, amphibians, and reptiles, all sorts of insects including butterflies live within Hulah Reserve. But the first mammal I saw that morning happened to be an alien. As I was crossing the bridge to the swamp trail, I looked down and saw a hairy body plying the water. It was a mammal quite familiar to me, one I had last seen in the bayous and swamps of the Mississippi Delta.

About the size of a beaver but with a long, rat tail, the nutria is a large aquatic rodent from South America. The nutria was introduced into Israel with the idea that it could be bred for its fur. The project failed, some animals escaped, and now nutrias have settled in the waters of Hulah, a perfect habitat for them. Nutrias were brought to the swamps of Louisiana with the same purpose in mind. The same thing happened, and now swamps in the southern United States are full of nutrias.

Still clouded by a thin veil of morning mist, the waters below the bridge were full of fish, the most obvious fat carp, another species introduced for commercial purposes. Gambusia, brought from North America, are too small to be obvious. The 2.5-inch-long fish were introduced because they feed on mosquito larvae, scooping them up with an extended lower jaw. Used here and throughout North America, gambusia are a more environment-friendly solution to controlling mosquitoes than the toxic pesticide DDT.

On another visit, the central figure on this watery stage was a three-foot-long catfish, thrashing frenetically, flicking its long, Manchu mustache as it consumed a small fish. The huge catfish of the Hulah, like tilapia and plants such as papyrus, migrated from Africa, making their way north up a flooded Great Rift in the distant past.

Walking along the trail, I noticed a shrub whose leaves looked familiar, reminding me of childhood and my mother's garden: Persian lilac. Another interloper, albeit a sweet one, lilac made its way to Hulah as seeds in the fill dirt for Hulah's dikes. Plants and animals have become international travelers whether we mean for them to or not. They have hitchhiked with us since the time of camel caravans, but now with planes, boats, and trucks, the pace is considerably faster.

Hulah Reserve provides a fine bird list to carry along the trail, but I had run across a much older one. Leviticus 11:13-19, in spelling out the birds that shall not be eaten, provides an abridged millennia-old bird list:

> They shall not be eaten . . . the griffon vulture, and the bearded vulture, and the lappet-faced vulture; the kite, and each kind of buzzard; all varieties of raven; the ostrich, and the nighthawk, and the seagull, and hawks of every kind; the little owl, and the osprey, and the short-eared owl; the barn owl, and the pelican, and the Egyptian vulture; the stork, and each kind of heron, and the hoopoe, and the bat.

Bats are mammals, nocturnal mammals, and there were none at this time of day. But papyrus-edged water channels, like long narrow rooms, revealed teals here and a rust-colored shelduck there, both tardy in their summer trip to Europe. A group of shovelers spun in tight circles on the water, perhaps practice for soon to come breeding displays. Named for their shovel-shaped bills, the ducks use their bills to scoop up mud and water, filtering it to find insects, duckweed, and other food. Graceful warblers sang from the willows, and on every available floating log, turtles lined up like dark green coins.

A lone white egret stalked the shallows, and, nearby, a coot floated. **231** Where there is one coot, there are bound to be more. Small, chunky, and soot-colored with white bills, coots group together in especially large flocks during winter, then move north to Europe in spring.

Emerging from the papyrus marshes, the trail opened to views of much-reduced Lake Hulah. Cattle egrets skimmed low, flapping sparingly. A pair of mallards, rising from the water at my approach, took off with that overly energetic flap-flap-flap of ducks built more for floating than flying. High above, buzzards circled.

In the middle distance, over the open water, a vortex of storks rose. Just below them, a neat line of white pelicans flew only inches above the water before landing on a narrow bar of land jutting into the lake. A pas de deux of species.

At the far end of the trail, overlooking the water, is a long, covered blind. On one of the benches within, I sat with my binoculars, desultorily watching a raft of gulls floating across the way, wondering where all the cormorants were.

I had drifted into a daydream when a soaring figure caught my eye. I looked, and looked again. It was an exceedingly large raptor with a white fantail soaring skyward. Only one bird fits that description—the white-tailed eagle, the very bird that helped save this swamp. An endangered species throughout its range, the eagle is being reintroduced in the Hulah.

The white-tailed eagle is still a rare sight. Excited, and afraid to look away and lose the bird, I continued to stare until the eagle became a dot, and the dot disappeared into the sky. I wanted to tell someone, but there was no one to tell. I stored the memory and drifted back to the serene scene before me.

Sometimes a panorama presents lush ripeness rather than the stark drama of, say, a mountain. This is Hulah in the warmth of summer, when it takes on a sultry cast. Papyrus flourishes, creating emerald thickets where winter's thatch lay brown and broken. Rising eight or nine feet and topped by feathery umbels, the papyrus reeds rustle together like knots of people murmuring under green parasols.

By the time I left the blind, plenty of people walked the paths, many of them families with children, in a nation that delights in its children. Young brothers, sisters, and cousins ran back and forth, clattered up the stairs of the observation tower, then raced down, daring each other, whooping with the pleasure of motion. Of course they did not realize that such jubilant shouting scares away the birds, but for them birds took a back seat to sheer exuberance.

232

I, too, climbed to the top of the observation tower. The soft-focus view reminded me of another critical and incomparable marshland: Florida's Everglades. A sea of tall grasses growing from shallow water, the Everglades were drained and channeled: more than 90 percent of wading birds are now gone from the Everglades. Wetlands of India and South America—wetlands worldwide—face similar manipulation and ruin. The importance of wetlands, those subtle, watery ecosystems that serve as nurseries for a rich array of wildlife, is underestimated everywhere.

Fortunately, life can renew itself given half a chance. Along a Hulah dike, at the water's edge, yellow flag irises hold up sunny flowers. Lying atop Hulah's waters, fluid gardens of yellow waterlilies are making a comeback after the disruptions of the past.

Bladderwort, a carnivorous plant, is a nearby resident. It also floats on water, its leaves supported by air-filled sacs set with trap doors. When a tiny insect touches the sensitive hairs on these doors, the doors instantly drop inward sucking water and insect inside. The plant then uses digestive juices to consume the insect.

Water buffalo, who lived within the Hulah Valley historically, have their own paddock in the reserve. Water buffalo had been domesticated in India for thousands of years and were brought to this region in about 600 C.E., just before the rise of Islam. In Egypt they were used extensively as draft animals and still are.

Crusaders, whose communities were enriched by arts and cultural ideas brought back from the Middle East, brought back the water buffalo, too. Classic Italian mozzarella cheese is made from water buffalo milk. Tolerant of weather and water, and able to forage on most plants, water buffalo have been employed all around the Mediterranean.

Other hydrophilic plants crowd the waters of the Hulah Reserve, from giant reeds to duckweed, one of the world's smallest flowering plants. Some European reeds live here at their southern limit, and some African reeds at their northern limit. Boars, and otters, and marsh cats, small wild felines that hunt at the edges of wetlands, are among the mammals that inhabit Hulah Reserve.

Not all of the animals that once lived in the Hulah Valley survived the draining of the swamp. Although extirpated from Hulah, the purple coot and the anhinga, a black and silver fishing bird, live elsewhere in the world. Hulah's Rhyothemis dragonfly and round-tongue frog were not so fortunate. Both are now extinct, expunged from the line of the living.

233

Smaller reserves protecting other remnants of the swamp lie nearby. In the mid-1990s, the Israel Nature and National Parks Protection Authority, with the help of the Jewish National Fund, began flooding another section of what was formerly Hulah Swamp. The first time I tried to find the "new" Hulah, I ended up in what looked like the parking area of an industrial plant, so I turned back. The next time I went with Roni, the SPNI guide I had met on the Golan, and who consumes natural history with the energy and enthusiasm of a twenty-something. She knew the way. I had just not gone far enough.

The new Hulah lies less than three miles north of Hulah Reserve and about a mile south of Ko'ah Junction, where a dirt road loops around open waters dotted by small islands of papyrus. The place has a languid feel and few enough visitors that birds are not shy.

Marsh hawks flew low, looking for prey. Gray herons, purple herons, and black-winged stilts slowly explored the water's edge on their

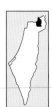

long legs, looking for a fat frog or fish to spear. Moorhens, coots, and garganeys floated in inlets, each species grouped with its own kind. Wagtails, blackcaps, bee-eaters, and spur-winged plovers were among the many other birds in view. It seemed that if we went slowly enough and were so inclined, we could check half the species on the bird list.

Jordan: River of Memories

The Jordan is one of the most celebrated rivers in the world, glorified in psalms, stories, and history. It is mentioned almost two hundred times in the Bible, more than any other natural feature. The river has associations that resonate for Jews, Christians, and Muslims. But for scores of first-time visitors who expect a river of mythic proportions, this slender stream—so imbued with meaning—comes as something of a disappointment.

"Jordan River's deep and wide . . ." goes the gospel song, a description better suited to the lower Nile. More accurate is another verse, "Jordan River's chilly and cold, it chills the body but not the soul."

Certainly, born of spring water, the Jordan is chilly. Certainly, it has captured imaginations and souls. But the Jordan is, after all, a real river and a modest one at that. The lowest river in the world, the Jordan is nearly two hundred miles long, dropping more than two thousand feet over its length. It is little more than thirty feet at its widest. Its width and length are constantly changing in small ways as banks erode and collapse, altering the many bends in the river.

Of late, the Jordan has seen other changes as well. Increasingly, river rafting and tubing have become popular. Some changes have been more intrusive. With the draining of the Hulah, whose spongy breadth served as a natural reservoir, sections of the Jordan had to be widened and dammed to stem flooding.

The Jordan is most easily and naturally experienced along the stretch between Gadot and Bet Tseda (Bethsaida) Junctions, where Routes 918 and 888 parallel the river. The dirt road that also parallels the river and leads past Kefar ha-Nasi allows views and rambles down to the Jordan along the way.

Near Gadot, where paleontologists discovered fossils of hippopotamus and elephant, lies the Benot Ya'aqov Bridge. Below, the mountainous Jordan tumbles along, cutting through rock, its banks tight with vegetation. A trail just south of the bridge follows the racing river downstream.

As it makes its way south, the Jordan becomes more mild-mannered, flowing smoothly toward Lake Kinneret. Just north of Bet Tseda Junction lies Jordan Park, cooperatively run by the Israel Nature and National Parks Protection Authority, the Jewish National Fund, and the Sea of Galilee Administration. The park includes some of each group's spheres of interest: a section of the Jordan River, its wild banks and side channels, pleasant picnic grounds, ancient ruins, plus kayak and food concessions.

Tel Bet Tseda, where Apostles Peter and Andrew were born, lies within the park. A lovely spot to grow up, with the rushing Jordan only paces away, shaded by willows whose limbs lean

With its ruffled scarlet flowers, lustrous green leaves, and large globes of red fruit, the pomegranate looks a tree worthy of honor. In Greek legend it was guarded for the gods: Persephone, daughter of the goddess Demeter, was punished for eating the fruit of one. The red rind peels back to reveal juicy seeds the color of rubies, so many hundreds of seeds that the pomegranate has long been a symbol of fertility. Even today, young women wear gold earrings fashioned as pomegranates.

Although the pomegranate has thrived in Israel for millennia, it was introduced probably from Iran, where it grows wild. Persian recipes, among the earliest food recipes recorded, used pomegranate juice as a base for sauces: those classic dishes endure.

over the water. The river, reflecting the dense vegetation, is colored a soft blue-green. Lines of boulders beneath the surface create riffles of whitewater, eddies, and quiet backwaters. In spring, wildflowers bloom where the Jordan's banks are open to the sun.

Pomegranates grow within the park, the remains of Arab orchards. They were one of the seven species mentioned by the spies Moses sent to scout Canaan. And they have been honored since at least the time of the Exodus, when the hem of the high priest's robes were ornamented with bells and pomegranates (*rimmonim*) fashioned in gold. Sculpted stone pomegranates decorated the capitals of columns that supported the Temple. The Bible speaks of Solomon's orchard of pomegranates, and later: "I would let you drink of the spiced wine / Of my pomegranate juice" (Song of Songs 8:2).

After the destruction of the First and Second Temples, *rimmonim* were incorporated in the ornamental crowns atop the Torah. From

intricate, filigree Yemeni silverwork to spare Bauhaus design, To-rahs around the world are crowned by this fruitful imagery.

Myrtles add their fresh and fragrant leaves to the green tapestry that lines the Jordan, growing where the banks are steep. A symbol of success, myrtle branches are woven into wedding wreaths for good luck.

In addition to willows and myrtles, palms grow here, too. To-gether, these three make a lulav, specified in Leviticus 23:40 for celebrating Sukkot, one of the oldest Jewish festivals. With Pesach and Shavuot, it is one of the three pilgrimage-harvest holidays, the first holidays mentioned in the Bible.

During the autumn holiday of Sukkot, people live and eat in sukkot, temporary dwellings partially open to the sky. Life is temporal; we should be glad and grateful for what we have. The Sukkot ritual requires holding the bound sheaf of palm fronds, willow, and myrtle together with an aromatic etrog. The etrog, or citron, is a fruit that may have entered Israel from Persia when the Jews returned from exile in Babylonia in the fifth century B.C.E. As the lulav is waved to the four directions, plus the sky and the earth, it makes a whispery, hypnotic sound and makes clear how much nature has influenced the spiritual.

In Jordan Park, where grass runs down to the banks of the Jordan, I had settled with a book, intending to spend some time toward the end of an afternoon. But rain changed my plans, and I got in the car, turning it north through the Hulah Valley and the gloom created by gray skies.

As I returned toward Mount Meron, the clouds parted and the sun cast a brilliant rainbow against the Golan, each leg of the bow plunged into the Jordan River. Looking up, I saw gilt-edged, God-speaks clouds. Rays of sunlight piercing the clouds poured down on the mountains of Meron, especially one peak whose crown is Safed, the city of holy men and mystics. It happened just that way.

Canyon of the Woolen Mills

Safed is inextricably tied to Nahal Ammud, a stream that has cut a lovely canyon through the hills south of Safed. For residents of sixteenth-century Safed, Nahal Ammud was a walk away. And they walked there often, for they had business in Nahal Ammud.

The highest perennial stream west of the Great Rift, Nahal Ammud flows southeast, entering Lake Kinneret near Ginnosar. Like most of the rock associated with the Meron Range, the walls of Nahal Ammud are limestone. The name *ammud* means "pillar," referring to the pillar of limestone that rises alongside the stream in the lower reaches of the canyon.

The limestone pillar stands alone in the spare openness of the lower Ammud, separated from the nearby cliffs by thousands of years of erosion. When Canon Tristram ventured through here in the mid-1800s, he noted the many vultures roosting on the pillar and the cliffs. Near the pillar lie caves where archaeologists have found bones and artifacts of prehistoric humans.

Whereas the lower Ammud is a sunny, rock-walled gorge, the upper Ammud is shaded by trees. The hillsides overlooking the stream-bed are full of almond and calliprinos oak, broom, and thorny green cushions of poterium. Among the trees and shrubs, wildflowers scatter themselves: red poppies, rose-colored bear's-breeches, pink orchids, and, nestled in its rosette of sword-shaped leaves, the exquisite, pure white star-of-Bethlehem, a relative of the lily.

As much as it is a walk in nature, Nahal Ammud is a walk into the past. In addition to wildflowers, an old British fortification, left from the Mandate period, overlooks the streambed. The Ottoman Turks held the Middle East for four hundred years, but after they were defeated in World War I, the British took over Palestine. They mounted pillboxes and other fortifications along roads, and the hills of Galilee are still dotted with these structures. The one at the head of Nahal Ammud was built to control Safed's water supply.

237

The descent toward the streambed passes terraces where Arabs once tended their orchards. Fig trees and old, twisted olive trees grow wild now. Ein Tina, one of many springs whose name means Spring of the Fig in Arabic, is marked with a huge fig tree.

Water races through a centuries-old aqueduct paralleling the stream. Its tumultuous energy powered flour mills used by Arabs before 1948, the year of Israel's independence. Even earlier, the water powered flour mills and woolen mills built by the renowned six-teenth-century Jewish community of Safed. The water still runs past these ancient mills through the aqueduct whose stone sides are edged by green maidenhair ferns. Berry brambles grow thickly along the path that parallels the aqueduct.

The flowers of wood-sorrel, an immigrant from South Africa, add small, low spots of yellow to the shaded undergrowth. The cloverlike plant was spread throughout moist, shady areas of Israel by mole rats, which bring wood-sorrel bulbs into their burrows, inadvert-ently "planting" them.

Mills Ruins, Nahal Ammud

A robust styrax tree leans toward the path. Goats and other mammals, knowing the styrax is poisonous, do not browse its leaves, so where styrax grows it usually looks healthy. Ground styrax fruit once was used as a poison to kill mice, perhaps in these very flour mills.

One side of the streambed is shaded by its own high walls. The other side is baked by the full force of the sun. The difference between the two is striking. On the shady side, trees, shrubs, ferns—all manner of greenery grows. On the south-facing slopes, dazzling sunlight dries out all but low, meager vegetation. Sabra cactus, poppies, and tall blue hyacinth squill manage to grow on the sunny side amid ranks of glinting white limestone.

Atop one ancient wall, the aqueduct channels water to a narrow shaft where it drops straight into the ruins of a mill, providing all the energy the mill owner needed. Twenty-four mills once lined Nahal Ammud, so it was also called Wadi of the Mills. How the mills came to be here is intriguing history.

After 1492 and the beginning of the Spanish Inquisition, Jews fled persecution by immigrating to Turkey, Italy, other areas of Europe, and to Spanish colonies in what is now Mexico and New Mexico. They also returned to Israel. In Safed, a remarkable group of learned rabbis gathered and began enriching the mystical kabbalistic tradition.

At their center was Rabbi Isaac Luria, called Ha-Ari—the Lion. **239** In order to support themselves, many of Safed's kabbalists became master woolmakers, including Ha-Ari. Their fabrics were of such quality that they became known throughout the Mediterranean, although it probably helped that coreligionists in Europe marketed their goods. What remains of their mills still lines Nahal Ammud.

The mills used water to power long wooden paddles that pressed the wool in water-filled vats. The wool was shrunk to make it water resistant, then dyed. Rabbis would regularly make the two- to three-hour walk from Safed to check on their mills. Along the way, they passed terraces full of fruit trees.

In those days, as in the days of the Nabateans and Byzantines centuries before, the hills of Israel were much more heavily cultivated than now. Gas-powered equipment cannot manage the steep slopes, whereas animal-powered effort could manage almost any gradient. With orchards, mills, and workers coming and going, this narrow wadi must have been a busy place.

Nahal Ammud is busy still. Where the wadi widens and a grove of

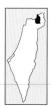

Ferns and moss are uncommon in Israel, yet they are found in the heart of Nahal Ammud and other moist, tree-shaded canyons.

tall plane trees shades the splashing, mountainous stream and its cool banks, schoolchildren—fifth-graders by their looks—were eating lunch. I stepped over and around, opting for a quieter spot just below.

After lunch, when the children hiked back to their bus, cellophane snack bags, candy wrappers, tissues, and plastic bags layered the ground. SPNI was wildly successful in its wildflower protection campaign but, so far, much less successful in figuring out how to stanch the garbage that litters the most popular hiking trails.

Pulling out my usual lunch of olives, dates, and mango yogurt, I looked up into the oriental plane trees that grow sixty feet high here at the southern limit of their range. Odd for them to be in such a place, but the streamside setting was right. Through the broad, maple-shaped leaves I could make out the bark of the high limbs, patterned in the familiar tan, cream, and pink patches.

240

The spring-fed stream at my feet runs cold and wild, spilling over boulders like a true mountain stream. Clusters of leathery ferns grow at the base of moss-covered rocks. An arum opens its pale green hood to reveal a tall purple spike at its center.

Aerie of Mount Meron

Israel is said to have some of the world's worst drivers. Far more people are killed in traffic accidents each year than by terrorists. Choosing discretion over valor, I made my way up Mount Meron from the Hulah by joining a line of sedate drivers on the wide highway shoulders. Let the road warriors joust in the middle lanes.

On a clear day, one lookout point on the road winding up from the Hulah Valley allows a view of both Mount Hermon to the east, shining above the Golan, and the blue Mediterranean Sea on the west. And, as always in Israel, matching the natural is the historic.

Rabbi Simeon bar Yohai survived the Bar Kokhba Revolt then evaded a Roman death sentence by escaping to a cave on Mount Meron with his son, where it is said they subsisted on the fruit of the carob tree for thirteen years. Although scholars say the Zohar was written in medieval Spain, others believe this mystical Torah commentary was written by Rabbi Simeon while he lived in the cave. Tradition puts the anniversary of the rabbi's death on the holiday of Lag ba-Omer, a holiday of weddings, picnics, and tree planting. On that day, the Mount Meron groves surrounding his tomb are filled with the faithful.

Near the Meron Junction on the way to SPNI's Mount Meron Field School, lies the tomb of Rabbi Simeon (Shimon) bar Yohai.

Soon after the community of Sasa, a small road branches off toward Mount Meron Field School, nestled among a grove of trees within the Mount Meron Reserve. The field school is not far from the top of Mount Meron, at nearly four thousand feet Israel's second-tallest peak and the tallest peak west of the Great Rift. The cool moist air of the mountaintop allows lichen to flourish in the oaks. Long feathery strands of gray lichen, sometimes called Spanish moss, and tight clusters of bright yellow lichen provide natural decoration.

Where the grove opens to let in spring sunlight, anemones brighten the grasses in tones of blue, purple, pink, and white. From gravelly soils grow blue afternoon iris, so named because each flower lasts only an afternoon. Jays wing between oaks, announcing themselves with raucous calls. Doves and blackcaps live among the trees as well.

I stayed for a time on the mountain and came to recognize a pair of Syrian woodpeckers living nearby. One or the other of the black-and-white-patterned birds was always visible hopping up a trunk, the male distinguished by the smudge of red decorating the nape of his neck. Woodpeckers' short stiff tails make a tripod with their sharp-taloned feet, allowing them to walk up trunks and balance while they hammer at bark, looking to winkle out tasty insects. In order to absorb the trauma of continuous pounding, the woodpecker's brain-pan is held in place by an avian version of high-performance shock absorbers.

Syrian woodpeckers live throughout northern and central Israel, but their numbers are dependent on the numbers of their preferred trees: almonds, oaks, and pines. They also have included the recently

241

introduced eucalyptus among acceptable tree types. During the first half of the 1900s, when trees were cut during the two world wars, woodpecker numbers fell. Since the 1950s, forest groves and orchards have been planted, so woodpecker numbers have risen.

Among the gentle grasses and groves, field school buildings fit unobtrusively: offices, a dining room, a tiny museum, and a scattering of low white modules. Like an aerie, the modest complex sits high above the rest of northern Galilee, quiet during the day but for the birds and the wind. The office manager said that once an Englishman came to Mount Meron and rented a room for the summer in order to finish a book he was writing. An ideal location.

During school holidays, however, the nights are anything but quiet. High-school students spend a night or two at the field school, hiking around the reserve during the day. During my stay, their buses often arrived late in the evening, but I could always distinguish between Arab and Jewish teens by the type of music that blared through windows and walls until near midnight. What they had in common was the decibel level.

In the dining room I often sat with teens working in the reserve for a few months between Army and university. At dinner, big bowls of soup and platters of vegetables and meat were passed around the table. The family-style meals encouraged conversation.

242

Returning one evening minutes before the field school gates closed, I hurried up the path to the dining room, relieved to find that I had not missed dinner. High-school teens milled around, engaged in high-pitched social interactions. A slight apricot glow at the edge of the sky showed me which direction was west. I looked up and saw that the dark, moonless sky was smeared with a large thumbprint of white light.

Thinking my eyes were tired, I looked away, rubbed them, then looked again. The luminous thumbprint remained. I asked a group of teens nearby if they knew what it was. They had been so engrossed in talking they had not noticed the sky and now were as puzzled and fascinated as I. Excited speculation buzzed through the group. The next day, a field school staffer nonchalantly explained that what we had seen was a comet.

The field school serves as the gateway to the Mount Meron Reserve. At twenty-five thousand acres, the reserve is the largest north of the Negev because the terrain has always been too difficult to cultivate. The Israel Nature and National Parks Protection Authority decided to preserve nearly the whole mountain, which is ringed with a variety of trails. Sinkholes and caves tell a story of karst formation, of limestone dissolving and reforming as stalactites, of water percolating through the hills to burst forth as springs. It is a story common in the hills of the Galilee, although springs are not as common here as in some parts of the north.

Polecat and marten live within the forests of Mount Meron. Bear and leopard once lived here, too. Salamanders and green lizards, uncommon in Israel, occasionally can be spotted: the former near streams, the latter zipping among rocks. Rare flora includes round-leaved cyclamen, orchids, and the wild peony. The peony, with its rose-colored blossoms, is at its southern limit on Mount Meron, the only place in Israel where it grows.

Near the head of the trail leading to the top of Mount Meron, I was greeted by a huge olive tree, twisted by age and surrounded by clumps of its own shoots. "Your sons are like olive saplings around your table," says Psalms 128:3, with as much accuracy as elegance.

A canopy of moss-hung oak arches over the trail, intimate as a wedding huppah. Small arbutus trees with red peeling bark and strawberry-red fruit, rockrose shrubs with rose-petaled flowers, and vining greenbrier crowd together in the understory.

The soil under the oaks had been roughed up, and not one acorn lay on the ground. Wild boars were here, eating the acorns, and a few tufts of gray boar's hair caught on a greenbrier gave away their presence.

243

Where the trail opens up, see-forever views of the rest of the Meron Range are framed by wild almond trees with delicate white flowers. In these sunny areas, the trail becomes a narrow track hugging the side of the mountain. Low mounds of poterium and broom muscle against each other alongside the trail. In the sun-warmed soil grow tall spikes of lavender sage and pink Anatolian orchids, whose dainty white throats are dotted like a landing strip, showing insects where to pick up and deposit pollen.

As the trail winds upward, it passes in and out of forests of Boissier oak and pine. Young Atlantic cedars, with clusters of blue-green needles, have been planted near the top. These are from North Africa's Atlas Mountains but are related to the cedars of Lebanon that King Solomon imported for the First Temple.

A cobbled circular overlook announces Mount Meron's peak. At eye level, a short-toed eagle hovers over a giddy drop-off as scarves of gray cloud swirl in, obscuring the summit and the military post there. Always, in Israel, nature and security meet at the top.

CHAPTER TEN

Western Galilee and Mount Carmel:

Where Mountains and Mediterranean Meet

Qeshet Cave

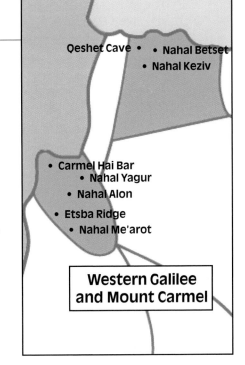

Western Galilee and Mount Carmel

Qeshet Cave • • Nahal Betset
• Nahal Keziv

• Carmel Hai Bar
• Nahal Yagur
• Nahal Alon
• Etsba Ridge
• Nahal Me'arot

AT FIRST GLANCE, WESTERN GAL-
ILEE looks like a dense mix of
towns, farms, and industrial
zones. It is hard to imagine where the
natural areas might be hiding. But they
are there, and those who search them
out are rewarded.

Although the region's southern limits are fuzzy, the rest are clear. To the
north, western Galilee is defined by
the hilly border with Lebanon. On the east, the massive wall of Mount

Meron divides western Galilee from northern Galilee. On its western flanks, Mount Meron's foothills merge into coastal plain that
spreads to the Mediterranean Sea.

The western flanks of Mount Meron, the foothills, and the hills at
the Lebanese border all conceal alluring natural areas. Part of their
charm is their obscurity.

Because the hills and high country of western Galilee are mostly
porous limestone, the region is dotted with caves and, in places, layer
springs rush forth. Catching moisture sweeping in from the sea, the
heights of western Galilee are enveloped with Mediterranean vegetation: oaks and pistacia, hawthorn and pine. Laurel and oleander
settle close to streambeds. Carob, which prefers drier terrain, lives
on sunny slopes.

Roe deer and fallow deer once hid among the forests. Perhaps one
day they will again. Leopards lived here, too; some say they still do.
The animals that do inhabit western Galilee include fox and wild
boar, hyrax, porcupine, dormouse and other rodents, reptiles, cuck-
oos, jays, and a host of woodland birds.

The streams that pour down the eastern side of Mount Meron have a steep but short, wild ride down to the Great Rift. The streams on the western side are more leisurely. Nahal Keziv, which drains the western flanks of Mount Meron, meanders approximately twenty-five miles to the Mediterranean Sea.

As Nahal Keziv rambles toward the coast, the terrain flattens out, becoming a broad, low plain as it approaches the coastal cities of Nahariyah and Acre (Akko). If the image of Israel is one of rocky hills covered with low, thorny bushes or desert oases dotted with palms and acacia, Nahal Keziv feels like an afternoon in European woods. The evocative ruins of a Crusader fortress, preserved in Montfort National Park, overlook the forested gorge of Nahal Keziv Reserve, which lies about halfway between Keziv's headwaters on Mount Meron and its meeting with the sea.

Although winter floods can swell the stream to rampage proportions, Nahal Keziv is usually gentle, rippling over stones, its banks shaded by tall plane trees and laurels. Arbutus trees, their bark exfoliating in soft, reddish strips, arch from the hillside like languid dancers, giving the landscape a gauzy feel. Farther up the slopes, oak and pistacia, which are better at taking the heat, spread green arms.

A few flour mills remain from the days when water, rather than fossil fuels, powered a slower-moving way of life. Where the stream spreads out, pools form, and, among the rocks, small green lizards chase each other. They look like they are playing, but their games are tests of territory here near the southern limit of their range. The Palestine viper, the only poisonous snake found throughout Israel, is another reptile that lives here. Vipers, like many snakes, hide unseen among rocks.

Madonna lily blooms within the canyon of Nahal Keziv, but perhaps not quite here or at this season, or perhaps it, too, is hiding among the rocks. Hiding is a good strategy. In the past, pilgrims to Palestine would pluck out the plant to carry home, seeing the magnificent pure white trumpets with yellow anthers as a symbol of chastity. Madonna lilies, which grow sparsely on Mount Carmel and in the more northern parts of the Galilee, are now rare because they were so treasured.

The singular voice of a cuckoo sounds somewhere in the trees, either on passage to Europe from Africa or to stay briefly and mate. With buff breast, long tail, and a pattern of white dots spanning its gray wings, the cuckoo is pleasant-looking—but a negligent parent. Once a pair has mated, the female lays eggs, one per nest, in the

246

nests of other birds. Then she abandons the eggs, leaving hooded crows, pipits, or certain warblers to raise her babies.

Once it hatches, the baby cuckoo may destroy the unsuspecting mother's legitimate eggs or nestlings so that she will devote all her energy to feeding the cuckoo. Although the cuckoo's deceptive and murderous behavior seems repellent, it is a successful strategy.

Cave of the Djinn in Nahal Betset

Long ago, near Banias in northern Galilee, there lived a prophet named Ido. I had met his namesake in the Judean Desert, where Ido was working as a guide for SPNI. Sometimes, with his red beard and thin, ascetic face, Ido looked like a biblical prophet, but a prophet with a touch of Pan, constantly belying the stern visage with songs and jokes. We had decided to be friends as well as hiking partners because it is rare to find someone who appreciates both plant arcana and bad puns.

Our goal was Nahal Betset, western Galilee's northernmost river system, which drains into the Mediterranean near Rosh ha-Niqrah. We started in a small, quiet tributary, Nahal Sharakh, a tributary longer than its parent and named for the many ferns that adorn its shady depths. Nahal Sharakh begins near the Lebanese border, but we began farther downstream, where the *nahal* is crowded with Boissier oak and pistacia—mastic pistacia with strongly aromatic leaves.

247

In the dappled light, sinkholes greeted us, a sure sign of karstic activity and caves to come. Sinkholes form where dissolving lime-stone creates a funnel into the earth. The Hebrew word for sink-holes means "swallowers," and the shadowed slopes of these funnels provide a home to a host of shade-lovers: ferns and mosses, lichen and fungi—plants not often seen in Israel.

Close to the stream, which rippled with springtime water, grace-ful laurel trees grow, scenting the air with spicy sweetness. Behind their glossy leaves, birds sang songs of information and exultation in languages I do not know but can appreciate.

Forest dormice live here, in nests among the branches, hidden from our sight. Hyraxes also keep out of sight among the rocks. Undoubtedly they heard us but would not appear again until the crunching and crackling of our footsteps faded. Beyond happy acci-dent, the best way to see wildlife is the patient way. Pick a spot and sit there; become part of the background until wildlife feels safe

enough to emerge from hiding. Wildlife biologists can match moments of animal sightings with hours of cramped muscles.

A short distance before the confluence of the Sharakh and Betset streams, the small, dark mouth of a cave pierces the rocky walls of the streambed. Outside the cave, three young men with climbing ropes were eating lunch, sitting on rocks under the trees. We exchanged greetings, passed them, and, as we entered the cave, switched on small flashlights that shed just enough light for us to see our way but not enough to dispel the cave's mystery. We turned off our lights as Ido told the story of the cave—for every cave has a story:

Long ago, a young Arab met a beautiful young woman. He fell in love with her and she with him, but they belonged to rival tribes. Still, the young man's father was sympathetic to his son's infatuation and agreed to speak with the girl's father. Her father grudgingly agreed to hear the young man's plea, but he had one condition.

"You may have my daughter as your bride," he said, "if you agree to spend a night in the cave." The cave was reputed to be the home of a fearful djinn, and no one dared enter alone or at night. The father thought this would quash the suitor's ardor. But no. The young man's love made him brave.

The next night he entered the cave with his *shabaria* ("knife"). In the deep of the night a storm raged in from the sea, clouds tossed and thundered, and torrents of rain darkened the sky. The young man could hear the thunder rolling closer and closer, thrilling him with fear.

248

Suddenly, lightning flashed, illuminating the cave and the tall, menacing figure of a djinn. The terrified young man tried to strike with his knife, but he lost his grip, and the knife fell. Terrified, he tried to rush from the cave, but he could not tear himself away from the djinn. His heart burst from fear.

The next day, the sheik sent some of his men into the cave to see what had become of his daughter's suitor. They found him dead, pinned to the floor of the cave by his own knife and his fear. There, in front of him, stood the djinn.

At that, Ido flashed his light on the "djinn," a water-molded giant of a stalagmite cloaked in a robe with many folds. Sheer theater.

Near where Nahal Sharakh meets Nahal Betset, the canyon widens, allowing views of its slopes, thickly wooded with oak and pistacia and studded with caves. The canyon closed in again, and, as we walked under a green canopy of trees, we talked of nature, travel, families, and the complexities of raising teenagers.

In Nahal Betset proper, a line of plane trees marks the stream. Below the tall trees grow laurels and snarls of berry bushes, which the birds would soon raid. Sage and stalks of blue hyacinth squill sprout in patches of sunlight that spot the banks. A Syrian woodpecker ignored us to work at drilling a hole in a Syrian ash tree.

The stream slipped glassily over lips of rock, providing pleasant background music. Suddenly, the stream seemed to disappear into a tunnel of tall pink-blossomed oleander shrubs. Beyond the tunnel of oleander stood a few huge European hackberry trees, their smooth gray trunks so old and deformed they looked like evil fairy-tale trees from a Disney movie. Balanced at the edge of Nahal Betset, the hackberries' bare roots wrapped their woody tentacles around streamside boulders.

Small pools, caves, and dense vegetation mark the canyon of Nahal Betset, which flows west to the sea.

In counterpoint to the sound of the stream, we heard lovely lilting music ahead. Around the bend we came upon a man and woman sitting on rocks, facing each other, she playing a guitar and he a clarinet. He saw us first, blushed, and stopped playing. Too bad, their music fit the moment. But almost immediately Nahal Betset ended as well, its waters drawn off through a sluice gate to enter one of the branches of the National Water Carrier, the system of canals that disperses water throughout this water-scarce country.

Our few hours of separation from the urban world seemed too short. So we headed up the tight switchbacks of Route 8993 toward Adamit and the trail to Qeshet Cave.

From the shoulder of the mountainous road, we could see across deep, narrow Nahal Namer to where a cavernous hole pierced the canyon wall: Cave of the Leopard, to match the name of the stream-bed. Nahal Namer winds south into Israel from Lebanon, and we could plainly see villages dotting the Lebanese hills only a few miles away.

In the mid-1900s, before roads were cut through this difficult terrain, Arab shepherds still encountered leopards in Nahal Namer. Some animals, such as porcupine and fox, can tolerate intense human intrusion. Others, like the leopard, cannot.

Arab shepherds still refer to Nahal Namer as Wadi Dalem. Although the words share the same meaning, language can claim a place. In his book *The Israelis: Founders and Sons*, Amos Elon says that the names the early settlers gave their children had the power to transform immigrants to people of place:

> In other countries, mountains are sometimes called after great men; in Israel, men more often call themselves after great mountains.
>
> For many settlers, the new surnames were mythic symbols of a personal and collective rebirth; for a few, they served compensatory needs. The widespread adoption of local flora and place names reflected the frantic desire of the settlers to become one, in body and name, with the landscape of their regained patrimony, its rivers and mountains, its trees and its thorns.

250

So family names were changed from Schwartz and Stern and Belinsky to Hermon, Gilboa, and Tavor. Children were named Yael (ibex), Dov (bear), Rimon (pomegranate), Alon (oak), and Dafnah (laurel). My friend Talia's siblings have such names. Ido's children have such names.

From the hillside parking lot, we walked to the top of the trail. In this remote place some government agency is at work making "improvements." Their goal: make the natural more orderly. Bulldozers have scraped boulder-strewn slopes into tidy terraces, planting them with row upon regulation row of pine saplings, whose tender trunks are protected from gnawing animals by plastic tubing.

Below the new, improved park, lies the earlier, natural version: green cushions of poterium, pink and purple bindweed twining around big cobbles of white chalk, blue bellflowers, and small white crocuslike flowers growing in cracks scattered with snail shells.

Stepping down among the boulders, we came to the edge of a sheer cliff and a view of fields and forests reaching across the flat coastal plains. A glint of sun caught our eyes—the sea, the Mediterranean, a calm sheet of blue at the horizon sparked by spots of sunlight.

We walked farther, stopping atop a massive stone arch, the largest in Israel. On one side we looked out toward the Galilee, on the other we peered down into what is left of Qeshet Cave. Soaring over open space, this arch, or *qeshet*, was all that remained after the roof of the cave collapsed. Far below, where sunlight lit what was once the dark interior of a cave, grasses had attracted a small herd of black goats whose shepherd we could not see.

We watched a pair of Egyptian vultures glide by, a few feet below the clifftop, when the phone rang. Ido pulled a cell phone from his backpack to find a crisis brewing with the builders working on his home: a stairwell, bad measurements, low clearance, decisions and changes necessary and immediate. Enough of the natural for one day.

Mount Carmel: the "Nose of the Gazelle"

Mount Carmel builds slowly, starting from the south where Route 70 swings in to meet the coast roads: scattered outcrops become low ridges, low ridges become hills, gaining momentum, growing massive until the mountainous uplift crests above the Bay of Haifa.

Like much of Israel, the mountain is made of sedimentary layers that have been heaved up, crumpled, and worn by time. Mount Carmel **251** actually is an extension of the Samarian Hills, which parallel the Great Rift for a bit then angle toward the Mediterranean. At the sea, the range ends with evergreen Mount Carmel, but the mountain is separated from the rest of the Samarian Hills by a distinct stream valley.

So Mount Carmel stands alone. Its southern boundary is the valley through which Route 70 runs. To the west, beyond the strip of coastal plain, stretches the Mediterranean Sea. On its eastern side, the mountain drops precipitously toward the Zebulun and Jezreel Valleys. On the north, Mount Carmel thrusts into the sea, forming the "fishhook" of the Bay of Haifa.

At nearly eighteen hundred feet, Mount Carmel is less than half the height of Mount Meron, but it seems high because it rises dramatically from surrounding lowlands. Seen from the sea, the point projecting into Haifa Bay is so prominent that an inscription on an Egyptian tomb, referring to a military venture in the third millennium B.C.E., mentions it as a landmark: "the nose of the gazelle's head." Over the centuries it has remained a landmark for sailors.

Once wooded, the extreme tip of Carmel is now filled with the stair-step streets of Haifa. And the most prominent feature on the mountain is Eshkol Tower, the tall box of a building that dominates the University of Haifa. Below Carmel's serene heights, smoggy air spews from industries rimming the Bay of Haifa, causing residents lung disease two and a half times that of other Israelis.

The bulky middle of Mount Carmel, however, is filled with stream-beds and forests kept green all year by moisture-laden winds sweeping in from the sea. Like much of the north, winters are often cool and rainy and summers warm and humid. Moist sea winds bathe Carmel with more rain and humidity than anywhere else in Israel.

A lack of springs plus a thick Mediterranean maquis of pistacia, oak, carob, and shrubs preserved Carmel from development. At the foot of the mountain, the coastal plain and Zebulun and Jezreel Valleys have been used for as long as people have known how to use land. Unlike Carmel, they are well watered and level. The dawn of agriculture occurred about ten thousand years ago in the Middle East, in river valleys such as the Tigris-Euphrates. For nearly as long, people have been raising crops and herding animals on lowlands surrounding Carmel. As human use grew, wild plants and animals found refuge on the mountain.

252

Today, badgers and gazelle, foxes and jackals, wild boars, rare salamanders, bats, warblers, jays, other woodland birds, a variety of rare orchids, and the country's largest old pine forests live on the Carmel. Wolf and leopard lived here long ago. Fallow deer lived here until the late 1800s and roe deer until the early 1900s. They were destroyed as guns made killing easier and more efficient.

Mount Carmel National Park, the largest in Israel at twenty thousand acres, preserves much of the mountain for wildlife and antiquity. By comparison, Yellowstone National Park, one of the largest in the United States, is about two million acres. But, as a percentage of its country's size, Carmel is far larger. The national park includes archaeological, historical, and sacred sites plus picnic areas and other recreation.

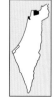

Within the national park lies a number of nature reserves—protected habitat for wildlife. The slopes of Carmel hold a place even more aggressively bent on saving species. Carmel Hai Bar's fifteen hundred acres provide wildlife refuge in contained natural habitats. Carmel's wildlife park also incorporates breeding programs for species such as the wild goat, which once roamed natural Israel and may again.

People began domesticating the wild goat in the Middle East about eight thousand years ago, and the dramatic success of those efforts is sorely ironic. Israel is now replete with domestic goats, but wild goats were eliminated from the area long ago. A relative of the ibex, the wild goat once lived throughout the eastern Mediterranean and western Asia but is becoming rare everywhere.

A subspecies closely related to the wild goat of the Levant still lives in dwindling numbers on the island of Crete, however, and in the early 1980s the Israel Nature and National Parks Protection Authority brought some to Carmel Hai Bar. University of Haifa zoologists and others have been monitoring the wild goat breeding and reintroduction program.

Among their findings: wild goats are picky eaters, preferring sage-leaf rockrose to most other fare. With their browsing and trail cutting, wild goats also open up the dense maquis, allowing wildflowers to flourish where once thickets of rockrose, poterium, and other shrubs defied penetration. Perhaps the goats will provide competition for the boars that churn up the earth in their search for acorns and roots.

Wild sheep and roe deer, once native to Carmel, live at the Hai Bar and are in breeding programs designed to return them to the wild. As these animals were eliminated in recent centuries, raptors had less food, thus the raptor population plummeted. As the mammals return, biologists hope the raptors will, too.

253

Another problem plagued the Mount Carmel raptor populations: agricultural pesticides. Pesticides sprayed to kill rodents and other pests in nearby croplands did a fine job of killing the rodents. But raptors feeding on these rodents absorbed the poison in their bodies and passed it along to their offspring. The deadly results were eggs too fragile to sustain developing chicks. Chicks that did hatch were weakened by the poison and often died. The worst of these pesticides have been banned.

As raptor populations fell, reptile populations rose. Snakes have few natural enemies besides raptors, mongooses, and us. Once the balance of nature is distorted, it is hard to make right.

Not long before the Shah of Iran's regime fell in late 1979, Israeli conservationist Abraham Yoffe, working through Dutch agronomist Michael van Grevenbroek, made contact with a brother of the Shah. Between political upheaval and war with Iraq, Iran's fallow deer populations were in danger. At the same time, conservationists were trying to reestablish fallow deer in Israel in an effort to restore all

ISRAEL NATURE AND NATIONAL PARKS PROTECTION AUTHORITY

Fallow deer, only three feet high at the shoulder, are little bigger than goats. They were once native to woodlands of Israel and are being reintroduced at Carmel Hai Bar.

the wildlife mentioned in the Bible.

An agreement was worked out to relocate some Iranian fallow deer to Israel, but mention of the word *Israel* enraged both customs officials and residents where the animals were caught. So bribery, hours of argument, and a story of sending the deer to the Netherlands—via Israel—were employed to bring four female fallow deer to Carmel Hai Bar.

Not much more than three feet high, an adult fallow deer would hardly reach the waist of an adult human. Its antlers resemble those of a moose, in miniature, and its tan coat spotted with white helps camouflage the fallow deer as it browses through forest and brush.

From the start, restoring species at Carmel Hai Bar has been a multicultural effort, both outside and inside Israel. The Druze, who live throughout the mountains of Lebanon, also live in two large villages on Mount Carmel. Some among the Druze community have been instrumental in reestablishing wildlife populations at Carmel Hai Bar.

Close to Carmel Hai Bar is Little Switzerland, an area so named because it is green and mountainous. Nahal Kelekh and Nahal Galim 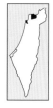 form the main drainage system, whose upper reaches are blanketed with Mediterranean flora, which is still recovering from arsonists who torched the forest in 1989. Although scientists still can measure the extent of the fire's disturbance, the regenerating forests meander down the mountain, forests of pine, pistacia, and calliprinos oak.

The Hebrew name for calliprinos oak means "common" because

it is the most common oak in the country. The pistacia that most often accompanies calliprinos oak is *Pistacia palaestina*. The pistacia, which was given its taxonomic name in the 1800s, was tweaked by politics when it was given its Hebrew name: *elah erets-yisraelit*.

Laurels and other water-loving plants grow where the Kelekh-Galim streambeds are moist and shaded. Mosses add an emerald glow. And, among the cliffs, patches of white Madonna lily bloom in late spring. From giant fennel (*kelekh*) near the top to sea waves (*galim*) at the bottom, the views of cliff, forest, and coast along the Nahal Kelekh-Galim route are spectacular as it winds down Carmel's western flanks to the sea.

A Leisurely Descent Along Nahal Yagur

The eastern flanks of Carmel, which look down on Haifa Bay and the Zebulun and Jezreel Valleys, are much steeper than those facing the sea. Ido and I had arranged to hike the long Yagur trail down Carmel's eastern flank. So we would not have to hike back up after descending the nearly four-mile trail, we came in two cars, parking one at the top and one at the bottom of Nahal Yagur. We began near the crest of Carmel at the mountain town of Isfiya, one of the two Druze communities on Carmel.

Druze have lived on Mount Carmel for hundreds of years, part of the cycle of peoples in this venerable land. Established around the twelfth century B.C.E., the kingdom of Israel eventually came under a succession of Babylonian, Persian, then Roman rule. Byzantine Christianity reigned in the region from the early-300s until the rise of Islam in the mid-600s. Crusaders took over Carmel in the Middle Ages, until they were defeated by Saladin, the Syrian-born ruler who led Muslims to victory. At the start of the 1500s, Ottoman Turks gained control of the Middle East. Not long afterward, Druze from Lebanon made their way south to Carmel, some say to escape overbearing overlords.

But the past remains. In 1933, the mosaic floor of a Byzantine-era synagogue was uncovered in Isfiya. The tiles depict a shofar, a menorah, and other symbols plus the legend "Peace on Israel," and inscriptions thanking and blessing the donors who contributed to the synagogue. One of the donors named was a woman, a dedication unusual in those days. A section of the mosaic was moved to the Rockefeller Museum, now part of Jerusalem's Israel Museum.

What we saw in Isfiya when we began our hike down Nahal Yagur

255

was very much the present: a clutch of little children on tricycles played an inadvertent version of bumper cars while older men sipped morning coffee on vine-covered patios.

Starting from a small memorial to a soldier who died in 1970, the path leads through an open, parklike forest. A teenage shepherd drove a herd of black goats and white sheep ahead of him. We waved and went our separate ways, we into thicker forest.

When the rains come, Nahal Yagur is punctuated by a series of small waterfalls. Rainfall, more than thirty inches per year, is what keeps Carmel so green and allows such a wealth of flora to flourish. Everywhere arbutus trees lean out over the trail, their smooth red bark peeling in coils. Small white flowers dangle like lilies of the valley, followed by strawberry-red fruit, which gives the tree its pseudonym, "strawberry tree."

In Hebrew, the arbutus tree's name is *qetalav*, the "slain father," said Ido. Oh?

As with many such stories it is a tale of love and death. In the legend, a young shepherd falls in love with a beautiful girl, who neither rejects nor encourages his advances. But he is besotted with her. One day, approaching a grove, he sees the girl making love with a man. The shepherd comes closer and sees that the man is his own father. In a murderous rage, he kills his father, and blood sprays all over the trees. The red-barked arbutus tree is still marked by that murder.

256

Arbutus is a tree of cool, moist shade and chalk soils. So, it is found on north-facing slopes near the top of Mount Carmel, where the chalk layer lies. Californians walking through a Carmel forest might think they were seeing Pacific madrone. The trees are related, of the same genus, although they live half a world apart.

Arbutus, with its red bark, bell flowers, and the thoughtless grace of a Degas ballerina, caught my attention and I backed up, came close, moved around one arbutus then another, camera to eye, as if they were celebrities or runway models, never satisfied that I had shot the tree's best side. Ido was amused.

We passed other typical residents of this ecological neighborhood, fingering old yellow crabapple-sized fruits on a hawthorn, whose twisted branches are covered with orange lichen and guarded with long, sharp thorns. Because apples do not grow naturally in Israel, some believe the fruit of the hawthorn was the apple in the Song of Songs (2:3): "Like an apple tree among trees of the forest, so is my beloved among the youths."

Aleppo pine (also known as Jerusalem pine) grows near the top of Nahal Yagur as well. The woods are full of calliprinos oak and its companion, pistacia, whose new red leaves give it a fiery glow. Arum, greenbrier, and long tendrils of wild asparagus flourish in the understory. Chopped-up earth hints at rooting wild boars.

Winding our way down Mount Carmel, we passed from forest to meadows and back again into forest, from rock-rimmed dappled shade to open, sloping parklands. Fewer walks in Israel are more pleasant. In filtered light, where forest meets meadow, two types of rockrose grow, one with pink, roselike flowers, the other with white flowers and wrinkled leaves similar to sage.

On the sloping meadows, grasses and wildflowers ramble down the incline among white boulders. We found hairy pink flax; afternoon iris; tall, spicy horn-leaved sage; red anemone; and the chartreuse flowers of spurge mounded between the rocks.

In the valley far below, the sun played over orderly fields, and before us soared a trio of long-legged buzzards, their pale bodies seemingly bleached by the sun. In the low light of the next patch of woods, I saw something familiar and rushed to greet an old friend.

"What are *you* doing here?" I asked the small, silent tree in disbelief. I had seen wild relatives of this tree in the Appalachian Mountains, but was surprised to discover it here. Ido pulled out his field

---

With big barrel bodies, wild boars are among the largest mammals extant in Israel and are native to the Middle East as well as to parts of Europe and Asia. Between four and six feet long and weighing up to six hundred pounds, these predecessors of domesticated pigs forage in forest underbrush looking for acorns, carob pods, leaves, roots, bulbs, and tubers. But they are not fussy. Eggs, fungi, insects, reptiles, small mammals—wild boars, will eat almost anything.

The flexible, disklike cartilage at the tip of their nose plus a unique nose bone allows them to root up ground like earth-moving machines. With black-brown hair, tusks, and sometimes a mane on neck and shoulders, boars look—and occasionally can be—dangerous. But they avoid human contact, traveling in family groups mostly at dawn and dusk. Colonists brought them to North America, where they have spread throughout the southeastern United States, becoming formidable pests.

guide and we began keying it out: leaves, alternate or opposite; oval or ovate; leaf margins, smooth or serrate. Indeed, it was an arrow-wood viburnum, with large white lacecap flowers, which become blue-black fruit beloved by birds. A true beauty.

The way through the woods was full of pink cyclamen—*raqefet*—tucked into rock crevices and, at one point, Ido leaped ahead, singing in engagingly rhymed Hebrew:

> From under a stone
> A miracle grown
> A very lovely *raqefet* . . .

The song of the *raqefet*, who wears ". . . on its head a pink crown," is learned in elementary school by almost every Israeli. Just humming it elicits looks signaling quick trips down memory lane.

The next couple of openings in the woods brought dainty yellow Jacob's rod; lizards scurrying over rocks at our approach; lances of pink sword lily, a type of gladiolus; red tulips, singly and in patches; and Carmel garlic's purple ball flowers.

As we made our way down the mountain, the sun became hotter and the trees sparse. A raptor hung in the hot air as if magically suspended. The thick woods were replaced by scattered patches of olive, carob, and mastic pistacia. A narrow chasm to the north showed us we had reached the dolomite layers. Across the chasm, tall white cliffs were hung with greenery and studded with the mouths of numerous caves. Some may once have housed primitive hunter-gatherers in the dim, prehistoric past.

258

Mastic pistacia is a tree with survival skills. Ido pointed out that the leaves are coated with a waxy cuticle, so it does not burn easily. Goats and sheep do not like to browse it. And it can withstand salt spray. Mount Carmel's western slopes, facing the salt-laden breezes coming off the Mediterranean, are covered with this tough carob-pistacia community. In Second Temple times, mastic resin derived from the pistacia was mixed with fig or date honey to make a type of chewing gum.

Like mastic pistacia, the carob is a tough tree that can withstand drought and abuse. Although carob trees have been in Israel through most of written history, they probably were not present during the biblical period because they are not mentioned in the Bible. References to carobs began to appear during talmudic times.

The end of the Nahal Yagur trail is marked by a large old carob.

At this point, the slope of Carmel fades onto the plain and into parking lots and playgrounds. Water from Nahal Yagur and other streams of Carmel's eastern flanks eventually pour into Nahal Qishon, the river that drains much of the Valley of Jezreel into the Bay of Haifa.

Ido had a long drive east through the valley before he reached home. I took the narrow road up Carmel from Nesher, driving with the mountain on one side and a sheer drop-off on the other. A series of dramatic switchbacks provides views of the Bay of Haifa and the valley below. Butterflies float past, and at every intersection a possibility arises to explore nature.

In the curve of one switchback I could see the crest of Mount Hermon shining to the north. In the curve of another, I caught a glimpse of some Carmel bee-orchids. A line of cars was less than a switchback behind me. I weighed the options: stop and get a good view of the orchids versus car collision. Live to see them another day, I decided.

According to Christian tradition, carob is one of the foods Saint John subsisted on in the Judean Desert, so it also is known as Saint John's bread. And it is one of the fruits associated with Tu bi-Shevat, the Jewish New Year of the Trees. Loaded on Tu bi-Shevat seder (ceremonial dinner) platters heavy with figs and grapes, dates and plums, walnuts and pine nuts, carob pods make a surprisingly sweet treat.

About the size and shape of a banana, but flat and dark brown, carob pods are fibrous and require vigorous chewing—worth the effort because the pods contain 55 percent sugars. Health food stores sell carob bars and chips as a natural substitute for chocolate.

Smooth, round carob seeds are ground to make a flour that is 60 percent protein. In fact, the seeds of *Ceratonia siliqua* are so uniform in size and weight that at one time they were used as jewelers' measures. The term *carat*, still used to measure gold and precious stones, comes from the name ceratonia.

Israel is full of orchids—thirty-one species plus another dozen or so natural hybrids and subspecies. Some, such as the pink butterfly orchid, are common. Many are rare. But orchid populations rise and fall according to a number of factors. Some orchids are self-pollinating, but some are pollinated by just one species of insect. If pesticides kill off too many of that insect, the orchids will decline as well.

Sometimes, buried orchids burst into life when a fire sweeps away

underbrush, allowing light to awaken the orchid bed. Sometimes, if brush grows unchecked, a healthy orchid population will disappear completely.

Mount Carmel is a haven for orchids, especially bee-orchids. Of these, the Carmel bee-orchid is the most common and one of the most dramatic: the reddish-brown flower is shaped and marked to mimic a female bee. An amorous male bee, thinking he is mating, lands on the orchid, inadvertently picking up pollen and carrying it to the next orchid. Clever orchid.

Musing about orchids, I reached Damun Junction, near the crest of Carmel. There stand the guard towers, floodlights, blank walls, and barbed wire of Damun Prison. Orchids and prison. It is always such a shock to see prisons and nature juxtaposed, they seem so antithetical. Yet, for the sake of isolation, prisons are often located in the most idyllic of places.

Finding the Symbol of Israel in Oak Canyon

The insistent "hoo" of an eagle owl woke me at dawn, and I walked out under the pines at Bet Oren, a kibbutz near the top of Mount Carmel. Sprawling redbud trees, densely twining greenbrier, and the limbs of the pines provided perches for myriad birds, so the morning was full of song.

260 Tiny wrens, their tails hoisted like flags, trilled from tree and bush. Goldfinches, doves, and crow-sized jays with their blue wing patches and black "mutton chops" throat patches were all busy.

I had planned to walk down nearby Nahal Alon in the Har Alon Reserve, but a dirt track at the top of the streambed, shaded by a broad Aleppo pine forest, lured me. Extensive old-growth pine forest, with airy understory and the feel of a quiet sanctuary, is now rare in Israel. Mount Carmel National Park protects the best of what is left, so the opportunity to walk beneath the pines was a treat.

Eventually the pines gave way to more open terrain. Where the sun broke through, butterfly orchids and three-toothed orchids bloomed, pink dotted with purple. I walked a bit farther until I was arrested by the sight of a salvia: Jerusalem sage. One of about twenty salvia species growing in Israel, Jerusalem sage puts out salmon-pink flowers, each wearing its own curved petal cap. That, however, was not what caught my attention. The plant, with three arms branching symmetrically from each side of a central spire, looked exactly like a menorah.

I certainly was not the first to be struck by this resemblance. Much has been written about the simple salvia and how it served as the model for the first menorah, fashioned by the artist Bezalel for the Tabernacle (Exodus 25:31–36). But this particular salvia looked archetypical.

The natural world served as the model for much of ancient Israel's art. Synagogue walls, coins, and mosaics were decorated with grape vines, pomegranates, stalks of wheat . . . and salvia. The famous Arch of Titus in Rome depicts Romans carrying away the menorah, a symbol of the kingdom of Israel. Today, the menorah is again a symbol—of the State of Israel.

The Israelites were a people who lived close to the earth and who lived in accordance with rules protecting the earth. A fruit tree could not be harvested for general consumption until its fifth year, allowing the tree to grow strong in its youth. Even during war, fruit trees could not be cut. There is a statute for humane ways to gather eggs and practices to assure that the land is not overworked.

I was feeling full of fine sentiments about floral simplicity—a feeling easy to come by when you are out in it. I decided to turn back, find Nahal Alon, and continue walking. Nahal Alon twists and turns through a rocky canyon: broad enough so that blue, yellow, red, and pink wildflowers strew themselves across sunny, sloping meadows where butterflies dance, but narrow enough to make it seem private, away from the world of people. This quality was put to use during World War II.

261

Nahal Alon ("oak"), which starts near the crest of Mount Carmel, is linked to Nahal Oren ("pine"), which runs down to the coast. During World War II, when the British governed Palestine, they refused entry to Jews fleeing the Holocaust in Europe. Palestinian Jews defied the British immigration blockade and smuggled in Jewish refugees by boat, then walked them over Mount Carmel. One of the main routes was up through the canyons of Nahal Oren and Nahal Alon, then down Nahal Yagur into the heart of the land. The walk still feels like a secret passage, now more a green and white delight than desperate sanctuary.

After leaving Nahal Alon, I took some time to drive the narrow roads that curve along the top and sides of Mount Carmel. Along the side of the road I saw a dead animal, probably struck by a car. It looked like a fox and, indeed, foxes are closely associated with Mount Carmel in biblical verse:

Mount Carmel's Nahal Alon was a surreptitious route for Jews escaping Nazi Germany.

262

> The blossoms have appeared in the land,
> The time of pruning has come;
> The voice of the turtledove
> Is heard in our land.
> The green figs form on the fig tree,
> The vines in blossom give off fragrance . . .
>
> Catch us the foxes,
> The little foxes
> That ruin the vineyards—
> For our vineyard is in blossom.
>
> (SONG OF SONGS 2:12–15)

Carmel—*kerem El*—the vineyard of the Lord, it was called. Isaiah compared the people Israel to the vineyard of the Lord. He cautioned that, without vigilant tending, a vineyard will produce poorly and eventually vanish. The metaphor must have been particularly compelling to eighth-century B.C.E. Israelites of Isaiah's time when the surrounding lowlands and terraces built on Carmel were full of olive orchards and vineyards.

If the grapevines that once grew here have vanished, remnants of those days are still visible in agricultural terraces dating from the time of the Bar Kokhba Revolt.

The Qeren Carmel Reserve not only preserves fecund woods bedded with nodding pink cyclamen, but also the Muhraka Monastery, a memorial to another, even older event. It was on Carmel, according to 1 Kings 18:19–38, that the prophet Elijah bested the magic of four hundred fifty priests of Ba'al, brought to Israel by Jezebel, the pagan queen of King Ahab.

Muhraka means "place of burning" because tradition says this is where the four hundred fifty priests set their sacrificial bull atop an altar laid with wood. The priests shouted and gashed themselves all day long, but their gods did not send fire to consume the sacrifice. At the end of the day, Elijah built an altar and laid it with wood and a sacrificial bull, both purposely drenched with water. Then he asked God to turn the people's hearts away from idol worship and set fire to the water-soaked wood. Thereupon, the wood and the bull slain for the sacrifice were consumed by fire.

To defy hundreds of the queen's priests took chutzpah, which Elijah had in abundance. Even so, he had to flee to the Negev to escape Jezebel's wrath.

Centuries later, Carmelite monks built Muhraka Monastery to honor Elijah's fight against idol worship. The monastery bears an Arabic name for a Catholic order honoring a Jewish prophet.

Bats Get Respect on Etsba Ridge

The scenic route over Mount Carmel is exceptional from either direction. Driving westward down Mount Carmel, however, the incline is less severe and the curves more leisurely. As on the east side, every intersection brings an opportunity to see something natural—or near-natural. The sheer limestone walls of the mountain draw rock climbers with their coils of orange and blue nylon rope and their carabiners. My husband and I could see them—brightly colored flyspecks on a far limestone wall.

He had joined me toward the end of my travels, and I had to drive him around Mount Carmel, showing off its fine attributes as if I had something to do with them. He was indulging me. He did not want to retrace my steps in Carmel's nature reserves. In fact, I knew he was anxious to arrive at the sea, throw a towel on the sand, and fall asleep in the sun, a book shading his face. As we neared the coastal plain, where Mount Carmel begins to level out, a parkland and picnic ground along the road signaled the trailhead to Etsba Ridge, a place I had not yet visited.

"Etsba Ridge!" I exhaled dramatically. "What a place! And we're right here. Oh, Michael, you really don't want to miss this."

He sighed, probably imagining the beach and, later, the beer that would be delayed by Etsba Ridge.

The trail begins across an old stone bridge, leads up past stone-work and the remains of other military construction. The British fortified Carmel here and elsewhere against possible German attack during World War II. The Jewish underground, too, prepared to fight to the last life to turn back the Nazis if they reached Mount Carmel.

Benign in light of what could have been, Etsba Ridge's forests are dominated by carob and mastic pistacia where slopes face the sun, oak and Palestine pistacia where slopes face north. The rocky path upward is rife with wildflowers and small plants, especially soft gray-green mounds of hyssop, a relative of marjoram, that grows from rocky crevices over much of Israel. I picked a leaf, crushed it so Michael could inhale its aroma and nibble it.

Hyssop, called *zatar* in Arabic, has been used for centuries as a remedy for stomachaches. More immediately important, *zatar* was what flavored the top of the pita we packed for lunch. Hyssop is so popular as a flavoring that many people picked slopes clean of hyssop, to sell and export. To save the wild plant from "industrial" harvesting, the government declared hyssop a protected species.

Hyssop is translated from the Hebrew *ezov*. In cooking and medicinally, it has been used since the time of the Exodus. This was the plant the Hebrews used to daub lamb's blood on their lintels so the angel of death would know to pass over their homes the night before they left Egypt.

Hyssop was used ceremonially as a purifying agent in Temple sacrifices because, as a small, low plant, it was the symbol of humility. Purification rituals also included hyssop's antithesis, the lofty and proud cedar.

In extolling King Solomon's wisdom, 1 Kings 5:12-13 states: "He composed three thousand proverbs, and his songs numbered one thousand and five. He discoursed about trees, from the cedar in Lebanon to the hyssop that grows out of the wall."

Hyssop seems healthy on Etsba Ridge, tumbling from rock crevices along the trail. Although the route from streambed to the top of the pine-covered ridge is steep, it is replete with views of banana groves, beaches, and the sea.

Halfway to the top, the mouth of a cave gapes black and cool against the hot Mediterranean sun. Just as we were about to enter, a

Bats are among the most maligned of animals, associated with vampires and witchcraft. Little is said of the good bats do—and they do quite a lot. Certain insectivorous bats can consume more than six hundred mosquitoes per hour. Colonies of just a few hundred bats, each bat itself weighing just a few ounces, can consume as much as ten pounds of insects per night. Bats not only help check insect-borne disease but also diminish the number of agricultural insect pests.

Hundreds of plant species, from tropical rain forests to deserts, depend on nectar-sipping bats to serve as pollinators or fruit-eating bats to serve as seed dispersers. Carob, date, fig, banana, mango—in the wild, all depend on bats for pollination or seed dispersal.

young couple, in their twenties, charged up the hill behind us. We said hello all around and looked each other over. Then, with metabolism to spare, they marched into the cave and out of sight.

Inside, water-slicked rocks angle upward through a series of three stalactite-hung rooms. The cave is called Etsba because it is like a long, narrow finger pointing upward, and the ridge takes its name from the cave. Archaeologists have discovered pottery, flint tools, and remains of prehistoric people who lived in the cave tens of thousands of years ago. Now, the cave is home to both fruit- and insect-eating types of bats.

265

Because of Israel's position at the meeting of three continents, it has an unusually broad range of bats, from long-nosed tropical species to long-eared desert species to European free-tailed bats. Thirty-three species of bats live in Israel, the same number that live in all of Europe and twelve less than the number of species in the United States. Yet Israel is only the size of New Jersey.

Israel's thirty-three bat species comprise about one-third of the country's mammalian species. Like many bat populations worldwide, Israel's are threatened by habitat loss, pesticides, and wanton destruction. Dr. Benny Shalmon, an esteemed zoologist with SPNI's Mammal Information Center, considers bats and their precarious situation so important that his work has focused on them, along with Israel's most famous endangered mammal, the leopard.

Diligent parents, bats nurse one pup per year and live in colonies of several dozen to several hundred to several million. They search

for food at night and maneuver in dark caves using precise echolocation. Researchers associated with Bat Conservation International, a prominent bat protection organization, have found that, from six feet away, African heart-nosed bats can hear the footsteps of a beetle walking on sand. Fishing bats can detect a minnow's fin protruding two millimeters above a pond's surface.

Conducting rough, anecdotal tests of their accuracy, I've slept in a hammock on hot nights, hearing the flutter of bats all around me. Never did a bat graze me in the dark.

We and the other couple exited the cave at the same time, but they disappeared so quickly I could not tell whether they went up or down. We pushed on to the top, climbing over rocks, following the trail through a thick maquis of pistacia and carob until we reached the pine-shaded crest of Etsba Ridge. There we stopped to drink some water before making our way down and onward to the beach.

Nahal Me'arot: Home to the Most Interesting Mammal

The renowned caves of Nahal Me'arot Reserve lie at the western foot of Mount Carmel within sight of the sea, just off Coast Route 4. More formal than most reserves, Nahal Me'arot (River of the Caves) has a small visitor center cum restaurant near the parking lot. Having just driven north from Tel Aviv, I was told a tour would begin in English in an hour, so I sat down in the restaurant to nurse a glass of iced coffee.

Half an hour later found me pacing at the beginning of the trail up to the caves. I was joined by a family of four who had recently immigrated to Israel from Ohio. They were accompanied by a friend who was considering making the same move.

The two children, a girl and a boy, about five and seven, were jittering around with the excess energy of children, and I was wired on coffee. We needed a focus, and an agama lizard accommodated us. Tantalizing us, the half-foot-long lizard darted a few feet ahead and looked back. The chase was on. We dashed along a low rock wall, following the leaping lizard. Our chase ended almost immediately when our guide appeared, and we started up the walk.

He directed our attention north, to a huge humped ridge of dark rock that is possibly the finest rudist reef in the world. Cone-shaped mollusks, rudists lived in shallow seas one hundred million years ago. They are long extinct, but in their time they lived in dense colonies, forming reefs similar to those of present-day corals. By press-

This towering rock formation at Nahal Me'arot Reserve once lay beneath tropical seas. It is the remains of millions of rudists, now-extinct animals who lived in colonies like corals.

ing together in reefs, rudists could withstand the force of the sea as it crashed toward that long-ago coastline.

The fossil formation that arched against the blue sky is the remains of one of those reefs—millions of rudists from a time when the sea surged farther inland. Rudists, like dinosaurs, became extinct suddenly, at the end of the Cretaceous period. Scientists now believe that the impact of an enormous asteroid, possibly combined with intense volcanic activity that darkened the atmosphere with debris, caused the extinction of much of that period's fauna.

267

The reef and limestone cliffs at Nahal Me'arot now provide purchase for today's species. Rare flora, such as Cretan cabbage, a relative of the common cabbage, grow from the cliffs overlooking the Mediterranean. So does navelwort, whose name in English, Hebrew, and Latin means "belly-button plant."

The story goes that when navelwort, which has a drab spike of green-white flowers, saw all the colorful flowers around it, it complained that it had nothing nice to show off. In response, this plant with a self-esteem problem got a poke in the belly, so to speak. Its mark of distinction is its dimple, right in the middle of each round, succulent leaf.

At the base of the Me'arot cliffs stand spiny walls of sabra cactus.

Raptors and other birds sweep by the outcroppings at Nahal Me'arot Reserve. But, by far, the most fascinating species here were our fore-bears, the antecedents of humankind.

Low on the slopes of Mount Carmel, facing the sea, the beings who would give rise to human civilization eked out a hunter-gath-erer living at a time when they were only a few stages more ad-vanced than the animals they hunted. The yawning caves that line the hilly paths at Nahal Me'arot were home to a continuous march of prehistoric peoples. Along this spectrum, the line between natural history and cultural history blurs.

Our guide explained that although bones of ancient humans were discovered at the caves in 1856, systematic archaeology did not be-gin until the late 1920s, when a feminist group in England funded an all-woman team to begin excavations. At that point, an expedition headed by English archaeologist Dorothy Garrod began uncovering some of the most seminal findings on early people.

Over decades of investigation, what archaeologists have found is an unbroken line of culture beginning with the early Stone Age at least two hundred thousand years ago. Teams of archaeologists and anthropologists representing many nationalities have uncovered layer upon layer of artifacts and bones, nearly seventy feet thick, one of the most complete records of human existence known.

Since the 1920s and 1930s, a near-continuous stream of research teams has discovered strata of human cultures at other sites on and around Mount Carmel. The collection of about two hundred fifty sites makes the mountain one of the richest areas on Earth for early hominid findings.

The most ancient human progenitor—discovered in Africa—was of the genus *Australopithecus*. An evolving succession of upright primates, barely more than four feet tall, *Australopithecus* roamed eastern African forests about four million years ago. Two million years ago, early tool-using hominids emerged. Archaeologists call them *Homo habilis*, "handy man," the first of the human line.

As brain capacity grew, *Homo erectus*, "upright man," developed about a million years ago. These hominids had the ability for speech and learned how to use fire at least three hundred thousand years ago. Remnants of a *Homo erectus* culture, the oldest human arti-facts found at Nahal Me'arot, were uncovered in Tanur Cave, the lowest cave on the slope.

The stone tools found in Tanur Cave are part of what scientists call Acheulian culture, which thrived approximately two hundred thousand years ago. These early people used hand axes—roughly shaped stones—to dig and to skin and cut up game in the area around Nahal Me'arot.

Although now the Mediterranean lies nearly two miles west of the caves, a warming period between Ice Ages raised the seas, bringing the Mediterranean nearly to Acheulian man's "door." During this warming period, elephant and rhinoceros lived in Israel.

In addition, Tanur Cave (also called Tabun Cave) contains artifacts from Tabunian culture, a step closer but, like Acheulian culture, part of the Lower Paleolithic period. Dating to about one hundred fifty thousand years ago, Tabunian hominids made technological progress, developing slightly more refined stone implements: their axes were almond-shaped, with the broader base of the rock fitting into the palm of the hand.

Although the cave often was occupied, Tabunian bands hunted far afield after game and wild plants. As the climate cooled, elephant and rhino retreated south, replaced by fallow deer, gazelle, and wild cattle in the woodlands around Nahal Me'arot and in cave-dwellers' diets.

From one hundred thousand to about forty thousand years ago, as glaciers crept over the northern hemisphere during the most recent Ice Age, Mousterian culture of the Middle Paleolithic period inhabited the caves. Both Tanur and Nahal Cave, higher up the cliff, have revealed much of Mousterian culture, which was, perhaps, the most fascinating period at Nahal Me'arot.

By the Middle Paleolithic period, early people had developed pressure-flaking techniques that allowed far more advanced stone implements than crude axes. They learned to chase deer over the cliffs to obtain meat. They buried their dead, something not seen in previous cultures.

As our guide explained the shift from Lower to Middle Old Stone Age, our small group stood in Tanur Cave. I tried to see through Acheulian eyes and imagine the Mediterranean lapping near the cave entrance where a stalwart carob tree now stands, then fast-forward from Acheulian to Mousterian culture.

As we picked our way up the trail, I ceased playing time traveler. These are leaps too hard to make while plodding up a stony slope. The guide caught my attention, though, when he said that researchers had been astonished to find the skull of a Neanderthal woman in Tanur Cave.

Until recently, Neanderthal had been thought to be a dead-end spur of the *sapiens* line, thick, brutish hominids who were adapted

Nahal Me'arot caves, with views of rudist reef, coastline, and sea, were the front doors of prehistoric peoples dating back more than two hundred thousand years.

to surviving the last Ice Age in Europe and elsewhere. Neanderthals appeared about the start of the last glaciation, which began one hundred thousand years ago and ended little more than ten thousand years ago.

270

What is startling about finding a Neanderthal skull is that *Homo sapiens*, who were our direct predecessors, lived here about the same time. This remarkable discovery suggests that the two species may have coexisted.

Another dramatic insight was gleaned from Kabarah Cave on Mount Carmel: the first find of a Neanderthal tongue bone (hyoid), which revealed that Neanderthals had the capacity for speech. If Neanderthals could talk and lived side by side with our *Homo sapien* ancestors, archaeologists wonder if the two species communicated? Shared knowledge? Mated?

Although Gamal Cave, whose cavity is shaped like an enormous camel's hump, has not revealed evidence of early man, a slide show imagines prehistoric life. The dim light cast by the slides is reminiscent, perhaps, of the low glow of the campfires that lit these people's cavernous dwellings. In the caves of Nahal Me'arot, they cooked their meat and laid out sleeping blankets of fur-lined hide.

During daylight hours they hunted, gathered berries and nuts, caught fish in the sea, and spent hours honing the simple tools that allowed all of their industry. Our guide explained that the rock here is full of flint, so early hominids had the makings for tools at hand.

And tool-making abilities progressed apace. People of the Aurignacian culture, which began the Upper Paleolithic period about forty thousand years ago, had become skilled at flint-knapping. During this time, flint blades knapped with chisels replaced flakes chopped off with rocks. Upper Paleolithic people made all sorts of blades, from spear-throwing points to etching tools.

Cultures found in Carmel caves from about twenty thousand to thirteen thousand years ago show steady development toward civilization. From the number of animal bones found, researchers deduce more intensive hunting. Detritus of a new invention, grinding stones, reveal an increasing focus on gathering wild nuts and grains. With their stone mortars, they ground wild almonds, wild wheat, and other foods.

In Natufian culture, from about twelve thousand to nine thousand years ago, people began to develop the first flush of an agricultural society. They gathered grains with sickles whose large flint blades were hafted onto bone handles—a relatively sophisticated tool. They also created art and jewelry.

We walked up to the highest and longest of the caves, Nahal Cave, with its imposing entrance hall and interior corridors and halls that measure more than two hundred feet long. The people who lived here at the dawn of civilization, probably in groups of twenty-five to fifty, hunted deer and gazelle, avoiding the lions and leopards that lived throughout Israel up until modern times. They could roast and stew their meat and eat meals that included grains and vegetables.

271

Natufians initiated terrace farming on aprons of land near Nahal Cave. And they buried their dead with ceremony, fastening bands of seashell jewelry around the heads of those who died. Nearly a hundred Natufian skeletons were found here, ritually folded in the fetal position, the guide said, adding that perhaps the fetal position was to remind themselves of the cycle of life, from birth to death.

Our tour had ended. As I walked down the trail to the base of the cliffs, I thought about our connection to these ancient cultures.

Nahal Me'arot is a poignant site of past peoples, balanced on the brink of civilization. Not quite us, but like enough that we can imagine their lives. So close to the Mediterranean, they must have watched the sun set just as we do, the glowing golden sphere dipping into the waves as though the water would extinguish its fire, their sense of the magic of that view no less than ours.

CHAPTER ELEVEN

The Coast:
Coves, Dunes, and Sun-Soaked Beaches

Dor ha-Bonim

FROM ROSH HA-NIQRAH'S TALL CHALK CLIFFS in the north to softly rolling sand dunes in the south, Israel's coastline sweeps in a one-hundred-eighteen-mile arc around the southeastern end of the Mediterranean Sea. Along this path lay the Via Maris, one of the world's first commercial routes.

Punctuating this ancient coastal route are the ruins of millennia-old cities, mighty fortresses, and imposing palaces, telling of Israel's glory at the center of the early civilized world: Caesarea, Herod's magnificent Roman tribute, built upon the foundations of an even older port; Akhziv, along the northern coast, containing ruins from Canaanite, talmudic, and Crusader periods; Ashqelon, already old in the time of the Philistines; as well as Dor and the tells of other ancient cities that are just beginning to be uncovered.

To the north lie Netanyah, Haifa, Acre (Akko), and Nahariyah. To the south lie Ashdod and Ashqelon. Most of these cities are a mix of old and new. Some cities, such as Tel Aviv, the epitome of Israel's pulsing modernity, are entirely new, hoisting themselves up faster than the ancient world could have imagined. Some cities are still to come: white apartment complexes and high-rises seem to spring from the sands every month. Ports and power stations, marinas and military bases eat up more of the coastline.

Sweeping back toward the hills, in an arc matching the coastline, the Sharon coastal plain is covered with crops and orchards, industry, kibbutzim, moshavim, and towns of all sizes. Like spaghetti, roads tangle across and up and down the coastal plain.

Fully 70 percent of Israel's population lives along the littoral.

Yet . . . the natural still exists. Although pressure from developers is tremendous, approximately half of Israel's coastline remains

relatively natural. At the Lebanese border, Rosh ha-Niqrah's high white cliffs stand against the sea. Stretching south from there, rocky limestone outcrops and natural arches are lashed by waves. Washed by ebbing and flowing water, tide pools harbor myriad life.

Beaches provide nesting areas for sea turtles and food for shorebirds. Reaching inland, low kurkar ridges bloom riotously with wildflowers. In the other direction, offshore islands succor nesting birds.

Up and down the coast modest rivers pour into the sea: Keziv, Qishon, Tanninim, Poleg, Yarqon, Sorek, and others. Some maintain a bit of dignity and still attract migrating birds to their shrubby banks. Most, however, have been dirtied and weakened by use.

Israel's southern shores are a mix of golden beaches and low sand dunes, home to endangered lizards and turtles. The dunes, Israel's most endangered ecosystem, roll in gold and silver rills inland from the sea, occasionally mounding as large hills covered with dune grasses, shrubs, and flowers—a sun-warmed landscape soothed by sea breezes.

Even a busy urban seafront is enhanced by the natural: freshening winds wafting in from the sea temper the heat-heavy humidity blanketing Tel Aviv in summer. Of course people want to be by the sea.

Rosh ha-Niqrah's Sea Caves and Grottoes

274 Rosh ha-Niqrah is as close to both the Mediterranean Sea and Lebanon as it is possible to be. If you do not turn off the coast highway at Rosh ha-Niqrah, about a mile to the north you will be stopped at the border checkpoint. Rosh ha-Niqrah, however, is hard to miss. The cliffs are a smaller-scale match with the white cliffs of Dover, and the sea-scoured grottoes are exquisite. But, as a cranky purist, I was put off by the tourist paraphernalia that shouts "You Are Here": cable car, cafe, and *tchotchke* shop. Oh, all right, I did have some decent eggplant salad in the cafe. And the view from the cable car wasn't bad.

Deposited by the cable car on a rock platform at the foot of the cliffs, my view straight up was striking: two hundred thirty feet of blinding-white chalk cliff beaded with dark flint. Where niches provide purchase, pigeons gather. Beyond what is visible, the cliffs rise higher still, covered with low, wind-sculpted pistacia and other plants. Below the platform, the cliffs plunge directly into the sea.

Known in antiquity as the Ladder of Tyre, Rosh ha-Niqrah was the most obvious impediment to travelers heading north on the coast route. They had to mount these tall cliffs in order to reach Tyre, one of the most important ports of the ancient world. Steps carved in the rock allowed caravans from Egypt and Arabia to climb the "ladder" to Tyre, which lies about fifteen miles north on the Lebanese coast. Hiram, the Phoenician king of Tyre and an ally of both King David and King Solomon, sent cedars and cypress for David's palace and for Solomon's Temple—probably by this route.

Because the middle sections of cliff are composed of softer chalk than top or bottom, the sea has pounded away over the years, eroding the chalk and creating a series of grottoes. The name Rosh ha-Niqrah is derived from the site's Arabic name, which means "head of the grottoes."

Like the cliffs of Dover, England, the chalk cliffs of Rosh ha-Niqrah rise tall and white from the sea. Gorgeous sea-carved grottoes etch these cliffs at Israel's northwest corner.

As the sea has carved through the chalk, so have people. In 332 B.C.E., Alexander the Great began his successful campaign to conquer the Mediterranean and western Asia. It is said that, after overtaking Tyre, Alexander had his troops excavate a tunnel through Rosh ha-Niqrah to expedite the route south. During World War II, the British dug a railroad tunnel through the same cliffs to connect Haifa and Beirut. Although now gated and blocked to visitors, the tunnel entrance is still visible.

Unlike Rosh ha-Niqrah's human amendments, the sea grottoes are uselessly splendid. From the open platform at the bottom of the cable lift, a rock path leads into a labyrinth of pathways. These paths, cut alongside and at the back of the sea-cave walls, allow tourists to view the grottoes from a series of perspectives.

I walked, leaving the bright light reflecting off the chalk cliffs for the dim interior of the grotto path. A finger of sea reached into the cave. Calm, the color of milky jade, the water lapped against the rock a few feet below where I stood.

I followed the path around the back of the first grotto and could see, through a window that water had cut in the rock, another scalloped grotto next door. The path led there and I followed. Sunlight slanted into the watery cave, and I watched as it played a pattern of light and dark across water that now had a lapis hue.

Steps led to other viewpoints in other grottoes, where seawater the deep, rich color of semiprecious stones swayed with the tide. From the cool gloom of the caves I could see the Mediterranean beyond, pricked with light as bright as diamonds.

As the tide rose, waves washed into the caves rhythmically, beating against the back of the grottoes like low drumrolls. I made my way back to the cable car.

At the top of the lift, I struck up a conversation with some touring Swiss and German women. I happened to mention that when my daughter was in Israel for a semester during high school, she had sent a postcard telling how the sea had come crashing through the grottoes, splashing the footpaths, snarling at their feet, and the park staff made them leave. This was just the sort of high drama meant to scare a parent, I told the women.

276

The women assured me it was true. They had been at Rosh ha-Niqrah only the day before and had been turned back by a minor storm. From where we stood now, they had looked down on the rock platform below to see every tenth wave or so crashing over its surface. I learned later that it is in winter, when the rains begin, that the sea really goes to work, storming the rock, eating away at it bit by bit.

From the overlook, I watched terns and other sea birds circle over Rosh ha-Niqrah, some coming from rookeries on offshore islands. The beaches just south of the cliffs are divided by low rock ledges reaching into the sea. Once, this was the realm of the tribe of Asher.

I had no idea what I was gazing down upon, but the ledges looked like they might hold tide pools and, by now, the tide was ebbing. I asked one of the staff at Rosh ha-Niqrah and she said that just south of where we stood SPNI's Akhziv Field School sits alongside the beach and the Rosh ha-Niqrah Marine Reserve.

A marine reserve—what luck! They told me how to reach the unpaved, sandy road that intersects with Route 4 a few miles south, and I pointed my car that way. The field school looked closed, and

Rosh ha-Niqrah Marine Reserve's tidepools are full of barnacles, mussels, anemones waving flowerlike tentacles, and other sea life.

most of the beaches were populated only by birds. I drove to a spot near a broad bank of ledges where I could keep my car and the surrounding area in clear view. Impetuous, maybe. Foolhardy, no.

I barely noticed the tufts of wildflowers growing from the low dunes, so anxious was I to reach the tide pools. The rocky ledge closest to shore was already dry in the light of the bright sun. As I walked farther out, the broad and damp limestone shelf became carpeted in spots with barnacles and mussels.

The glossy black mussel shells and cones of barnacles ringed tide pools brimming with life. Each watery pocket in the limestone was full of tiny forests: small sea plants and scarves of green, translucent seaweed. Among these emerald beds shrimp and snails slowly grazed while anemones—like large undulating dahlias—waved flowery tentacles. I went from pool to pool, stopping for minutes at each, entranced by these miniature worlds.

Near the water, an elegant great white egret stood motionless atop long, spidery legs, its eye fixed on fish, waiting for the right moment to strike. Farther out, gulls bobbed on small breakers; inland, hooded crows complained about nothing.

Walking back to the car, I finally noticed the line of low dunes tumbling down from the road. Spur-winged plovers and bulbuls

277

picked through sea holly, dune grasses, and sea squill, which form the first line of plant defense against the sea.

In winter, daffodils or, more properly, narcissi light up the narrow apron of coastal plain in nodding white-and-yellow bunches. In spring, clumps of sapphire sea lavender spill over the sands in bouquets mixed with purple clover and yellow birdfoot trefoil.

Blue afternoon irises, whose flowers last only an afternoon, poked through thorny cushions of poterium. Poterium, also called spiny burnet, grows on fallow land all over central and northern Israel and is one of the first shrubs to move in when a field is abandoned or fire chars wild lands. Although a lowly shrub in every sense, poterium is mentioned in the Bible and its commentaries.

Farther down the coast, where tide pools give way to sandy beaches, some of the world's most endangered species haul themselves ashore to lay their eggs. All seven of the world's sea turtle species are endangered. Sea turtles nest from the southeastern United States down along the east coasts of Central and South America. Others find beaches along southeast Asia and Australia and on the west coast of Africa. The eastern Mediterranean, including Israel, sees some turtle nesting.

The loggerhead is the species most likely to lay eggs on Israel's beaches. The loggerhead also is one of the largest sea turtles, with females weighing in at about five hundred pounds; males are even larger. A loggerhead shell is the size and shape of a giant shield—about four feet long.

278

Guided by stars and moon, female sea turtles haul up on beaches during late spring and summer, dig a deep hole above the tide line, and lay a hundred or so rubbery eggs the size of ping-pong balls. Using her flippers, the female turtle covers the eggs with sand. Then, her job done, she slips back into the sea.

The eggs incubate for about two months. As they incubate, the temperature in the sand-covered nest rises, and it is temperature that determines their sex. Eggs near the warmer top of the nest become female turtles. Lower, cooler areas of the nest produce males.

Once the turtles hatch, they make a life-threatening run for the sea. From nest to sea can take a clutch of a hundred turtles about three minutes. Those who linger surely will be eaten. The size of large coins, baby sea turtles have enemies everywhere. Crabs and gulls are especially fond of eating them. Once in the water, the turtles are powerful swimmers for their size, but everything in the sea wants to eat them as well. The few that survive their first year have a decent chance of reaching maturity, which can take up to twenty years.

Poterium's name refers to the small, pot-shaped fruit it bears—not only the fruit's shape, but its color. As poterium fruit matures, it changes from green to red and, finally, to the burnt umber color of a fired pot.

To see poterium in the burning heat of summer is to see a silvery-white skeleton of a plant, bony and thorny. When dry like this, poterium makes excellent kindling and has been used to start fires since biblical times. When lit, all its little "pots" pop like popcorn.

Ecclesiastes (7:5-6) says of sputtering poterium, "It is better to listen to the rebuke of a wise man than for one to listen to the song of fools, for like the crackling of poterium under a pot, so is the laughter of the fool."

In those days, living fences of poterium guarded grape orchards against "the little foxes that ruin the vineyards" (Song of Songs 2:15). Today poterium serves other functions. Because of a suggestion made by Nogah Hareuveni, founder of Neot Kedumim Biblical Landscape Reserve, Israeli Defense Forces use poterium as impromptu mattresses. Hareuveni thought poterium's pillowy limbs might keep troops above cold or wet ground and provide a bit of springy comfort as well.

It worked. Step on piled-up poterium limbs and the thorns break off. After a comfortable night's sleep, the mattress cleans up as kindling for heating breakfast coffee.

By far, people are their worst enemy. People trap adult turtles for their shells and meat. In some parts of the globe, poachers dig up turtle eggs to sell as delicacies. The biggest threat, however, is loss of habitat. As we build up coastal areas with homes, industry, and bathing beaches, turtle nesting sands disappear. Brightly lit coastal areas also throw off a turtle's sense of direction. After laying her eggs, a female may wander inland, mistaking bright lights for the wash of moonlight on the sea.

South of Akhziv, south of Nahariyah, near the horseshoe coastline that curves between Acre and Haifa, Ein Afeq Reserve is what remains of the Na'aman Swamps. In the lowlands of the Zebulun Valley, the springs that give rise to Nahal Na'aman, once a true river, have been trained and contained in channels and ponds.

Before the Na'aman Swamps were drained, water buffalo and

waterfowl inhabited the spongy area. The waterfowl were attracted by hoards of insects, including malaria-carrying mosquitoes, which afflicted settlers. Nearby lie the remains of ancient Afeq. (A town also called Afeq, whose remains now lie within a national park, existed on the Plain of Sharon east of Tel Aviv.)

Today, near old mills and other ruins at Ein Afeq Reserve, paths and boardwalks lead past pools where coot and heron, stilt and pelican find refuge. Tamarisk and brambles create green confusion. Above it all, the millhouse ruins make a comfortable viewpoint from which to watch the swamps and birds of Ein Afeq.

Radiant Carmel Coast

South of Haifa, where part of the Carmel coast skirts the towering headlands of Mount Carmel, the coastal plain is little more than a mile wide. But fewer seaside areas are more beautiful than the Carmel coast. Cove upon small cove, each with its own sandy beach, lies between the curving arms of rocky kurkar ridges that reach into the sea with platforms greened by seaweed and full of tide pools.

Kurkar ridges are low, sedimentary plateaus of limestone cemented atop sandstone. Remnants of earlier beach lines, they lie along much of central Israel's coastline. Most kurkar ridges are little more than thirty feet high. Where waves have been hard at work, the ridges simply erode into beach, the sedimentary rock crumbling to sand. Atop the ridges, wildflowers abound. In spring and early summer, these headlands are painted with swaths of yellow, white, pink, and blue.

280

Early in modern Israel's history, construction companies removed millions of cubic feet of sand to use as building material. So much sand was removed from the beaches of Atlit, just south of Haifa, that the shoreline receded more than two hundred feet between 1945 and 1963. Since 1964, law prohibits quarrying beach sand, so the further erosion of kurkar and beaches has been halted.

South of Atlit is the seaside community of Nahsholim. I had arrived at Kibbutz Nahsholim near evening, planning to stay a few nights in beachside rooms. After dinner at the kibbutz restaurant and an hour or so of reading, I wanted a short stroll. The night was dark, lit only by stars, and the short, thick grass that weaves through the complex was already dewy. As my eyes adjusted to the dim light, I could see a low, rounded shape on the lawn to my right. A hedgehog. I moved close enough to watch the hedgehog, but not so close as to scare it off. A nocturnal species, the gray, spiny ball placidly roamed over the grass, grubbing for insects.

Three types of hedgehogs live in Israel: two of Saharan desert origin, and one from Europe. The Nahsholim variety is European: sweet-faced with a body like a small spiked ball. When threatened, it rolls up, exposing only its spikes. Using this technique, a hedgehog sometimes will attack and eat small snakes, rolling itself around the snake as it begins to eat it. The hedgehog is protected from the snake's bite by its spines and, like the mongoose, by a certain immunity to snake venom.

The sun was burning off mist early the next morning when I joined a desultory group of walkers. A couple here, a trio there, all of us strolled along the beach, up over a kurkar ridge, down to the next beach, north from Nahsholim into the Dor ha-Bonim Beach Reserve. Turquoise lagoons sparkled in the sunlight. Half-moon coves embraced their own beaches. In small inlets, roiling whitewater crashed against the rocks.

From a sea of yellow chrysanthemums atop a kurkar plateau, I stepped down from ledge to ledge to where a long mantle of rock points into the sea. Waves have eaten away a portion of the rock, creating caves and an arch that frames sea and sky. This crenelated sea castle, pounded by surf, was guarded by a slender white egret, whose bill pointed into the wind.

Beyond, where the shore straightens, the sea became calm. I followed ribbons of seashells that marked high tide on the broad sandy beach. I took off my shoes and dug my toes into the sand, now warm on top but still cool and moist beneath the surface. Ahead of me, small groups of plovers and pipers raced along the water's edge, stopping to probe for small crustaceans and other morsels of food.

Among the low dunes at the back of the beach, sea grasses had rooted, anchoring the sand and forming soil. As soil forms, low shrubs take hold. From such simple beginnings, a shoreline can eventually reach a climax community of trees, shrubs, wildflowers, grasses, and all the animals that inhabit such seaside ecosystems.

The smell of sun-warmed beach grasses lulled me, and I sat awhile on the sand, letting groups of strollers pass before I put on my shoes to walk to the top of the next kurkar ridge. Atop this ridge, cushions of purple clover and white chamomile grew directly from the sand, scattered among yellow daisies. Later in the year, cheerful narcissi would serve as reminders that even come winter there is something lovely to look at along the shore.

At Dor ha-Bonim Beach Reserve, cove beaches reveal offshore islands where the Mediter-ranean Sea has battered at the rocks, forming caves and arches.

282

Some beaches are covered with shells, some with garbage. Even though I was within reserve boundaries, the next beach was littered with plastic bags and bottles, rusting cans, and other unsightly stuff. In Israel, the garbage issue is a difficult one. Stricter fines have been in force since the late 1990s, but it will take time and education to make a significant dent in this problem. The garbage was offensive enough to turn me back to Nahsholim.

At Nahsholim, the beach widens. Edged by grassy areas and a few open-air restaurants, the swath of sand adjacent to the kibbutz attracts picnicking families, people playing Frisbee and paddleball, children building sand castles. At the southern edge of Nahsholim, small boats bob in shallow water; others lie upturned on the beach.

Where Dor ha-Bonim Reserve and Nahsholim meet, excavations are teasing away centuries of detritus to reveal the thirty-five-hun-dred-year-old metropolis of Dor, once a prominent port city. To learn more, I went to the Nahsholim Museum. Located on the kibbutz, the museum presents an intriguing and comprehensive portrait of Dor: the city, the coast, and its history.

The skeleton of a Phoenician woman was found at Dor under a

house that had collapsed in an eleventh-century B.C.E. earthquake: fault lines at work. In display cases, tiny jugs from pre-Roman times once held pharmaceuticals, such as extract of boxthorn, a coastal shrub that yielded a remedy for eye infections.

The museum exhibits ancient bones used to play dice games and metals smelted from rock, used by early peoples for a variety of purposes. A more recent flintlock musket pulled from the waters off Dor, encrusted with shells, is a remnant of Napoleon's 1799 campaign against the Turks here.

Some three thousand years ago, Phoenicians ruled the coast and traded goods across the Mediterranean. They spread the concept of syllabic writing, which we use today, and learned how to produce glass. They also learned to extract a purple dye from *Murex trunculus*, a sea snail with an elaborately ridged and frilled shell.

Phoenicians were sophisticated enough to know the photochemical processes for producing a range of purple tones from the murex extractions, from reds to blues. Because the dying process was tedious and difficult—from gathering thousands of snails to extracting the dye—purple was extremely costly to produce. The dye became known as "royal purple" because only kings and other high-ranking individuals could afford to wear cloth of that color.

At Dor, murex snails were collected and held in rock pools until the dye masters had a sufficient amount. The snails were then crushed in order to release the purple dye from a gland within the gastropod. A rock dye vat, still faintly tinged with purple, was found at Dor.

283

Royal purple also was the color specified by the Bible for the four-cornered, fringed ritual garment, the tallit: ". . . let them attach a cord of blue to the fringe at each corner. . . . That shall be your fringe; look at it and recall all the commandments of the Lord and observe them . . ." (Numbers 15:38–39). In fact, a form of the Hebrew word *segol* ("purple") came to mean "exceptional" or "select." The phrase "chosen people" comes from the Hebrew *am segulah*.

Later, during the first and second centuries C.E., indigo dye derived from the leaves of a mustard plant, *Isatis tinctoria*, began to replace expensive Tyrian purple, both in the tallit and in other garments.

In the time of the Phoenicians, both linen and wool were well known in the Middle East, as cloth production dates to approximately 6000 B.C.E. Egyptians wrapped their mummies in linen. The covering for the Ark of the Covenant and the robes of the priests of Israel were of fine linen. Linen, produced from the flax plant, is a material whose excellence is still unmatched by synthetic fibers.

Linseed oil as well as flax are derived from the wildflower *Linum usitatissimum*. Early people learned to sow flax seeds as crops. When the plants were ready, they were pulled from the ground, dried, soaked to loosen the outer husks, then stripped of their fibers. The fibers were then combed and spun into thread much as sheep's wool is. Anyone who has seen golden strands of flax, called "tow" in English, understands immediately where the term "towhead" comes from.

Using simple wood implements, women would spin out flax thread from a distaff onto a spindle. Once enough thread was spun, the material was woven into fabric. In the earliest method of weaving, warp fibers probably were suspended from a tree branch and the weft fibers threaded through them. The first looms date to the fifth millennium B.C.E. and consisted simply of wood frames holding parallel threads.

By biblical times, flax was a staple crop. Before the battle of Jericho, Joshua sent spies to reconnoiter the region, and they lodged at the house of a harlot name Rahab. When officers of the king of Jericho came looking for Joshua's men, Rahab "had taken them up to the roof and hidden them under some stalks of flax which she had lying on the roof" (Joshua 2:6).

In Roman and Byzantine times, flax was an important crop in the Bet She'an and Jezreel Valleys. Flax-soaking vats have been discovered, and the Talmud advises that one should rotate fields used to grow flax because the plant depletes soil nutrients.

284

Although these seminal inventions took place over hundreds, even thousands of years, the ideas involved in making linen—from stripping a plant for its fibers to weaving—is reminder that though our ancestors lived lives far more primitive than ours, their brains were just as fertile.

Of Birds and Crocodile Rivers

Only a few miles south of Nahsholim, Kibbutz Ma'agan Mikha'el raises carp, gray mullet, and Saint Peter's fish. SPNI's Carmel Coast Field School sits on a hill overlooking Ma'agan Mikha'el's fish ponds to the north and Nahal Tanninim to the south. To the east of Ma'agan Mikha'el, beyond the Tel Aviv-Haifa highway, lies southernmost Carmel and the Manasseh highlands. To the west lies the Mediterranean Sea.

Not many decades ago, marshes filled much of the lowlands here, but they were drained to create agricultural fields. Now kibbutz fish ponds fulfill a function of the swamps. Surrounded by rushes and reeds, the large ponds attract myriad bird species. In summer, parts of Ma'agan Mikha'el are closed to the public so as not to disturb nesting birds.

In spring and autumn, however, the place is a frenzy of migrating birds. Although birds migrate along both coastal and inland routes, ornithologists believe that many soaring birds migrating north from Africa in spring choose the desert route along the Great Rift. The reason is that desert cliffs heat air currents faster, and birds such as storks need rising currents to soar on. With mating hormones pushing them north to nest, some birds choose the faster route. As a result, autumn sees storks migrating through Ma'agan Mikha'el while spring does not.

Early one evening, I took a slow walk on the paths and dikes that separate the fish ponds. The company of birds included sandpipers, great white egrets and golden-slippered little egrets, blackcaps, yellow wagtails, and mallards, to name a few. A night heron hid among the giant reeds. Fat moorhens, red face stripe bright against their black bodies, floated quietly, picking among plants near the edge of a pond. One of the males flashed its white rump feathers in flamboyant display. A duck, a red-crested pochard, dove again and again. Above, a vulture circled.

As evening waned and night approached, I returned to the Carmel Coast Field School, where simple rooms surround pleasant terraces. Walkways lined with flowering shrubs and trees smelled sweet in the cooling evening air. A Palestine sunbird sipped nectar from the showy rose-pink flower of a Chinese bauhinia, a tree now grown in warm climates throughout the world.

285

In the afternoon, I had visited Bet Gail, the field school building honoring Gail Rubin. A New Yorker who began visiting Israel in 1969, Rubin had turned her photographer's eye to Israel's natural history. In 1978 Rubin was here, at Ma'agan Mikha'el, photographing birds when some men approached from the direction of the sea. They spoke with her briefly, then shot her dead. They went on to attack a public bus before being overcome by security forces. Yet, Gail Rubin's vibrant images of Israel's wildlife will outlive the terrorists who took her life.

As night gathered the world in darkness, I walked in the direction of the sea, a broad black band of velvet under the moonless sky. I could hear the faraway sound of waves, rhythmically breaking on the beach. During the night, I awoke several times and stepped outside just to wrap myself in the rare blanket of serene darkness.

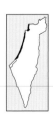

Although Palestine sunbirds are only as big as hummingbirds, the male is unmistakable: a darkly iridescent blue-purple with flashes of shimmering green. Sunbirds sip nectar by dipping their long, decurved beaks into tubular flowers and sucking up the sweet liquid with long, brush-tipped tongues.

Like hummingbirds, Palestine sunbirds are attracted to brightly colored flowers, especially red flowers. The classic image is of a sunbird with its head buried in the tubular crimson flower of a strapvine, the semiparasitic plant that rambles over acacia trees.

The sunbird's efforts are mutually rewarding. As it buries its head in the flower to drink nectar, pollen brushes off on the bird. The sunbird then flies to the next flower and unknowingly deposits some pollen, thus fertilizing that flower.

Canon Henry Baker Tristram identified the Palestine sunbird in the 1860s. In 1908 Israel Aharoni was working for the Turkish government as its official zoologist. When he went out looking for sunbirds, he could find only four pair, near Jericho. But, over the century, flowering shrubs have been planted throughout the country, tempting Palestine sunbirds to expand their range from the confines of the Great Rift. Now they appear most everywhere.

Birds are crepuscular creatures, best seen at dusk and dawn, so early the next day I visited the fish ponds again to see what I could see. Just inside the gate, I met an older British couple who were toting some serious photographic equipment. Birding seems to be a British national hobby, the country full of knowledgeable amateur ornithologists who will travel the world to see a bird.

As we walked toward the ponds, a pair of mongooses, low slung and sleek, chased each other over the dikes. Crested larks and spur-winged plovers ran ahead of us. Ponds erupted, one after another, 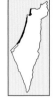 with the chuckling of frogs. A "graceful warbler" gracefully warbled from among the pink and white flowers of a tamarisk.

The couple and I continued walking until the husband stopped suddenly and stared. His wife immediately followed his gaze. Silently they indicated to me where to look, and she whispered, from the side of her mouth, "little bittern."

Bitterns are common during migration and otherwise rare in Israel. They hunt the margins of freshwater, looking for fish and frogs. When disturbed, they stand stock-still at water's edge and imitate a reed. The bittern's trick is to extend its long neck straight up, sharp beak pointed at the sky. Light and dark stripes on its neck extend down over its belly, making the bird look like just another long, slender reed at the edge of a pond.

We saw kingfishers on a telephone wire, black-and-white pieds and a turquoise-backed white-breasted. And on an embankment edging one of the ponds we could see the kingfishers' nest holes. A gray water rail with a red beak stalked the reeds, looking for a tasty dragonfly or water strider.

Along a canal I showed the British couple the prickly leaves and fuchsia-colored flowers of alkanet, whose name comes from the Arabic *alkhenna* because it was once used as a dye. They, in turn, pointed out a Cetti's warbler. It is one thing to spot a big raptor—raptors are hard to miss. It is quite another to discover a warbler and instantly know which of the dozens of small, look-alike warblers it is. The secret is in the song. Good birders track as much by ear as by eye.

We parted, they to focus their camera lenses on the bittern, while I walked out toward the beach. In an area between the ponds and beach, field school staff have found patches of brush where African monarch butterflies breed. African monarchs are also found along the Great Rift, where the caterpillars feed on the leaves of the Sodom apple. The monarch, immune to the plant's poisonous sap, itself becomes a bitter meal. After pupating, it advertises its toxicity with brilliant orange wings veined with black.

287

At Ma'agan Mikha'el, a colony of African monarchs lays jewel-like green eggs on the undersides of a patch of stranglewort vines. The smooth-skinned caterpillars, yellow with black stripes, feed on the plants, becoming sleek and fat until each wraps itself in a chrysalis the color of a leaf. There they pupate until they are ready to emerge, unfold their wings, and fly off, fully formed butterflies.

Closer to the beach, poterium trimmed low by the salt spray borders the soft path of white sand. Red poppies, sunny yellow daisies, and blue bugloss surround poterium's green mounds.

As I strode along the sandy beach, groups of sanderlings skittered ahead on short, quick legs, chasing the tide to see what delicacies each new wave washed ashore. Sanderlings, sandpipers, and other shorebirds are equipped with long, probing beaks, each designed to reach prey at a different level in the sand.

The sea was a quiet blue with a white line of foam where the waves broke. A noisy cloud of gulls argued overhead. And a snipe, its brown-and-white patterned body wide and low to the ground, scuttled off toward the brush.

Offshore lies Dove Island, a rocky outcrop where a few hundred terns nest each summer. There, they lay their eggs in shallow depressions on the bare ground, safe from mongooses and other mainland predators. The nesting terns also are safe from human intrusion, the island being off-limits to people. If a raptor or other predator should approach, the terns find safety in numbers, rising up as one to attack the intruder.

Dove Island lies not far from the mouth of Nahal Tanninim. Where the fresh water of the river meets the salt water of the sea, a variety of fish thrive. Schools of fingerlings crowd the brackish mix of waters and serve as a constant food supply for adult terns and their growing chicks.

Nahal Tanninim means "Crocodile River." The last crocodile was killed on the river in the early 1900s. It is hard to imagine such huge reptiles along such a humble waterway. Like all rivers in Israel, not too much emphasis should be put on Nahal Tanninim's size or strength.

The stream and its banks are the last of Israel's undisturbed coastal riverine habitats, so it is protected as a nature reserve. Preserving

288 Nahal Tanninim and the springs that feed it is a struggle in the face of unrelenting development.

This river reserve also reveals pieces of the past, including ruins of the Roman town Crocodilopolis. The parking lot at the beginning of the river reserve lies a walk away from the Carmel Coast Field School. Across from the parking lot a low cliff is notched by ancient burial chambers, long empty after centuries of other uses.

The field school director had mentioned a rookery, so I ventured along the path toward a grove where I hoped to see nesting birds. Planted after the Kabarah Swamps were drained in the 1920s, the grove of tall eucalyptus indeed serves as a nursery for egrets and night herons, who flew in and out of the trees' upper branches, cackling and squabbling. The path south from the grove parallels an ancient Roman aqueduct that once carried water to Caesarea, about two miles away. In between lies the Arab village of Jiser al-Zarqa.

I walked back to Nahal Tanninim and the bridge that spans the small river. The bridge was once a Roman dam, but stones from the bottom have been removed to let the river run through. Agama liz-

Ma'agan Mikha'el fish ponds attract hosts of birds and bird-watchers. Beyond the ponds, sandy paths lead past mounds of daisies to beaches and shorebirds.

ards raced over the timeworn blocks, their bodies colored with mating advertisements, stereotypic blue head for male, pink for female. A female also sports orange stripes that advertise the fact that she has a belly full of eggs to be fertilized.

289

I was reminded of a story told to me at Bio Ramon wildlife park near Makhtesh Ramon in the Negev. In the agama enclosure lived three males of various sizes plus one female. When the female produced her orange stripes, the two largest males faced off and started fighting for the right to mate with her. While they were battling, the smallest male snuck in and took care of the mating.

The edges of the Roman bridge were decorated with white-flowering garlic and asphodel's candy-striped flowers. Against the blue horizon, a dark line of glossy ibis flew low over the coast. A hoopoe landed on the ruins, flattening its comb, then launching itself again in a whirr of black-and-white wings as I stepped down toward the river path below. At the head of the trail stand ancient mills.

The river trail parts thick brush. Tamarisk and silvery saltbush bend toward the water, and a few palms moor the damp ground. These three salt-tolerant plants hint that the Tanninim, at this point,

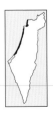

is brackish. Mint grows along the water's edge and within the water live crabs, mollusks, and timorous soft-shell turtles. Gambusia, the small fish that feasts on mosquito larvae, was introduced because the former marshes attracted malaria-bearing mosquitoes.

Tilapia and eel live in Tanninim's waters as well. Catfish cruise the river. Like the crocodiles that once lived here, they are an African species that migrated north eons ago. At this meeting of the continents, crocodiles sunned themselves on the riverbanks while, just to the east, European roe deer roamed the hills.

Goldfinches and other small birds flit among the brush until a kestrel swoops in. Instantly, the small birds fall silent and seem to disappear. Farther on, the Tanninim is joined by the Adah River, and together the widened waters meander through sunny meadows to the beach and sea.

Roses and Other Remnants of the Plain of Sharon

Josephus wrote, "If ever a man was full of family affection, that man was Herod. In memory of his father he founded a city, choosing a site in the loveliest plain in his kingdom with an abundance of rivers and trees, and naming it Antipatris."

Herod was a ruler who let nothing, not even relatives, stand in his path. Although no one would want to be on the receiving end of Herod's "family affection," it would be wonderful to see "the loveliest plain . . . with an abundance of rivers and trees." The well-watered woodland Josephus wrote of was located near present-day Petah Tiqvah on the Plain of Sharon.

Writing fifteen hundred years later, the Italian poet Tasso called the Plain of Sharon an "enchanted forest." And when Napoleon arrived in 1799, one of his generals spoke of a bivouac in "the forest." Until the 1830s, the Plain of Sharon still appeared much as it had in ages past: a rolling plain covered with groves of Tabor oak interspersed with meadows.

The broad plain that lies just east of the coast looks nothing like an enchanted forest today. The seeds of destruction were planted in the early 1800s, when a Macedonian officer rose to the top of the Ottoman military structure. The Ottoman Turks, who had ruled the Middle East since the 1500s, made him viceroy of Egypt. Muhammed 'Ali Pasha, often called Egypt's first modern leader, then began his own campaign to govern not only Egypt but the entire eastern Mediterranean.

In the 1830s, the forests of the Sharon were cut to provide fuel and building materials for Muhammed 'Ali's campaign to conquer. After ten years of advance into Syria, Muhammed 'Ali was defeated and retreated to Egypt. Ottoman rule, though waning, again filled the power vacuum in the Levant. In their battle for supremacy against the English during World War I, the Ottomans stripped what remained of Sharon forests to build and fuel railroads through Palestine.

Today the Plain of Sharon is full of orchards, industry, towns—the full complement of human activity. The "rose of Sharon" is hard to find and, now, the most obvious wildlife is the hooded crow.

But the prophet Isaiah (35:2) wrote of the "splendor of Carmel and Sharon." Song of Songs (2:1) sings, "I am a rose of Sharon, a lily of the valleys." In those days, crimson Sharon tulips lit up Sharon meadows. *Havatselet*, translated as "rose," was possibly this brilliant flower. The "rose" may also be a narcissus, perhaps the radiant white sea daffodil that blooms along the coast.

The lilylike sea daffodil also may be the "lily of the valleys," the lilies whose artless beauty Matthew (6:28-29) mentions as example: "Consider the lilies of the field, how they grow; they toil not, neither do they spin: And yet I say unto you, that even Solomon in all his glory was not arrayed like one of these."

All of these were once part of the varied flora of the Sharon. Their beauty now is confined to the few natural places that survive. Afeq National Park, which preserves the remains of Herod's Antipatris, also preserves some natural terrain and is a good place to watch the autumn bird migration.

Along the shore north of Netanyah, Nahal Alexander National Park is more about recreation than nature, but it does preserve the remains of Nahal Alexander. This stream, named for the ruthless Hasmonean king, Alexander Yannai, cleaves cliffs near the shoreline as it carries water from the mountains of eastern Samaria to the sea. Nearby is an echo of the original forest. Just north of Netanyah, Berekhat Ya'ar Reserve, the Sharon's last natural pool, attracts migrating waterfowl.

South of Netanyah, adjacent to the Wingate Institute for Physical Education and Sport, Nahal Poleg Reserve preserves what little remains of Poleg Stream, its surrounding dunes, and beach. What's left of the stream is sad, as it struggles past a pile of garbage here, some rutted jeep tracks there. Jeeps and dirt bikes have gouged most of Poleg's tall dunes.

I passed a woman and two children picnicking on a blanket. The blanket lay cozily on the sand among broom bushes, and the woman invited me to share some apple slices with them. She told me a little about her life, how she had moved to Israel from Houston, Texas, a decade ago, met and married an Iranian Jew. Now they were settled, with two school-age children.

Cheered by this unexpected meeting, I ventured into the dunes again and discovered a few pleasant sights at Poleg, including glittering purple Palestine sunbirds. Terns, white etched with black, wheeled exuberantly from dunes to sea and back. The chirruping of frogs rose from a portion of stream fringed by tall phragmites reeds. The few unblemished dunes, golden in late afternoon light, were capped with green boxthorn and broom.

Pink maresia, yellow daisies, white daisies, and snowy mounds of knotgrass scattered themselves in bunches through the sands. Deep blue flowers of wrinkle-leaf sage made a show and, hidden in the shade of a shrub, a cyclamen survived. The best saved itself for last. Just as I was leaving, I noticed a dark, almost black flower: an iris. The purple iris, which grows on Israel's coastal sands near Netanyah and Rishon le-Zion—and nowhere else in the world—is one of eight iris species unique to Israel. *Iris atropurpurea* is about as dark a purple as a flower can get.

Not surprisingly, the closer one approaches Tel Aviv, the less natural the coast becomes. In the Samarian foothills, Wadi Qanah feeds into Nahal Yarqon, the largest coastal river. Wadi Qanah, which once formed the boundary between the tribes of Manasseh and Ephraim, still looks like a natural waterway.

292

By the time Nahal Yarqon reaches the sea, however, it has been polluted, channeled, and much of its natural flow drawn off for irrigation. Lying along Tel Aviv's northern city limit, the Yarqon River threads its way past apartment buildings, marinas, power-station smokestacks, electric lines—urban wilderness.

Perhaps the most interesting natural history in the Tel Aviv metropolis is the handsome Geological Garden tucked away in a corner of huge and hugely popular Yehoshua Gardens in Ha-Yarqon Park. Every type of rock found in Israel is displayed here in superbly landscaped settings, so a trip to the Geological Garden delights while it informs. The rocks are surrounded with sweeps of native wildflowers, shrubs, and trees, making the park botanically interesting as well. The plants attract birds, another layer of natural history. And the whole is put together with such artistry that it feels like the natural equivalent of a sculpture garden.

At Nahal Poleg, a small coastal river struggles through nearby development to reach dunes and sea. Among the dunes grow endemic deep purple wild irises.

Beyond Ashdod: the Last Dunes

I was looking for the last dunes. I was told that the last large expanse of natural coastal dunes lay south of Ashdod, so I drove onto the Ayalon Freeway, heading south from Tel Aviv. The Ayalon is a familiar nightmare, much like Chicago's Dan Ryan Expressway, New York's Cross-Bronx Expressway, or Los Angeles's evil octopus of freeways.

Usually I panic on the way north into Tel Aviv. Faced with a convoluted interchange in snarling traffic, I get off at the wrong exit— always the same wrong exit so I have learned how to wend my way north on city streets from there. This time I panicked going south and spun off into the southern realm of Rishon le-Zion, along coastal sands where bright white apartment buildings, some nearly new, some

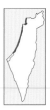

brand-new, some not quite finished marched in look-alike ranks along streets not yet marked on maps.

I seemed to drive around what looked like the same block for half an hour until I found myself in front of a police station. A patrol officer said she and her partner were headed to the Ayalon and would escort me. From there I continued south to Ashdod, but I knew what I had seen was a very visible demonstration of the dunes' demise.

A few miles south of Ashdod and just north of the community of Nitsenim, SPNI's Shiqmim Field School is the gateway to the Holot Nitsenim Reserve. *Holot* means "dunes," and between Ashdod and Nitsenim lie Israel's last, uninterrupted coastal dunes. These southern shores have another distinction. They and the southern California coast are the only places in the world where desert and Mediterranean climate mix.

The field school is called Shiqmim because nearby stand some of Israel's oldest Egyptian fig trees (called sycomore, or *shiqmah* in Hebrew). Because growth tissue lies just under the bark, some of these trees are hollow, yet they live. Wind can scour the sand from around their roots, and they will live. Shifting sand can sift over them, and they will live. The word *shiqmah* is related to the Hebrew word meaning "rehabilitate"; indeed, the Egyptian fig can revive from the toughest of circumstances.

Before wandering out among the dunes, I had stopped at the field school to get some advice on where to walk and what species might be about. Conservation stations are understaffed and overworked worldwide, and Shiqmim Field School is no different. I patiently waited for Shulamit, who teaches ecology at the field school.

She took me to her home, a bungalow in a line of small bungalows facing west toward the dunes. Inside, ecological papers and signs of children were scattered across tabletops. Shulamit had especially wanted to show me a photography book, *Mabat v'od Mabat* (*Look and Look Again*), by Jack Rubin.

In the book, Rubin compares aerial photographs taken in 1917 with aerial photographs he took from the same viewpoints in 1991. The changes that occurred in those seventy-four years are riveting. In the 1917 photograph, Tel Aviv is a small grid surrounded by dunes and open space. In the 1991 photograph, Tel Aviv is a huge spread of interlocking grids as dense as a computer circuit board. Open areas are hard to find. Page after page, up and down the coast, showed how much had been eaten by urban development in those intervening years. The pace has not slowed since 1991.

Egyptian fig's resinous wood is so light and durable that it was used in Egyptian sarcophagi and as beams in buildings of ancient Israel. Like the cultivated fig, the sycomore also was valued for its fruit. Dressing the fruit of the sycomore so that it would reach full ripeness was an occupation in early Israel, and the Prophet Amos declared, "I am a cattle breeder and a tender of sycomore figs" (Amos 7:14).

Egyptian figs are native to wet and tropical Sudanese regions, not to the more northerly coastal lands of Israel. Botanists believe this species of fig was brought to Israel by traders millennia ago. It must have been cultivated because, in this cooler, drier region, sycomore fruits need help in ripening.

Once Egyptian fig trees, as well as olive trees, were common on the coastal plain and in the Judean foothills. King Solomon "made silver as plentiful in Jerusalem as stone, and cedars as plentiful as sycomores in the *shefelah*" (1 Kings 10:27). But, after the Bar Kokhba Revolt against the Romans, the Talmud indicates that the plain's wealth of sycomores was greatly reduced.

Even the changes at Ashdod are astonishing. Preserving what is left of the Ashdod Dunes is critical from a number of perspectives. SPNI's Bilha Givon, who has been instrumental in saving many natural areas in southern Israel, points out that the intersection of desert and Mediterranean climate allows unusual adaptations in flora and fauna: Mediterranean species move into desert conditions, and desert species infiltrate Mediterranean conditions.

295

"Here," Givon says, "the massive golden sand dunes bordering the blue sea are still shifting and developing, thanks to a complex balance of natural factors. These dunes provide a last refuge for a rich variety of plants and animals, as well as a unique living illustration of geological processes."

Some geological processes have been changed, radically and recently. Southern Israel's sand washes in from the great delta of the Nile. But the Aswan High Dam, built in the late 1960s, has been holding back nearly 98 percent of the sediment that builds the Nile Delta and keeps it healthy. As a result, the Nile Delta is shrinking fast.

Egypt plans to capture what little sediment does reach the delta, which will prevent the natural flow of sand eastward. Beaches along

Sinai, Gaza, and southern Israel will suffer as a result. Gloomy news.

The best antidote to this news, I decided, was a walk among the dunes themselves. From the field school, I backtracked by car on a sandy road and parked at a fork: one direction leads to golden Nitsenim Beach, the other to the back dunes. The fork is marked by head-high stands of sabra cactus, which was introduced to Israel sometime after the 1500s when the Spanish colonized what is now Mexico and the American Southwest.

(Ironically, a number of those first Spanish colonists were conversos, Jews forcibly converted to Christianity. They had traveled to what is now Mexico and New Mexico trying to get as far from the center of the Spanish Inquisition as possible.)

Prickly-pear cactus has lived in Israel long enough that it is considered native. The first generation born to Jewish immigrants in modern Israel were called "sabras" because, like the cactus, they were said to be prickly on the outside, sweet on the inside. The fruit of the cactus is edible, and the peeled, paddle-shaped leaves are used to make candy. As living fences, walls of sabra cactus also reveal where Arabs marked land boundaries.

From the prickly-pear fork, I chose a sandy path leading into the back dunes. The dunes, some about twenty feet high, stand in tangled ranks and are covered with native acacias as well as weeping acacias. Like sabra cacti, weeping acacias are newcomers (in this case, from Australia) whose blue-gray straplike leaves are hidden by an explosion of yellow pompom flowers in spring. Beach peas sprawl across the sand, along with leggy, lipstick-pink storksbill.

Hooded crows and Palestine sunbirds flew by. I rounded a dune and met a group of kindergarten-age children and their teachers, returning from a field trip. As we passed and the high-pitched children's voices faded behind me, the insistent call of a white-breasted kingfisher took over, sounding from somewhere near the pool created by a quarry. Now edged with vegetation, the former quarry looks nearly natural, an eye-soothing pond of water on a hot desert day. On low dunes nearby, arching boxthorn and white broom bushes provide hideouts for tan lizards.

The most famous lizard of the dunes is the desert monitor, a three-foot-long relative of the Komodo dragon. A long log of a lizard with loose, leathery sand-colored skin speckled by a pretty pattern of dots, the desert monitor's largest population lives in the Ashdod Dunes.

It used to live as far north as the Yarqon River at the northern boundary of Tel Aviv. But development has taken over much of the

Brought to the Mediterranean long ago, North American prickly-pear cactus has natural-ized. Near Ashdod, huge stands of "sabras" line Israel's last best dunes.

sandy habitat monitors favor, so the reptile has become increasingly rare. Monitors, along with the rest of Israel's reptiles, are now protected by law.

297

Except during mating, these huge reptiles are loners and require large territories to track down enough protein to eat. Mice, geckos, snakes, hares, hedgehogs—a monitor will eat any animal big enough to fit in its mouth. Like a snake, it swallows dinner whole.

I walked back to the fork in the road and headed in the other direction, toward the beach. Between the high, shrub-covered back dunes and the flat beach lies a rippling sea of low, grass-covered dunes. This is where a monitor is mostly likely to roam. Of course, if you went looking for a monitor you would likely not find one. They see you before you see them, and, if you are too big to eat, they make themselves scarce. Not knowing our intentions, the eaters do not want to be the eaten.

Grasses are the most critical plants among the low dunes. They are the first to colonize bare sands, sending out vast skeins of roots that stabilize the tiny grains of quartz. Grass-anchored sand holds more moisture than shifting sand; as grasses die, the organic material helps build soil. With a bit more water and soil, the sand is on its way to becoming a stable dune.

Next in the march of plant succession—and the most obvious plant among the rolling sea of sand—is single-seed wormwood, or artemisia, which grows in squat, silvery clumps. Like other artemisias, single-seed wormwood thrives in these parched conditions and, like most dryland plants, its silvery leaves help retain moisture by reflecting sunlight. As I walked among the rills of dunes, I watched black darkling beetles scurry away, into the lacy shade of wormwood. They were the only creatures, besides me, moving on the hot, still day.

Feeling sticky with sweat, I thought of the Noël Coward line, "Mad dogs and Englishmen go out in the noonday sun," and made my way toward the sea from the solitude of the dunes. Where swells of sand merge into broad flat beach, people lay under umbrellas, watching others jump in the surf. Beyond the breakers, flotillas of gulls bobbed serenely. I laid down my gear and waded into the cool water.

A Final View from Dor

My time exploring natural Israel was drawing to a close. Time spent sleeping under the stars in the desert and following streams crowded with oleander and scented with mint would be supplanted by months of sitting in a room with a computer. My husband and I were preparing to depart in a few days when he suggested a farewell walk along the beach at Dor ha-Bonim on the Carmel coast.

298

Michael and I walked along the shoreline of one of Dor ha-Bonim's small, curving coves. I found a few cuttlebones that had washed up on the sand, the kind I used to put in my parakeet's cage when I was a child.

The north end of the cove was bounded by a kurkar ridge stepping down in increments to the sea. At sea level it formed a thick rock platform a few feet above the water. We scrambled onto its pocked and battered surface to find seaweed-lined tide pools where sea slugs and small crabs made themselves at home.

We climbed higher, to the top of the ridge. Below, a tumble of boulders divided the tide pool platform from the next beach north. Just visible above the boulders at water's edge was the simple dark arch of a long fishing pole and the capped head of the man who held it.

On a low wall of earth-encrusted rocks where wildflowers had gained purchase, we sat and watched the sea. Clouds raced against a pale blue sky. A few gulls swooped in, hovered, then finding nothing to scavenge, shrieked indignantly and flew off.

"I think you're sitting on something quite old," I said.

"You mean my behind?" Michael laughed.

He examined the ruler-straight rock wall. "Yes," he finally agreed, "these must be remnants of Dor."

And they were. We talked about this ancient city, a Phoenician port thirty-five hundred years ago, when people still sacrificed children to gain the gods' beneficence. Dor saw the world change: Phoenicians, Hellenists, the Jewish Hasmonean kings, Romans, the rise of Christianity, and, in the seventh century, the rise of Islam. Crusaders came and went. Napoleon's armada retreated to Dor in 1799.

Dor was an important link along the Via Maris. Shipwrecks off its shores reveal nearly four thousand years of maritime history: anchors from the dawn of the Bronze Age; Greek amphorae; ceramic lamps from Asia and Italy; three-thousand-year-old glass produced on this very spot; bracelets, coins, and precious stones from every age; eighteenth-century muskets; and twentieth-century submarines.

Dor arose as a seaport when merchant ships first set sail in these waters, among the first merchant fleets in the world. Its sailors carried purple linens and green glass bowls produced by Phoenician artisans to trade with peoples around the Mediterranean. Camel caravans with loads of frankincense from southern Arabia and silks from the far East stopped here to unload their goods. Two thousand years ago and more, farmers from the Judean Hills brought olive oil and almonds, dates and figs to sell. Innkeepers and merchants were busy for millennia.

299

Yet here lies Dor, conquered by daisies. In a pocket of crumbling wall kingfishers have dug a home.

Just down the road, Tel Aviv is now the eastern Mediterranean's bustling coastal city, full of commerce and crowds, derricks, bulldozers, and steamrollers building more skyscrapers and highways. Tel Aviv is less than two hundred years old, one-twentieth the age of Dor. How, I wondered, would future peoples fit Tel Aviv and what we think of as the modern world into this vast tapestry of humanity.

Israel has long been a place where nature as well as world cultures and peoples have mingled. I saw where mining was invented among the copper-filled rocks of the Negev; where olives were first cultivated in the Judean Hills and Galilee; where long-ago fishermen threw nets on Lake Kinneret; where the ancients, using papyrus and hide and early writing skills, left texts in the Judean Desert; and where

Stone Age people hunted and developed agriculture at the foot of Mount Carmel at the dawn of civilization.

It is hard to mesh our own history with the enormity of time. In this ancient land where so much human and natural history have converged, who knows what human works will cover this spot in the distant future.

Although nothing, including nature, remains static, the natural world seems ageless by comparison.

Near the rocks where the fishing pole arched, a heron bent its neck, also fishing. I expect, four thousand years from now, a long-legged heron will still probe the shallow waters against the rhythmic sound of the sea.

CHAPTER TWELVE

Resources

WHEN CONTACTING ISRAEL BY TELEPHONE or fax from North America, add the international prefix 011 followed by the country code 972 and delete the 0 that precedes each regional exchange. For example, 03-638-8666 becomes 011-972-3-638-8666. Phone and fax numbers are subject to change. Because of the time difference, fax or email is often more efficient than phone. And most Israelis know English. Some reserves do not have visitor centers, so no contact point is given.

To make excursions as safe and pleasant as possible, bring a hat, sunscreen, and sunglasses. Bring—and drink—plenty of water. Check your plans with SPNI or a similar organization and let people know your itinerary. Don't hike alone. Carry adequate maps, wear proper footwear, dress in layers, and stay informed about the weather. For long hikes, extra food, a flashlight, an emergency blanket, a pocket knife, and a basic first-aid kit may prove useful. Avoid feeding or approaching too close to wildlife. Few experiences offer as much pleasure as an outing in the natural world, but always use common sense.

To protect the beauty and integrity of the natural world, observe the hiker's creed: "Take only photographs; leave only footprints."

301

Nature Organizations, Reserves, and Parks

Society for the Protection of Nature in Israel (SPNI)
4 Ha-Shfela St., Tel Aviv 66183, Israel
tel: main 03-638-8653, tours 03-638-8674 or 03-638-8677;
fax: tours 03-688-3940; email: tourism@spni.org.il;
Web: www.teva.org.il

American Society for Protection of Nature in Israel (ASPNI)
28 Arrandale Ave., Great Neck, NY 11024
tel: 212-398-6750, 800-411-0966; fax: 212-398-1665;
email: aspni@aol.com

SPNI Israel Nature Trails and Tours
Ami Travel
6200 N. Hiawatha Blvd., Suite 625, Chicago IL 60646
tel: 800-323-0035; fax 773-777-4921; email: tours@amitravel.com;
Web: www.amitravel.com/spni

Israel Nature and National Parks Protection Authority
3 Am Ve'Olamo St., Givat Shaul, Jerusalem 95463, Israel
tel: 02-500-5444; fax: 02-652-9232; email: info@parks.org.il;
Web: www.parks.org.il
Formerly two agencies, Israel Nature Reserves Authority and Israel
National Parks Authority, this government agency provides a packet
of information on the most popular reserves and a detailed map and
highlights of the national parks, which focus on archaeological and
historical sites as well as recreation. The Website offers plenty of
general information as well as information on specific parks and
reserves.

Israel Ministry of Tourism, North America
800 Second Ave., 16th Floor, New York, NY 10017
tel: 888-77-ISRAEL, 212-499-5660; fax: 212-499-5665;
Web: www.goisrael.com

302

Camel Riders Desert Exploration Tours
Shaharut Mobile Post, Eilat 88865, Israel
tel: 07-637-3218; fax: 07-637-1944; email: camel@inter.net.il

Timna Park
Hevel Eilat Regional Council 88820, Israel
tel: 07-631-6756; fax: 07-635-6215

Coral Beach Reserve
South Beach, Eilat 88105, Israel
tel: 07-637-6829; fax: 07-637-5776

Coral World Underwater Observatory and Marine Park
Almog Beach, P.O. Box 829, Eilat 88106, Israel
tel: 07-636-4200; fax: 07-637-3193; email: cwe@netvision.net.il;
Web: www.coralworld.com/eilat

International Birding and Research Center in Eilat
P.O. Box 774, Eilat 88106, Israel
tel: 07-633-5339; fax: 07-633-5319; 07-637-6922

Yotvatah Hai Bar
Yotvatah 88820, Israel
tel: 07-637-3057; fax: 07-632-6172

Bio Ramon
Mitspeh Ramon, Israel
tel: 07-658-8755; fax: 07-658-8754

Ramon Reserve Visitor Center
P.O. Box 340, Mitspeh Ramon 80600, Israel
tel: 07-658-8691, 07-658-8698; fax: 07-658-8620

Avdat National Park
P.O. Box 650, Mitspeh Ramon 80655, Israel
tel: 07-658-6391; fax: 07-655-0954

Ein Avdat National Park
P.O. Box 44, Midreshet Ben-Gurion 84990, Israel
tel/fax: 07-655-5684

Arad Visitor Center
28 Elazar Ben Yair St., Arad 80700, Israel
tel: 07-995-4409; fax: 07-995-5866

Masada National Park
M.P. Dead Sea 86950, Israel
tel: 07-658-4207; fax: 07-658-4464

Ein Gedi Reserve
tel: 07-658-4285; fax: 07-652-0228

Matsukei Deragot Center for Desert Tourism
Kibbutz Mitspeh Shalem, M.P. Dead Sea 86983, Israel
tel: 02-994-4222; fax: 02-994-4333; email: metzoke@netvision.net.il
Web: www.metzoke.co.il (Hebrew)

Avshalom Reserve (Sorek Cave)
P.O. Box 302, Bet Shemesh, Israel
tel: 02-991-1117; fax: 02-999-0215

Amatsyah Caves (Hazan Caverns)
Moshav Amatsyah, Mobile Post Lachish Darom 79365, Israel
tel: 07-660-3264; fax: 07-660-3256

Neot Kedumim Biblical Landscape Reserve
P.O. Box 1007, Lod 71100, Israel
tel: 08-977-0777; fax: 08-977-0766; email: gen_info@neot-kedumim.org.il;
Web: www.neot-kedumim.org.il

International Bird-watching Center/Jordan Valley
Kefar Ruppin 10850, Israel
tel: 06-606-8396; fax: 06-648-0612;
email: dglasner@kfar-ruppin.org.il;
Web: www.kfar-ruppin.org.il

Yehudyah Reserve
tel: 06-696-2817; fax: 06-696-1166

Gamla Reserve
tel: 06-696-3721; fax: 06-696-1166

Golan Archaeological Museum
P.O. Box 30, Qatsrin 12900, Israel
tel: 06-696-9636; fax: 06-696-9637

Ancient Qatsrin Park
Qatsrin 12900, Israel
tel: 06-696-2412; fax: 06-696-2277

Nahal Hermon Reserve (Banias)
tel: 06-690-2577; fax: 06-690-4066

Tel Dan Reserve
tel: 06-690-2754; fax: 06-695-0128

Beit Ussishkin Museum of Natural History and Archaeology
Kibbutz Dan, M.P. Upper Galilee 12245, Israel
tel: 06-694-1704; 06-695-1703; fax: 06-690-2755

Hurshat Tal National Park
tel: 06-694-2360; fax: 06-695-9360

Ayun Reserve
tel: 06-695-1519; fax: 06-695-0128

Hulah Reserve
P.O. Box 340, Sedeh Eliezer Jct., Yesod ha-Ma'alah 12105, Israel
tel: 06-693-7069; fax: 06-693-0706

Mount Carmel National Park
P.O. Box 36, USAFIA 30090, Israel
tel: 04-823-1452; fax: 04-832-2287

Carmel Hai Bar
M.P. Carmel Coast, Haifa, Israel
tel/fax: 04-984-1750/2

Nahal Me'arot Reserve
M.P. Carmel Coast, Ein Carmel, Israel
tel/fax: 04-984-1750/2

Rosh ha-Niqrah
M.P. Western Galilee, Eilon 22825, Israel
tel: 04-985-7108/9; fax: 04-985-7107;
Web: http://yaron.clever.net/nikra

Nahsholim Museum
Kibbutz Nahsholim, M.P. Carmel Coast 30815, Israel
tel: 06-639-0950 (museum); 06-639-9533 (kibbutz); fax: 06-639-7614

Ein Afeq Reserve
tel: 04-877-9992; fax: 04-877-4052

Alexander River National Park
tel: 09-866-6230

Geological Garden/Yehoshua Gardens
Ha-Yarqon Park, P.O. Box 24052, Tel Aviv 61240, Israel
tel: 03-642-2828

SPNI Field Schools

The SPNI field schools below provide accommodations and dining.
The number of rooms range between twenty-five and fifty, depending
on the field school, and rooms usually must be reserved in advance.
For reservations, contact specific field schools or SPNI in Tel Aviv.

Hermon SPNI Field School
Mobile Post Upper Galilee 12240, Israel
tel: 06-694-1091; fax: 06-695-1480

Golan SPNI Field School
P.O. Box 100, Qatsrin, Golan Heights 12900, Israel
tel: 06-696-1352; fax: 06-696-1947

Mount Meron SPNI Field School
Mobile Post Meron, Galilee 13870, Israel
tel: 06-698-0023; fax: 06-698-7723

Akhziv SPNI Field School
Mobile Post Western Galilee 22817, Israel
tel: 04-982-3762; fax: 04-982-3015

Alon Tavor SPNI Field School
Mobile Post Lower Galilee 14101, Israel
tel: 06-676-6250; fax: 06-676-6272

Carmel Coast/Ma'agan Mikha'el SPNI Field School
Mobile Post Menashe 37805, Israel
tel: 06-639-9654; fax: 06-639-1618

Har Gilo SPNI Field School
Mobile Post North Judea 90907
tel: 02-676-8678; fax: 02-993-2644

Ein Gedi SPNI Field School
Mobile Post Dead Sea 86980, Israel
tel: 07-658-4288; fax: 07-658-4257

Har ha-Negev SPNI Field School
Mitspeh Ramon 30600, Israel
tel: 07-658-8615; fax: 07-658-8385

Sedeh Boqer SPNI Field School
Sedeh Boqer College 84990, Israel
tel: 07-653-2902; fax: 07-653-2721

Ha-Tseva SPNI Field School
Mobile Post ha-Aravah 86815, Israel
tel: 07-658-1546; fax: 07-658-1558

Eilat SPNI Field School
P.O. Box 204; Eilat 88101, Israel
tel: 07-637-1127; fax: 07-637-1771

Related Sites and Organizations

306

There are countless overnight accommodations in Israel, including hotels, kibbutzim, and bed-and-breakfast inns and homes. Those listed below are just a start. The list also includes natural history museums, zoos, and botanical gardens. Occasionally, telephone numbers will be answered by Hebrew voice-mail.

Israel Youth Hostels Association
Youth Travel Bureau, International Convention Center
P.O. Box 6001, Jerusalem 91060, Israel
tel: 02-655-8400; fax: 02-655-8432; email: iyha@iyha.org.il;
Web: www.youth-hostels.org.il

Kibbutz Hotels Chain
1 Smolanskin St., P.O. Box 3193, Tel Aviv 61031, Israel
tel: 03-524-6161; fax: 03-527-8088; email: yael@kibbutz.co.il;
Web: www.kibbutz.co.il

Israel Camping Union
P.O. Box 53, Nahariyah 22100, Israel
tel: 04-992-5392

Jewish National Fund
42 East 69th St., New York, NY 10021-5093
tel: 800-542-TREE, 212-879-9300; fax: 212-517-3293;
email: communications@jnf.org; Web: www.jnf.org

Jewish National Fund-Keren Kayemeth LeIsrael
1 Keren Kayemeth LeIsrael St., P.O. Box 283, Jerusalem 91002, Israel
Web: www.kkl.org.il

University Botanical Gardens—Jerusalem
Hebrew University Campus, Givat Ram, Jerusalem 91904, Israel
tel: 02-679-4012/3; fax: 02-679-3941; Web: www.botanic.co.il/english/

Tel Aviv University Botanic Gardens
Department of Botany, George S. Wise Faculty of Life Sciences,
8 Klausner St., Tel Aviv University, Tel Aviv 69978, Israel
tel: 03-640-9151; 03-640-9910; fax: 3-640-9380;
email: garden@post.tau.ac.il; Web: www.tau.ac.il/botany/Gardens

Tel Aviv Zoological and Botanical Gardens
155 Herzl St., Tel Aviv 68101, Israel
tel: 03-682-2352, 03-681-3966; fax: 03-518-1099

Zaparri Bird Park
P.O. Box 24049, Tel Aviv 61240, Israel
tel: 03-642-2888; fax: 03-642-0546

Museum of Nature
P.O. Box 30805, Kibbutz Ma'ayan Tsvi 30805, Israel
tel: 06-639-5156; 06-639-5111 (kibbutz office); fax: 06-639-1018

307

Tisch Family Zoological Gardens
P.O. Box 898, Manhat Rd., Jerusalem 91008, Israel
tel: 02-675-0111; fax: 02-643-0122

Hulah Valley Museum of Prehistory
Ma'ayan Baruch 12220, Israel
tel: 06-695-4611

Man and the Living World Museum
P.O. Box 947, Ramat Gan 52109, Israel
tel: 03-631-5010; fax: 03-631-5103

Man and the Environment Museum
16 Sharett St., Petah Tikva 49100, Israel
tel/fax: 03-921-9201; tel: 03-924-5708

Bet Rishonim Geological Museum
12 Ha-Palmach, Ramat ha-Sharon 47203, Israel
tel: 03-549-7185; fax: 03-540-8425

Stekelis Prehistory Museum and Gan ha-Em Zoological Garden
124 Ha-Tishbi St., Haifa 34455, Israel
tel: 04-837-1833 (museum); tel: 04-837-2886 (zoo)

The Natural History Museum in Jerusalem
6 Mohaliver St., Jerusalem 91081, Israel
tel: 02-563-1116; fax: 02-566-0666

Bet Gordon Natural History Museum
Kibbutz Deganyah Aleph, Jordan Valley 15120, Israel
tel: 06-675-0040; fax: 06-670-9514

Eretz Magazine
5 Ma'avar Yabok, Tel Aviv 67440, Israel
tel: 03-691-2211; email: eretz@eretz.co.il

Websites

www.infotour.co.il
In addition to providing links to many of Israel's nature reserves and national parks, Infotour includes a host of other tourist categories and information.

www.israel-mfa.gov.il
Israel Ministry of Foreign Affairs' Website provides a "Hot List" with links to the most useful Israeli Websites, including Israel government tourist offices worldwide. Look for "Our Bookmarks."
Email: ask@israel-info.gov.il

www.environment.gov.il
Although rarely updated, this site does list environmental organizations in Israel as well as telling something of government policies on the environment.

www.coejl.org
Maintained by Coalition on the Environment and Jewish Life (COEJL), this Website also provides links to Israeli environmental organizations.

www.birds.org.il
The main Website of "Migrating Birds Know No Boundaries" offers information on specific birds, tracking birds, and educational activities relating to birds and Israel, path of one of the world's major flyways.

www.birds.org.il/bulbul
The Jerusalem Bird Observatory tells about open space and bird life in Jerusalem and how to get to its site near the Knesset where nearly two hundred birds have been spotted.

Bibliography

Tanakh, the Holy Scriptures. Philadelphia & Jerusalem: The Jewish Publication Society, 1985.

The Holy Bible (New Testament, authorized King James version). New York: The World Publishing Co. [c. 1970].

Alon, Azaria. *The Natural History of the Land of the Bible.* London & New York: The Hamlyn Publishing Group, 1969.

Alon, Azaria. *300 Wildflowers in Israel.* Bnei-Brak, Israel: Society for the Protection of Nature in Israel/Steimatzky, 1993.

Bar-Am, Aviva, and Shalem, Yisrael. *Guide to the Golan Heights.* Safed, Israel: Safed Regional College/Bar Ilan University, 1995.

Barnavi, Eli, ed. *A Historical Atlas of the Jewish People.* New York: Schocken Books, 1992.

Bar-Yonah, Rabbi Benjamin. *The Itinerary of Benjamin of Tudela.* Translated by Marcus Nathan Adler. New York: Philipp Feldheim, Inc., reprinted from 1907 edition.

Ben-Tor, Amnon, ed. *The Archaeology of Ancient Israel.* Translated by R. Greenberg. New Haven: Yale University Press, 1992.

Dafni, Jacob. *Eilat: Routes and Trails in the Eilat Region.* Jerusalem: Nature Reserves Authority and Gefen Publishing House, 1995.

Devir, Ori. *Off the Beaten Track in Israel.* New York: Adama Books, 1989.

Dorst, Jean. *Field Guide to the Larger Mammals of Africa.* Boston: Houghton Mifflin, 1970.

Elon, Amos. *The Israelis: Founders and Sons.* New York: Holt, Rinehart & Winston, 1971.

Eretz Magazine. *Spring Fever: Eretz Guide to the Sources of the River Jordan.* Givatayim, Israel: Eretz Ha-Tzvi, Inc., 1991.

Feliks, Yehuda. *Nature and Man in the Bible.* New York: Soncino Press, 1981.

Gauthier-Pilters, Hilde, and Dagg, Anne Innis. *The Camel: Its Evolution, Ecology, Behavior, and Relationship to Man.* Chicago: University of Chicago Press, 1981.

Ghisotti, Andrea. *The Red Sea.* Florence, Italy: Casa Editrice Bonechi, 1995.

Glueck, Nelson. *Rivers in the Desert: A History of the Negev.* New York: Farrar, Straus & Cudahy, Grove Press, 1959.

Hareuveni, Nogah. *The Emblem of the State of Israel.* Translated by Helen Frenkley. Kiryat Ono, Israel: Neot Kedumim Ltd., 1988.

———. *Nature in Our Biblical Heritage.* Translated by Helen Frenkley. Kiryat Ono, Israel: Neot Kedumim Ltd., 1980.

———. *Tree and Shrub in Our Biblical Heritage.* Translated by Helen Frenkley. Kiryat Ono, Israel: Neot Kedumim Ltd., 1984.

Jonsson, Lars. *Birds of Europe, with North Africa and the Middle East.* Princeton: Princeton University Press, 1992.

Josephus. *The Jewish War.* Translated by G.A. Williamson. London: Penguin Books, 1970.

Livneh, Micha. *Hikes and Rambles Along the Northern Border and the "Finger of Galilee."* Booklet translated by Joseph Shadur. Israel: Society for the Protection of Nature in Israel, circa 1990.

Marcus, Menachem. *Granite Garden: Eretz Guide to the Eilat Mountains.* Givatayim, Israel: Eretz Ha-Tzvi, Inc., 1992.

Orni, Efraim, and Efrat, Elisha. *Geography of Israel.* Jerusalem: Israel Program for Scientific Translations, 1966.

Oz, Amos. *Touch the Water, Touch the Wind.* Translated by Nicholas de Lange. New York: Harvest/HBJ Book, Harcourt Brace Jovanovich, 1973.

Roman, Yadin, and Shkolnik, Ya'acov. *Primeval Paradise: Eretz Guide to Ramon Park.* Givatayim, Israel: Eretz Ha-Tzvi, Inc., 1992.

Roskin, Joel. *A Guide to Hiking in Israel.* Jerusalem: The Jerusalem Post, 1991.

Shadur, Joseph, ed. *Israel: Land and Nature, the Quarterly Journal of the Society for the Protection of Nature in Israel.* Jerusalem: SPNI.

Horesh, Tzvi, "Robber Jackals at Ein Fashkha," Vol.3, No.1

Halevi, Dov, "Of Chukar Partridges and Francolins," Vol.4, No.2

Ilani, Giora, "Protecting Israel's Carnivores," Vol.4, No.2

Leshem, Yossi, "Zoological Treasure in Jerusalem," Vol.4, No.2

Amit, David, "Of Dyeing Vats and Olive Presses," Vol.4, No.3

Nir, Ya'acov, "Delicate Balance of Israel's Beaches," Vol.4, No.4

Eshbol, Yossi, "Observing Kingfishers," Vol.8, No.4

Leshem, Yossi, "Centenary of Israel Aharoni," Vol.8, No.4

Mendelssohn, H., "Herpetological Nature Protection," Vol.9, No.1

Paz, Uzi, "Portrait of the Palestine Sunbird," Vol.9, No.1

Siegelmann, Asriel, "Flax Growing and Processing in Roman Palestine," Vol.9, No.4

Karschon, R., "Who Deforested the Plain of Sharon," Vol.10, No.1

Bouskila, Yonah, "A Closer Look at the Striped Hyena," Vol.10, No.2

Keynar, Doron, "Ancient Agriculture at Ein Gedi," Vol.12, No.1

Ortal, Reuven, "Israel's White Acacias," Vol.12, No.2

Ben-David, Zechariah, "Crocodile River: Last Unpolluted Coastal Stream," Vol.12, No.4

Weigler, "Israel's Coastal Plain: An Endangered Landscape," Vol.12, No.4

Chaver, Yael, ed. *Israel: Land and Nature, the Quarterly Journal of the Society for the Protection of Nature in Israel.* Jerusalem: SPNI.
Shalmon, Benny, "The Aravah Gazelle," Vol.13, No.1
Danin, Avinoam, "Harvest Ant and Milky Thistle," Vol.14, No.2
Cohen, Ofer, "Atlantic Pistachios in the Golan: Part I," Vol.14, No.4
Silberstein, Dalia, "Loggerhead Sea Turtles in Israel," Vol.15, No.2
Ben-Mayor, Yossi, "Butterfly Breeding on the Beach," Vol.16, No.1
Danin, Avinoam, "Origins of Israel's Sycomores," Vol.16, No.2
Hofshi, Hana, and Katzir, Gadi, "Infanticide by Tristram's Grackles," Vol.16, No.2
Givon, Bilha, "Saving Israel's Last Coastal Dunes," Vol.16, No.3
Shmida, Avi, "Tamarisks in Israel," Vol.16, No.3
Aronson, Len, "Cretan Wild Goats on Mt. Carmel," Vol.17, No.1
Shalmon, Benny; Kofyan, Tatiana; and Hadad, Ezra. *Field Guide to Land Mammals of Israel, Their Tracks and Signs* (Hebrew). Jerusalem: Keter Publishing House, 1993.
Shirihai, Hadoram. *The Birds of Israel.* London & San Diego: Academic Press, 1996.
———, and Bahat, Ofer. *Bird-watching in the Deserts of Israel.* Israel Ornithological Center (Tel Aviv), Israel Raptor Information Center (Har Gilo), and International Bird-watching Center (Eilat), 1993.
Shmida, Avi. *Handbook of Trees and Bushes of Israel* (Hebrew). Jerusalem: Keter Publishing House, 1992.
Shkolnik, Ya'acov. *Desert Waterways: Eretz Guide to the Nature Reserves of the Dead Sea Valley.* Givatayim, Israel: Eretz Ha-Tzvi, Inc., 1991.
———. *Evergreen Mountain: Eretz Guide to the Carmel Park.* Givatayim, Israel: Eretz Ha-Tzvi, Inc., 1992.
———. *The Hula Nature Reserve: An Eretz Guide.* Givatayim, Israel: Eretz Ha-Tzvi, Inc., 1994.
Smith, George Adam. *The Historical Geography of the Holy Land.* New York: Harper Torchbooks/The Cloister Library, Harper and Row, 1966, reprinted from 1933 edition of 1894 book.
Twain, Mark. *Innocents Abroad.* New York: Signet Classic, New American Library, 1966.
Walker, Ernest P., et al. *Mammals of the World,* Vol II. Baltimore: The Johns Hopkins Press, 1964.
Wilson, Edward O. *Sociobiology: the New Synthesis.* Cambridge, Massachusetts: The Belknap Press of Harvard University, 1975.
Yosef, Reuven. *Bird-watching in Eilat.* Eilat, Israel: International Bird-watching Center, 1995.
Zohary, Michael. *Flora Palaestina.* Jerusalem: The Israel Academy of Sciences and Humanities, 1966.

Species

In the lists below, mammals are organized in taxonomic orders and families according to the checklist devised by scientists and followed by field guides. The list begins with members of the Insectivora order, continues through Rodentia and Carnivora, and ends with the ungulates. Birds are organized according to the checklist accepted by the American Ornithologists' Union and other such organizations. Because plants may each have a number of common names, plant species are organized alphabetically according to scientific name. The index, however, lists plants by their common names. Some species mentioned briefly in the text do not appear below in an effort to keep the species lists to a manageable size.

MAMMALS

ENGLISH	SCIENTIFIC	HEBREW (transliterated)
European hedgehog	*Erinaceus concolor*	qipod matsui
desert hedgehog	*Paraechinus aethiopicus*	qipod midbar
Egyptian fruit bat	*Rousettus aegyptiacus*	ataleif peirot
Kuhl's pipistrelle (bat)	*Pipistrellus kuhlii*	atalefon leven-shulayim
brown hare	*Lepus capensis*	arnevet metsuyah
Persian squirrel	*Sciurus anomalus*	sena'i zahov
vole	*Microtus* sp.	navran
lesser Egyptian gerbil	*Gerbillus gerebillus*	gerbil deromi
jird	*Meriones* sp.	meriyon
fat sand rat	*Psammomys obesus*	pesamon midbar
golden spiny mouse	*Acomys russatus*	qotsan zahov
dormouse	*Dryomys nitedula*	namneman eitsim
mole rat	*Spalax ehrenbergi*	holed
nutria*	*Myocastor coypus*	nutriyah
Indian crested porcupine	*Hystrix indica*	darban
wolf	*Canis lupus*	ze'ev
Negev wolf	*Canis lupus pallipes*	ze'ev
jackal	*Canis aureus*	tan
red fox	*Vulpes vulpes*	shu'al matsui
badger	*Meles meles*	girit metsuyah
marbled polecat	*Vormela peregusna*	samur
stone marten	*Martes foina*	dalaq
otter	*Lutra lutra*	lutrah
Egyptian mongoose	*Herpestes ichneumon*	nemiyah

313

* Indicates nonnative

MAMMALS (continued):

ENGLISH	SCIENTIFIC	HEBREW (transliterated)
striped hyena	*Hyaena hyaena*	tsavo'a mefuspas
wildcat	*Felis silvestris*	hatul bar
marsh or jungle cat	*Felis chaus*	hatul bitsot
sand cat	*Felis margarita*	hatul holot
caracal	*Felis caracal*	qaraqal
leopard	*Panthera pardus*	namer
hyrax, rock badger	*Procavia capensis syriaca*	shafan
onager; wild ass	*Equus hemionus*	pereh
wild boar	*Sus scrofa*	hazir bar
camel	*Camelus dromedarius*	gamal
roe deer	*Capreolus capreolus*	ayal ha-karmel
fallow deer	*Dama dama*	yahmur
mountain gazelle	*Gazella gazella*	tsevi yisraeli
Aravah gazelle	*Gazella gazella arabica*	tsevi ha-aravah
dorcas gazelle	*Gazella dorcas*	tsevi ha-negev
ibex	*Capra ibex nubiana*	ya'el
Arabian oryx	*Oryx leucoryx*	re'em arvi
water buffalo*	*Bubalus bubalis*	te'o

BIRDS

ENGLISH	SCIENTIFIC	HEBREW (transliterated)
ostrich	*Struthio camelus camelus*	ya'ein
little grebe	*Tachybaptus ruficollis*	tavlan gamadi
cormorant	*Phalacrocorax carbo*	qormoran gadol
pygmy cormorant	*Phalacrocorax pygmaeus*	qormoran gamadi
white pelican	*Pelecanus onocrotalus*	saqnai matsui; qa'at
little bittern	*Ixobrychus minutus*	anafit gamdit
black-crowned night heron	*Nycticorax nycticorax*	anafit lailah
squacco heron	*Ardeola ralloides*	anafit suf
cattle egret	*Bubulcus ibis*	anafit baqar
little egret	*Egretta garzetta*	levanit qatanah
great white egret	*Egretta alba*	levanit gadolah
gray heron	*Ardea cinerea*	anafah aforah
purple heron	*Ardea purpurea*	anafah argamnit
black stork	*Ciconia nigra*	hasidah shahorah
white stork	*Ciconia ciconia*	hasidah levanah
glossy ibis	*Plegadis falcinellus*	maglon
spoonbill	*Platalea leucorodia*	kapan
ruddy shelduck	*Tadorna ferruginea*	qazrakah
teal	*Anas crecca*	sharshir
mallard	*Anas platyrhynchos*	berakhiyah
garganey	*Anas querquedula*	qarqir
shoveler	*Anas clypeata*	marit

BIRDS (continued):

ENGLISH	SCIENTIFIC	HEBREW (transliterated)
red-crested pochard	*Netta rufina*	netah
black kite	*Milvus migrans*	dayah matsuyah
white-tailed eagle	*Haliaeetus albicilla*	eitam leven-zanav
Egyptian vulture	*Neophron percnopterus*	raham
griffon vulture	*Gyps fulvus*	nesher
lappet-faced vulture	*Torgos tracheliotus*	ozniyat ha-negev
short-toed eagle	*Circaetus gallicus*	hivya'i
marsh hawk	*Circus aeruginosus*	zaron suf
steppe buzzard	*Buteo buteo*	aqav horef
long-legged buzzard	*Buteo rufinus*	aqav ayiti
lesser spotted eagle	*Aquila pomarina*	ayit horef
steppe eagle	*Aquila nipalensis*	ayit aravot
golden eagle	*Aquila chrysaetos*	ayit sela'im
Bonelli's eagle	*Hieraaetus fasciatus*	ayit nitsi
osprey	*Pandion haliaetus*	shalakh
lesser kestrel	*Falco naumanni*	baz adom
kestrel	*Falco tinnunculus*	baz matsui
chukar	*Alectoris chukar*	hoglah
sand partridge	*Ammoperdix heyi*	qora
black francolin	*Francolinus francolinus*	franqolin
quail	*Coturnix coturnix*	selav
water rail	*Rallus aquaticus*	relit
moorhen	*Gallinula chloropus*	sufit
coot	*Fulica atra*	agamit
black-winged stilt	*Himantopus himantopus*	temiron
spur-winged plover	*Hoplopterus spinosus*	siqseq
sanderling	*Calidris alba*	hofit levanah
snipe	*Gallinago gallinago*	hartomit bitsot
sandpiper	*Actitis hypoleucos*	bitsanit levnit batan
black-headed gull	*Larus ridibundus*	shahaf agamim
tern	*Sterna hirundo*	shahafit yam
rock dove	*Columba livia*	yonat sela'im
turtledove	*Streptopelia turtur*	tor matsui
cuckoo	*Cuculus canorus*	quqiyah eiropit
Scops owl	*Otus scops*	sa'ir
eagle owl	*Bubo bubo*	o'ah
white-breasted kingfisher	*Halcyon smyrnensis*	shaldag lavan hazeh
pied kingfisher	*Ceryle rudis*	perpur aqod
little green bee-eater	*Merops orientalis*	sheraqraq gamadi
bee-eater	*Merops apiaster*	sheraqraq matsui
hoopoe	*Upupa epops*	dukhifat
Syrian woodpecker	*Dendrocopos syriacus*	naqar suri
crested lark	*Galerida cristata*	efroni metsuyats
swallow	*Hirundo rustica*	senunit ha-refatot
yellow wagtail	*Motacilla flava*	nahli'eli tsahov

315

BIRDS (continued):

ENGLISH	SCIENTIFIC	HEBREW (transliterated)
yellow-vented bulbul	*Pycnonotus xanthopygos*	bulbul
wren	*Troglodytes troglodytes*	gidron
blackstart	*Cercomela melanura*	shahor zanav
black-eared wheatear	*Oenanthe hispanica*	salit qa'its
mourning wheatear	*Oenanthe lugens*	salit levnat-kanaf
northern wheatear	*Oenanthe oenanthe*	salit eiropit
blackbird	*Turdus merula*	shahrur
Cetti's warbler	*Cettia cetti*	tsetiah
graceful warbler	*Prinia gracilis*	pashosh
blackcap	*Sylvia atricapilla*	sibkhi shahor kipah
Arabian babbler	*Turdoides squamiceps*	zanvan
rock nuthatch	*Sitta neumayer*	sitat tsuqim
wallcreeper	*Tichodroma muraria*	katili
Palestine sunbird	*Nectarinia osea*	tsufit
great gray shrike	*Lanius excubitor*	hanqan gadol
woodchat shrike	*Lanius senator*	hanqan adom rosh
jay	*Garrulus glandarius*	orvani
hooded crow	*Corvus corone cornix*	orev afor
fan-tailed raven	*Corvus rhipidurus*	orev qatsar zanav
Tristram's grackle	*Onychognathus tristrami*	tristramit
Dead Sea sparrow	*Passer moabiticus*	deror yardan
goldfinch	*Carduelis carduelis*	hohit

316

OTHER ANIMALS

ENGLISH	SCIENTIFIC	HEBREW (transliterated)

Reptiles and Amphibians:

ENGLISH	SCIENTIFIC	HEBREW (transliterated)
desert monitor	*Varanus griseus*	qo'ah
Egyptian dabb lizard	*Uromastyx aegyptius*	hardon tsav matsui
agama lizard	*Agama sinaita*	hardon sinai
pygmy sand viper; sidewinder	*Cerastes vipera*	akhan qatan
desert racer	*Coluber rhodorachis*	za'aman
Burton's carpet viper	*Echis coloratus*	efeh
horned viper	*Pseudocerastes fieldi*	shefifon
Clifford's snake	*Spalerosophis cliffordi*	nahash holot
cat snake	*Telescopus dhara*	ayin-hatul
Palestine viper	*Vipera palaestinae*	tsefa matsui
desert cobra	*Walterinnesia aegyptia*	peten shahor
eyed skink	*Chalcides ocellatus*	nihushit einunit
fringe-toed lizard	*Acanthodactylus boskianus*	shenunit nahalim
loggerhead sea turtle	*Caretta caretta*	tsav-yam hum
hawksbill sea turtle	*Eretmochelys imbricata*	tsav-yam qarni

REPTILES AND AMPHIBIANS (continued):

ENGLISH	SCIENTIFIC	HEBREW (transliterated)
soft-shell turtle	*Trionyx triunguis*	tsav rakh
Egyptian tortoise	*Testudo kleinmanni*	tsav yabashah midbari
chameleon	*Chamaeleo chamaeleon*	ziqit
green lizard	*Lacerta trilineata*	leta'ah yaroqah
fire or spotted salamander	*Salamandra salamandra*	salamandrah

Fish:

sergeant major	*Abudefduf saxatilis*	difduf
clownfish	*Amphiprion bicinctus*	shoshanon eilati
slingjaw wrasse	*Epibulus insidiator*	shalfan
eel	*Anguilla* sp.	tselofah
coral grouper	*Cephalopholis miniata*	daqran adom
butterflyfish	*Chaetodon semilarvatus*	parparon
Napoleonfish	*Cheilinus undulatus*	tifar anaq
catfish	*Clarius gariepinus*	sefamnun matsui
angelfish	*Pomacanthus imperator*	qeisar ha-dor
Picasso triggerfish	*Rhinecanthus assasi*	netsran piqaso
parrotfish	*Scarus gibbus*	tukinon giban
Saint Peter's fish	*Tilapia zilli*	amnun
yellowtail surgeonfish	*Zebrasoma xanthurum*	natahan segol
trout*	*Oncorhynchus mykiss*	forel; terutat ein-ha-qeshet
gray mullet*	*Mugil cephalus*	buri; qifon
carp*	*Cyprinus carpio*	qarpion
gambusia*	*Gambusia affinis*	gamvuyah

317

Invertebrates:

yellow scorpion	*Leiurus quinquestriatus*	aqrav tsahov
harvester ant	*Messor semirufus*	nemlat ha-qatsir
weaver ant	*Oecophylla* sp.	nemlat ha-oreget
darkling beetle	*Blaps* sp.	shahrurit
black river snail	*Melanopsis* sp.	shahrir ha-nahalim
locust	*Schistocerca gregaria*	arbeh
dragonfly	*Anisoptera* sp.	shapirit
African monarch butterfly	*Danaus chrysippus*	danayit tapuach-sedom

PLANTS

ENGLISH	SCIENTIFIC	HEBREW (transliterated)

Trees and Shrubs:

white acacia	*Acacia albida*	shitah malbinah
weeping acacia*	*Acacia saligna*	shitah makhilah
umbrella acacia	*Acacia tortilis*	shitat ha-sokhekh

TREES AND SHRUBS (continued):

ENGLISH	SCIENTIFIC	HEBREW (transliterated)
Syrian maple	*Acer obtusifolium*	eder suri
almond	*Amygdalus communis*	shaqed matsui
chapter plant	*Anabasis articulata*	yafruq matsui
arbutus	*Arbutus andrachne*	qetalav matsui
saltbush	*Atriplex halimus*	maluah qipeah
balanites	*Balanites aegyptiaca*	zakkum mitsri
Chinese bauhinia*	*Bauhinia variegata*	bohineyah meguvenet
Sodom apple	*Calotropis procera*	petilat ha-midbar ha-gadolah
thorny broom	*Calycotome villosa*	qidah se'irah
caper (green)	*Capparis cartilaginea*	tsalaf sehusi
caper (blue-green)	*Capparis spinosa*	tsalaf qotsani
Atlantic cedar	*Cedrus atlantica*	erez atlanti
European hackberry	*Celtis australis*	ma'ish deromi
carob	*Ceratonia siliqua*	haruv matsui
redbud	*Cercis silliquastrum*	kelil ha-horesh
sage-leaf rockrose (white)	*Cistus salviifolius*	lotem marvani
rockrose (pink)	*Cistus villosus*	lotem varod
etrog; citron	*Citrus medica*	etrog
snail-seed vine	*Cocculus pendulus*	saharon meshulshal
hawthorn	*Crataegus aronia*	uzrar qotsani
cypress	*Cupressus sempervirens*	berosh matsui
eucalyptus*	*Eucalyptus camaldulensis*	eiqaliptus ha-maqqor
fig	*Ficus carica*	te'enah
Egyptian fig; sycomore	*Ficus sycomorus*	shiqmah
Syrian ash	*Fraxinus syriaca*	meilah surit
doum palm	*Hyphaene thebaica*	dom mitsri
laurel	*Laurus nobilis*	dafnah; ar atsil
henna	*Lawsonia inermis*	eshkol ha-khofer
strapvine	*Loranthus acacia*	harnug ha-shittim
boxthorn	*Lycium europaeum*	atad eiropi
moricandia	*Moricandia nitens*	moriqandyah mavriqah
moringa	*Moringa peregrina*	moringah ratmit
myrtle	*Myrtus communis*	hadas matsui
oleander	*Nerium oldeander*	hardduf ha-nehalim
flowering tobacco*	*Nicotiana glauca*	tabaq ha-siah
rikhpetan	*Ochradenus baccatus*	rikhpetan midbari
olive	*Olea europea*	za'it eiropi
sabra; prickly-pear cactus*	*Opuntia ficus-indica*	tsabar matsui
date palm	*Phoenix dactylifera*	tamar matsui
Aleppo pine	*Pinus halepensis*	oren yerushalayim
Atlantic pistacia; terebinth	*Pistacia atlantica*	elah atlantit
mastic pistacia	*Pistacia lentiscus*	elat ha-mastiq
Palestine pistacia	*Pistacia palaestina*	elah erets-yisraelit
plane tree	*Platanus orientalis*	dolev mizrahi

318

TREES AND SHRUBS (continued):

ENGLISH	SCIENTIFIC	HEBREW (transliterated)
Euphrates poplar	*Populus euphratica*	tsaftsefet ha-perat
pomegranate	*Punica granatum*	rimon matsui
Boissier (Cyprus) oak	*Quercus boissieri*	alon ha-tola
calliprinos (kermes) oak	*Quercus calliprinos*	alon matsui
turkey oak	*Quercus ceris*	alon shasua
Tabor oak	*Quercus ithaburensis*	alon ha-tavor
Look oak	*Quercus libani ssp. look*	alon ha-levanon
white broom	*Retama raetam*	rotem ha-midbar
buckthorn	*Rhamnus palaestinus*	eshar erets-yisraeli
rose	*Rosa sp.*	vered
holy bramble	*Rubrus sanctus*	petel qadosh
willow	*Salix acmophylla*	aravah mehudedet
white willow	*Salix alba*	aravah levanah
poterium; spiny burnet	*Sarcopoterium spinosum*	sirah
greenbrier	*Smilax aspera*	qisusit
styrax	*Styrax officinalis*	livneh refui
tamarisk	*Tamarix sp.*	eshel
rope plant	*Thymelaea hirsuta*	yitran; mitnan sa'ir
viburnum	*Viburnum tinus*	moran
chaste-tree	*Vitex angus-castus*	siah-avraham matsui
grapevine	*Vitis vinifera*	gefen
jujube	*Ziziphus spina-christis*	shezaf matsui
bean caper; couple plant	*Zygophyllum dumosum*	zugan ha-siakh

319

Wildflowers and Grasses:

bear's breeches	*Acanthus syriacus*	qotsits suri
pheasant's-eye	*Adonis dentata*	demumit meshunenet
hollyhock	*Alcea setosa*	hotmit zifanit
dyer's alkanet	*Alkanna tinctoria*	alkenet ha-tsaba'im
Carmel garlic	*Allium carmeli*	shum ha-karmel
Naple's garlic	*Allium neapolitanum*	shum mishulash
scarlet pimpernel	*Anagallis arvensis*	marganit ha-sadeh
rose of Jericho	*Anastatica hierochuntica*	shoshanat yeriho
androcymbium	*Androcymbium palaestinum*	betsaltseyah erets-yisraelit
crown anemone	*Anemone coronaria*	kalanit matsuyah
chamomile (white daisy)	*Anthemis leucanthemifolia*	qahvan ha-hof
snapdragon	*Antirrhinum majus*	lo'a ha-ari ha-gadol
white wormwood	*Artemisia herba-alba*	la'anat ha-midbar
single-seed wormwood	*Artemisia monosperma*	la'anah had-zarit
arum	*Arum palaestinum*	luf erets-yisraeli
asparagus	*Asparagus aphyllus*	asparagus
yellow Jacob's rod	*Asphodeline lutea*	irioni tsahov
asphodel	*Asphodelus microcarpus*	irit gadolah

WILDFLOWERS AND GRASSES (continued):

ENGLISH	SCIENTIFIC	HEBREW (transliterated)
maidenhair fern	*Asplenium adiantum*	sa'arot shulamit
milk vetch	*Astragalus callichrous*	qadad yafeh
Cretan cabbage	*Brassica cretica*	keruv kereti
blue bellflower	*Campanula rapunculus*	pa'amonit qafahet
field chrysanthemum	*Chrysanthemum coronarium*	hartsit aturah
desert broomrape	*Cistanche tubulosa*	yahnuq ha-midbar
autumn crocus	*Colchicum hierosolymitanum*	sitvanit yerushalayim
Negev colchicum; sand lily	*Colchicum ritchii*	sitvanit ha-negev
round-leaved cyclamen	*Cyclamen coum*	raqefet yevanit
cyclamen	*Cyclamen persicum*	raqefet matsuyah
papyrus	*Cyperus papyrus*	guma ha-papirus
Queen Anne's lace; wild carrot	*Daucus carrota*	gezer ha-ginah
shield fern	*Dryoperis villarii*	sherakhyah ashunah
globe thistle	*Echinops adenocaulus*	kipodan matsui
Judean bugloss	*Echium judaeum*	akhnai yehudah
horsetail reed	*Equisetum telmateia*	shevatbat gadol
desert storksbill; erodium	*Erodium touchyanum*	maqor ha-hasidah ha-midbari
Jerusalem spurge	*Euphorbia hierosolymitana*	halavluv migubeshesh
fagonia	*Fagonia mollis*	fagonyah rakhah
giant fennel	*Ferula communis*	kelekh matsui
yellow gagea	*Gagea commutata*	zehavit ha-sheluhot
geranium; cranesbill	*Geranium libani*	geranyon ha-levanon
sword lily	*Gladiolus italicus*	saifan ha-tavu'ah
tumble thistle	*Gundelia tournefortii*	akhuvit ha-galgal
afternoon iris	*Gynandiris sisyrinchium*	ahi'iris matsui
sunrose	*Helianthemum vesicarium*	shemshon ha-shelhofiot
barley	*Hordeum vulgare*	se'orah
henbane	*Hyoscyamus aureua*	la'ana
shikor sinai	*Hyoscyamus boveanus*	shikor sinai
purple iris	*Iris atropurpurea*	iris ha-argaman
Grant-Duff's iris	*Iris grant-duffi*	iris ha-bitsot
Gilboa iris; Haynei's iris	*Iris haynei*	iris ha-gilboa
Hermon iris	*Iris hermona*	iris ha-hermon
Yerukham iris	*Iris hieruchamensis*	iris yeruham
Lortet iris	*Iris lortetii*	iris hadur
yellow flag iris	*Iris pseudoacorus*	iris anef
Vartan iris	*Iris vartanii*	iris ha-sargeil
dead nettle	*Lamium moschatum*	nezmit lofetet
dotted mallow	*Lavatera punctata*	me'ug menuqad
lentil	*Lens esculenta*	adashim
lion's leaf	*Leontice leontopetalum*	artanit ha-sadot

WILDFLOWERS AND GRASSES (continued):

ENGLISH	SCIENTIFIC	HEBREW (transliterated)
ivory leopoldia	*Leopoldia eburneum*	metsilot shenhav
Madonna lily	*Lilium candidum*	shoshan tsahor
sea lavender	*Limonium sinuatum*	adad meforats
hairy pink flax	*Linum pubescens*	pishtah sa'irah
birdfoot trefoil	*Lotus creticus*	lotus makhsif
lupine	*Lupinus philosus*	turmos he-harim
purple loosestrife	*Lythrum salicaria*	shenit gadolah
hyssop; zatar	*Majorana syriaca*	ezov matsui
maresia	*Maresia pulchella*	maresyah yefefiyah
mint	*Mentha* sp.	qoranit ha-nahal
michauxia	*Michauxia campanuloides*	mishoyah pa'amonit
narcissus	*Narcissus tazetta*	narqis matsui
yellow waterlily	*Nuphar luteum*	nufar tsahov
cotton thistle	*Onopordum cynarocephalum*	hohin ha-qinres
Carmel bee-orchid	*Ophrys carmeli*	devoranit dinsmur
Anatolian orchid	*Orchis anatolica*	sahlav anatoli
butterfly orchid	*Orchis papilionacea*	sahlav parperani
three-toothed orchid	*Orchis tridentata*	sahlav shalosh ha-shinayim
star-of-Bethlehem	*Ornithogalum montanum*	nets he-halav
Mutel's broomrape	*Orobanche mutelii*	aleqet mutel
wood-sorrel*	*Oxalis pes-caprae*	hamtsits natui
peony	*Paeonia mascula*	admonit he-horesh
sea daffodil	*Pancratium maritimum*	havatselet ha-hof
poppy	*Papaver subpiriforme*	pereg agasani
mountain knotgrass	*Paronychia argentea*	almot ha-kesef
phragmites reed	*Phragmites australis*	qaneh matsui
polypody fern	*Polypodium vulgare*	rav-regel pashut
red buttercup	*Ranunculus asiaticus*	nurit asyah
Maltese cross	*Ricotia lunaria*	karmilit na'ah
snow romulea	*Romulea nivalis*	romulit ha-sheleg
white salvia	*Salvia dominica*	marvah reihanit
horn-leaved sage	*Salvia fruticosa*	marvah mishuleshet
Jerusalem sage	*Salvia hierosolymitana*	marvah yerushalayim
wrinkle-leaf sage	*Salvia lanigera*	marvah tsamirah
hyacinth squill	*Scilla hyacinthoides*	ben-hatsav yakintoni
sedum; stonecrop	*Sedum* sp.	tsurit
milky thistle	*Silybum marianum*	gedilen matsui
field mustard	*Sinapis arvensis*	hardal ha-sadeh
sternbergia	*Sternbergia clusiana*	helmonit gadolah
purple clover	*Trifolium purpureum*	tiltan ha-argaman
emmer (wild wheat)	*Triticum dicocoides*	hitat ha-bar
mountain tulip	*Tulipa agenensis*	tsivoni he-harim
Mount Hermon tulip	*Tulipa lownei*	tsivoni ha-hermon

321

WILDFLOWERS AND GRASSES (continued):

ENGLISH	SCIENTIFIC	HEBREW (transliterated)
Sharon tulip	*Tulipa sharonensis*	havatselet ha-sharon
desert tulip	*Tulipa systola*	tsivoni ha-midbar
navelwort	*Umbilicus intermedius*	taburit natuyah
sea squill	*Urginea maritima*	hatsav matsui
stinging nettle	*Urtica* sp.	sirpad
Syrian veronica	*Veronica syriaca*	beroniqah surit

Index

NOTE: Page numbers in italics indicate illustrative material. Species are listed by common name; more complete information can be found in the species lists (pages 313–22). Nature reserves are listed not individually but together under "Nature reserves." Similarly, national parks are listed under "National parks."

324

Neot Kedumim Biblical Landscape Reserve, *136*, 147, *148–50*, 279
Nepeta, 206
Netanyah, 273, 291
Nettle, 206
New Moon (Rosh Hodesh), 23
Nezer Cave, 225
Nile River, 295
Nimrod Fortress, 212–13
Nitsenim, 294, 296
Noah, 4, 74
Northern Galilee, 211–43
   animals, 233, 243
   archaeology sites, 212–13, 216, 235, 236
   birds, 212, 223–24, 229–34, 241–42
   fish and marine life, 218, 230
   geology, 229, 236–37, 243
   plants, 215, 218–19, 222, 228–29, 232–33, 235–43
Northern Negev, *front matter*, 60, 81–99
   animals, 81, 90, 94, 95
   archaeology sites, 70, 84–85, 90, 92, 93–94, 97–98
   birds, 86, 87–88, 89–90, 92, 94
   caves, 94
   geology, 90
   plants, 81–84, 87–88, 92–96, 98–99
Nose of the Gazelle, 251–52
Numbers (book of)
   animals, 78
   geography, 67
   land of milk and honey, 2
   purple dye, 283
Nuthatch, 206
Nutria, 229

O

Oak (*alon*), 139, 168, *204–205*, 207, 215, 245–46, 248, 252
   ancient forests, 5, 137, 139, 178
   Boissier (Cyprus), 191, 201, 243, 247
   calliprinos (kermes), 191, 201, 219, 237, 254–55, 257
   Look, 191
   turkey, 191
   Tabor, 185, 191, 192, 196, 219, 290
Oak Canyon (Nahal Alon), 260–61, *262*
Oases, 99, 101, 111
Odem Forest, 201, 203, *204*
Oleander, 173, 177, 185, 198, 222, 245, 249, 298

Olive, 4, 61, 165, 219, 237, 243, 258
   cultivation of, 145, 165, 299
Onagers (wild asses), 50, 51, 52, 62, 70
Orange groves, 83
Orchids, 198, 203, 221, 225, 237, 252
   Anatolian, 202, 243
   butterfly, 259, 260
   Carmel bee-orchids, 259–60
   three-toothed, 260
Oren. See Pine
Oryx, 50, 51, 52
Ospreys, 160
Ostriches, *40*, 50, 52–53
Otters, 172, 178, 212, 221, 232
Ottoman period, 37, 173, 178, 237, 255, 290–91
Oven Falls, 224
Owls, 163–64, 212, 225
   eagle, 52, 260
   Scops, 163
Oz, Amos, 1

P

Paleolithic period, 269, 270
Palestine Exploration Fund, 127
Palestine Liberation Organization (PLO), 160
Palestine sunbirds, 57, 101, 162, 285, 286, 292, 296
Palestinian Autonomous District, 128
Palestinians, 153, 155
Palmach, 88, 160, 161
Palms, 99, 101, 118, 120–23, *148*, 173, 236, 289
   date (*tamar*), 49, 50, 83, 121–22
   doum, 41, 48–49
   fan, 223
Palm Sunday, 122
Pan, temple to, 216
Papyrus, 211, 226, *228–33*, 299
Parkinsonia, 223
Parrotfish, *43*, 46
Parsat Neqarot (Horseshoe Crevice), 67, 68
Partridges, 116, 118, 135
Passover, 87
Peace Bridge, 158
Pelicans, 161, 231, 280
Peony, 243
Persia, 236
Pesticides, impact of, 163, 230, 253, 259
Peter (apostle), 235

About the Author

MICHAL STRUTIN has been involved with nature writing from her time as an editor at *Outside* and *National Parks* magazines. Her books on natural history include two volumes of *Smithsonian Guides to Natural America* and the award-winning *Places of Grace: the Natural Landscapes of the American Midwest*, with photographer Gary Irving. *Chaco: a Cultural Legacy* and *A Guide to Northern Plains Indians* focus on cultural history. She has worked for *Rolling Stone* magazine and written for *The New York Times, Modern Maturity*, and many others. She is an avid gardener, and her love of the outdoors has taken her into backcountry areas across America, in the Himalayas, and in Israel. She lives with her husband near the Great Smoky Mountains of Tennessee.

341